Fulfilling Lives

Douglas H. Heath

with the
Assistance of

Harriet E. Heath

FULFILLING LIVES

Paths to
Maturity and Success

 Jossey-Bass Publishers

San Francisco • Oxford • 1991

FULFILLING LIVES
Paths to Maturity and Success
  by Douglas H. Heath with the Assistance of Harriet E. Heath

Library of Congress Cataloging-in-Publication Data

Heath, Douglas H.
   Fulfilling lives : paths to maturity and success / Douglas H.
  Heath, with the assistance of Harriet E. Heath.
       p.   cm. — (The Jossey-Bass social and behavioral science
  series)
   Includes bibliographical references and indexes.
   ISBN 1-55542-309-4
   1. Success — Psychological aspects.   2. Maturation (Psychology)
  3.Self-actualization (Psychology)   I. Heath, Harriet.   II. Title.
  III. Series.
  BF637.S8S365   1991
  155.6 — dc20   90-20556
                                                                    CIP

Manufactured in the United States of America

The paper in this book meets the guidelines for permanence and durability of the Committee on Production Guidelines for Book Longevity of the Council on Library Resources.

JACKET DESIGN BY WILLI BAUM

FIRST EDITION

Code 9110

THE JOSSEY-BASS
SOCIAL AND BEHAVIORAL SCIENCE SERIES

Contents

Preface xiii

The Authors xix

**Part One
Understanding Maturity and Success 1**

1. Growing Up to Succeed 3

2. Billie Leighton: Succeeding on Her Own 20

3. Key Paths to Maturity 33

4. Eight Myths About Maturity 60

**Part Two
Succeeding in Personal Relationships 73**

5. Andy and Marty Miller: Finding Their Own
  Paths 75

6. Andy: Mature Androgyny 95

7. Marty: Growing into Her Own Vision 103

8.   Eleven Insights into Becoming an Adult   113

9.   Becoming a Successful Marital Partner   118

10. Successful Parenting: Making the Commitment   137

11. Finding Sexual Fulfillment   148

12. Succeeding as a Friend   161

13. Fulfilling Personal Relationships   169

Part Three
Succeeding at Work   **175**

14. Jane Allen: She Knew What She Wanted   177

15. Earning It the Old-Fashioned Way   187

16. Making Work a Calling, Not Just a Job   199

17. Reflections on Vocations and Intimacy   215

Part Four
Enhancing Other-Centeredness and Well-Being   **221**

18. Harry Barnett: A Model Citizen   223

19. Religious and Virtuous Individuals   231

20. A Toast to Good Health and Happiness   243

21. Male and Female Paths to Physical Health   253

22. Ten Facts About Other-Centeredness and
     Well-Being   260

Part Five
Paths to Adult Success and Well-Being 263

23. Harry Barnett: A Loving, Democratic, Firm
Parent 265

24. Mothers of Children Who Grow Up to Succeed 273

25. Fathers of Children Who Grow Up to Succeed 282

26. School and Adult Success 291

27. Adolescents Who Become Successful, Healthy,
and Happy Adults 299

28. Men Growing into Mid-Life 309

29. Women Growing into Mid-Life 315

30. Ten Prescriptions for Building a Strong Family 328

31. A Perspective on Hope 331

Notes 341

Appendix: The Study of Adult Development 363

References 385

Index 399

To the one hundred and five men and women
whose lives made this book possible

Preface

A Citicorp TV ad asserted that "Americans want to succeed, not just survive." What did the bank's ad really say? That the Chinese and Panamanians who use its services want to "just survive" and not succeed? Scarcely. Or that Koreans don't want to succeed as much as Americans? Not true. Or that Americans want to achieve some goals more than others do? Like what? Be blissfully married? Raise healthy and happy children? Have frequent sex? Be fulfilled? Doubtful. Well, was the ad saying that Americans want to be wealthy more than the Japanese, Germans, or Sicilian Mafia do? Or that Americans want to enjoy a comfortable life now by spending their wealth — and borrowing from the bank what they have not yet earned?

I don't know what Citicorp intended to say. Maybe the ad's ambiguity was its real (though unintended) meaning: that we are confused about what we want; that we don't know what success means; or that, as some social critics claim, we have substituted immediate pleasure — this quarter's "bottom line" — for earlier American visions of "success": the Pilgrims' New Jerusalem; the colonists' "life, liberty, and the pursuit of happiness"; the pioneers' new beginnings at the western frontier; the immigrants' hope of opportunity upon reaching the Statue of Liberty; the astronauts' exploration of space's mysteries.

This book is about the character necessary to succeed in our principal adult roles and to be healthy and happy adults. It has

grown out of research initiated in the 1950s in an attempt to
understand the meaning of mental health, competence, and self-
actualization. In the 1950s, I undertook an in-depth study of
young men, first when they were seventeen and again when they
were twenty-one, who varied in how successfully they were
living their lives. In 1965, *Explorations of Maturity* described a
model of growing up healthily that emerged from this study.
The model demonstrated that, in maturing, our minds and
character become more present to our awareness and develop
into being other-centered, well integrated, stable, and autonomous. In 1968, *Growing Up in College* reported that this model
predicted quite well how other groups of students actually matured between their freshman and senior years. In 1971, *Humanizing Schools* drew out the implications of this research on
healthy growth for practicing educators. And then, in 1977,
Maturity and Competence showed that the model, based predominantly on the lives of Protestant and Jewish young men, also
described young men who were Catholic Sicilians and north-
ern Italians and Muslim eastern and western Turks.

To learn how and why men grow from twenty-one to succeed by their early thirties, during the late sixties I restudied
the participants. I secured valuable information about them from
their closest friends, colleagues, and wives, many of whom I
also interviewed about their relationships with their husbands.
The model of maturing not only described how they had grown
since they were twenty-one but also had predicted who would
succeed twelve years later. The technical articles I wrote between 1976 and 1983 (see References) reported what I found.

In the early 1980s, I returned to restudy the men for a fourth
time, this time when they were middle-aged. I welcomed the
request by the men's wives that they be allowed to participate
as fully as their husbands in the middle-age phase of the study.
(Because the same model of maturing described their growth
into middle age and predicted how well they succeeded, I question the currently fashionable idea that women grow *healthily*
in different ways from men.)

Why write about happily married persons, good lovers, competent parents, community leaders, and vocationally success-

ful men and women when hundreds of articles have already been written about these and other adults who have succeeded? I do this because researchers have not heretofore identified the core character strengths necessary to succeed in all of our principal adult roles, examined how success in one role is related to success in others, and explored the meaning of success in as much depth. Most have examined *only* marital happiness, or *only* parenting, or *only* vocational success. We have a psychology of each role but not a psychology of persons who succeed in many roles.

Because the research encompassed all aspects of the character of successful middle-aged men and women, we can now answer questions that we could not before. Are there core character strengths that contribute to success in numerous adult roles? Do vocationally successful men and women make good marital partners, parents, and lovers? Are virtuous persons more likely to succeed and be healthy and happy? Are feminists who espouse androgyny right to argue that it is a characteristic of healthy and successful adults? From what kinds of homes do men and women come who succeed in their familial *and* vocational roles? What adolescent strengths (and weaknesses) might determine how successful and happy a youth will be when forty-five years old?

Overview of the Contents

To answer these and other provocative questions about adults who create fulfilling lives for themselves and others, the book is organized into five parts. The first describes the study and the model of maturing. The second describes the character of persons who succeed in creating intimate marital, parental, sexual, and friendship relationships. The third examines the character of those who succeed vocationally by making a lot of money, exercising power and leadership, enjoying their work, and being fulfilled and competent in their colleagues' eyes. The fourth describes those who extend themselves beyond their immediate familial and vocational roles to serve their communities and devote themselves to religious and ethical ideals; it also discusses the character of mentally and physically healthy and happy persons. The last part tracks the roots of success and well-being. It describes the contributions of mothers and fathers, schools, and adolescent and adult experiences, and concludes with some reflections about growing up successfully and healthily in these days.

Young adults, parents, and teachers who have heard me speak about the study have urged me to write for them, not just for professionals interested in adult development. Without violating the research's scientific integrity, I have tried to translate complicated and technical terms, methods, and statistical results into ordinary language. Readers of the book's earlier drafts disagreed about what they wanted from a study about personal, sometimes troubling, ideas and results. Most wanted me to speak directly to them: informally, colloquially, and concretely. Some wanted more and longer examples from the lives of the study's 105 men and women; others wanted fewer and shorter ones. Some asked for more in-depth and specific results; others asked for simpler and more general comments, not always qualified by an anemic "some," "could be," or "more likely than not." Psychologists wanted more technical detail; others wanted less.

To meet such contradictory requests, I begin Parts Two through Five by describing the most successful exemplar of the roles each part examines. I conclude each part with capsule summaries of the points that may be most useful to remember. You may wish to skim these capsules before delving into the chapters of greatest interest to you. The research literature about many of the topics I examine is vast. In the notes I report primarily the work of those researchers who have studied adults over long periods of time. To satisfy those who want more of the study's background and technical detail, I include an Appendix that describes the participants, measures, and types of analyses. I abbreviate in parentheses citations to specific sections of the Appendix as "A" followed by an outline number, to guide the reader to a description of the method or score whose result I describe in the text. To avoid clogging the chapters, I omit citations to a specific Appendix section after I have referred to it a few times. After reading Chapter One, you may wish to skim the Appendix in order to better understand the information on which the book is based. Researchers can secure a copy of the study's principal unpublished methods and their associated statistical information, as well as the statistical results supporting the book's generalizations, from the National Auxiliary Publications Service (NAPS).[1]

Acknowledgments

I dedicate the book with affection and gratitude to the men and women who so openly shared their most personal feelings and experiences with me. I am especially indebted to the principal leads of the book — Billie Leighton, Andy and Marty Miller, Jane Allen, and Harry Barnett — for letting me use their lives to illustrate what men and women who succeed are like and why they accomplished what they did. While their names and potentially identifying circumstances have been changed so that these individuals cannot be recognized, their characters have not. I am also grateful to Roger Blake, a thirty-two-year-old former student, who critiqued the study's findings from his generation's perspective about fulfilling lives. All of these people have given me permission to publish what I have written about them.

The book has benefited from the careful and thoughtful reading of many others. Michael Murray helped me sharpen the book's focus; I greatly appreciate his perceptive analyses, as well as those of Charles Abelmann, Donald Barkin, Molly Conrecode, Russell Heath, David Mallery, Carol Mann, Barbara Morrison, and Dwight Raulston. I am also indebted to Mark Aymar, Dave Bickel, Peter Buttenheim, Peter Hanson, James Lee, Margaret Linn, Steve Morrison, Stephen Siwinski, and Mary Wilson for their comments and support. I am particularly grateful to Kenneth Clark and Robert Sternberg for their critiques and to Thomas Williamson for his persistent support. The research has been guided over the years by the comments and suggestions of Jack Block, Robert Holt, Bernice Neugarten, M. Brewster Smith, and George Vaillant. I also thank Emily Kingham, who has faithfully and efficiently helped me for more than twenty years with the research; Joan McKoy, who scored the Rorschachs; Jane Loevinger, who advised me about her Ego Development Scale; and Deborah Browning, who scored them. The editors and staff of Jossey-Bass have been exceptionally dedicated at every stage of the editing and production process.

My wife, Harriet E. Heath, has been indispensable. She not only kept our family going for the years I traveled to all parts of the world to locate the men and women of the study but also contributed professionally to the book. As an expert on child development and parenting, she created the study's key measure assessing parental satisfaction. She also critiqued my interpretations, particularly about women and their roles as wives and mothers.

Haverford, Pennsylvania   Douglas H. Heath
December 1990

The Authors

Douglas H. Heath is professor emeritus of psychology at Haverford College. He received his B.A. degree (1949) from Amherst College in psychology and both his M.A. (1952) and Ph.D. (1954) degrees from Harvard University in social relations, majoring in clinical psychology. As a National Science Foundation Fellow, he did postdoctoral work in statistics and research methodology in the Department of Psychology at the University of Michigan, Ann Arbor (1957).

Heath's principal research has focused on developing a model of psychological maturity that describes optimally functioning, competent, and self-actualized men and women. He has tested the model transculturally, as well as longitudinally from adolescence to middle age, on effectively functioning persons to understand the whats and whys of their well-being, success, and happiness. He has applied his research methods to the study of such educational issues as faculty and student morale, the changing character of students, and institutional ethos.

Worldwide, Heath has lectured at and consulted with more than 800 schools and colleges, as well as youth, religious, and business groups, on the implications of his research on establishing institutional goals, assisting organizations to establish means to assess their effects and advising them on how to create more effective learning environments to further the continued psychological maturation of their members.

He has authored six books, including *Explorations of Maturity: Studies of Mature and Immature College Men* (1965), *Growing Up in College: Liberal Education and Maturity* (1968), *Humanizing Schools: New Directions, New Decisions* (1971), and *Maturity and Competence: A Transcultural View* (1977). Results of his earlier longitudinal studies have appeared in numerous professional journals.

Harriet E. Heath, director of the Parent Center at Bryn Mawr College, received her B.A. degree (1949) from Cornell College in elementary education and her Ph.D. degree (1976) from Bryn Mawr College in human development. She has authored *Parents Planning: A Manual for Parents* (1983) and *Learning About Parenting: Learning to Care* (1983), a curriculum for kindergarten to twelfth-grade students.

Fulfilling Lives

Part One——————————————

Understanding
Maturity and Success

1

Growing Up
to Succeed

To grow up to succeed and be happy is to develop the mind and character necessary to satisfy our needs, achieve our goals, and fulfill our dreams. But what needs and which goals and dreams? That is the first question we must answer. Only then can we seek to discover what kind of mind and character produce success and happiness.

What Does Success Mean to Us?

When we are young, few of us know who are we and what we shall want when we grow up. In 1950, Erik Erikson told us we should basically solve our identity crisis by our late teens. Erikson also told us that even when we are adults our ideas about who we are and what we want continue to evolve as we encounter new crises. Our marriages flounder. Our children leave home. We achieve our ambitions; our callings become only jobs. We wake up one morning to that proverbial mid-life crisis. Our stamina and potency begin to fade. We anticipate death and ask, "What's been the point of it all?" We must refashion and refashion again our wants and goals from one crisis to the next.[1]

Forty years and much societal turmoil later, Erikson's timing does not fit many of our lives very well. More freedom and choices complicate and slow growing up rather than simplifying it. Parents and society no longer prescribe as clearly what we should and should not be, certainly about sexual impulses and gender roles. The number of our options and lack of experience with their requirements have exploded, especially about vocations and marital relationships. We postpone commitments, certainly about marriage and children. Living has become more contingent; identities are more transitional and less societally prescribed for everyone.

My studies of how we grow from adolescence into middle age tell me how uncertain and untidy growing up has become. By their early thirties, about a quarter of the men I had been studying since they were seventeen still had not solved their identity crisis. Yes, most had married and begun to raise children and flourish vocationally. You might say they had grown up to succeed as adults, but they would not have agreed. They still questioned who they were and what they wanted out of life. By their mid-forties, however, all but one had created vocational identities that integrated their talents and values. Though more had become uncertain about their marriages, only a few felt empty and discouraged. Some had had what they called their "mid-life crisis" when they were thirty-three, others when they were forty-two. Others wondered when theirs was to be.

By their late twenties and early thirties, most of the women I interviewed had accepted that they were wives and mothers. They seemed to be stronger, more together, than their husbands. Twelve years and the women's movement later, however, the majority did not know who they were or what they wanted. I asked, "Where is that strong sense of self I saw just a few years earlier?" Why did a middle-aged wife, mother, and remarkably successful community leader tell me, "All I am is a collection of roles put together by a committee"?

Three men from three different generations and an Escort's bumper sticker recently reminded me once again how problematic growing up has become. Tom, a former student, visited me. Now in his mid-twenties, he had become a successful group manager monitoring the quality of computer chips in a Silicon Valley factory. His first words were, "Doug, I want to grow up but I'm stuck. I don't like my job but I don't know what I want to do; I've struck out with every girl I've ever met; my sex life is dead; all I have each night is TV and pot. I can't give up either. I'd have nothing left."

Peter, a forty-two-year-old physician whom I had known for twenty years, surprised me five years ago when he confided that he was an alcoholic. He had felt torn for years being so hypocritical with his patients when telling them not to drink or smoke. Shortly after Tom's visit, Peter shocked me when with no self-pity he matter-of-factly said, as best I remember his words: "At last I feel I've finally begun to grow up. I learned last month that I had terminal cancer of the liver. I've finally found the courage to tell my patients how divided I've felt being their doctor. Most have been understanding. I finally feel I'm now living with integrity. I really feel at peace now. I don't fear what I feel coming."

I then received a letter from Roger Blake, a thirty-two-year-old former Peace Corps volunteer in Ecuador and now a popular high school teacher of American history and literature. He wrote:

> I always seem to need an "out," a vision of change, a new destination. That's the restlessness I feel. Why do I feel so vaguely dissatisfied with my job that could inspire and stretch me for years to come? And Beth! Why do I wonder if I can find someone *better* when we have such a passion for each other and have shared so much? Why do I imagine other places to live when the mountains of Colorado are such a source of joy? When I have a fine apartment and a loving group of friends? Restlessness haunts me.
>
> . . . It all comes down, I guess, to what I value. Maybe I don't know what I value, really. Maybe I haven't been honest with myself all these years. Here I am, thirty-two, and I don't know what I really want. . . . I've got to prioritize my life. . . . Do I want a relationship I can fully commit myself to? Beth wants children; I don't. I'm not into being a father — married or not . . . but I would like to work with Quito's street kids.
>
> It's time for me to grow up, but how?

Ford Escorts are also confused about what they want. The bumper sticker of one I followed read, "When I grow up, I want to be a Cadillac." Almost a pathological identity confusion, isn't it?

Tom, Peter, Roger, and the Escort sparked these ideas about growing up successfully. Success means a lot more than just living out a vocational, marital, or other adult role. What others may view as success, like becoming a group manager by the age of twenty-eight, we may view as failure. Our visible success may not reflect our hopes and dreams. Our success may not be enjoyable, fulfilling, or even feel right for us. To understand the mind and character necessary to succeed, we must evaluate success not just on society's but also on each individual's terms.

Growing up successfully does not happen naturally or effortlessly any more — if it ever did. Western societies no longer provide clear guidelines or dictate what we are to do, whom we are to marry, or how many children we should want. My twenty-three-year-old Nepalese treking guide told me that it was time for him to marry. No, he didn't want to marry until he could support a wife, but his younger brother couldn't marry until he did. No, he wasn't looking for a wife; in his country, mothers arranged the marriages of their children. Yes, he would see whom she chose for him, but only briefly, before the marriage. Maybe in time they would love each other — even become good friends. No, he couldn't divorce her if he didn't like her. Tom and Roger, however, must work much more self-consciously to create their goals and the mind and character to achieve them. Success isn't just a matter of luck, family privilege, or society's program; it has become more a matter of our character and the way we use it, for example, learning how to be persons of integrity.

Growing up also means deciding what is more and what is less important, such as not wanting to father one's own children but wanting to work with street kids instead. It means accepting that we cannot be everything we would like to be, as William James, one of America's most influential philosophers, told us 100 years ago when he wrote psychology's first textbook.

I am often confronted by the necessity of standing
by one of my empirical selves and relinquishing the
rest. Not that I would not, if I could, be both hand-
some and fat and well dressed, and a great athlete,
and make a million a year, be a wit, a *bon-vivant,*
and a lady-killer, as well as a philosopher, a philanthropist, statesman, warrior, and African explorer,
as well as a "tone-poet" and saint. But the thing is
simply impossible. The millionaire's work would
run counter to the saint's; the *bon-vivant* and the
philanthropist would trip each other up; the philosopher and the lady-killer could not well keep house
in the same tenement of clay.[2]

Harriet, my wife, questions James's idea that we have to have
a Number 1 Self, or one identity. "Why couldn't James be si-
multaneously fat, a wealthy philosopher, and a lady-killer?" I
think she says this because she's having trouble juggling being
married to me, devoting herself to our three children (and now
our two grandsons), and enjoying being so needed in her consulting work on parenting in schools. She wants to do everything as well as she'd like, so she argues that James's belief that
we must have a Number 1 Self is a male view of growing up.
Men have always had one identity — their vocations; women have
had at least two — wives and mothers — until recently. Super-
woman now wants three. Not even Superman could manage
two successfully; he lost his superhuman power to work good
when he chose to marry Lois Lane.

The Escort's bumper sticker provokes such questions as: What
is success to mean to us? Are our goals genuinely ours, project-
ing into the future our own identity's potentials? Or are our goals
only grafts of others' expectations, pushing us to become what
our potentials aren't — a Cadillac rather than a Lincoln Con-
tinental?

What does success mean to you? Why not rank the following
twelve goals that most people would like to achieve? Then you
can compare your personal meanings to those of college-going
adults who have similarly ranked their values. Rank your most

important goal or value a 1, the next priority goal a 2, and so on. Try not to give tied ranks; discover just how clearly ordered your priorities are.

Leadership-power   ——
Happy marital relationship   ——
High income   ——
Competent and satisfied parenting   ——
Psychological maturity; good mental health   ——
Self-fulfillment; happiness   ——
Religious-ethical ideals   ——
Fulfilling sexual relationship   ——
Competence in a satisfying vocation   ——
Being a contributing citizen to the
   community-nation   ——
Having a close friend of the same sex   ——
Physical health   ——

Let's see how your priorities compare to those of several thousand college-educated thirty- to fifty-year-olds. The adults I have surveyed rank the following as most to least important:

Self-fulfillment; happiness
Psychological maturity; good mental health
Physical health
Happy marital relationship
Religious-ethical ideals
Competent and satisfied parenting
Competence in a satisfying vocation
Being a contributing citizen to the community-nation
Fulfilling sexual relationship
Having a close friend of the same sex
Leadership-power
High income

Men and women reliably differ in a few of their priorities. Men value a fulfilling sexual relationship and high income more than women do. Women rank a close friendship with another woman and contributing to society more highly than men do.

(Parenthetically, every dogmatic-sounding statement about what I have found is a reliable statistical result — unlikely to have occurred by chance. I shall tell you when I am giving an opinion that is not well backed up by firm results.)

Although every group I have spoken to ranks these values similarly, the order of the priorities doesn't ring quite true to me.[3] (You may be asking yourself the same questions.) Surely the unemployed or those trying to support a family on a McDonald's hourly wage or Chinese peasants planting rice shoots day in and day out would order their hopes differently. Is wealth generally ranked last because the adults who have ordered these goals are economically comfortable? Or do they feel guilty being so? Do well-educated and prosperous Americans *really* believe that wealth and vocational and sexual satisfaction are less important than religious and ethical ideals? What about those advertisers who presumably know what we want — or at least know what they want us to have? Status? A Porsche or BMW? A Gold American Express card? Sex? X-rated cassette tapes and TV soap operas? Are we saying something important to them and our leaders about what we really want for ourselves and, I assume, for our children? About what our "basic values," our priority selves, really are? About what success means to us? Or are we unconsciously deceiving ourselves by professing one value but living out another?

I have grouped these twelve values into three parts that organize the book's discussion of the character and mind needed to achieve them. In the first part belong the values about fulfilling our intimate and personal relationships, such as creating marital, parental, and sexual ones, and close same-sex friendships. Second, there are the values about succeeding vocationally — achieving wealth, leadership, power, satisfaction, and competence. In the third part go the values about committing ourselves to other-centered activities, like contributing to our communities and holding religious and ethical ideals, as well as the values about enhancing well-being — being physically and mentally healthy, self-fulfilled, and happy.

If we are clear about our priorities, we now can ask what mind and character are necessary to achieve them.

Understanding the Mind and
Character Necessary to Succeed

Before previewing the strengths needed to succeed in our intimate relationships and work or to be healthy and happy, I must answer the questions I am most frequently asked about the study and how I got my information. If my answers are too brief or raise other questions, you may wish to read the Appendix, which gives more technical information about the study and its methods.

Why Did You Do the Study? The study was undertaken to find out what successful and fulfilled people are actually like and how they got that way, to test the principal hunches of clinicians and researchers about what middle-aged men and women are like, and to discover if men and women mature similarly.

Who Are the Study's Men and Women? They are primarily college-educated men and women; many have secured graduate and professional training. They are physicians, scholars, ministers, journalists, engineers, research scientists, mathematicians, poets, singers, lawyers, managers, entrepreneurs, and owners and presidents of business firms. About two-thirds of the women work outside of the home.

The sixty-five men are more homogeneous as a group than their partners. All are white. Most came primarily from middle- and upper-middle-income families; all attended the same small liberal arts college (Haverford), though not all graduated. They were selected from five successive classes, either randomly or nominated by judges for their interpersonal, extracurricular, and community success or failure. I had extensive information about them when they were about seventeen, twenty-one, and thirty-two. When studied for the fourth time, they ranged in age between forty-two and forty-seven.

The forty women are the partners of the men. They vary more than the men in their ethnic, national origin, and social class backgrounds. They attended diverse colleges and ranged in age from twenty-six to fifty-two though they averaged thirty-nine when studied. I had known two-thirds of them when the men were in their early thirties. At that time they had completed extensive questionnaires about their husbands and more limited questionnaires about themselves; I had also interviewed many of them in their homes.

All but five of the men had married. Thirty percent had been divorced, most since I had seen them when they were in their early thirties. All but four couples had children who ranged in age from two months prenatally to twenty-six years.

Isn't Your Group So Atypical That Generalizations to Other Persons Are Precarious? Yes. I cannot assert with great conviction that some of these results would also describe blue-collar steel workers, unemployed inner-city blacks, or migrant Hispanics. I don't know, for example, how great disparities in education limit what I found about the character of vocationally successful persons.

Possibly. The past decades' remarkable changes in women's roles may limit some findings, such as those about the character of good lovers, to women in their thirties and forties. The equally as profound changes in the structure of the family may make findings about the parents and homes that contribute to adult success questionable.

And no. The men and women are human beings who had to learn to cope successfully with universally shared life-tasks, such as marriage, children, and vocations. Since I wanted to know about successful persons, I needed exemplars of different successes. The men and most of the women had gone to colleges that had carefully selected them for character strengths and promise as well as academic achievement. Most had been favored by excellent preparations likely to increase success in some areas of their lives. So the likelihood was high that I had some who approached the ideally successful person of their generation.

I took several steps to check how their "atypicality" might limit my generalizations. I included questions from a national survey of mental health. The men and women did not noticeably differ from other highly educated persons in how satisfied and happy they were about their various roles.[4] I also compared the group's statistical results with those of the few other longitudinal

adult studies that used either randomly selected or similarly atypical samples. Studies like the Intergenerational Studies (IGS)
at Berkeley and Vaillant's study of Harvard graduates (which
I describe in the Appendix) used many more researchers, elaborate methods, and participants. What is remarkable, however,
is that despite such differences our findings are so similar. I shall
alert you about others' findings that contradict what I discovered.

*How Can You Make Generalizations from Describing Unique
Persons, Such as Roger and Peter?* This superb question, most
frequently asked by humanists, requires a longer answer about
how psychologists go about their business of understanding human nature. Freud revolutionized our understanding of ourselves by developing a psychological cosmology based on clinically studying only a few unhealthy patients and himself. For
more than fifty years, researchers have tried to determine how
true his conclusions were for the rest of us. Abraham Maslow,
the first influential psychologist to describe fully developed and
self-actualized adults, did the same thing.[5] But psychologists have
been much less interested in testing his ideas; I now understand
one reason why. Successful adults are extraordinarily involved
and busy people. Scheduling thirteen to fifteen hours of questionnaires, tests, and interviews into their calendars tested not
only their commitment to our study but my own. It would have
been infinitely easier to have studied "actualized" but captive
white rats, college students, and hospitalized patients.

Although Freud, Maslow, other psychologists, and popular
writers vividly describe interesting people and then induce ideas
from their lives about what the rest of us are like, they do not
answer satisfactorily whether what they found can explain others'
lives. I too shall describe individual men and women who succeed and identify the salient strengths that account for their success, but I must go beyond this more literary approach if I wish
to maintain that such strengths are necessary for others to succeed. I must check out statistically how *common* the strengths
are in the lives of other successful men and women. If I do not,
I will have no reliable clue about which strengths are unique
to a particular person and which are shared by most who suc-

ceed. To answer the question "What are the core strengths we need to succeed and be happy?" I shall return over and over to the larger group to search out which strengths most consistently appear in the lives of successful men and women.

What Is So Special About the Study? Some ask a more stringent question, "What is unique about the study?" I risk seeming to be immodest, but I believe that it is the most systematic and theoretically organized long-term study of adults yet completed. It is also the most thorough study of the fullest range of different adult successes of which I am aware. More than any other study of such long duration, it has used the same core battery of measures for at least three of the four times the men have been assessed.

Compared to the few other longitudinal studies of adults that have been reported, it has relied on the judgments of the three persons — marital partner, closest friend, and colleague — who knew most intimately how successfully the participants fulfilled their principal adult roles. Most studies of adults rely almost exclusively on the participants' own descriptions of their personalities, relationships, and achievements.

I can more comfortably answer the question, "How rare is the study?"

There are only a few comparable intensive longitudinal studies, though the most prominent ones, such as Terman's of intellectually gifted persons, the Intergenerational (IGS) studies of Californians, and Vaillant's of Harvard alumni, have gone on for longer periods of time. The Appendix describes these and other supportive studies.

The study's design and methods enabled me to objectify and quantify for statistical analysis even its most subjective measures, like focused interviews on how and why adults change over time. Consequently, it is possible to identify personality changes from ages twenty-one to forty-five, their causes, and principal maturing effects of such determinants. However, I won't elaborate in detail on this aspect of the study; this book is about successful middle-aged persons rather than about their development from seventeen to middle age.

Because the study included different ways of assessing how successfully each person achieved each of the twelve goals that you rated, I was able to check the results of one measure against the results of several others. For example, I measured marital success by each participant's ratings, each partner's ratings about the other, and their closest friends' ratings. Each also completed a comprehensive marital scale about his or her marriage that described in detail what researchers had previously found described happy marriages. Each also answered interview questions about the marriage, as well as created an imaginative story in response to a picture portraying a middle-aged man and woman embracing, thus revealing (so clinicians believe) less conscious feelings and attitudes about such relationships. Finally, I lived with most of the couples for several days and observed how they got along with each other.

Mental health and psychological maturity were similarly assessed in as many different ways as possible: psychology's most widely used questionnaire and projective measures of mental health; self-, partner-, and close-friend ratings of psychological health; interview questions about coping ability; transculturally validated measures of maturity; and behavioral tests of different aspects of maturity, among others.

Casting such a wide net increased the odds that I actually measured success. Combining such diverse measures of each of the twelve goals into summary scores increased my confidence in the reliability of the results.

The study is rare in another way as well. I have known the men for twenty-five to thirty years and many of the women for twelve years, been the only person who has studied them, and lived with most for several days in their homes. I have, therefore, probably as ideal a trusting and open relationship with them as is possible for a researcher to have. I have also administered all tests in precisely the same way each time, and so it is probably not possible to secure a more ideal methodological basis for comparing results over the years.

Why Do We Know So Little About Well-Functioning Adults?

Numerous formidable hurdles make such intensive longitudinal studies difficult to initiate and maintain. Realistic problems are daunting. Longitudinal studies are expensive and funding agencies shy away from supporting them. They are also very time consuming; they don't lend themselves to rapid and frequent publications that may emerge, like this book, only after many years of work. Securing the cooperation of just one partner, let alone two, as well as of close friends and colleagues, demands much patience and persistence; incomplete information about some types of success bedevils data analysis and increases the unreliability of some findings. The physical stress of travel for weeks at a time or for weekends for several years can cause severe health problems.

For me, the emotional stress of becoming so involved in the inner dramas of others is the most compelling reason why our knowledge about adults is so thin. I'll tell you about a few of my many adventures to illustrate why psychologists have avoided going "out into the world" to study individuals intimately for long periods of time.

My visit to see Marc Taylor and his wife illustrates the logistical problems of such research. I taught Thursday afternoon and just made my flight to Brazil, which arrived early Friday morning. When he met me at the airport, he was prominently wearing a shoulder holster and gun. Being pacifistically inclined, I apprehensively asked why.

"We're driving into the jungle. Bandits have been reported in the area."

I shrank. Great. Just what I need. Will I get home in time for my seminar Monday evening? (I had promised myself I would never let the research usurp my commitment to my students. It never did.) And then I said to myself, "If we're attacked, I'll whip out my Rorschach inkblots, flash them at the bandits, and promise to tell them their fortune, which will include a happy future if they let us go unscathed." (Only on the return flight did I remember that I couldn't speak Portuguese.) I returned emotionally exhausted, but I was prepared for class Monday night.

Another tale explains why researchers know so little about the most personal lives of effective adults. It is emotionally risky to enter as deeply as I did into the inner secrets of families, and I found no family that was secret free. Since I (and the IRS) paid for my own research expenses for the study of the middle-aged, I tried to see more than one person who lived in the area during the same visit. On one of several trips to the Chicago area I saw Barb and Bob Henry and John and Mary O'Neil. When I first saw Barb, whom I hadn't met before, I felt that she was subdued and preoccupied. She smiled dutifully, almost plaintively, but I sensed some inner dark cloud that I had little inkling of from the hours of preliminary test and questionnaire material. After the first twenty minutes or so of our first interview, I began to feel sad.

When I asked what she was most proud of in her life, she answered, "Nothing. I've a lousy marriage; I love my kids but I sometimes wish I didn't have them."

A few minutes later, she broke in to ask, "Everything I tell you is just between us, isn't it? Bob won't know?"

"Yes. I feel strongly about that," I responded.

At the end of the interview, she tearfully said, "I've had enough. I'm thinking of ending it all."

I couldn't sleep that night. What should I do? I had no question about what was most important: Barb, not the study. I decided to ask her if she really wanted to continue. The next morning, without my asking, she drew me aside to say she wanted to go on. "I just needed to feel understood." But we worked on the pain later. (No one in the study has committed suicide, though one child of the participants has.)

Late the next day I arrived at the O'Neils'. John's first comment was, "I'm awfully sorry. I hope we haven't messed up the study. We didn't have time to let you know. Martin [their fourteen-year-old son] ran away from home last Tuesday, stole a car, and cracked it up. He refused to tell the police his name. We've been going crazy. Mary's had a rough time. We just found him. He's okay now but he doesn't want to meet you." How could I help John and Mary? All I could do was to be there for as long as they needed me, and for several years after, whenever they needed support.

A Preview of the Personality
of Successful Men and Women

To share the results of a comprehensive study of twelve different values like a happy marital relationship and a high income may tax your patience and dampen your interest. To provide a general framework with which to remember and make sense of the detailed results, I shall now begin to build the overall psychological scaffold of the mind and character of persons who grow up to succeed.

I ground the scaffold on the men's and women's own judgments about the strengths necessary to succeed in their principal adult roles as citizens, marital and sexual partners, parents, friends, and workers (A4b). They agreed that eleven core strengths are necessary. Note the ones that are missing that our society values highly. The most important strengths are *caring* and *compassion, honesty and integrity,* and a *sense of humor.* Every major adult role involves other persons; our success depends upon the quality of our relationships with them. When we care, we affirm to others that they count, are important, are valued, or are even loved. When we speak honestly and act out of our hearts with integrity, we create trust. And when we bring the perspective of humor to our relationships, we help each other transcend the pain of frustration and anger that inevitably arises in our relations with others.

The next core strengths needed to succeed are *openness and undefensiveness* about sharing our feelings and *tolerance and acceptance* of others' quirks and failings.

Other strengths are *dedication and commitment* to fulfill our different roles well. Without such commitment, work becomes sloppy, marriages are unstable, good parenting is unreliable, sex is only sex and not intimacy, friendships are untrustworthy, and community contributions are ineffective.

The men and women then identified the interpersonal strengths of *understanding, respecting, and empathizing with others,* and rounded out the list with *adaptability and self-confidence.*

I had not anticipated that so many interpersonal skills would be so critical for success in *all* of our adult roles. Unless one is a hermit, however, works by and for one's self, is single, childless, and avoids doing anything for any other nearby hermit, strengths like caring, openness, tolerance, and honesty are essential.

Are you now as troubled as I that intellectual skills and knowledge are not at the top of the list? They are important, but are not even as important as patience. Is it not ironic, and un-settling, that not one of the principal strengths that contribute to adult success is directly measured by the academic grades and the achievement and scholastic aptitude test scores that create so much anxiety in young people, parents, and commissions that seek to improve our schools? Instead of measuring the likelihood of adult success, these tests humble our children, enhance self-centered competitiveness, and undermine their confidence in their ability to learn and educate themselves. It is not that the kind of intelligence that they measure is unimportant; grades and scholastic aptitude scores tell us how rapidly we can learn, particularly abstract ideas. It is just that they do not measure well the rich variety of skills and character strengths, particularly interpersonal and ethical ones like caring, empathy, and honesty, that contribute most to adult success.

The foundation of the scaffold of success has been based on the men's and women's reflections about the strengths most necessary to succeed. To make it more firm, let's find out what you would *actually* be like if you and your partner, closest friend, and colleague believed that you had such strengths. If you scored high on the strengths you identified as necessary to succeed, you would undoubtedly be happy and fulfilled; your partner, friend, and colleague would agree (A11). You would also be an ethically sensitive and idealistic person (A31), happily married (A7), interpersonally intimate (A8), and vocationally successful in the eyes of the colleague who best knew your work (A26).

If you want a simplified prescription for how to grow up to succeed, the two most noticeable personality strengths would be your maturity and androgyny. More than any other of the numerous personality traits I measured, they predict best who will succeed and be happy. My previous research had alerted me to the importance of psychological maturity (A12). Mature men and women are more likely to be happily married (A7); good parents (A4b,c); sexually fulfilled, compatible with and faithful to their partners (A4e); vocationally satisfied (A6); and healthy, happy, fulfilled (A29), and virtuous (A31). Overall, our maturity impressively contributes to success in our major adult roles. No wonder adults select it, after happiness and self-fulfillment, to be their most important value. They are right to do so. It is the most important key to success in most areas of life.

I had had no clue from my earlier research that androgynous, particularly interpersonally feminine, skills (A10a) would also consistently predict who would succeed. By androgynous, I mean persons whose peers rate them to show many of the strengths associated with *both* masculinity *and* femininity. Some stereotypic masculine strengths are self-reliance, independence, and ambition; some typical feminine strengths are sensitivity to the needs of others, loyalty, and compassion.[6] Among other things, androgynous men and women feel fulfilled (A11) and make good marital partners (A7), vocational colleagues (A6), close friends (A26c), and responsible community members (A4g).

I have to confess that years of studying how we grow up healthily did not prepare me for how much an androgynous character contributes to success and fulfillment. The result — one of the study's many surprises — taught me about a blind spot in my own thinking about growing up. For thirty years, I had taught my students about yin and yang, the feminine and masculine principles, and Carl Jung's notions about the individuation of anima and animus in the adult years. I knew the feminists' arguments that we must become more androgynous to be healthy persons. But I had never really believed such ideas since no one had ever given me the scientific evidence that I require to support my beliefs. So I never studied androgyny earlier. I included measures of it in the middle-age phase of the study to check out Jung's notions, but I never expected they would be useful (A10). Was I wrong! For the first time, we now have good consistent evidence that documents the wisdom of such religious and clinical insights. The feminists of the past decade were right to focus on the importance of androgyny.

You may have found the description of the study too abstract and the preview elusive because I have not told you how I actually studied how a living, full-bodied, mature, and androgynous person succeeds. I'll introduce you now to Billie Leighton, the study's most successful woman, and tell you about how we worked together to understand the strengths that enabled her to work her own miracle of growing up.

2

Billie Leighton:
Succeeding on Her Own

If any one of the women in the study merits the label of "super-woman," Billie does. But before I can tell you why, I have to tell you more about Abraham Maslow, the first psychologist to try to understand well-functioning and self-actualized persons.

Do you remember that Maslow was the psychological guru for many Americans during the tumultuous sixties and seventies? Even today he is referred to as the father of humanistic psychology. His idea that self-actualization is the ultimate goal of living justified for many "doing their own thing."[1] While psychologists studied white rats, pigeons, and their freshman students in the forties, Maslow pioneered the study of the fully developed adult. He first identified such persons as Abraham Lincoln, Eleanor Roosevelt, others he personally knew, and unabashedly, so I am told, himself. Then he impressionistically drew from their lives the traits he believed they shared, such as self-acceptance, spontaneity, and need for privacy, to paint the portrait of a self-actualized person. Although they are perceptive and wise, Maslow's ideas have been questioned by psychologists; his personal biases and values intruded too insistently into his choices of self-actualized persons, as well as into his method and conclusions.[2]

I have tried to avoid his mistakes when studying well-functioning adults. The men were originally selected randomly or by knowledgeable judges; the women were selected by the men as their spouses. The five stellar examples of the different successes the book describes scored highest on objective tests and the judgments of the three persons who knew best how well they succeeded: their partners, closest friends, and professional or community colleagues.

Even Maslow would have selected Billie Leighton to be the most all-around successful and self-actualized of the study's forty women. She had created one of the happier marriages, become a successful physician, and scored among the top three in her judged leadership, ethical character, and tested maturity. She, as well as her peers, rated herself to be very happy and fulfilled. Maslow might say that she fell down only in her satisfaction as a mother. She scored "average" on a measure of parental fulfillment, largely because she felt torn between her strong need to be a "nurturer," as she labeled it, to her daughter and a caring physician to her patients. So she is not entirely the archetypal superwoman.

How and what did I learn about Billie Leighton? What lessons does her struggle to grow up healthily teach us about the strengths of those who eventually achieve what they've worked a lifetime for? You might enjoy looking for clues in her story that explain why she succeeded so eminently and then compare your clues to those Billie and I came up with.

Billie was the second wife of Allan Leighton, a successful lawyer, whom I had studied when he was seventeen, twenty, thirty-one, and again when he was forty-three. Although I never met her until early Friday evening of one late April day, I knew a great deal about her from the questionnaires and tests that she had promptly completed and returned several months earlier (A1-17). I don't recall now what I expected she would be like when we met, but she appeared younger than her forty-one years. Though she was five feet nine inches tall she seemed more petite, due to her carefully trimmed auburn hair, lissome, willowy movements, and simple, almost severely plain dress. She was not a frilly woman; she seemed to be very much a piece of her St. Louis town house, which was understatedly decorated with modern Danish furniture. The smell of blueberry muffins lingered in the kitchen where we began our work together about

7:30. Her aura, not her appearance or that of the house, captured my memories that spring day: calm, composedly controlled, "down-to-business," efficient, purposeful.

In my study visits, perhaps because I and the men and women
had so little time for a leisurely visit, and because they were
willingly open with me, I tended to ignore the social graces that
people typically use to circle around each other, sensing what
they can and can't say and ask and so seldom ever knowing how
each really feels. As with every person in the study, within the
first hour I gave Billie the Rorschach inkblots test, one of psychology's most intimately revealing personality tests (A19). I
asked her to tell me everything that she saw in each of its ten
cards. To make sense of a vague inkblot or a summer's cumu-
lus cloud, we must find images in our minds to project onto
the blot or cloud. Such images are openings to our inner lives.
They can reveal our unfulfilled urges and fears, the intensity
of our energies, the cast of our minds that organizes our images, and our ways of coping with stress.

After the hour dedicated to the Rorschach, I gave Billie other
tests as well as the first of two several-hour interviews, which
I taped and typed, that focused on her past history of accom-
plishments and worries, ways of coping with them, and present
feelings about her work, marriage, family, and friends (A21).
In the first few minutes of the interview, she said, "A lot of people who know my family story believe that it was very unlikely
that I'd grow out of it. As a child, I truly believed I never would
become old enough to be a parent, probably because of my fear
of not surviving. . . . When my mother was murdered by her
fourth husband, my first husband said, 'Given your relation to
your mother, you're better off that she's dead.'" So Billie in-
troduced me to her family story. No self-pity. No dramatics.
No blame. No excuses. Acceptance. Matter-of-fact. A "What
do I do about it?" attitude. This was the way it was.

Billie's family life had been abysmally capricious. It had few
of the loving, democratic, and firm values that mark the homes
that I have found contribute most to later adult success and happiness. She declared that her beautiful mother's artistic talents
had led her into an erratic, even chaotic, bohemian way of life.

When Billie was five, her mother had divorced her husband because he physically abused her. She subsequently remarried three times; each new husband reminded Billie of her own father. He had also remarried but shortly afterward divorced his second wife to marry another. Billie was shuffled back and forth between her mother, father, and grandparents during these marital games of musical chairs. On the previsit questionnaires, she had rated her parental home as tense and conflictive; her parents had argued frequently about her and about money and had never given her the feeling that they had enjoyed being parents to her (A1a).

As Billie said (which was later confirmed by her test scores), she still felt deeply ambivalent about her mother and women who took the role of a "mother" to her. She had rated her mother as a socially outgoing, effervescent, actively energetic woman who enjoyed exploring new ideas and encouraged her independence. But she also recalled that her mother had been sexually maladjusted, physically unhealthy, and so mentally unstable as to be twice hospitalized for depression. Too self-absorbed, her mother seldom made herself available or accessible when Billie really needed her. Though she emphasized that Billie should do well in school, she never, for example, helped her daughter with her homework. To the item, "I felt rejected by my mother," Billie checked "Quite true." However, she felt more gently ignored than hostilely rejected. Her mother had not been an authoritarian or severe disciplinarian. Billie didn't feel particularly close or temperamentally similar to her mother; she only moderately respected her as a model of the woman she should become. But she still was not emotionally free of needing her (A4i). To an incomplete sentence that began, "When she thought of her mother, she . . . ," Billie poignantly wrote, "wanted more" (A16).

Billie talked much more about her father than her mother in the first interview, perhaps because he was no longer an *unresolved* painful presence in her life. She felt that he really loved her when she was a child, but he had later run out on her. "As a little kid, he loved me; he paid attention to me and provided for my physical needs through my teenage years. He stimulated me intellectually; we'd sit at the dinner table and talk about theories of evolution. That was important to me."

He, however, as well as both stepmothers, who she felt didn't like her, became more authoritarian, severely disciplining and regulating her personal and social life in her teenage years. He enforced "ridiculous rules, like I could go out only one night a week, and restricted me in other ways not at all in line with my peers." She felt that her father was more loyal to his wives than to her, which he later admitted after his second divorce. He never sided with her when she desperately needed his support. On Billie's seventeenth birthday, he told her that she was now "emancipated"; it was time for her to be on her own. Billie returned to her grandparents, who have remained her "real" parents to this day. Regrettably, I didn't inquire more deeply into their character to understand their support that she knew she could always rely on.

Without rancor, Billie said she had never been important to her father. To a questionnaire item, "I felt rejected by my father," she checked, "Quite true" (A1a). Not actively concerned about her or her welfare, he, like her mother, never made himself accessible when she needed him. Billie felt that he did not understand her, perhaps because they were so dissimilar temperamentally. Nevertheless, he felt more warmly toward her than her mother had; so she felt closer to and loved him more than she had her mother. Though she still visits him several times a year, he has never visited or telephoned her. He has emotionally passed out of her life.

Despite her unsettled home life, Billie enjoyed school, where she did so well that she became overly sensitive about appearing to be too smart and competent. Believing that "the only pathway to love and approval was through perfect performance," she participated in every challenging academic and extracurricular activity she could. She made the state's debating team, became a leader in her state's athletic association, and won awards for scholarship as well as leadership. Excelling in school and extracurricular activities and assuming household responsibilities in her father's house left little time to develop other interests. Although sharing interests typical of girls her age, she felt that she was different, a feeling that has persisted to the present. She had some close friendships with other girls and boys but was not sexually active until she married in her mid-twenties.

Needing the security of her grandparents, she remained home with them while attending what she called a "mediocre" state-run college with "very mediocre teachers," rather than going the several hundred miles to the university, which would have been more appropriate for her talents.

Growing up in a stable and conservative Catholic neighborhood with an eventually thrice-divorced mother and then father had made her feel that she "was from the wrong side of the tracks." So after graduating from college and marrying Frank Peters, who came from "the good side," she felt a special duty to prove to him her own credentials. She supported him during his graduate work for the five years they stayed together, but the marriage became rockier and rockier.

When her mother was murdered by her fourth husband in an ugly drunken brawl, Billie inherited some money from a small insurance policy that (unknown to her at the time) eventually became her life-raft to a much happier and more productive adult life. Doubtful about her future, increasingly unhappy with a marriage that wasn't meeting her needs, feeling stuck, and unable to grieve her mother's death, she used the insurance for short-term counseling from a local community clinic. At one point, her counselor asked her, "What is it you really want?" For forty-five minutes, Billie talked about what her grandmother and husband wanted of her. He re-asked the question. "What do *you* want?"

> I burst into tears for no one had ever asked before what I wanted. When he then said, "I hear you saying you are in a terrible marriage and really want to get out," a light bulb flashed. He was giving me permission to ask something for myself. It took me another year and a half to get out. My husband didn't pass his grad school prelims. I bought him a car and got him an apartment so I could leave him as free of guilt as possible. I left and felt free for the first time in my life.

Deciding to go to medical school, she paid her own tuition and living costs by working at odd hours at any job she could find. (A "miracle," her adviser later told her.) She got her M.D., married a successful lawyer, and took time out to have a child. She had resumed her career working with three other physicians in a nearby suburb shortly before I saw her.

So began my intensely concentrated visits — first, the Rorschach, then some other tests, and then the first of two taped recorded interviews. Unfortunately, my visit, as was so frustratingly typical, was regulated by a tight plane schedule and teaching responsibilities. I couldn't relax and be sociable that evening for I had to analyze Billie's Rorschach and integrate its results with an interpretation of her other personality tests that I had completed prior to my visit. Since I don't like to take from another without giving in return, I offered Billie, as I had everyone in the study, an analysis of all of her test results after completing the two interviews (A25). The next day's interview would focus on how and why she had changed during the past decade, and, because her reflections might influence my interpretation of the Rorschach, I had to complete its analysis before that interview. (This precaution was most needed in my work with the men who had taken many of the same tests, including the Rorschach, when seventeen or twenty-one and also in their early thirties.) After completing the typed sixteen-page analysis of Billie by two in the morning, I wearily drifted off to sleep.

After Saturday morning's fresh orange juice and blueberry muffins, Billie and I got right to work to complete several other questionnaires and the second taped interview about how her mind, values, relationships, and attitudes about herself had changed in the past ten to twelve years. We then explored systematically which of fifty possible events, such as her type of occupation or role as a wife, had influenced her most and how they had changed her (A23). She next answered other questions about how the changing roles of women and men had affected her (A24). I then reviewed with her the report about her tests that I had completed the night before (A25).

That afternoon I began to work with Allan, who in the morning had considerately taken their daughter on an outing to the arch along the river. I don't remember now what happened, but I got caught for time and couldn't stay for the special Sunday dinner that Billie had prepared. We raced to the airport where I just made my flight back to Philadelphia in time to prepare for Monday's classes.

As others had done, both thanked me for the "gift" my visit had been — for what, I wasn't sure. Perhaps it was because I genuinely tried to listen and understand without making judgments even about what they might have felt were awful, perverse, or wicked wishes and deeds. However, it was really I who had been given the most precious gift a person can receive: the sharing of another's most personal life. It was a measure of Billie's maturity to so trust me — almost a stranger — and be so open and honest and to agree to share her life so publicly with you, the reader.

Why Billie Grew Up to Succeed

If you enjoy figuring out Agatha Christie's mysteries and working with Jessica Fletcher to solve her weekly murders in CBS's *Murder, She Wrote,* then become a psychological detective and join Billie and me as we look for hunches about why she succeeded the way that she did. Her life story defies the lessons that our Dr. Spock and other psychologists have taught us about the families that help us to grow up healthily. How could Billie, given a disruptive family, rejecting parents, mediocre schooling, and a failed marriage, pull herself up by her bootstraps to become the study's most competent, mature, and fulfilled woman? What strengths enabled her to resist and free herself of the potentially damaging effects of her early life?

Most of my hunches are based on the tests I gave Billie. You may feel they are arbitrary, even dogmatic, pronouncements, but Billie (like the others of the study) had asked for my ideas about how and why they were growing, knew that I cared, and realized that my ideas were only hunches. Billie agreed with them and amplified them with other examples from her life.

The summary of her tests that I completed early Saturday morning identified the core strengths that contributed to her success. "She has an unusually rich number of intellectual and personality potentials to use for adapting. Her most salient specific strength can only be described as an androgynous judiciousness. What is most striking is her accessibility in a balanced way to stereotypical feminine and masculine strengths. She is one of the more psychologically healthy, emotionally stable, and mature persons of the entire group." Billie's success and fulfillment were due to at least three prominent strengths: her cast of mind, her androgynous character, and her maturity.

I could not tell how much her genes, constitution, family climate, parents, schooling, and other events separately contributed to how she turned out. Surely she must have inherited some impressive intellectual and energetic genes that enabled her to withstand and overcome the corrosive effects of her early family life. What is important is how she developed and made use of her potential intellectual strengths.

What strengths of mind contributed to her ability to cope? She herself identified her principal ones, which were independently confirmed by the tests. "Ever since I can remember as a child, I have been both very introspective and very socially outgoing. I have an analytical side to me. When I had a bad relationship with someone, I'd think about it, work it through in my mind until I understood it and why it happened. It helped me to change my behavior. I did a lot of analytic work when younger; I kept a log, not exactly a diary, in which I wrote about what was troubling me and how to change myself."

Billie coped with her disruptive family life by consciously developing what she called a "problem-solving" approach to living. She must have had a lot of practice trying to understand her discordant family life, making sense of what was happening, and adjusting to each new stepfather or -mother. The Rorschach showed she could note details and put them together in clear, realistic, and practical ways—hence her judiciousness. Her mind was more practical than fanciful. I wrote, "She has beautiful control as well as resiliency, but her inner clarity seems to preclude the turmoil and disorder as well as the strange and bizarre" (qualities that tend to mark the minds of imaginatively creative persons).

She spoke of the intellectual strengths that contributed to her adult success this way: "I was always very good at remembering things and making relationships between things. Now I am much better able to do the next step of analysis . . . the grander relationships. One skill I have is being able to see a patient, analyze seemingly separate and discrete symptoms, pull them together in a whole, and then bring out the various approaches to treat the problem."

Years of practice trying to figure out each of her four fathers and three mothers and how to get along with them must have strengthened her reflective problem-solving skills, such as planning "proactive" steps, as she called it, to resolve family strains and anticipating their consequences.

High intelligence, introspective and reflective control, analytic ability, and practical problem-solving skills aren't enough to account for her success, however. We must look to her character. Billie shared the typical strengths of both women and men to an unusual degree. Her androgyny consistently emerged in three different ways. She populated the vague Rorschach inkblots with well-defined wolves, bears, giants, and alligators — all typically aggressive images that males tend to give. But she also saw princesses, bunny rabbits, sea cows, and a baby's head — images that females typically see more frequently in the blots.

She was also temperamentally similar to persons successful and happy in *both* typically feminine and masculine occupations, as measured by a widely used vocational interest scale, the Strong-Campbell (A3). Unlike others of the study, she resembled successful persons of her own sex in most fields of endeavor: in the expressive arts, probably reflecting her mother's bohemian inclinations; in mathematics and science, reflecting her father's scholarly temperament; in entrepreneurial activities like business, politics, and law; and even in adventurous, risk-taking vocations like the military.

I had selected Billie to describe before I had examined how she, Allan, her closest friend, and a colleague had rated her on 100 personality traits (A10; A13). Twenty of them measured typical masculine strengths like assertiveness and self-reliance;

twenty measured typical feminine ones like compassion and sensitivity to others.[3] Such strengths are not exclusive to one's sex; every man and woman share to different degrees both masculine and feminine ones (A10). Allan, her friend, and a colleague rated her to be not only the most masculine of the study's women but also its third most feminine woman. Adding these two high scores together made her the most androgynous woman. That three diverse measures — an inkblot test, psychology's most reputable vocational interest scale, and judgments of the three persons who knew her most intimately — identified her to be androgynous, rather than only feminine or masculine, suggests that her androgyny was probably close to the core of her identity. Billie did not dispute these objectively based hunches. She told me, "My colleagues tell me that I don't think like a woman. I think like a man. They mean it as a compliment, not realizing it is insulting. I've also been very aware that my name is androgynous. That must've influenced me in some ways when growing up."

The tests suggested that her androgyny may have influenced her growing up this way. In her growing-up years, she developed both masculine and feminine strengths without clearly emotionally identifying with either a fixed female or male sexual role. So she is open to and accepts the potentials of both. What is intriguing from a developmental view is that this amalgam did not result in a diffuse sense of self or identity, lack of a strong will or ego, or paralyzing emotional conflicts. Instead, she learned when young how to reflect judiciously, analyze, and integrate such potentially contradictory strengths in very healthy and mature ways. In some ways, her basic identity is organized around her own image of herself as a problem solver who can cope, not around her femaleness or maleness. Her stereotypic female and male strengths are not ends in and of themselves but means to adapting. Her androgynous character provided her with rich and diverse gifts on which to draw to succeed in her familial and vocational roles.

That her psychological maturity was so formative didn't surprise me. My earlier research had amply showed over and over that more mature youths continue to grow more rapidly and healthily than immature ones; they cope with adversity more effectively throughout their lives. Maturity is its own condition for further maturing. Billie's maturity enabled her to use her intellect in the way that she did to succeed.

When asked of what she was most proud in her life, Billie instantly replied, "I feel that I've now come to terms with what I am and am functioning as a healthy adult for the first time in my life. I am ambitious, set high goals for myself, and work hard to get there. But I don't walk over other people. I really have a strong need to be loved and have loving friendships. Because of that I have sought out mother- and father-figures in my friends and colleagues." I shall describe her maturity in more detail in the next chapter, which summarizes what we now know about healthily growing persons.

So why did Billie turn out so successfully, overcoming seemingly impossible and devastating odds? We don't know with great certainty, for her early childhood and other influences remain too obscure, as well as much too complicated. Native talent and temperament contributed to her special coping skills. Probably, in a perverse way, her parents, by not being emotionally compelling and respected models, didn't confirm her in either a rigidly feminine or masculine sexual role. Familial insecurity was the goad to learn how to survive. School was where she succeeded and discovered her own competitive worth. Supportive grandparents provided the safe harbor to which to retreat and from which to sail forth.

Billie learned to survive and flourish on the basis of her *own* maturity and determined will to produce that "miracle" of putting herself through medical school to which her adviser had referred. By the time she remarried, she had developed the good judgment to marry a man who, sensitive to her needs, supported her professional career by making adjustments in his own life.

Her story suggests ideas about maturing, success, and fulfillment that we should keep in mind when we later sort out what is unique to Billie and what is common to those who succeed in their different adult roles.

• Destructive and unhappy families do not inevitably doom us to stagnation and failure.

- It can take a long, long time of hard personal work to really feel "grown up."
- Too rigid demands to be a typical male or female can get in the way of developing the rich strengths needed to succeed later in life.
- Psychologically mature adolescents have the skills and values to take charge of and direct their own growing up.

Does not Billie's identity as a problem solver model the character we need to develop to adapt to the uncertainties of the twenty-first century? It transcends the traditional role categories that have become increasingly dysfunctional in our gender-related relationships. Her life is really a story about hope. It tells us that we don't have to succumb passively to today's dismally disintegrating families and societal values. It begins to illuminate the critical character strengths necessary to create healthier, more fulfilled lives. We can summon the will to assert control over our lives and work to change them for the better. This sounds like a sermon, but it expresses what Billie reaffirms for me.

Let's now examine in depth the meaning of Billie's maturity — the principal key to her growing up to succeed and be happy.

3

Key Paths
to Maturity

Each of us can tell our own special story about how we have grown up. Billie's may feel foreign, even unbelievable, to you. Although few of us have had seven "parents" raise us or have witnessed the murder of our mothers, each of us walked a common psychological path when growing up healthily.

The great religions believe similarly and urge us to take this path. Whether they call it the path to "maturity," "salvation," *Sahaja,* or "Enlightenment," most identify similar signposts along the way. Their view of how humans grow healthily tells us to become more aware, other-centered, harmonious, committed, and self-disciplined persons. Furthermore, whatever their century or background, people have highly valued that path. Buddha, Jewish prophets, Christ, Mohammed, liberal educators, philosophers, Dewey, Maslow, and the men and women I have canvassed around the world have agreed, though each in his or her own words, that becoming more mature is an important goal for living. Wise observers of those who have lived their lives well intuitively sense, with good reason, that this is the *key* to the good life, and research agrees. Maturity predicts who will marry happily, feel fulfilled vocationally, and act virtuously.

The map below (Table 3.1) describes maturity's principal markers. To make the map vividly "real" for you, ask yourself questions like those I asked Billie. "How have I changed since I graduated from school?" "How has my partner's personality or my divorce

Table 3.1. Model of Maturing: Attributes That Contribute to Adapting Effectively.

Developmental Dimensions of Maturing

The Person	Symbolization	Other-Centeredness	Integration	Stabilization	Autonomy	Effects of Successful Adaptation
			Mind			
Cognitive skills	Is imaginative; Has precise control of words-numbers; Comprehends oral and written word; Speaks-writes articulately; Is reflective; Is inductive	Takes multiple perspectives; Analyzes well; Is realistic and objective in judgment	Has relational, synthetic, organizational skills; Developed hypothetical-deductive and logical reasoning skills	Knowledge is accurate, precise, broad, organized, readily accessible, resistant to interference; Skills resist disruption; if not, can recover resiliently	Judgment is independent, critical, and appropriate; Knowledge and skills are mobile, readily transferable, and available for self-educating and creative purposes	Increased mastery, competence, and sense of power
			Character			
Interpersonal skills	Is sensitive to and perceptive of others and of relationships; Is psychologically minded and understanding of others	Empathically feels for, cares about, respects, and enjoys persons who differ from self	Is not defensive but genuinely open and spontaneous in relationships; Is able to create cooperative mutual work and intimate relations	Is loyal and faithful to friends and organizations; Has enduring friendships and work relations not readily broken by argument and strain	Can be independent, self-reliant, and tolerate aloneness if necessary; Selectively forms interdependent relationships	Increased ability to create intimate and love relations

Values	Is aware of and articulates biases, values, and assumptions	Accepts and appreciates diverse viewpoints Has humane values	Sets priorities among values Has values and acts consistent with each other	Has values that endure Persists purposefully to achieve long-term goals	Motivated by considered principle rather than by impulsive wish or environmental pressure	Released energy for new interests, enthusiasms, and adaptive efforts to meet new problems
Metavalues	Honesty Truth	Fairness Compassion	Integrity	Commitment	Courage Freedom	
Self	Has accurate self-insight and understanding	Accurately understands how others view self Identifies self with increasingly diverse others	Strives to unify component selves: private, private and public, actual and ideal Acts spontaneously for has resolved conflicts over divided selves	Sense of self is strong and stable; identity is firm Positively values and is confident of self	Discriminatingly accepts and rejects others' views of self Can affirm own worth independently of others' valuations Believes can direct and control growth of own self	Heightened capacity for self-transcendence and sense of humor

changed me?" "What gift of character or mind would I most value my children thanking me for when they reach thirty?" Then see if you can locate your changes or gift in the table. Or you might even rate on a five-point scale just how much of each strength you have, then ask which strengths have contributed most to your own success. I shall use Billie's map to illustrate other signs of maturity.

The model of maturing summarizes the core strengths needed to adapt successfully.[2] The first column, *The Person,* lists the four principal facets of the whole person: mind's skills, character's interpersonal skills, values, and attitudes about self (self-concept).

The next five columns, labeled *Developmental Dimensions of Maturing,* identify the underlying organizing principles that guide our growth. Our minds and characters mature in five predictable interrelated ways. As we grow, we become increasingly more able to put our experience into some kind of language; we also become more other-centered, integrated, stable, and autonomous, as shown in the way we use our minds and express our character.

The model's last column, *Effects of Successful Adaptation,* lists the principal visible signs of our maturity. When asked by business leaders, school admissions officers, or superintendents for criteria to select managers, students, or teachers for their maturity, I suggest looking for such signs.

If you want a glimpse of your own maturity, first look at how effectively you have fulfilled your responsibilities, say as a lawyer or a citizen. A history of doing many things well tells me that you are on top of your talents and can make them work for you.

Then ask how excited, even passionate, you are about your work, hobbies, community, or world events and whether you have energy left over for initiating new friendships and interests. A mature person's energy is available for spontaneous adventures and new commitments, not tied up in conflict, intellectualized, limited, or exhausted by day-to-day tasks. I once was chairman of a committee to nominate seniors for prestigious international awards. We turned down the college's most distinguished scholar, primarily because he reacted to the question "What have you contributed in the four years you've been here to the life of the college?" with "I've been so busy with my academic work I've had no time or energy to get involved."

The next question to ask is how fully present you are in your relationships with others. I'm not talking about infatuations, sexual affairs, or transitory lover relationships. I mean sensitively aware, compassionate, cooperative, sturdy, nondefensive ones, including those with your own children and parents — probably the most difficult persons with whom to get along maturely.

And finally, ask yourself how well you keep your sense of humor, even in distressing relationships or situations. Do you have enough perspective about a troubling issue to laugh at yourself? A hearty laugh from deep in your gut about yourself and current predicaments with your colleagues or partner is not just cathartic and health sustaining but also a sign that you have transcended pride. Mature persons can also spontaneously play; they don't have to use drugs to anesthetize their consciences or dissolve their self-control. As Jesus implied, they can act like children again. Though I wish Jesus had laughed and played more like a child. He was much too serious for me.

As I now describe each of the five developmental principles that organize the growth of our minds and character, keep the whole person in view. Remember what St. Paul told us in 1 Corinthians 12:12, 17:

> *For as the body is one, and hath many members,*
> *and all the members of that one body, being many,*
> *are one body . . .*
> *If the whole body were an eye, where were the*
> *hearing? . . .*
> *If the whole were hearing, where were the smelling?*

He is right. We grow healthily as persons, not just as minds or in personal relationships. Growth in one facet on one dimension affects growth in other facets on other dimensions. So we are not just eyes or ears, bits and pieces — we are adapting, whole persons. As Maslow once said, we are like indivisible, multifaceted crystals. We sparkle differently depending upon which facets the light strikes, but each facet, whether our minds, interpersonal skills, values, or self-attitudes, is an integral part of the whole crystal. I shall be somewhat arbitrary as I tell you about each in isolation from the other, but I have no other linguistic option: I must focus first on one facet and then another to describe each sign of our maturity clearly.

Becoming More Reflectively Aware: Symbolization

Mind Becomes More Reflectively Aware of Itself. Growing persons like Billie become more aware of how their minds work. Billie reflected about how she went about solving problems. In her own words, she described how our minds mature on all of their dimensions. "I've become increasingly reflective and analytical in my work as well as in my personal relations. I've learned how to approach a problem in a very ordered way. . . . I know now how to analyze and clarify a problem, collect information from others, find a way to reconcile the different viewpoints, and then try testing them out to see which one really works. I do that in my personal relations as well as in my work with patients." Shades of Dewey, who, in 1922, described solving problems similarly. Billie perceptively tells us how a maturing person turns her awareness back on itself by reflection, seeks out information from others and then analyzes it from different perspectives, imagines a course of action that integrates her and others' views, repeatedly tests the proposed line of action to see if it fits, resolves the problem, and so stabilizes the new solution. Billie self-consciously applies this mature way of using her mind to her relationships. She has made the process so much her own that she can autonomously apply it to most domains of living.

Our ability to use symbols to reflect about our experience is the most important adaptive power that distinguishes us from other animals. We can put into words, figures, art, music, and gestures the most simple to the most complicated ideas. We can mentally represent what we feel and think or what our senses see, hear, and touch and then think back in time about it. To describe precisely how to drive from Denver to Miami; recall where we were last Christmas; imagine, anticipate, and plan for the birth of our child; or monitor our ongoing arguments or plans gives us extraordinary power to adapt more effectively. To represent and then manipulate reality imaginally before we must act is a remarkable and immeasurable strength. Mature persons like Billie, who have perfected their awareness of how they can use their mind's coping skills, can therefore adapt more successfully.

Interpersonal Relations Become More Reflective. Maturing persons, like Billie, also become more sensitive to and reflective about their relations with others. Billie's maturity was most pronounced in her ability to reflect about and figure out why she was having difficulties in her relationships. She scored highest on items measuring interpersonal reflectiveness such as "I usually can understand why I have misunderstandings with my partner." "I could describe in detail my feelings and thoughts I had several years ago about my relations with a close female friend" (A12).

Not knowing how to understand others and reflect about our relationships can undermine being successful in our key adult roles. Do you remember Roger Blake, the high school teacher, who wrote, "Restlessness haunts me"? After he wrote that, his relationship with Beth became increasingly more tumultuous and painful. Mystified by what he called her "guerrilla campaign" to make him more sensitive and responsive to her needs, he asked me what she meant by the following excerpt from one of her letters:

> You are easy to love on the one hand and yet difficult to love on the other. Easy because you ask for nothing and yet accept whatever you are given at a shallow level. I give and give to you and it all seems to go down a black hole. Difficult because your soul, your very being, seems enclosed so very deeply, hidden by layers and layers that even to catch a glimpse of a flicker of its flame is rare. In times of stress you seem to sink even further into

yourself. . . . I so desire you to be fully alive, to feel
the pain and the joy but most of all to be there 100%
and not only just a flicker.

Roger dismissed what I felt was a devastatingly accurate
description of him and their relationship by pushing it down
his "black hole." Puzzled about what she really wanted from him
and hurt by her persistent attacks, he decided several months
later to leave her. He had not yet learned what Billie had taught
herself for years to do: to reflect about his relationships with
others and why they were so disruptively painful.

Values Become More Symbolizable. Another maturing change
that contributes to how successfully we adapt is our increasing
awareness of our values. The word *values* refers to what initi-
ates and steers what we do: our goals, preferences, motives, biases, and prejudices. Growing up means becoming more aware
of what is more and less important to us and why. To be aware
of what we want and don't want and why we believe and act
or do not believe and do not act as we do vastly increases our
ability to adapt appropriately. Not until Billie's counselor prodded her to reflect about what *she* really wanted out of her marriage did she feel "free for the first time" to plan her future to
fit her own needs.

Freud taught us how powerfully our behavior can be influenced by wishes and needs of which we are not aware. Repress-
ing desires or impulses into our inner "black hole" can so drain
our vitality that we become just a "flicker" of what we could be.
Like Roger, we don't understand why we are restless, indecisive, and act in ways that aggravate others.

Roger had begun to get glimmers that he didn't know what
he wanted. "Maybe I don't know what I value, really. Maybe
I haven't been honest with myself all these years. Here I am,
thirty-two and I don't know what I really want."

In the mysterious way that our unconscious self communi-
cates to us, Roger and I got clues about his future growth and
why he acted as he did with Beth from three different types of
drawings he had been experimenting with. The first were meticu-

lously precise, over-controlled, literal black-and-white pen sketches devoid of all life. The next were watercolors, explosive, barely controlled riots of color that gave the impression of disruptive passion that hadn't yet been channeled well. The last paintings beautifully integrated the disciplined control of the black-and-white pen sketches with the vivid yellows, oranges, browns, and blacks of his watercolors. The artwork heralded his growing intellectual and emotional integration.

But it was the theme of passages that struck me in the last series of three watercolors. The first showed in perspective a black mine-shaft tunnel with a blocked door at the end. The second was of the same door, closer up, but now partially opened with light shining around it. The last was even closer up, with brilliant yellowish, orange light streaming through the completely opened door gloriously illuminating the tunnel's rich brown-and-black beams and walls.

Intuiting that his pictured passages might reveal something about his restless indecisiveness, I asked Roger to make up a story about his pictures. He said that an old man dressed in black wearing a tall black hat was standing in the doorway and a thirteen-year-old boy holding a burst balloon stood next to him. Suddenly, several playful dogs bounded out of the door. The boy began to play with them but the dogs began to snap and growl at each other so viciously that he became scared, cringed, and backed through the open door, which he managed to shut.

I asked, "What are the first words that come to mind when I say 'dogs'?"

"Passion. Degenerate," he instantly replied, in that order. Then I said, "Old man."

"Superego." Roger impulsively added, "Dogs are id" — Freud's words for conscience and animalistic impulses.

What might such rich and suggestive symbols mean? Could Roger's accepting, "easy to love" persona be shielding him from aggressive, sadistic male impulses that scare him and that his conscience keeps from bounding out of him because such intense passion is "degenerate"? To understand why he closes the door to them, I would ask what happened in his relationship with his father when he was thirteen. Whatever his drawings may mean, they beautifully portray how what is unconscious begins to sneak into awareness, though still in disguised form. As we become more mature, our inner doors open up and our darker passions as well as repressed goodness become accessible for more conscious and constructive use.

Accurate understanding of our motives enables us to be more intellectually honest with ourselves. Roger was psychologically right when he wrote, "Maybe I haven't been honest with myself all these years." He had much growing up ahead of him to better understand his own motives and apprehensions.

Self-Concepts Become More Accurate. A classic sign of growing up is increasing *self*-insight and self-understanding, not just of our relationships and values but also of our personality and how we have become what we are. Accurately understanding our strengths and weaknesses contributes immeasurably to how well we adapt. The study showed that men and women who accurately understand themselves succeed in their principal adult roles, as they and their spouses rated their success (A4c and A26c; A13a).

The roots of our maturing self-awareness reach far down into our earliest years. We learned in first grade, for example, why we were put in the bunny rabbit reading group but not the teddy bear one. I learned in third grade that I might become a teacher when Mrs. Simpson asked only me to read to the rest of the class when she had other things to do. When in adolescence our reflective ability begins to approach that of adults, we turn inward to make sense of our changing selves. One self-conscious, introspective teenager told me, "Well, any sort of criticism, even if somebody curses me out and calls me a dogmatic bastard, which happened recently, I think about. You see, I try and see why am I really a dogmatic bastard."

Helen, when asked what had contributed most to the change in her attitudes about herself since I had seen her twelve years earlier, chose the demands of her community activities.

> What I discovered was that I couldn't be all things
> to all people and I didn't want to. That is my flip

answer. I discovered that being as intense a person as I am, I can't necessarily do as much as other people. [She paused for a moment and frowned.] "Much" is a funny word. I may be even doing more than most. I am chairman of a local community group that works with the elderly. The government gave us 2,000 pounds of cheese to distribute to 400 low-income older citizens. They felt humiliated waiting in line to get cheese; some didn't even know how to sign their names. There were six of us passing the cheese out. Afterwards, this other gal and I really were drained; the others were tired but not drained like us. Only we were flipped out. Then I realized why. We had talked to every one and tried to decrease their discomfort and humiliation. What this tells me is that I really have to be very deliberate and selective about what I do.

Billie's years of laborious effort to understand herself and her relationships with her parents may account in part for the singular inner clarity that I noted in her reactions to the Rorschach. She knew herself so well that the tests I had given her told her nothing that she had not already discovered about herself. With a minimum amount of training in understanding symbols, she could have interpreted her own images. (Roger probably couldn't.)

The study reconfirmed my earlier findings with younger Italians and Turks.[3] Mature, middle-aged persons accurately understand themselves (A12; A13a).

Becoming More Other-Centered

Mind Becomes More Relativistic and Empathic. The course of healthy growth moves from self- to other-centeredness. Intellectually, a child sees the world only from his or her point of view. As five-year-old Jimmy was departing after our neighborhood party, his mother told him, "Tell Mr. and Mrs. Heath 'goodbye' and thank them for the ice cream and birthday cake." Jimmy turned to ask us, "Where are you going?" An adolescent acknowledges others' viewpoints but still believes his or hers

is *the* right one. A mature adult knows that others have their
own views about an issue, each of which may contain elements
of the truth. The mature mind thinks more relativistically. Our
judgment and objectivity improve as we grow beyond thinking
in terms of either/or and black-or-white positions. We learn from
discussions and arguments how to analyze and don't accept simplistic dichotomies, such as "You're either for or against me;
you're a communist or a real American."

Some women told me that their husbands and children prodded and encouraged this growth of their minds.

> My husband is a lot more direct, concise, penetrat-
> ing, down-to-earth. So I look to him for answer-
> ing the question of how do I see what I see . . . like
> to check out reality with him . . . I have taken in
> his way of looking at the world, so it also affects
> my way of looking at the world. He is rather ana-
> lytical. This has been foreign to me. He has showed
> me how to break down a problem into stages with-
> out becoming confused and how to work to a logi-
> cal conclusion.

Another woman said of her thirteen-year-old son:

> He is more of a challenge than I really need. I really
> need to know what the hell I am talking about to
> communicate with an adolescent. He's so sharp that
> he picks up any loose pieces in my thinking. So I
> have to learn how an adolescent would think, put
> myself in his shoes when we disagree. He can drive
> me nuts. [She laughs.] Not really. He's an interest-
> ing little person. Take his snakes. I'd never ever
> look at a snake or rodent and now I realize that
> they can be very interesting things. He brings them
> home. Just as long as they are not contagious, I
> don't care now.

A sign of becoming more other-centered is not just an increasing ability to think like another but also to feel what another

feels. Beth may have been complaining that Roger wasn't entering into *her* world, understanding *her* needs, feeling what *she* was feeling. If Roger had been empathic, he might have talked for Beth this way. "I'm now thirty-four, have been your faithful lover on and off now for more than twelve years, may never have another, and face a 'maritally' empty and childless future as time runs out for me to fulfill my dreams. You keep coming back to my bed, but I still don't know your real 'intentions' or if you'll ever commit yourself to me or anyone else."

Interpersonal Relations Become More Caring. It takes a lot of maturity to value and then develop more other-centered relations in which we genuinely care for and are compassionate with persons who differ from us. Billie Leighton and her peers believed that she was caring and compassionate. Though in conflict about how much time she could give to her daughter and her patients, she valued most highly being a nurturer (so much so that she couldn't leave her first husband until she had bought him a car and an apartment). On one scale measuring her other-centered maturity, she gave herself the highest score for having done things for Allan, even though it was at the expense of her own interests and desires (A12).

Empathy, sympathy, and caring are typically feminine interpersonal strengths. The men did not stand out as mature in their empathy (A13b), possibly because American males have not been expected or taught to develop such other-centered skills. Being a parent contributed to the empathic growth of about 25 percent of them, however (A23). They had to learn such skills "on the job," so to speak, as one father said about his three-year-old son. "He taught me . . . that being a little tiny guy, while I'm a great big guy . . . that a tiny guy has feelings, thoughts, and reasons for doings things, too. And because he is tiny and little and inexperienced does not mean that he is stupid or insensitive. Brought a greater sense of empathy and sympathy for him." The study's three judges reliably agreed that the mature women *and* men were more typically feminine in such interpersonal skills than the immature women and men (A13e; A10a).

Values Become More Humane. Learning how to take someone else's point of view, to analyze a problem from different perspectives, also affects our values. When we truly understand others' viewpoints, we can emotionally appreciate their values and interests, and we more readily tolerate views that disagree with our own. We begin to value giving to others, even though we have no personal relationship with them and may have to sacrifice some of our own interests and desires. Mature Haverford alumni, for example, give more to their college's annual giving fund and to charity than immature alumni. Vaillant found the same result when studying Harvard alumni.[4]

We develop more humane values when our role prods us to learn how to care. A new father eloquently described how his child had begun to affect his values this way. "The feeling that you have toward a helpless baby and later growing child of enormous protectiveness and affection and love and wanting to shield and ensure happiness for her can't help but make you feel a little better and more home-conscious — and less pleasure oriented too" (A23).

Self-Attitudes Become More Other-Centered. Mature persons also have more other-centered images of themselves, images which become broader and more self-acceptant over time. They have shed their adolescent self-image that they are so unique no other person can understand them. By accepting more of their own humanness, they rejoin the human race and become less self-righteous. By seeing everyone in themselves, regardless of their sex, ethnic background, or nationality, they gain access to a wider range of adaptive potentials. By accepting her masculine strengths, Billie developed the assertive will to compete successfully in a male world.

Mature persons, therefore, have a more universal identity that enables them to identify sympathetically with diverse peoples. I think the planet's youth may be spurting ahead of their parents in defining themselves more as human beings than as black or male or American Catholic. Such extensions of our selves' boundaries prepare us to lead less parochial lives. Jews marry Catholics nowadays; blacks marry whites; President Bush, Harriet, and I now have grandchildren of different colors.

Our ideas of ourselves become more other-centered as a result of our relationships with others. Becoming parents not only can nurture our empathic skills and alter our values and priorities but also can change our attitudes about ourselves.[5] Another father captured how his view of himself had changed in his beautifully insightful comment, "I'm certainly different now in that I approach selflessness with my child more than I do at any other time . . . I'm also now more concerned for people other than myself. You become oblivious to yourself . . . your attention becomes focused on the children and you are concerned with their development and really for the first time in your life, your self really drops out of your own thinking" (A23). My daughter, reflecting on what Benjamin, her first child, had done to her, also said, "He's made me much less selfish and self-centered. He comes first now."

As we mature, we not only develop more other-centered self-concepts but also understand more accurately how others view us. This empathic understanding of others' opinions about us powerfully predicts our maturity[6] and success in our marital roles as we and our partners evaluate them (A4c).

Becoming Better Integrated

When Roger was a freshman, he told me, "I feel like a thousand bits and pieces going in a thousand different directions." I recall at the time that I felt he was painfully trapped in an inner maelstrom, but it was a good kind of turbulence. He was in a state of high educability and potential growth, as when we are in love: vulnerable, hypersensitive, flooded by poetry, coursed by strong emotions, confused, awed, and asking, "What is happening to me?"

Such times of personal chaos are potentially precious gifts that can promise new integrations and so new growth. It is agonizing to feel we are only bits and pieces of contradictory values and habits that undercut each other and trip us up as we try to become as decisive and successful as we feel we could be. But it is also exhilarating, for example, to be so possessed by love for another that we become unrealistic, preoccupied, inefficient — even so irrational that Freud likened falling in love to becoming psychotic.

We are built to make sense of our pains and exhilarations, to order and make more consistent our views of ourselves, to create coherent meanings about our world. When religions talk about becoming more inwardly harmonious, as most do, they acknowledge the ontological principle that a healthy growing person becomes more consistently integrated. Biographers also know this truth. They search for the fewest themes that organize, make sense of, give consistent meaning to the persons they are bringing to life. I similarly tried to make sense of Billie and will try also for the other principal actors and actresses of the book by identifying the organizing keynotes of their success.

As we mature, our values, temperaments, interests, and personalities increasingly come together to help us achieve our goals; parts of ourselves don't work against and undermine other parts. I remember watching my youngest teach herself to play the piano when she was seven. I heard a particularly discordant note, saw her slap her left hand, and then heard her indignantly exclaim, "Stop doing that." Her two hands had yet to work well together and with her brain.

Mind Becomes More Relational and Contextual. I'll go back to mind's earliest signs of integration. A newborn infant takes no more than a few days to convert his first clumsy efforts to suck at the breast into an efficient, seemingly reflexive effort. He quickly learns how to bring his thumb effortlessly to his mouth to suck when his mother is not present, and eventually he watches his thumb as he waves it back and forth. Wiggily Benjamin, two and a half months old at the time, taught me again how early such integrations occur. While I was babysitting him, he reached for the first time to some colorful keys hanging on a string over his head and pulled them to his mouth to suck. He had never done that before. I witnessed the birth of a new, more complex visual-motor skill that combined looking, grasping, pulling, locating one's mouth, and sucking.

Out of such beginnings and subsequent practice will later come more complex adult physical and mental skills. When he was twenty months old, Benjamin was fascinated by trucks with hitches that pulled trailers. He loved to attach his toy trailer to his truck. When visiting me he saw my trailer parked under the trees and my Escort on the other side of the driveway. Guess what he mentally put together? Right. He pulled me over to the car, pointed to the hitch, and looked at the trailer. The mind's miraculous ability to generalize and put things together blossomed right in front of me.

Such early visual-motor coordinations provide the templates of how we become more and more integrated as we adapt. Piaget, psychology's most careful observer of children's growing minds, showed us how an adult's cognitive skills evolve out of such early experiences; they are the roots of our ability to combine ideas, take them apart, and recombine them to make different patterns or hypotheses.[7] We actively seek more information and learn new skills to increase our perspective and create new meanings and philosophies (or even books like this).

The mature person's mind is relational and contextual. A business manager selected his community's choral group as one of fifty more influential causes of his mind's maturing, and then he explained how it had enriched him. "I just got a broader and broader based frame of reference; while you learn the music strictly speaking, you also get a commentary about interpretation, comparative analyses of the piece's similarity to other pieces we have done, which is very satisfying and stimulating. My musical background just has a richer context to it." The principal growth of the men from thirty-two to middle age was their increased ability to organize, synthesize, and relate ideas with other ideas and to apply them in their work (A23).

Billie has already told us how skillfully she could put ideas together to form hypotheses about her patients' illnesses as well as her own interpersonal troubles with others.

Interpersonal Relationships Become More Cooperatively Mutual. The men and women, as well as their peers, all agreed that mature persons create open, cooperative, harmonious relationships with others. At ease with themselves, they are nondefensively open with others. Mature persons, like Billie, feel comfortable sharing their feelings about even the most personal of topics, such as their dreams, failures, and sexual wishes, with their partners and trusted friends — and with me (A13e, f; A8). They trust themselves to be themselves; they don't try to seem what they aren't in their relationships.

Their genuineness makes possible a deep mutuality, or "we-ness." Such times of communion occur in many different situations: five basketball players effortlessly playing as one unified team; the elderly couple gracefully and flawlessly waltzing in the Ice Capades; the shared mutuality I felt with eight rebellious Jesuit priests in the early seventies illegally taking communion while circling their makeshift altar under the eaves of their monastery; the corporate pride of a Vietnam combat platoon that never left a wounded buddy behind; the gathered meeting of Quakers experiencing a corporate mystical experience; the class coming together as a unified group of reciprocally vulnerable and cooperatively educating students.

Although episodes of mutuality may be transitory or longer lasting, their occurrence is enhanced when the participants have the maturity to transcend their own imperious needs to become attuned to and adapt to those of the group. Not unexpectedly, it was the mature men and women who created more enduring and happy marital and sexually compatible relationships[8] (A4e).

Values Become More Consistently Organized. Growing up means making one's values and acts more consistent with each other. We act with greater integrity; we develop priorities; we figure out what is most important to us. A forty-one-year-old woman in the study had had breast cancer, which had altered her perspective about time. "It caused me to rethink what was important to me and what I truly valued about what I wanted in my own life. So it opened me up and made me more aware, alert, more thinking about how important time was and how I needed to get more control over my time to be able to do what I really wanted to do."

Consider Dave Corcoran, a seemingly successful corporation lawyer who had been deeply divided for years between what he thought he should be and what he wanted to be. He wrote me on his thirty-eighth birthday to say that he had just abandoned his lucrative seventy-hour-a-week practice to "have a

bash!!!" He had *adjusted* very well to his career's expectations:
He was highly skilled and competent, thorough, reliable, responsible, respected by his clients and colleagues (even by his parale-
gal aides), and wealthy. But Dave had not *adapted* as well to his
career. He had become more and more restless and dissatisfied.
For years he had gotten out of bed each morning feeling that
life was passing him by.

Why? Programmed to be a lawyer since he had been just an
idea in his lawyer father's head, he had adjusted too well during his high school and college years. Dave had worked compulsively in high school to get into Haverford and while there
diligently pursued a narrow prelaw program. In law school, he
kept his nose in his books and made the law review. Too obsessed vocationally, he had never explored his other potentials
and interests — even his own adolescence. He had too many wild
oats left to sow. So one morning, upon awakening, he had his
mid-life crisis. He impetuously decided that the day had arrived
to have his long delayed "bash!!!" and satisfy his increasingly
clamorous need for adventure.

Self-fulfillment temporarily triumphed over adjustment. It
took Dave several years of self-indulgently reliving his teenage
years and trying different jobs before he discovered how to
balance his needs with those of a career and family. Learning
that he had a flair for administrative leadership, he secured a
position in a large bureaucratic insurance company that gave
him more time to be with his family and to indulge his new-
found passion for fly casting. He had become better integrated
after his "crisis."

I don't know how you will react to Dave Corcoran's story.
Do you envy, disapprove of, or condemn him, or judge him
to be a sick, self-seeking neurotic because he abandoned his
lucrative law practice? From his view, he felt that he wasn't
together and was stuck. He had the strength to give up a way
of life that he knew did not fit what he could be, but at the age
of thirty-eight he endured the anxiety of not knowing how he
might come out of his own self-induced chaos.

Though educators and philosophers say that mature persons
develop a coherent philosophy of life, few of the men and women

could articulate a well-thought-out *weltanschauung* that integrated their talents, needs, and personalities (A21). Jim Pryor was an exception. When I saw him, he had become dissatisfied with his real estate business and was struggling to create a new way of life that brought together his strong, sensuous, esthetic sensibility and acute mind under the guidance of an embracing religious philosophy. Fragments from my Rorschach analysis reveal the measure of his effort to create a philosophy that made sense of his mind and character.

> He is a basically stable, highly imaginative, and very bright person whose mind is inseparable from his esthetic feelings. Objective reality is strongly colored, infused, by feelings that are largely benign and sexual. He may well dramatize life which for him certainly is not dull, flat, without spice and verve. I don't mean he can't be realistic; he can make good judgments. I see no bizarre or disorganized ways of thinking. His mind is open to hunch, intuition, and mythic, primitive, even divine inspiration.
>
> His mind is more appreciative than critical, more tender- than tough-minded, more dramatic and colorful than disciplined and precisely crafted. Its flexibility enables him to see issues from different perspectives. He has good analytic skills and can be accurately self-critical. He is introspective and able to put intellectual distance between himself and his impulses to which he can accommodate in conventional ways if he has to.
>
> My concern is that given his obvious talents, impressive esthetic sensitivity, and the maturity to be so open to his impulses and feelings without distorting most of his judgments, he may not find a way to integrate his esthetic sensuousness with some fulfilling channels to the world of work.

"Absolutely true," he exclaimed. An evolving religious philosophy became his integrative route and provided him with the strength and serenity to endure what I learned later was the severe stress of being imprisoned for bringing into the country what a judge thought were pornographic films.

Self-Concept Becomes More Integrated. Finally, a growing person develops an increasingly coherent and consistent view of himself. My studies of Americans, Italians, and Turks clearly show that what mature persons think they are is what they predict others think they are; mature persons don't play roles and put on masks to appear what they aren't. Traits like genuineness, naturalness, and spontaneity describe them.

Billie thought of herself as one piece. She gave herself the highest score possible when rating how accurately statements like the following described her: "I seldom feel I am a divided, inconsistent, and contradictory person. I am reasonably sure of what I am and what my direction is." "I actually am what I believe other people think me to be" (A12).

I have often wondered if Norma Jean Baker committed suicide because she had always been a deeply divided person. She had never found a way to bring together her private self-image as Norma Jean Baker and her public one as Marilyn Monroe. She reputedly didn't feel she could be herself wherever she was.

Perhaps we can get a deeper insight into how obscure the route to personal integration can be from the analysis of a college senior's Rorschach. He saw himself as an esthete — a bohemian writer — but an emotionally empty one. "He may assume the sophistication of the esthete to mask the intensity of his feelings. He has considerable humor and a sense of the delightful to get away with it, [but] his feeling life gets very quickly super-refined, involuted, and convoluted into an abstract esthetic humanism. . . . Does he play the role of the 'cool intellect, the refined esthete' at the expense of the vigorous and vital part of his personality, namely, a strongly competitive masculine assertiveness?"

Literature is replete with examples of divided souls, like the hero of Dostoevsky's *Crime and Punishment*. Wouldn't you say that Reverend Dimsdale in the *Scarlet Letter* is the best example in American fiction? Hawthorne brilliantly described how the Reverend's divided soul produced his psychosomatic symptoms.

Remember that the puritan divine got Hester pregnant. She
refused to name him as the father, was imprisoned in the stockade for adultery, emerged wearing on her breast the brilliant
scarlet A that she had embroidered, and was ostracized to an
isolated house on the outskirts of the community. He, on the
other hand, the most respected member at the heart of the puritan community, did not confess his sin. Never betraying the
Reverend, Hester grew in inner strength and saintliness throughout the book, while the divine's guilt slowly split his righteous
public self and his sinful private one. His suffering, witnessed
by incapacitating physical symptoms and paralyzing despair,
powerfully depicts the consequences of a divided self.

Becoming More Stable and Autonomous

I discuss how we become more stable and autonomous together, not because they cannot be theoretically distinguished,
but because I have had a lot of trouble untangling them empirically.

Mind Becomes More Resiliently Stable and Mobile. Benjamin's
rapid growth in his early months illustrates how our two last
organizing principles, stabilization and autonomy, guide maturing. To enable him to survive outside the womb, his neurologically wired sucking reflex had to be strengthened immediately.
However, he could not initially nurse successfully at his mother's
breast, so she wore a breast shield. The next day at home, he
didn't work hard enough at first to fill himself up, but after a
lot of wailing and maternal frustration, his skills of rooting and
sucking became graceful and efficient. Later, after stabilizing
the skill of looking at his thumb, grasping it with his other hand,
and bringing it to his mouth to suck, he instructed his grandfather how to reach for the dangling keys and bring them to
his mouth to suck.

One night, months later, after Benjamin had stabilized many
more complexly integrated skills, he was squirming in his chair
at the dinner table when his mother hastily ran to a pot boiling
over on the stove. Curious Benjamin seized the opportunity to

pull the tablecloth to his mouth to chew. Plates crashed to the floor. Frightened, Benjamin fell apart; he then giggled. Piaget would say that he had learned to use skills originally learned to satisfy his hunger needs to create crashing effects. His grasping, pulling, and chewing skills had become freed, more mobile, and autonomous of the original needs whose satisfaction had led to their stabilization. He now could explore his world by looking at, grasping, sucking, chewing, banging, and dropping any toy he found in his crib. He could freely use his skills any time, any place, with any other skill, and with any object he wished to explore, know, or destroy or to which he was attracted.

Mature persons have more stable and autonomous intellectual skills available for adapting than immature persons. Their skills have become an integral part of their personality. In a new situation or crunch, they don't fall apart; their skills and knowledge are readily on tap. My senior students got angry at me when I held to this principle by refusing to read their unproofread papers. They remonstrated that they knew how to write but my classes were psychology, not English, courses. I insisted that if they had really mastered our language and made it their own, they should be able to use it correctly in any course—even unconsciously. They called me compulsive. I thought I was just consistently supporting my English brethren, as well as teaching them something about growing up.

Stable and autonomous skills enable us to resist or quickly recover from the disorganization that stress can cause. To test the idea that mature persons efficiently cope with stress, I gave mature and immature American, Italian, and Turkish students personally threatening problems to solve. One of three types of problems was to give in five minutes as many realistic stories as possible to a picture of a small boy attacking an older woman with a stick. Sure enough, in every culture, the mature youth not only solved the threatening problems efficiently but, when temporarily disorganized by the stressful content, resiliently recovered his mental efficiency.[9]

Surgery, probably more than most professions, demands that feelings and apprehensions be kept from interfering with one's mental efficiency under unpredictably stressful conditions. The study's one heart surgeon claimed that operating every day had

> forced me to become very good at what I do. I am much better now in my judgment and technique. I've learned from my mistakes and am now very efficient. Surgery is a decision business; you are constantly making decisions. How should I make this incision? How deeply should I cut? Should I take this cancer out in this elderly person? I make such decisions much more easily now. I could always make decisions easily but now I am not afraid to deal with the unexpected; I don't get flustered, even when a patient is close to dying on the table, as happened this afternoon when I was inserting a pace-maker.

"What happened?" I asked.

"He died," he replied, almost too calmly. I felt more troubled than he did.

As our intellectual skills become more stable and autonomous, so that we no longer have to pay attention to their use, energy becomes available for other purposes. What we do becomes automatic, like reading or typing. We take such skills with us wherever we go. We don't have to use energy to be aware of them; we use them with minimal attention. Habits free our energies for other activities.

Interpersonal Relationships Become More Enduring and Selective. Mature persons develop more stable and loyal relationships but can endure aloneness if necessary. Billie saw herself as loyal to Allan and her friends; her peers agreed with her. Mature men and women create more sexually compatible and faithful marriages (A4e). I don't know if this result will hold in the future, given changing values about extramarital relationships, but the model suggests the hypothesis that immature more than mature persons seek out and run from one "friend" or lover to another.

Other signs of immature autonomous relationships are excessive "neediness" (incessant demands that others approve of and love us) or falling apart when alone or not being circled by admirers. To get along with aloneness is a great test of our interpersonal maturity, *providing* we can still love another.

Values Lead to Commitment and Courage. Growing up also means deepening our interests and values, which we pursue more persistently, even though we may not fulfill them for years. We make our values so completely our own that we accept full responsibility for their consequences. Billie tested her maturity by putting herself through medical school. She had what our society used to value — an old-fashioned calling that supported her heroic determination. To be steadfastly committed and to persist in the face of criticism and adversity is a hallmark of a mature person.

John, a vice-president of a college, picked becoming middle-aged from the list of fifty events that most influenced how he had changed in his values since his early thirties. When asked how he had changed as a result, he said that becoming middle-aged "has given me much more experience and opportunity to test my values. I am now much more definite; I have very strong views; I am less tolerant of faculty views that I regard as downright nonsensical. If someone can't give me a good intellectual argument, I tell him, 'Let's drop it. Otherwise we will just shout at each other.' I don't resist arguments. I just want reasonable arguments." Anyone who knows how emotional college faculty become when arguing with deans and vice-presidents can appreciate just how maturely John dealt with argumentative faculty.

Self-Concept Becomes Stronger and More Autonomous. Finally, growing up means feeling a sense of continuity and being in charge of one's self. Erikson's idea of "identity" refers to just such a strong sense of self. Our self yesterday was what it is today and what it will be tomorrow. Billie learned what she could and could not do, accepted and liked herself, and felt confident in her ability to succeed. The Turkish, Italian, and American studies taught me that one of the most reliable signs of maturity

is whether persons will describe themselves several weeks or
months from now in roughly the same way that they describe
themselves today (A13d). Middle-aged women who have a
strong sense of themselves (A13d) are mature (A12), succeed
in their principal roles (A4c), devote themselves to their communities (A4g), and have been predictably happy and fulfilled
since their teenage years (A4a).

Stability is not rigidity in mature persons; they are open to
new ideas about themselves. Their mature autonomy enables
them to discriminate which ideas are true or worthwhile and
which aren't. Mature persons can act independently of the opinions that others have about them, affirming their own worth
even in the face of their in-laws', lovers', and friends' doubts
and criticisms.

Seeking to understand the sources of Albert Einstein's genius
from his collected papers, a reviewer identified both his strong
sense of self and his autonomy to be its roots.

> Albert had an early, strong sense of autonomy as
> expressed by his leaving home [early] . . . refusing
> to let his mother dictate [his] personal relations. [His]
> sense of self-worth had much to do with a support-
> ive home environment. His mother was immensely
> proud of Albert's early intellectual achievements. . . .
> What Einstein had was the special balance of in-
> tense early nurture and autonomy that gave him
> a self-esteem that would carry him through the years
> when he was homeless, degreeless, and jobless. He
> was consequently never hopeless or loveless.[10]

This insightful comment illustrates the balance between other-
centeredness, stability, and autonomy that we need to grow
healthily.

Such are the signposts that guide growing up. Reassuringly,
others studying adult development, using different methods with
different persons and unaware of this model, also identify similar dimensions to describe maturing from adolescence into adulthood.[11]

The model codifies and makes explicit the wisdom of novelists, religionists, and philosophers, as well as psychologists and the results of years of research about what growing up means. It provides a comprehensive but manageable map to guide efforts to understand healthy growth. It has produced many interesting discoveries. For example, I know now that measures of our self-concept's accuracy, other-centeredness, integration, and stability powerfully predict a person's effectiveness.[12] I know that the model's theoretically generated measure of maturity (A12) predicts healthy adult outcomes far better than psychology's traditional tests, such as the Rorschach, Minnesota Multiphasic Personality Inventory (A2), and sentence completion measures of ego development (A16). I also know now that maturity as a teenager predicts maturity when one is thirty-two, which in turn predicts maturity when one is forty-five.

I have also learned about the ways that growing up gets off track and about what I now consider to be myths about maturing that are still being perpetuated by popular writers and psychologists. Let's now turn to these issues.

4

Eight Myths
About Maturity

I shall comment first about how we stay healthy, discuss next
the ways that growing up can go wrong, and then defend my
belief that some popular ideas about growing up healthily are
myths.

Walter Cannon, a physiologist, proposed that healthy living
systems have internal regulating principles that maintain or recover their physiological balance when they are too stressed.
An analogous psychic equilibrating principle similarly protects
us from breaking apart when psychologically "stretched" too far.
We can be emotionally pummeled, hurt, and squashed just so
much before we resist, rebel, and compensate, sometimes in extreme, seemingly unacceptable, and self-destructive ways. Sometimes, like a rubber band stretched too far out of shape, we either
break or resist further stretching by unexpectedly shooting off
in unpredictable directions. Dave Corcoran's precipitate decision
to abandon his corporate law practice told me just how far he
had been stretched out of shape for years.

Whether we deliberately disrupt our existing way of living,
as Billie and Dave Corcoran decided to do, or are upset by
others, as Roger was by Beth, the equilibrating principle is the
steward of our psychic health. It doesn't always intervene as dramatically in our lives as it did in Dave's. More often than not
it speaks softly — so quietly we may not hear it clearly. After
an intense lecture schedule last spring, I took to our Maine

coastal retreat two computers, boxes of research, and numerous books, some of which I've carried back and forth unread now for three summers. After the first few days of doggedly working at my computers and writing, what predictably happened? My thoughts wandered to the dying trees outside my window that the family of porcupines who nested under our cabin during the winter had stripped of bark. They needed to be cut up into firewood. I dreamt of laying up a stone fireplace for our guest cabin; I yearned to survey a road I've wanted to put in. Instead, I forced myself to write this book. My system rebelled, its equilibrating principle noisily warning me that I needed to live in my body all year around, not just in my head during most of the winter and spring.

Excess in fundamentally healthy human systems naturally provokes warnings that we must change our life styles. If only we had listened more sensitively to what we could be hearing, we might not have been so prone to that heart attack, ulcer, or depression. I listened last May. So I worked ten hours a day for several weeks cutting the trees down and surveying another portion of the road. I just wish I could have exorcised the guilt I felt about how slowly my writing was going. And each year my body tells me a little sooner that it is getting too much of this compensatory physical trauma and that I should run my life differently during the winter to avoid being so strenuously stretched out of shape by May.

Ways Growing Up Goes Off-Track

How does growing up go wrong psychically and impair our adaptation? I shall mention a few examples. If you have also felt stretched out of shape at times, you might want to figure out why you have sometimes been knocked off-track on each of the five dimensions of maturing.

Inadequate or excessive *symbolization* limits our ability to adapt. Unreflective persons take a long time to learn from their mistakes. Roger needed to become more adept at reading the signs his unconscious broadcast so loudly while he produced his artwork. If he does not become more psychologically minded, he may repetitively get lost in the same emotional black tunnels with his next lover.

Awareness can also be forced or excessive, relative to maturing on other dimensions. We become obsessionally introspective, or hyperaware of our motives, or self-conscious about our relationships or ourselves. We become paralyzed and can't act. Like the typical academic faculty, we see so many ins and outs of an issue that we can't commit ourselves wholeheartedly to any decision except to return it to our inner debating committee. A student sought my advice. He had stewed for weeks about dropping out of college; then he had begun to fret about his stewing. He went over and over every macro- and microscopic reason why he should and shouldn't drop out, and then he started over again, criticizing his reasons and his indecisiveness. He began to pace so frantically around my office that I thought he was working himself into an anxiety attack. His central issue was not whether to drop out or not; it was his inability to decide — about anything.

The second way we grow — becoming more *other-centered* — can also be under- or overdeveloped and so limit our ability to achieve what we want. American males are traditionally undersocialized and females oversocialized in other-centeredness. I know many more egocentric males than I do females, and I know more accommodating females than males. Roger paid a steep price for his lack of empathy and sensitivity to Beth's needs. I have also for not keeping you and your interests constantly in mind while writing and rewriting this book. I have revised it several times because I let my scientific conscience insist that I include too many technical details about the study that *I* would want to know about but you might not.

I don't need to belabor how excessive other-centeredness can distort healthy growth, since Billie has told us of its dangers. Remember how she felt compelled to set up her first husband in his own apartment and even buy him a car before she could divorce him. Caught up in the grip of her need to nurture and please, for years she could not develop a well-integrated, strong sense of herself and become healthily autonomous.

We can also be inadequately or overly *integrated*. While Reverend Dimsdale's psychosomatic descent, due to his divided soul, was dramatic, the effects of poor integration on our adaptation are typically more subtle: unpredictability, inefficiency, emotional sloppiness, or the restlessness of a Roger. Paradoxically, we can be too well integrated relative to growth on other dimensions. Though compulsively efficient automatons or machines in our work, we may lack spontaneity, earthiness, and warmth in our marital or love relationships. Drugs and alcohol deceptively make such persons feel less uptight, more loose, free, "together." Maturely integrated persons do not need such crutches to play spontaneously and childishly. They can will their own temporary "disintegration," for they can confidently recover their integration by their own willpower. Not surprisingly, those who report transcendent mystical experiences are, as Maslow declared, more mature;[1] they can allow their controls to dissolve, surrender, even disintegrate in the presence of the ineffable.

Too developed *stability,* again relative to growth on the other dimensions, is rigidity and thwarts further integration and new growth. Eventually, rigidity brings boredom, stasis, deadness, predisposing us to throw over the traces, injudiciously seek new experiences, and act out of character. The media delight in titillating us with tales of impeccably righteous TV evangelists like Jim and Tammy Bakker, who are suddenly wallowing in sin. Such unexpected acts are tell-tale signs that the sexual puritan and drug "prohibitionist" are not what they had tried to be. They had failed to integrate healthily what they had labeled "morally wrong" into their values and personalities.

Overexaggerated *autonomy* leads to narcissistic self-sufficiency. It brakes further growth, especially in other-centeredness. If such persons escape becoming loveless hermits, their love selfishly takes more than it selflessly gives. The Achilles heel of the typical masculine male is his overdeveloped self-sufficiency and of the typical feminine female her underdeveloped autonomy. Can you think of examples from your life of autonomy gone off-track?

If we accept that to grow healthily we must grow wholly, not just partially, and that the equilibrating principle naturally guards our health, then we can understand why some of today's popular opinions about maturing are myths.[2]

Myths About Maturing

Myth #1: Women Mature Differently from Men. It is fashionable to argue that women's maturity differs from men's, but this
myth egregiously ignores how systemic healthy growth is, as
well as its guardian, the equilibrating principle. The argument
is flawed; it confuses what is with what should be. To assert
that women mature differently than men risks confusing phenotypic or seeming female and male differences with healthy growth.
Because women are nurturers and communion oriented, other-
centeredness becomes the sine qua non of maturity. Or because
men are self-reliant and self-sufficient, autonomy becomes the
key to maturity. By not locating female and male development
within a comprehensive and valid dimensional model of healthy
growth, only one dimension, like other-centeredness or autonomy, is elevated to the keystone position of a woman's or man's
maturity. By ignoring the multidimensional complexity of the
maturing process and taking a tunnel view of healthy growth,
we risk ignoring the equilibrating principle. Billie scored high
on nurturing and saw herself as a nurturer. But she discovered
in counseling that her other-centered maturation had been too
much; it blocked the healthy growth and fulfillment of her other
impressive potentials.

The argument that women and men mature differently is
flawed for a second reason. Because men are viewed as more
autonomous and women are seen as more other-centered — and
my evidence supports this popular notion — doesn't mean that
if freed from their culture's procrustean molds of what they
should be, men and women would not mature similarly. Some
researchers who insist women mature differently base their
claims on studies of adolescent girls.[3] But I and the only other
researchers who have intensively studied adult women disagree.[4]
We think young girls have been so oversocialized on the other-
centered dimension that their maturation has been limited and
so doesn't predict their adult maturity. Billie is a good example. It took her forty-one years before she could assert, "I feel
that I now have come to terms with what I am and am functioning as a healthy adult for the first time in my life." Or it took
Jane Allen, a high school dropout who became a successful

entrepreneur, thirty-five years before she could say, "I like myself now. I didn't before . . . I'm more self-confident . . . I feel more confident to say, 'No.' I'm not afraid to offend others any more." Only after years of struggle did both develope stable and autonomous ideas of themselves.

Though some women have called me sexist to claim so, if we study how successful men and women actually adapt to their different adult roles, we discover that the men's and women's maturity predicts the same successes. This can only mean that maturity means the same for both.

Myth #2: Assessment of Maturity Is a Personal or Culturally Biased Opinion. If we value maturity as an important goal, as most adults do, then the personality traits we should nurture are predictable—whether in Chicago, Palermo, or Istanbul. I agree with Maslow's perceptive insight when he wrote, "I . . . maintain that science in the broadest sense can and does discover what human values are, what the human being needs in order to live a good and a happy life, what he needs in order to avoid illness, what is good for him and what is bad for him."[5] What has science since discovered? Young Protestant and Jewish American, Moslem Turkish, and Catholic Italian and Sicilian men from different regions and social classes, selected by friends and teachers to succeed in many areas of their lives, share similar traits of psychological maturity.[6] Science suggests that the idea of maturity may not be as arbitrary as the myth says; it may have some common core meanings among different religious and national groups. When I have asked Hindus, Saudis, or Indonesians to identify the qualities of the most mature person they know, for example, they mention similar ones, such as self-confidence, empathy, and a strong will.

True, different societies value some aspects of maturity more than they do others. The Japanese, for example, have historically valued other-centeredness more than autonomy; today, they value autonomy more. They believe that overdeveloped group conformity may be unhealthy for a future that will require more individual creativity; they must therefore educate their young to become more autonomous.

Myth #3: To Be Mature Is to Be Well Adjusted. I must make a technical distinction before you jump on me and accuse me of being another "headshrinker" urging you to become well adjusted by conforming to others' or our society's demands. To make my values exquisitely clear, I do not advocate adjustment; I advocate healthy maladjustment. I don't want us to accept and conform to an imperfect society; I want us to be dissatisfied enough to work maturely to make it a healthier one.

Maturity predicts how well a person *adapts,* not adjusts. Adjusting means conforming to and accommodating others' demands. Adapting means creating an optimal balance between adjusting to the demands of others, like a boss or a partner, *and* fulfilling one's own needs, interests, and talents. To only adjust risks incurring the wrath of our equilibrating principle.

Remember Dave Corcoran. He adjusted to his law practice and society's expectations of what a man should be like, but he was unfulfilled and therefore maladapted. Eventually, his equilibrating principle told him he had to have his "bash!!!" if he were to become better integrated and so healthier.

Billie told us the same thing happened to her when the counselor asked her, "What do *you* want?" She had been the dutiful wife, supporting her graduate student husband but feeling more and more miserable, stuck, purposeless, and empty. Her counselor's question permitted her to seek the freedom she needed to create a healthier balance between her self-sacrificing need to nurture (and so adjust to others) and her own undeveloped, imposing talents.

Dave and Billie illustrate how adjustment without self-fulfillment can lead to the potential frustration, even sickness, of what Fromm called the conforming or "marketing" personality. Yet self-fulfillment without adjustment can lead to the potential self-centeredness of what Freud called the narcissist. Adaptation results from balancing adjustment and self-fulfillment — a balance I, and I guess most others too, find difficult to approach and then sustain. The study's working women felt their imbalance most acutely. Few had found the center between the demands of their work, marriages, children, and their private selves.

Myth #4: Maturing Progresses Through Stages as a Result of Meeting Crises. Erikson, Levinson, and others identify a predictable sequence to the principal tasks or crises (some call these stages) to which we must adapt through life.[7] However, they are wrong to assume that an invariant order of crises fits everyone. The study's middle-aged men matured far beyond most of the women, excepting a few like Billie, in knowing who they were and what they could do; the women matured far beyond almost all of the men in intimacy. Erikson's belief that we must resolve the identity crisis before the intimacy crisis doesn't fit women at all, as I and other researchers have found.[8]

Those who have actually studied adults over long periods of time, which Erikson and other proponents of stages have not done, do not find the idea that all adults grow from one predictable and unvarying stage to another to be either valid or useful.[9] Nor can we understand the dynamic complexity of growing up by reducing it to a few sequential stages, like identity, intimacy, or mid-life crisis. What I do find helpful is the idea that regardless of what crisis or problem we encounter — whether the birth of a child, a divorce, or terminal illness — it will be the more mature person who will adapt to it more effectively. The model of maturing identifies the strengths necessary to resolve the crisis, as well as the signs that the crisis has been resolved.

The model of maturing predicts that the signs that a crisis has been resolved are a greater feeling of competence, released energy and enthusiasm for new adventures and interests, decreased ambivalence in one's intimacy relationships, greater playfulness, and a broader, even humorous, perspective about one's self. With these strengths, we are now ready to move on to the next crisis that may be looming over the horizon.

The spurs to continued growth don't have to wait, however, upon the great "crisis." Small and not-so-small unresolved problems provoke growth throughout our lives. We ceaselessly must learn to adapt to many dilemmas and problems each day. Some we resolve easily in a day or two; others not for weeks, months, or decades; some never. How successfully we adapt and so increase our maturity, perhaps only a mite, depends upon our maturity, which has been forged and consolidated earlier by all of our prior successes as well as those failures we have learned from.

If you are young, or like Roger, still groping around for your Number 1 Self, or middle-aged, or older and still growing, and you ask for advice about dealing with your day-to-day crises, I prescribe the following: Enjoy learning how to grow from them. They may be preparing you for the really big ones ahead: making a commitment to a calling, creating an enduring relationship with another, becoming a parent, assuming responsibility for your community, accepting the death of your parents, possibly living with crippling illnesses, losing your partner or a child, dying too slowly, and finding ways to keep from being bored in heaven for eternity.

Myth #5: A Person Can Reach Maturity. The myth that we can once and for all become mature assumes that there is an ideal end point, some destination that we can finally reach, where we can breathe a deep sigh, relax forever, and become blissfully comatose. However, mature persons learn that they can't take living for granted. We don't *reach* some pinnacle. Maturing is a process, not some blessed and exalted state that, once reached, never again needs to be striven for. I have perhaps talked too loosely of "mature" persons or "growing up," wrongly implying that there is an "up" to which to grow. I hope you will understand and be charitable when I seem to imply that there may be a final stage that we can come to: I don't intend that interpretation.

All of the men I studied when in their forties had continued to grow and become even more emotionally healthy than they had been in their early thirties, with only one exception. Their judgment had improved. They had become more concerned about their children, whom they also enjoyed more. They had gotten themselves more together. Like the women, they had become less concerned about what others thought of them. They were not more self-centered but more maturely autonomous and self-determining.

True, our rate of maturing may slow down, even slumber along on a plateau for years until some new change occurs, like becoming increasingly impotent, losing a parent or job, or finding our daughter makes more money than we. When life knocks us around like that, we have to adapt afresh and that can always become the spur to renewed maturing — or immaturing.

The mature persons thought of themselves as still searching, exploring, risking, and growing, not as arriving at some static place or finding *the* answer for the rest of their lives. Some, like Billie, made a conscious commitment to growing. Dave Corcoran deliberately upset his life to grow differently. Even Jim Pryor looked upon prison as an opportunity to develop new interests as well as test his religious commitment. They created their own goads to continued maturing. To want to know which pledge card to sign and so be *finally* saved may be the way to salvation; it certainly is not the route to maturity.

Myth #6: Maturity Is Not a General Attribute of a Person. As Saint Paul told us, we cannot glean from a few acts of a person his or her maturity. We don't discover those central organizing traits and motives that biographers use to describe a person by studying *only* Benjamin's fumbling efforts to coordinate looking with grasping or by observing *only* my daughter's efforts to make her wayward left hand work with her right one on the piano. Just so about our maturity. Though we may slip occasionally in how maturely we act, we can only assess our maturity by noting how consistently we act in many diverse and new situations. I knew that Benjamin had developed more stable and autonomous grasping skills when I saw him use them for the first time to grasp the key and later pull the tablecloth off to make the crash. Mature persons carry their maturity with them wherever they go because its attributes have become part of their enduring character. The word *mature* must refer to a person, not to a specific act. Failing to understand this can get us or others into a pot of scalding water. So shouldn't Saint Paul agree with me rather than the judge who plunked Jim Pryor into a federal pen for five years and fined him $100,000 for one poor judgment?

An avowed homosexual since he was thirteen, Jim, a successful real estate developer, enjoyed visiting and participating in the lives of South Pacific islanders to study their sexual customs. He was also one of the study's two most religious and ethical men — his friends rated him highly on honesty, integrity, and compassion. He never had had a court record, not even a traffic ticket.

The local police raided his apartment one day; his name had been found in the address book of a gay friend who had been charged with transporting pornographic pictures across state lines. They found Jim's films of his anthropological "participant-observer" relations, which the district attorney subsequently charged had been illegally brought into the country, showing "lewd" behavior with young-appearing boys. Jim had never known that bringing his films into the United States violated the law. A conservative judge refused to accept the fact that some Melanesian societies, as Jim wrote me and I later looked up to confirm,[10] believe that it is the duty of adolescent boys to offer themselves sexually to adult males and receive orally their semen, which their society considers to be the "essence of manhood." In court, the judge called Jim a "sick pervert who was a menace to the community," unfit to be let free. Jim's punishment was more severe than that of his cell-mate — a multimillionaire insider trader and political perjurer.

Appealing the sentence, Jim asked me to write the judge about his character. The law was the law — that I could not dispute. But I could dispute the judge's character diagnosis of "sick pervert" based on one specific act. From my thirty-year knowledge of Jim and the hundreds of personality measures that I had secured about him during that time, I felt confident that he had good control of his behavior and was not about to abuse children sexually. He was mentally healthy and of average maturity when compared to other competent adults. The judge had a moralistic bias about his act, but he had no basis to jump from one act of breaking the law to his character diagnosis that Jim was a "sick" person and therefore a "menace." Another person who might have broken the law similarly might well have been.

(Incidentally, Jim's general attribute of maturity sustained him. Without self-poisoning bitterness, he adapted with a lot more serenity to prison than yours truly would have. He became the chaplain's assistant, even the respected spokesman for the other prisoners. His appeal was denied; he served his full term: so much for justice. Better to be a thief of millions, a perjurer, even a murderer in some states, than a too zealous avocational "anthropologist" in others.)

As I wrote earlier, and Jim's story illustrates, we are not bits and pieces of indiscretions and poor judgments; we are adapting whole persons. Any assessment of our maturity must look at all of us, not just parts of us.

Myth #7: Maturity Cannot Be Measured. Rubbish. I hope *you* have never thought that. I am impatient with those who say that words like "maturity" or "creativity" or "happiness" are useless because they can't be *precisely* measured. Any trait that we can define with reasonable clarity can be reliably measured, maybe not with the precision of the grade of 91 that some English teachers give their students' papers, but certainly with the reliability necessary to emerge with the consistent and useful results I have found over the years. Is it not a sick American obsession to believe that important human strengths are inherently unmeasurable if we can't use decimals? Have you ever written a reference about someone you have known well? I wager you made comments like, "He is one of the most reliable persons I know." "She is as tenacious as a bull dog." All we have to do is put some numbers on words like "most" and "as tenacious as a bull dog" when compared with other persons and dogs, and we have numbers that communicate some valuable information. Too frequently, the bits and pieces of human behavior that we can measure very precisely, like our reaction times to flashing lights, predict little other useful information about a person. What in the world does a 65.5 percent score on an American history test predict? Almost nothing.

Myth #8: You Can't Learn to Become More Mature. I hope this is not another shibboleth that *you* believe. It has many disguises. One is the view of Rousseau and adherents of Summerhill that children just grow up "naturally." They should be allowed to do "their own thing," like go to school or read or help around the house only if they want to, write out of their hearts with no control of our language, and smoke dope. But just growing up naturally can retard growing up healthily. Premature autonomy can become self-centeredness.

Another disguise I have heard some teachers utter is that you can't teach students to become mature, even though educating for attributes of maturity has been the primary goal of liberal educators since Socrates. This myth is only a feeble rationalization to justify not being concerned about a student's character. If those who hold such a view about students are also parents, I wager they don't assume that they can't help their kids become more mature at home. Most parents are not so masochistic as to wish to enjoy the consequences of such a rationalization.

If I have persuaded you that such myths are in truth myths, then you might want to reexamine other questions or beliefs you have about growing healthily.

We are now prepared to learn what the study tells us about the character of successful men and women and why they turned out as they did. I shall begin by telling you about the Millers. Their tests and peers identified them to be the study's most all-around successful couple. They illustrate most of the character strengths that the statistical analysis of the entire group's results showed were necessary to succeed in our familial roles.

*Part Two*_____

Succeeding in Personal Relationships

5

Andy and Marty Miller:
Finding Their Own Paths

Do you remember how I selected Billie Leighton to be the study's most successful woman? I identified the Millers, as I did her, using only their objective test scores and peer judgments of their success. They are the couple that best represents the values you ranked in the first chapter. Neither Andy, a biological researcher, nor Marty, a feminist lawyer, is the study's most maritally happy, satisfied and competent parent, or sexually fulfilled person. However, as a couple, they *together* scored highest on all of the objective measures of the men's and women's marital, sexual, parental, and vocational success, as well as self- and judge-rated happiness and fulfillment.[1] I describe them now as a couple; I shall analyze why each succeeded in the next two chapters. Then I shall ask if their characters match the generalized statistical portrait of the strengths of successful men and women. If I didn't turn to the study's larger group to discover what happily married couples, for example, actually share in common, we couldn't tell with confidence just what it is about Andy and Marty Miller that contributes most to familial success.

Two warnings, though. Don't expect that a successful couple does not stumble along the way — even very badly, as Andy and Marty did. They illustrate the pain of deteriorating modern marriages and how a couple can work to create a happier and more fulfilling one. The route to marital, sexual, and parental success is not always a smooth one. Also, don't expect to meet two ordinary, typical, run-of-the-mill, Main Street Americans (whoever they might be — I don't seem to have any in the study, anyway; I'm not sure I would even recognize them if I did). Would you call yourself an "ordinary, typical, run-of-the-mill, Main Street American?" I doubt it. But when we go more deeply into the dilemmas the Millers faced trying to adapt to the changing role of women to create a viable two-career family, then I think you will see many of the issues that millions of other couples are currently struggling with, each in their own unique ways.

I can't emphasize enough, therefore, that Marty and Andy are every modern woman and man, despite how exaggerated and dramatic their lives may seem to be. They, as I believe most others will have to, worked to create a healthier marriage by reshaping centuries of emotional conditioning of what femaleness and maleness have meant. Just as Billie prefigured how many modern women may be growing in the future, so the Millers prefigure the route many couples may have to take also, if they want to remain a couple.

I had been fond of Andy ever since his college days, when he eagerly accepted my invitation to participate in the study. Though skeptical of psychology — "more like hocus pocus; not scientific enough" — he has consistently supported the study, as Marty, his second wife, has also. His sensitivity, even vulnerability, reflectiveness, and warmth have always lent a special aura to our meetings. The visit we had when he was forty-six was no exception.

Andy immediately completed and returned the preinterview questionnaire and tests. Marty's came back a week later, completed very frankly and in great detail. She had taken twice as long as I had suggested was necessary. Enamored by the questions, she had selected different ones throughout the week to reflect upon while driving to and from her office each day.

Both willingly interrupted their demanding careers to be available any time for my visit. A live-in couple freed them from immediate concerns about their two daughters and younger son.

Emerging from the plane one cool October Friday afternoon, I immediately recognized Andy. He was hovering along the crowd's edges, almost shyly; I knew he was trying to protect his shortened right leg, which had been partially paralyzed as a result of a crippling car accident when he was sixteen. Because he could feel few sensations from it, he never knew what he might be stepping on. He had to be constantly alert about where he put his cane to keep from tripping, losing his balance, and severely wrenching himself.

Limping beside me as we walked to his Buick, he seemed tired and in pain, though he had not mentioned either. (He had never complained about his disability; nor did he during my visit.) I'm quite direct, so Andy was prepared when I said, "Andy, you seem more thin and tired than I remember."

"Yeah. My muscles are weaker now. We're doing some tests to find out why I have so little stamina. I need to sleep now in the afternoon. And my headaches interfere with my concentration. They're the same symptoms I had when I was knocked out in that accident."

He later pluckily insisted on persisting with the six to eight hours of tests and interviews, despite frequently asking me to repeat the questions and occasionally grimacing and hiding his eyes as if he were in pain.

Marty was waiting for me when we reached their home, which was deceptively small on the outside, spacious but simply furnished on the inside, with the living room opening onto a swimming pool that Andy used daily. I had never met her before; Andy had married her after my last visit. Compared to Andy's gaunt, almost fragile gangliness that made me feel his tentativeness, Marty's five-foot-ten-inch frame, broad shoulders, flowing black hair, dancing eyes, earthy expressive voice, and expectant exuberance instantly gave me a feeling of rootedness, solidity, feminine power, even mystery. She immediately hugged me, saying, "I feel like I've known you for years." I felt similarly — and was already very much at home.

So began my intensely concentrated visit, first with Andy and then Marty, following exactly the same procedure that I had used with Billie and Allan Leighton. What routes had each taken before they began traveling together for the ten years before my visit?

Andy Miller

Andy was the fourth and youngest of a long line of Michigan Millers. His father, a small-town and not too successful Methodist minister, "never made enough money but always made me feel there was enough for the important things, like sending me to camp or allowing me to go to any school I wanted to." Andy felt that when he was an adolescent his father had been emotionally detached and uninvolved in the family and its conflicts. He was taciturn, and although he was not emotionally warm or expressive, he was not hostile and rejecting. To the phrase, "My father . . . " Andy wrote, "is a marvelous, lovable man but ill at ease with his feelings," and to "Remembering his father, he . . . " he wrote, "felt some sadness but deep affection and love" (A16). From his "impractical but high-minded" father, more interested in ideas and causes than in earning money, Andy got his social liberalism and interest in writing.

His mother, feeling neglected by her own mother (who had been married to an alcoholic husband and so had had to work), stayed home to be always available to her children, and, after Andy left home, to any stray hurt child who needed a temporary home. She was an active, energetic, and socially outgoing person, too attuned, according to Andy, to her social status among the neighbors. Again, to the phrase, "My mother and I . . . " he wrote, "are good friends," and to "When he thought of his mother, he . . . " he wrote, "remembered a strong, loving woman whom he admired." In recalling both parents, Andy said, "I felt loved and appreciated and got lots of strokes. My mother hugged me; my father never did. He really cared though; I know he cared. It wasn't until I took the initiative when I was thirty-five to embrace him that we ever touched each other. They didn't always understand me, but they stood by me through thick and thin. They've provided me a safe place to go back to."

Andy had been all-boy as an adolescent. He had enthusiastically participated in team sports and extracurricular activities, was elected president of his class, had close male friends, had begun to be drawn to girls, felt at home in social situations, and generally had the interests typical of boys of his age.

Then when he was sixteen his car accident, caused by one of his gang careening off of a curve on a rainy night, almost killed him and permanently changed his life, though not his basic psychic healthiness. Thirty years later I interpreted his frequent references to parts of the human body that he saw in the Rorschach inkblots. "It's as if his mind and self-awareness come constantly between his impulses and the external world, so diluting passionate spontaneity but also restricting aggressive energy for coping. . . . I feel this constant self-awareness and -monitoring may be limiting the full integration of his potential in action. It is as if he may need to always be aware of himself before he acts . . . the amount of energy tied up in awareness of and sensitivity to his body must take energy away from other activities. However, his basic concept of his bodily self seems to be quite healthy. I don't detect any morbid, self-rejecting, or negative feelings about his body that could undermine his self-esteem." Andy broke in at this point to say, "I am always aware of my body."

With prodigious determination, he recovered enough from the accident's maiming effects to teach himself to walk again before entering college two years later. Anticipating a medical career, he majored in biology. However, he discovered from work in the arts and English that he was a scientific humanist at heart and so decided, after a good but not stellar academic career, to get a Ph.D. in mammalian physiology. His evolving research interests eventually drew him into applied biohumanistic problems, such as developing therapeutic exercises for various sexual disorders. He regrets now that he didn't get his medical credentials so that he could work more comprehensively with clinical patients.

How successful did he become vocationally? Very. Like others of the study, he has been very productive and begun to receive national and, increasingly, international recognition for his work. He has reported his biomedical research in numerous technical articles, texts, and invitational lectures and received three or four job offers every year for the past five years. "Every time I open one door, five others are now available to me." His leadership potential has been recognized by appointments to national commissions in his area of expertise as well as to various university administrative positions. Research continues to be his first love, however, and he continues it to this day, here and abroad. More important, he feels good about his work, ranking fifth among the sixty-five men in his satisfaction with his vocational adaptation (A6). His earned income placed him in the top fifth of the men studied (A4d).

Andy's relations with women have been less successful. In graduate school he fell in love with a woman who after several months precipitously left him to marry a classmate. Two years after getting his Ph.D., Andy married, only to become increasingly unhappy. Four years later, unable to bear her interminable hostile sarcasm any longer, he persuaded his reluctant wife to see a marriage counselor with him. "In just a few sessions, the counselor convinced her of what I had known for a long time. We were incompatible. I felt good about it. It was a healthy step. Even though divorce had a negative stigma for me, I felt good that I had asserted myself and taken charge." Two years later he met Marty while working for the peace movement during the Vietnam War years.

Marty (Martha) Wood

Marty's route to her marriage with Andy had been filled with a different, less visible kind of hurt, so festering that she was still trying to heal it by psychotherapy when I saw her when she was forty-three. She had grown up in a rigidly conventional and culturally unstimulating home dominated by an unstable mother in constant conflict with an alcoholic husband (A1a). Marty, the eldest of five children, had had her parents to herself until she was five, at which time her first sibling was born. Her mother expected her to be her "assistant, not a daughter," and take care not only of the four rapidly appearing kids but also of her. She said of her parents: "At a time when I needed them, they were experiencing so much pain that they needed me to parent them. I've been resentful and angry all my life. I learned that men were incompetent and women were out of control. When my father wasn't drunk, he'd play with us, just as I now play with my kids. But mother . . . "

To the phrase "When she thought of her mother, she . . . "
Marty impulsively said, "cried" (A16). She replied similarly to
a similar item about her father, who she said "was a frightened
man." She felt that her mother and father had not enjoyed being parents; they had never respected, loved, or shared their
ideas and feelings with each other. A lingering special hurt for
Marty was that neither parent valued her mind nor encouraged
her to use it in school. In her mid-teens, they sent her to a girl's
religious boarding school and then to a women's college, where
she blossomed. Like Andy, she participated in organized team
sports and extracurricular activities, remained an active member of her church groups, and was looked to by the other girls
for leadership. Isolated from boys, very naive about sex, she
became emotionally attached in eleventh grade

> to a very cruel female teacher. She was a lot older
> and used my infatuation for her own purposes, I now
> realize. She then withdrew from me, shut herself
> away from me. I was crushed. I didn't know why.
> I blamed myself and felt terribly guilty and didn't
> tell anyone for a whole year. I thought I was going
> crazy. I couldn't sleep at night. I couldn't work. I
> went to a counselor who told me that there was noth-
> ing wrong and to use the experience as something
> to learn about my own intense needs to be close to
> other women. It sparked a wonderful change in my
> life. I started to collect very close women friends and
> learned what real friendship is all about.

After graduating from college she went to law school, from
which she graduated three years later. But law did not turn out
to be her vocation. She got swept up into the women's movement, joined the National Organization for Women, aided in
creating one of the country's most radical feminist groups that
rejected males and their domination, and used her legal talents
to further the cause of feminism. Her "calling" is to be a feminist.
When asked what was her bedrock, her strongest conviction and
commitment, the ultimate source of her energy and hope, she
instantly said (A21):

Fighting oppression of any kind. That just expresses itself in everything I do. I want to create a community of women. I want my girls to become strong women. Women who are physically strong can defend themselves. Big women who can walk with a strong stance; who have strong minds; who can take stands; who have strong spirits, strong emotions; who see their emotions as signs of strength, not weakness. Anger and sadness and joy and silliness. Everything.

How vocationally successful has Marty been? Very. She has preferred female clients and has gained a reputation in her metropolitan area for legal and, increasingly, marital and sexual counseling. She is an expert in cases of sexual abuse, harassment, rape, and other forms of oppression that women are especially vulnerable to. While she has continued to publish popular articles on women's issues, her principal influence has been through her public lectures, workshops, and organizational political activities. Her outspoken advocacy of feminist issues has propelled her into such prominence among women's groups that she has become a guru, even a priestess, for some women. Very satisfied with most attributes of her work, she ranked fourth among the women in her vocational satisfaction (A6), fifth in her colleague's assessment of her vocational adaptation (A26), and among the top four women in earned income.

Marty and Andy

After living with each other for two years, Marty and Andy married ten years prior to my visit. Their early marital years were happy and fulfilling, with one exception: Marty had trouble conceiving. Shortly after they decided to adopt, she became pregnant and had no difficulty with each of her rapidly appearing pregnancies. During the next several years, Andy was very productive and happy but Marty became increasingly troubled and dissatisfied with her life, the children, and Andy.

I felt trapped and that had a lot to do with Andy's disability. I survived the early years of our marriage because I was living out the typically feminine mode of thinking. I was a good person. I would take care of him. I was a sacrificing kind of person. A martyr. I really started to resent him tremendously. I thought he fell into that. We both just drifted into agreeing that I would be the one to take care of him. So I felt I had four kids again.

I know now that his disability does not make him a powerless person. But I used to see him as the person who was having just one fresh crisis after another . . . like newly handicapped every day. I'd work all day with women suffering as women and then come home to three screaming kids and a disabled husband who didn't, really couldn't, help much around the house. He couldn't easily lift the babies or change their diapers. Caused me to think more and more I was the victim of patriarchy. I didn't want to be just a wife and mother, a traditional homemaker, at that time of my life. But everything was pushing me that way emotionally.

Andy did not dispute Marty's description of their troubles. He was thirty-six when Jeannie was born and didn't have the stamina, or ability, to be physically involved with her and their later two children. He just didn't feel "bonded" to them. Besides, Marty breast-fed the children and ambivalently resented Andy's efforts to help as intrusions.

She was becoming more hostile and angry that I wasn't more involved. She saw it as part of a more general behavior pattern of mine, which she interpreted to mean I wasn't emotionally committed, that I didn't care, that she should do all of the work. Since she was the primary nurturer, she was the primary parent. All of the feelings she felt during her own childhood were coming back to haunt her.

Here she was living with a man who also wasn't
available or supportive.

At the same time she was being aggressive about
her nurturing role. She didn't make it easy for me
to be involved. She would jump in and take over
too quickly. She felt that only she could solve the
problem, only she could be the nurturer, only she
could provide the right amount of support and understanding and care and that automatically excluded anyone else from being involved.

Marty agreed. The shadow of her own mother and her own
childhood nurturing memories shrouded all that she did as a
mother.

I immediately felt out of control. When they were
babies and crying a lot, I couldn't stand their continuous demands. I couldn't stand that I couldn't
relieve their every cry. I would wake up in the middle of the night to their crying, which I couldn't
stop. I'd start crying, go into the kitchen to pound
the cabinets, run out of the house, fight with Andy,
blaming him for my being out of control. No matter what he did it wasn't good enough. Poor guy.
He didn't know what hit him. He withdrew more
and more and that made it worse. If only he had
gotten angry I would have felt better.

My main problem was that I was identifying with
my mother, who couldn't drive a car, had no college education, had five kids and an alcoholic husband. I started acting out all of her behavior; I felt
totally responsible for them and totally inadequate.

All the while, Marty found increasing support from her feminist friends and the ideology of the movement. Despite his sensitivity, Andy acted more typically male, an attitude that Marty
had begun not to value. She felt that he expected her to mother
him and didn't value women as women in their own right.

Though "he doesn't make comments like most men when driving along the street about a beautiful woman's tits, his first comment is about how attractive she is." Becoming increasingly sensitive to the subtle ways in which men have historically controlled women, she resentfully saw him playing out very old and familiar tapes, such as "Yes, I'll help around the house," but fading behind the newspaper after coming home from work, when the kids needed to be tended to, or dozing off when the table needed to be cleared.

Andy became more aware of a darker current troubling Marty that his own maleness had been unconsciously aggravating, more aware that what he called his "male strengths" had their own pathology. He knew that he was not carrying equal weight in running the house and providing Marty with the emotional support that she needed.

"How were you typically male in your thirties?" I asked Andy in an interview focused on the effects of our society's changing sexual roles (A24). He said

> I was very work-oriented, task-oriented. Very conscious of my role as principal provider. Aware that I was a person responsible for providing the main income and would be when we had a family and my wife had to stay home and raise the kids. I was very competitive athletically, and was always aware of the professional accomplishments of my colleagues. I was concerned about matching and surpassing those. I also wasn't aware of, in fact, didn't value, emotional kinds of behavior. I saw emotions as weak, womanly. I have to be dominant, in control, an expert at work before my peers.

He felt like a "victim" of his upbringing and cultural training as a male because he wasn't as demonstrative and effusive as Marty needed him to be. She saw him as "relatively aloof, cold, and uncaring," a view that he didn't fully share about himself. "She's been tough to live with and with her emotional crises. I've been a patient and understanding, sensitive person and willing to listen and take a lot of her verbal abuse. . . . She kept saying, 'If only you were more caring . . . ,' implying it was all my fault."

Not surprisingly, the doubts, strains, and accusations found their way into the bedroom. For Marty, sex eventually became the most available playing field on which to strike out at what she felt was patriarchal domination.

> I didn't enjoy sex at all, and I worried about this and thought about it a lot. I just grinned and bore it. After we got married, I never really enjoyed sex the whole time. I had always loved my sexual fantasies, enjoyed sexual play and its novelty. I enjoyed talking about sex but didn't enjoy intercourse. As I started to resent Andy for other things, I started to avoid sex even more. I hated its messiness, his thrusting, his dominating male violence. I felt no woman should enjoy that kind of violence. And that was part of what was happening when I tried to connect with women.

As Andy picked up the story,

> Marty had become increasingly involved in the feminist movement and more doubtful about her own feminine identity. One night she came home to tell me that she had "fallen in love" with a woman, had never been in love like this since high school, and wanted to remain living in the house but spend more time with her than with me. I said, "Absolutely not" and told her to get out. It was a difficult time, because she didn't want to leave. But she did and we separated. We got a housekeeper and agreed we would co-parent the children, each taking them half of each week. We were really headed for a divorce.

Marty's reaction to those bitter moments was, "We were ugly and cruel to each other. He cut himself off from me. I know

now he was very hurt because of what I was doing. He was very rejecting. We both got angry and screamed at each other and said things that were exaggerated. 'You don't really care about me.' 'You're selfish.'"

While listening to their stories, I wondered what they discovered in their relationship that brought them back together. Neither needed the other for financial security — the principal historical reason why women married and stayed married. They did need each other to help with the parenting — at least half of the time — but they didn't need to get back together to accomplish that. Marty didn't need Andy for status or social acceptance — she had achieved her own status in the city and created a community that did not devalue her single, separated role. Each found a way to deal with sexual needs independently of the other. So why get back together? Basically, each deeply loved and emotionally needed the other but couldn't face that fact until, paradoxically, they had outgrown the immature aspects of their needs for each other.

How did they deal with their pain? Marty turned to other women for the tenderness, intimacy, and support she felt she hadn't gotten from Andy. He was left, in his words, "bereft and lonely without the emotional and physical support Marty had provided." In the space of two years, his ratings of his energy, mood, productivity, and fulfillment plummeted on a ten-point scale from a 9 after the birth of his son to a 1 (A4a). Marty's ratings eroded more slowly, from a high of 9 shortly after her marriage to 0 when Andy told her to get out.

As I heard their stories, I felt I was reliving a Greek tragedy. They were like fated lesser deities being controlled by more powerful Olympian gods; they were neither fully responsible for nor had much control over the moves they were being forced to make. Just as humans have sensed for centuries that Oedipus, King Lear, and Faust of myth and drama are larger-than-life representations of themselves, so I felt that weekend that the Millers were magnified projections of so many torn contemporary couples that I knew.

How did their tragedy unfold? What route did each now take? How did they find a way to travel together again? What do their

lives tell us about how modern couples are resolving centuries-
old patterns that are now no longer adaptive?

Marty's Route. Marty said, "When I separated from Andy,
I deliberately threw all of my values to the four winds and
decided that I wasn't going to value anything. Probably didn't
throw all of them away. I sure acted like I did. I had a real 'I
don't care' attitude about what people thought I should do. I
was testing my values."

Marty returned to her happier college ways of living to plunge
fully into her feminist community of close friends. She said of
them:

> I had a fantasy that what I needed was to be with
> women all of the time, to be happy in women's bars.
> I would be happiest meeting radical feminists dis-
> cussing our oppression. But I found I wasn't. I don't
> know if this has to do with such feminists. They
> were very angry. I didn't enjoy that continuous state
> of anger. Also, it was very incestuous. Everyone
> knew everyone else's business and personal lives.
> It also affected my legal practice. I had a lot of
> clients who knew too much about my personal life
> and it became increasingly difficult to maintain my
> professional distance.

So Marty began to turn away from her more radical friends
to become closer to other feminists, particularly one married,
very reflective woman who helped her ground her feminism on
a less angry but much firmer spiritual basis. Her new network
of friends created religious rituals with each other to bond themselves together more communally.

She also turned back to men to satisfy her sexual needs,
though she later regretted that she had not really learned how
to become friends with them. Marty learned from these experiences that "I didn't absolutely need my husband and that
I could make friendships and relationships work with other men
also." She made up, so she said, for her delayed adolescence,

when she never had any close emotional or sexual relations with males in school or college.

Andy's and her earlier experiences at Esalen, a popular California human growth center of the sixties and seventies, and with similar groups created a common bond, to which they returned during the two years of their separation. They attended a workshop together where Marty was surprised to learn that her husband "was not the only sensitive man in the world," a revelation that some men had the courage to examine their own femininity and the meaning of their sexuality. She slowly became less hostile to men.

Her primary route back to Andy, however, was psychotherapy. She began to understand how her childhood and adolescent experiences had affected her marital and sexual relations. With Andy and then separately, Marty began to explore with her therapist the meaning of her relationships and feelings about the traditional roles of wife and mother, roles that she came to realize she really loved. "I learned that I try to make people dependent upon me and then I get angry at them and reject them. I also learned that I use sexual seductiveness when I want nurturing. I really do love my husband and like to feel safe in a family system."

About a year after their separation, Andy told her that he wanted a divorce, which "totally devastated" her. When asked why, she said that she had always viewed the separation as a temporary period during which each would learn how to grow up and become more healthy. She fell apart, couldn't go to the office, and "felt really knocked off center for several months."

To better understand Marty's less expressible feelings about Andy and their relationship, I gave her a picture of a woman holding onto a man who is intently looking toward the viewer. There is a picture of a partially clad woman in the background (A20). I asked Marty to tell as imaginative a story as she could about what these people were feeling and thinking. She spiritedly said:

> This is a story of a relationship. It has a pretty typical beginning. A woman is feeling like she needs

the man very badly. And he is . . . he looks like a
very harsh kind of person. Not in touch with any
kind of gentleness or sensitivity. There is a picture
on the wall that shows he views women as sexual
objects. And in his attempt to use this particular
woman that he loves, he is discovering some pain
in himself and that he would like to relate to her
in a more sensitive and caring way. And he doesn't
know how. And he's pulling away. He won't talk
to her about his feelings; he doesn't know how. She
is trying to understand him, trying to make contact with him in more mutually satisfying ways. I
think he's going to leave. He has been touched by
her in some way, but he can't put it all together.
He is going to spend some years struggling with
that, and she's going to need to let him go. But she'll
be all right.

Andy's Route. As his relationship with Marty "deteriorated,"
Andy turned to a close male friend for advice. He recommended
that he get counseling from a therapist who specialized in working with men "in crisis" and had an ongoing men's group that
met twice a week. Each man had the telephone number of the
others, whom he could call at any time. With this support, Andy
bounced back to begin dating again. He realized that he was
a "marketable single male" whom women still found attractive.

Andy initially found the responsibility of taking care of the
children to be unexpectedly arduous. But he also discovered that
he could be a very good parent, particularly when he could get
along with them on a more verbal level. He got in touch with
his feelings about how he wanted to raise the kids, and he felt
relieved not to have to discuss or argue with Marty about how
caring and firm he should be in setting limits for them.

But he emotionally held on to his relationship with Marty,
not only cooperating with her in taking care of their children
but also seeing the therapist together and hoping that they could
work out a different relationship. By focusing on Andy's half
of the responsibility for their rupture, the therapist refused to

allow Andy to blame Marty for the breakup. What did Andy learn about how he got along with women?

> I had become overly involved in Marty's life, as she had in mine. We lost our boundaries and became too fused and wrapped up in each other. I wasn't in touch with my strengths. I wasn't strong enough about my own territory, about my own role. I didn't stand up to her. I guess I tried to be sensitive and aware and flexible. She was testing me and interpreted my flexibility as weakness. The more she would test, the more I looked weak. Then she could despise me for that. It was during a period of maximum feminist rhetoric. She found it very easy to lump me with all other men as a chauvinistic pig and insensitive bastard. You know, all of that.
>
> I worked on becoming more self-contained, independent, until I emotionally felt totally separated and ready for the divorce. I took the initiative to get it started. She kept resisting, dragging her feet, and it wasn't until she was ready to get a legal divorce six to eight months later that she also began to feel free of me. We both felt so free of each other that we were able to say, "Hey, let's talk about starting over." I felt much better about myself. More self-reliant, independent, able to survive without Marty.

Andy and Marty Together. As Marty's imaginative story suggested, not until each, paradoxically, had become maturely more autonomous and free of the other could they return to walk the same path together, which they have now been on again for eight years. How successful have they been as marital partners, lovers, and parents?

I asked Marty to rate on a five-point scale how good a wife she felt she was (A21). She thought she was "quite good" but not "very good" and explained why.

Very good seems to be too good. If I were too good
a wife I would have too much invested in staying
a good wife. To be quite a good wife is as good as
I want to be because that means I'm taking care
of my needs as well. . . . I tried for a very long time
being a very good wife. Somehow that means to
me staying home more and taking care of all of the
needs of the family. But as a quite good wife I can
be successful in my work and feel good about myself and have some of that rub off on the family relationships.

Defining "marital success" is obviously going to be more complicated in the future for researchers studying happily married
women. Although Marty scored in the top 25 percent of the
women on a rather conventional marital happiness scale that
described all of the principal characteristics of happy marriages,
she felt extremely happy in her marriage at the time of the study
(A7). When rating how well Marty fulfilled the six most important attributes he had learned that a marriage required to
be happy and fulfilling, Andy gave her the highest ratings on
five of the six, including trust, shared values, common interests,
ability to grow, and ability to be her own person (A4b).

Though still feeling that he was not as emotionally demonstrative as Marty would like, Andy rated himself to be a very
good husband, mentioning that he has continued to co-parent
the children, thus showing his commitment to an equal division of family responsibilities (A7). He, as Marty, felt that he
was happily married. Marty saw both of them as sharing five
of her six attributes of a successful marriage, for example, good
communication skills, shared values, love, and mutual respect,
but she felt that he was less nurturing in the relationship than
she was (A4b). In these days, however, what more stringent
measure can there be of a man's success as a marital partner
than to have his spouse say of him, as Marty said of Andy,

He's a really sensitive and loving and strong person. And because he's stuck with me through all

of this I feel wonderful. I feel I have such a supportive and loving partner and that frees me up also
to make friends, to interact with other people without having to make that so intense. It's hard to put
into words. I feel so safe with Andy and so completely accepted by him. He's been so open to change
and to growth. He's taken so many risks with me
that I feel that I have not just a safe place but a
very real and honest relation. I now have more
energy to be friends with other people, because I
have a strong and caring partner.

Sexually, Marty rather dubiously enjoyed marital sex now,
varying in her ratings about how she felt (A4e). She rated him
to be high on the strengths that she believed described a good
lover: respect, self-confidence, playfulness, willingness to experiment, and giving (A26). Andy enjoyed sex with Marty and felt
she was a considerate and good lover: comfortable with sex, open
in talking about her sexual feelings, willing to give and be playful
sexually, which he valued highly (A4b).

Finally, both rated themselves and each other to be very competent parents (A4c). In terms of satisfaction and fulfillment in
the parental role, Marty ranked in the top 25 percent of the
mothers and Andy in the top 10 percent of the fathers (A9).
Both saw Andy as generally more "parental" than they saw
Marty, primarily because both agreed that Andy was more firm
and consistent in the way he reared the children. Marty pin-
pointed the differences when she said, "The kids will tell you
that I'm a softie. I'm not consistent and don't set limits as strongly.
He's much more patient. He can teach them. If they don't learn
fast enough for me I get angry. I'm much more physical and
do much more hugging and kissing [I also observed this; Marty
would wrestle with both her daughters and son on the floor,
which obviously Andy couldn't do] . . . Andy is very intensely
engaged with them now."

Numbers and percentages can't possibly express the messages
of the heart, of just what another really means to us. To Andy,
Marty

was a warm, caring, loving, giving person. She's a good mother, a good companion. She's been very supportive of me in my work, especially in terms of my emotional growth. She's helped me by sharing her own insights into feminism and what that has meant in getting in touch with some of my latent powers. She has the remarkable ability to face unpleasant things, to try to deal with emotional problems right now, not put them away and pretend that they're not there. We have an openness and ability to communicate that is really very remarkable. We can talk to each other about almost anything. That's what Marty has done for us.

And how happy were Andy and Marty? Very. Each felt happy and felt the other was, and their closest friends agreed (A11, A26). And how fulfilled and satisfied were they with their lives? Andy, Marty, and his closest friend all agreed: He and seven others in the study were the most fulfilled of the sixty-five men. Marty's restless dissatisfaction with herself, however, kept her only in the top 25 percent of the women.

Our question now is, "What are Andy's and Marty's strengths that enabled them to become the most successful two-career *couple* of the study?" After telling you my hunches about each, I shall turn to the results for all of the men and women to sort out which of Andy's and Marty's strengths more generally describe men and women who succeed in their familial relationships.

6

Andy:
Mature Androgyny

As with Billie, I knew nothing about how Andy's and Marty's genes, hormones, and constitution contributed to their success. Nor had I known or observed them as children in their early formative years. I know about them and their parents only through their adult eyes. Despite these limitations, the hours of tests and interviews generated the hypothesis that at least five roots nourished Andy's success:

1. Loving, basically respectful parents who had firm expectations of him and who steadfastly remained present to him when he needed them
2. An androgynous inclination both intellectually and emotionally
3. Adolescent and adult psychological maturity
4. Marty, who taught him how to continue to grow by way of his femininity
5. Much pain and an optimistic attitude that he could triumph over it himself

The first key to understanding Andy's growth was his feeling that he had grown up in an emotionally safe and loving home to which he could comfortably retreat when he felt so miserable and "emotionally wrenched" during his separation. His parents had always been accessible when he needed them. Actively concerned about his growth, they encouraged him to achieve in school and sports and become independent at an early age. While holding him to firm expectations, they had not severely disciplined him or ever given him the feeling that he wasn't accepted or loved (A1a).

I said that his parents "basically," not "fully," respected him, because of a central theme of Andy's Rorschachs that I must explain. His relationships with women were too mixed up with his relationship with his mother. He had changed from his early thirties to his late forties in his attitudes toward them. My report states:

> He still doesn't feel as connected and secure with women, who seem to be unpredictable to him. In contrast, however, to his early thirties, he has matured considerably, now seeing women more as adults, not just as mothers, having become much less dependent upon them for nurturance as well as less submissive in trying to please them. He is now more certain of his own sexual identity in such relations and has established a firmer sense of his own self in his relationships. The foundation for this movement is a growing confidence about his own sexuality.

I had not known that a focal issue in Andy's counseling had been his relationship with his mother. He explained it to me this way. He felt that she loved him but only "conditionally"; he had to earn her love by doing well, particularly in school. Although both parents expected great things of him, his mother had higher hopes and assiduously worked with him to attain them; for example, she helped him with his homework.

Two effects of her conditional love lingered into his middle age. We agreed that to get her love he had learned to dedicate himself ambitiously to work hard to succeed vocationally. Her less healthy effect intensified his emotional dependence on women, who he feared might not love him and so might abandon him. He needed to become part of them, in his words, to "fuse

myself with them," to continue getting their love. When a relationship started to go sour, he protected himself from any con-
firmation that he was not loved by initiating his separations and
divorce. His attitude was, "If I separate first then she hasn't separated from me, so she still loves me." Not until he left Marty
did he learn to let go of his need for her approval and so become his own independent man. His Rorschachs showed how
much he had grown as a result of his therapy and Marty's provocations during his late thirties and forties.

Andy felt more temperamentally similar to his father, whom
he respected, especially for his ethical idealism to which he traced
his own humanistic values about applying basic research to human concerns. But he apparently also learned from his father
that he should be an emotionally reticent, unexpressive, and
stoical male, traits that later got in the way of succeeding as
a husband and parent.

Andy explicitly singled out his androgyny as the second and
most important key to his success. He learned how to balance
his overdeveloped maleness by bringing what he called his hidden "feminine parts" into awareness so that he could more consciously use their strengths. As I've said, I had not anticipated
that the book's principal actors and actresses, selected solely by
objective indices of their success, would be so androgynous.

Raised as a typical male, Andy had learned to achieve, compete, and control, if not suppress, his emotions. He had participated in the usual adolescent male activities and cultivated what
he called his "male-dominated left-brain" strengths: analytic, objective, scientific modes of thinking. Andy was familiar with the
discoveries that the left and right hemispheres of the brain develop at different rates and abilities. The left brain mediates more
stereotypically masculine modes of thinking like analysis and
linear logic; the right brain controls more typically feminine
modes like empathy, intuition, aesthetic values, and contextual
thinking.

Andy had become unusually introspective and aware of himself, perhaps as a result of his accident, so he was not surprised
by what his tests showed. His "feminine mind," which he defined
for me as "the subjective, emotive aspects of my mind," was truer

to his given native talent than was his conscious analytical and conceptual mind. He had devoted most of his life to deliberately developing this more masculine way of thinking in order to be able to compete like a male. Clues to his undeveloped feminine mind's potential were his adolescent interest in literature, the discovery of an ability to learn and enjoy languages, and his movement away from "straight" biological research to its humanistic application in the area of sexuality.

The reasons for Andy's emerging vocational recognition are instructive, for they show just how one-sided his education had been and why traditional school credentials do not predict adult success very well. Schools value and measure stereotypical masculine talents, such as analytical, logical-deductive, and critical thinking, more than they do stereotypical feminine ones, such as empathic, intuitive, and contextual thinking. Identifying analytical conceptual thinking with intelligence, Andy thought he was less intellectually capable than his colleagues.

> I don't see myself as phenomenally gifted in intelligence or IQ. Yes, I'm bright and articulate and introspective. I like to write. I grew up in a left-brain environment. Most of my education and training also emphasized and focused on left-brain qualities. My intellectual abilities are primarily left-brain ones, and throughout my life I have compared myself with other academic colleagues primarily in terms of them. I don't feel that I'm in the 99 percent of left-brain performers and as a result have discounted my abilities. I have become more aware that I have right-brain emotional skills that may be stronger than my left-brain ones. These are valuable and important and it is the synthesis of the two halves that is most important. I feel I have an exceptional ability to synthesize the two halves.

Andy's synthesis of his femaleness and maleness, the yin and yang, Jung's anima and animus, became the pathway to increased creativity, as other researchers of creative persons have also noted.[1] His emerging vocational recognition paralleled his growing openness to and integration of his more feminine parts into his more masculine mode of research. Prodded by Marty, reinforced by Esalen and other similar group workshops, and furthered by his therapy, Andy said, "I became more comfortable with my own feelings and that made me more comfortable with issues in my professional life. I became more willing to look at my work from other perspectives. I became more open, accepting different approaches to problem solving, more tolerant of ideas I would have considered to be kooky, far-out, nonscientific when younger."

Andy's growth illustrates that when we grow healthily, we grow wholly. To mature, we must grow not only in our minds but also in our characters. Successes in our relationships, marriages, and vocations tend to go together because each draws upon the same underlying strengths that describe our maturity. Not only Andy's relations with Marty and the children but also his vocational achievement improved as he became aware of "the many dimensions of . . . (his) own sexuality." Paradoxically, but quite understandably psychologically, as he accepted and expressed his more emotional, affectionate, and feminine potentials, he became, according to Marty, more self-reliant, independent, and in more control of his own life. And, according to him, he became more creative in his research, for which he had begun to receive increasing professional recognition.

Andy was one of the two men described by three peers as equally balanced in their masculine and feminine strengths — another way to define androgyny (A10). Compared with the other men, he was more masculine than about a third and more feminine than 90 percent of them. As shown by the fact that he also scored higher than all other men in maturity (A12), his years of arduous growth had led to a healthily balanced androgynous personality.

The third key to Andy's success was his maturity, both as an adolescent and an adult. When he was a teenager, he ranked seventh among the sixty-five men in maturity (A31). Mature for his age in his relationships, self-aware and self-confident, determined and purposeful, Andy had the personal resources to learn to live with the shattering injury to his right leg (A1b). They enabled him to cope at the vulnerable age of sixteen, an age when its meanings for athletic skill and physical image are so traumatic. Andy did not resort to self-pity or neurotic withdrawal; instead he took himself in hand and taught himself how to walk again.

I wondered how his shortened, almost useless leg had affected his image of himself as a "regular guy." It could have turned him away from the rough and tumble of male competitive prowess, heightened his sensitivity to his body and therefore to his feelings and others', particularly girls', reactions to his disability. When I asked Andy directly about his accident's effects on his view of himself and his future, he replied, "There is no reason why I can't live a very full rich life in the domains of my life — the intellectual, emotional, and spiritual. I just have to live within a smaller perimeter." Andy never let his disability excuse his failures; instead, it prodded him to work even harder to succeed. But it did limit the perimeter of his effectiveness. Imagine so needing to protect one's useless leg that one fears picking up a three-month-old daughter or wrestling with one's older children.

Andy was the study's most mature middle-aged man, which gave him the strengths necessary to learn from his separation how to adapt to being a half-time father. Since maturity stimulates further maturing, it was not surprising that just as he grew as a result of adapting to his disability, he matured as a result of his separation.

> It had a profound impact on how I got along with my kids . . . in understanding the dynamics of child-rearing, the stages that children go through, and in being able to appreciate and experience how they felt and how to respond to them appropriately . . . the separation was a wrenching traumatic event and through getting insight into what led up to it and my contribution to it, I developed a better understanding of how I had been dealing with women. I became more comfortable as a husband

and a more effective one too, when she came back
to me two years later. It made me much more aware
of what other couples might be experiencing, more
empathic, and at the same time perhaps more inclined to encourage them to seek counseling, be
more persistent in their efforts to salvage their relationship.

Andy's maturity enabled him to adapt resiliently to one of the
most hurtful events of his life. He rapidly learned from his men's
group and counseling how to be more aware of and put into
words his feelings about Marty and their relationship. As a
result, he became even more interpersonally sensitive and effective in his other relationships.

But he still had unfinished growing up ahead of him. Two
of his answers to questions on the test measuring his maturity showed that he still had *not* transcended the effects of his
adolescence. Because of the ever-present physical reminder, he
might never overcome these effects. He agreed that "my ideas
about myself are still being shaped by experiences and feelings I had when I was much younger." "My beliefs and values
are still very closely related to experiences I had when younger" (A12).

The fourth key to understanding why he became so successful was Marty's confrontational feminism. Andy could not
escape her challenge to his maleness; fortunately, he had the
maturity to endure the suffering necessary to alter years of living as a typical male, the courage to risk refashioning his sense
of self, and the flexibility to persist in changing how he got along
with Marty and the children.

The last key to Andy's success is another offshoot of his maturity — one very similar to the one that aided understanding Billie's success. Andy is a hopeful person who highly values continued growth and feels he can control how he matures. He
believes living means growing and growing takes effort; it doesn't
just happen. In response to my question, "Where is your potential growing edge? Where could you be developing more?" he
replied (A21),

I am just aware that nothing is static. You don't achieve one level of excellence and move onto the next. You constantly relearn and repolish and re-practice skills that made you productive at a previous level. I am really aware that my past glories and triumphs either become memories or if I want to retain those skills and qualities that led to the triumph, I must work, constantly work. Like my marriage. Just getting back together was not enough. We have to keep working. The same is true in being a father.

I think I have lived life very fully. It has been a very rich life, full of a lot of pain and worry and setbacks, but what I haven't done very well is to integrate the pain and the triumph. I sort of see that as my next task.

I also asked him, "What role does faith play in your life?" He said, "I believe that humans are basically good and that collectively we are slowly and painfully learning from our mistakes. The majority of people in the world are interested in bettering life for their children and want to see life on the planet continue. I believe that we are evolving toward a higher state of raised consciousness, an awareness that we are a large family flying together among the stars."

Though Andy's story is as special as Billie's, I sense that, in addition, his has much to teach us men about our maleness. Andy shows us how we may need to alter its historic meanings if we are to become more whole and healthy in the future and succeed in our relationships with emerging modern women such as Marty. What does Marty's story tell us about why she succeeded as she did?

7

Marty:
Growing into Her Own Vision

I felt Marty to be special, different, even charismatically so, as her friends said of her. When I met her she was in psychotherapy, self-absorbed in exploring her "unordinariness," as she described it, as well as her feelings about her parents, particularly her mother. Since I had no measures of her pretherapy self, I could not determine how her therapy affected her judgment and views of herself and her parents. Therapists focus more on parents' and clients' weaknesses than on their strengths, more on what went wrong when they were younger than on what went right. Marty's complicated personality and history, combined with her therapy's effects, may have obscured psychologists' more conventional ways of understanding her evolving strengths.

Five keys—more complexly configured than Andy's—helped Marty and me understand her success:

1. Caring but unstable, powerless, and inept parents who propelled her to get in touch with her own resources in her early growing-up years
2. A sensitive, supportive husband, very similar in values and interests, ultimately responsive to the egalitarian, companionate, heterosexual relationship that she valued
3. A perhaps biologically given erotic intensity that opened her to archetypal sources of feminine insight and power, enabling her to articulate for other women their historic strengths and goodness

4. A temperamental, androgynous predisposition whose nur-
    turing femininity and independent masculinity were simul-
    taneously set when younger
5. An involvement with the feminist movement, which pro-
    vided her with the social forms and support to explore and
    integrate her refashioned identity as a woman called to an
    egalitarian vision whose time had come

The first key — Marty's caring but inept parents — contradicts
what psychologists have known and what the study's result of
its 105 men and women also confirmed: Favorable home environments produce successful adults. Since exceptions that violate our expectations frequently produce new insights, we must
closely examine Marty's unfavorable home environment. (Only
two other women reported as unfavorable a family during their
childhood and teens (A1a). Nine other women believed as firmly
that their mothers did not show the traits identified by researchers
as typical of the effective parent. Seven other women saw their
fathers as not effective.)

Just how unfavorable was her family in Marty's eyes? Very.
She reported few strengths in her parents and in her early relationships with them. Marty believed that both parents had poor
mental health. She regretted more what her parents did *not* do
than what they did do. Like Andy, she never felt that either
parent had severely disciplined or rejected her, but she was let
down that they had not loved her more or encouraged her athletic, outdoor, and especially intellectual activities. (A signal
event in her growth occurred when they went to one of her therapy sessions, during which she asked them to hug and love her
like a little girl again.)

Her alcoholic, physically unhealthy father and incompetent
and helpless mother did not give her models of a man and
woman to respect and emulate. Like Billie, she felt closer, though
ambivalently, to her father than to her mother. She depended
upon him emotionally but stubbornly rebelled against him.
(Only one other woman reported disagreeing more with her
father about vocational, political, and social values.) Therapy,
of course, seeks to resurrect our parents so that we can learn

how to get along with them more maturely or relinquish them as continuing influences in our lives. At the time of the study, Marty had not yet emotionally freed herself of her parents (A4i). She ranked six among the forty women in feeling her mother to be a strong, vivid, and internal presence still influencing her life.

We do not know the strengths Marty absorbed from her parents the first five years before her sister arrived. She must have become intensely uncertain, most likely jealous, about being displaced by her three sisters and brother. To then be expected by her mother to grow up overnight from being a child to being her "assistant," even a "mother," taking care of her rivals as well as her own parents, angrily galled her for years.

Sometimes, however, it is just such parental weaknesses that prod children to develop compensating strengths. As his father's taciturnity and emotional restraint caused Andy much later in life to learn how to be affectionate and even cry, Marty's out-of-control, powerless mother and weak, incompetent father may also have perversely provided the impetus to value and develop control, power, and strength.

Parents may indeed enable us with more strengths than we may be aware of or wish to accept. Marty's resentments when she was five colored for years her memories of her parents. Not until such feelings began to pass in her early forties did she begin to appreciate their strengths. Unanticipated by Marty, her mother demonstrated a nurturing competence by supervising visitors to patients in a local hospital; her father summoned the will to free himself from alcohol for seven years. And both parents came to her aid when she called out to them for help, even after Andy had told them why he had kicked her out of their home. So Marty began to accept and respect her parents, and as her anger abated she discovered that she too was a good person.

Psychologists only recently have begun to understand why some hurt children, like Billie and Marty, draw strength from their parents' weaknesses while others can't. Parentally hurt but resilient children have usually had at least one trustworthy, loving experience: for infants, a close bonding relation with a mother or, particularly valuable for vulnerable girls, an identification with a father; for older children, supportive siblings or adults (like Billie's grandparents), or even neighbors and teachers. Researchers also suggest that natural "self-righting" or equilibrating strengths can help children like Marty overcome the potential long-term damaging effects of their vulnerability.[1]

Caring teachers and rewarding school experiences can also provide hurt children the nurturing security they need to outgrow their parents' limitations. Unfortunately, Marty's female boarding school provided neither affectional security nor intellectual support. Hungry for affection, unsure of her own feelings and identity, isolated from boys and men, she was drawn into her romantic crush on an older mother-figure. Her teacher's cruel rejection of her, however, led her to discover and value later close female friendships, which became her principal path to growing up and provided the interpersonal model for her feminist vision.

Like Billie, Marty discovered her leadership strengths from her athletic and extracurricular activities, which opened up her vocational path to adult success. Although she was very bright, her intellectual strengths did not become a major route until she was older. Neither her parents nor her teachers modeled or encouraged her mind's growth. She didn't discover how much her teachers had let her down until she tried to argue logically with Andy. Like Billie, she felt her teachers had been mediocre, rigidly emphasizing memorization and never challenging her latent intellectual talents. So, again like Billie, Marty was forced to turn to her own resources. "Getting angry about all that they didn't teach me has sort of freed me up to be bright all on my own."

Marty agreed that another key to her success was her relationship with Andy. He adapted in ways that let her integrate her nurturing maternal needs with her achieving career desires. Psychologists have underestimated the maturing effects a loved partner can have on our growth. The study's women judged their partners' personality to be the most important of the fifty causes I examined of their continued growth (A23). In their thirties, the men rated their wives as most influential, but when they were middle-aged, their wives came second to their occupation in influence.

Others have had unfavorable family lives, incompetent parents, and uninspired teachers but not succeeded as Marty did. Why? The next two keys — her eroticism and androgyny — found their integration and social support in the last key, her involvement in the feminist movement.

Not until I had analyzed Marty's inner life as projected onto the Rorschach inkblots did I understand the third key to her success: why she felt different and valued strength and power so highly, and why other women called her their guru, even "priestess," during the heyday of the women's movement.

> She seems to have opened herself to what are typically less conscious and conventional images and sources of energy. A dominant theme in her imagination, almost of obsessional vividness, is her preoccupation with all varieties of erotic activity. She is in touch with sexual energies of all forms — voyeuristic and exhibitionistic needs, heterosexual and homosexual impulses, birth and menstrual fantasies — and can willingly allow their access into awareness without anxiety or defensive efforts to repress or avoid them.
>
> Now these erotic fantasies and needs seem to be vehicles for expressing forces even more primitive, archaic, and fundamentally human, which I have rarely seen expressed in the fantasies of most others. It is almost as if she has direct access to what Carl Jung calls "archetypal" sources of power. [Archetypes for Jung are inherited universal and primitive templates energized by instincts of such power to potentially overwhelm a person's control.] So she has available mythological, religious, universal symbols of great energy upon which to draw for insight and staying power. She is probably sufficiently aware of them to fear being taken over and lived through by felt transcendent powers. She could well emotionally identify with very primitive myths of the *magna mater*, the universal earth mother,

the power of middle earth, mother ocean, the life
energy — the sources of feminine mythological insight and power. Such images contain so much
energy and power that she may feel she is every
woman, rooted in and living out a centuries-old
myth of feminine mystery.

The quality of Marty's power that I am trying to communicate may seem elusive, even unfathomable, to you. If you are
a humanist, you can tell me that the power of Shakespeare, Hawthorne, or O'Neill comes from their access to such universal symbols of human passion and insight. It is the experience I sensed
behind the doors of Roger's watercolors, except that for Marty,
the door was wide open and she welcomed everything that
bounded through it. In its extreme uncontrolled form, such
power is seen in the mentally ill person who feels possessed by
demons or angels whose intensity is so great that they come alive
in hallucinations. In its public, more socially acceptable form,
the power is seen in religious and political leaders who are so
possessed that they move others to fanatic devotion, even self-
sacrifice. It is seen in creative persons who become transfixed
by an idea, a vision whose sources are felt to be transcendent.
It is seen in our daily lives when we are so caught by a feeling,
such as falling in love, that we are compulsively driven to act
beyond our rational control.

What implications does this way of understanding the roots
of Marty's familial and vocational success have for her? Three
questions immediately occur. What is the source of such felt
power? Does Marty have control over her inner myths or is she
controlled by them? What does feminism mean to her success?

I felt that there was a strong constitutional basis to Marty's
energy, dynamism, and earthy eroticism. In psychoanalytic language, she had a strong id. By erotic I do not mean simply sexual energy but an energy, as Freud used the term, that clamors,
excites, disturbs; an energy that impels to risk, to be attracted
to, to reach out to touch, to connect, to be a part of, to merge
with others, a cause, or a transcendent being. We know that
infants temperamentally vary greatly in the intensity of their
needs, energy levels, alertness, and outgoingness.[2] Such infants,

like my energetic grandson Benjamin who apparently needs only four or five hours of sleep a night, can drive their parents to distraction, as he does his sleepless, weary mother. Yet such vitality can be a priceless strength when appropriately channeled. Marty's erotic vitality was her great strength. It propelled her into the world of others, which became her route to growing up. In her words, she was a "networking" person, seeking to connect with others, creating groups, participating in communal rituals, nurturing other women, and learning from her own therapy to be nurtured by others. Marty's life-force was strong. Other women sensed it, were inspired by it, and sought her out as a counselor, not just for legal advice but for affirming support of their identities as women.

The fourth key to understanding her success is her androgynous predisposition, probably also temperamentally rooted. Children of such insistent vitality need help to learn how to control and use its associated intrusive, aggressive, self-assertive, frequently dominating energies. Girls in particular can become conflicted about such vitality when they are raised to be properly feminine, unassertive little ladies. Marty and I agreed that the early channeling of her vitality into becoming a nurturer when she was five had several enduring unhealthy effects. She became an "adult" before her psychological time. Her stereotypic feminine nurturing skills of reaching out and connecting with others were unduly strengthened, as were her stereotypic masculine initiating, assertive, independent, and self-reliant ones. So her erotically strong temperament combined with her early assumption of responsibility for raising other children strengthened her androgyny even more. She was described by her peers to be the second most androgynous and feminine and fifth most masculine woman of the study.

What happens to a young girl who must nurture others before she has had the opportunity to fulfill her own needs to be cared for and loved? These needs to be a child again linger on for years in adult fantasies, as Marty's story to a blank white card illustrates (A20).

There is a park or forest with a clearing in which there is a group of children playing, around whom

> are parents sitting watching them play. They are
> obviously ambivalent about whether they would like
> to play or go and work. The children beckon them
> to come and play with them. Little by little the
> adults move to the center to play with their chil-
> dren. They start to collect ribbons, putting them
> in each other's hair, and they learn they can go back
> and forth easily . . . back to their work and back
> into the circle . . . they decide to meet there every
> so often to remember how to play with each other.

The emotional price that Marty paid for the opportunity to
develop and stabilize her androgynous strengths too early was
high. It complicated her marriage and pushed her into therapy.

How vulnerable was Marty to being possessed by her archetypal power? Two strong bulwarks fortified her: her basically good health and the women's movement (the fifth key).
As an adolescent, she was quite mature, particularly in her interpersonal relationships (A1b). As a middle-aged woman, she
rated herself as more mature than only a fourth of the women
(A12), most likely because therapy unsettles clients and accen-
tuates weaknesses rather than strengths. Her Rorschach and the
other tests showed that she was basically healthy emotionally
and interpersonally mature, had good judgment and reflective
control, and excellent resiliency to resist being overcome by her
power. But in my concluding summary of all of her tests, I suggested "that the only limitation I could foresee, and it might
not be a limitation if she wished to move others, might be that
in her struggle to reconcile the opposites of maleness and femaleness under the dominance of feminism, she could be vulnerable to imposing arbitrarily a preconceived ideology on her
experience—and perhaps risk being possessed by the idea of being a great earth mother."

Marty emotionally understood my reservations. Unbeknown
to me, she had focused in therapy on how "to understand and
be more conscious of my charisma and always remember that
I am 'ordinary,'" that she was not the powerful great earth
mother, the priestess of all. "I'm not extraordinarily good and

holy and wonderful. I am not extraordinarily awful either." She succinctly and vividly interpreted the meaning of her own power. "I think much of my trouble has been a struggle with my power. I see myself as a powerful person and I need to make almost everyone else powerless to take care of them and I resented that because who would then take care of me?"

Marty's commitment to feminism was her way to integrate her own androgynous strengths; she used her masculine, forcefully assertive leadership talents to fulfill her feminine nurturing image of the ideal marriage and world. She could thus keep her intense feminism from leading to a single-minded fanaticism, as has occurred throughout history in members of religious cults, that could result in her losing control and so becoming unhealthy.

Just what did feminism, the fifth critical key to understanding her success, mean to Marty? Feminism provided her with the route back to the archetypal strength of her own femininity, which she had not seen in her own mother. She may have only begun to see it when she overcame her earlier childhood resentment that tenaciously held her in its blinding grip for some thirty years.

> I have made a commitment to women. I always will be committed to women. I believe by our nature as women that we are priestesses. Because of our cyclicity, the cycles we experience, the possibility of birth and death every month, we understand the cycles of the universe, the change of the seasons. We have the ability to celebrate life and death and all of their transformations. I celebrate all of the problems that have given women trouble in the past. I love that I can menstruate. I love that I am able to bear and nurse children. I love that I am empathetic, as long as I am taking care of myself. I love that I can connect with other women and form very supportive groups and experience a spiritual bond with my sisters. I love the history I have as a woman and all of the models I have of women throughout history.

Marty had a compelling vision that gathered up all of her talents and energies to which she felt called to devote her life. It was a vision of "total equality in which women are in all positions of authority in business and government, where other married couples are experimenting exchanging roles so ours doesn't look so strange. And where men can form their own brotherhood and not depend upon women to help them learn how to connect with each other and us."

I hope you have not thought of Marty's larger-than-life uniqueness, as well as Andy's and Billie's, as a reason to dismiss their stories as not helpful for understanding how to grow up to succeed. Why not draw some lessons from their lives and compare them with those of Roger and some others that I shall share with you in the next chapter.

8

Eleven Insights into Becoming an Adult

Each of us will take insights away from Billie's and the Millers' stories that speak to us at this time in our lives. After quoting Roger's thoughts, because they nicely capture what I hope most readers will remember, I'll add several of my own.

1. "Growing up is a lot more complicated than I had thought."
    Yes. There are no simple *Reader's Digest* formulas to become more mature. There are no easy ways to change our character.
2. "It's a damn slow process."
    There are no quick fixes, "maturing pills," adult education courses, psychic credit cards, weekend Esalen growth groups, or magical solutions for growing up that so many of us look for today. Miraculous conversions happen only to the few, like Saul of Tarsus on his way to Damascus; and their maturing effects probably endure for only a few of those few. Just how many converted nonbacksliding Saint Pauls do you know?
3. "Learn how to endure and use the pain that uncertainty, guerrilla attacks, and friends like Doug provoke to adapt more effectively. Persist like Billie to find that balance between adjusting to others and fulfilling my own needs."
    When we deny threats, flee into drugs, and withdraw to avoid frustration, anxiety, and boredom, we diminish the impetus to become more mature. To grow up to succeed requires the will to tolerate frustration and resist the temptation of self-indulgent escapes, as well as to persist and work hard.

4. "Growing up can go on every day. I don't need to wait for a 'crisis' to cope more successfully with my life."

Become a little more self-initiating, self-educating, and self-responsible every day.

5. "I'll never be finally 'grown up' because there'll always be some new challenge to stretch me. Even ones I'll create for myself."

I'd phrase Roger's insight somewhat differently. "I can continue to grow all my life. I don't have to say near the end of my life what Winston Churchill reputedly said of his, 'I'm bored with living.'"

6. "Many things can help me grow; but maturing goes fastest when I'm in-a-relationship-with-a-loved-one."

Almost everything that makes us human comes from our relations with others: our language, way of thinking, values, and attitudes about ourselves. Many experiences contribute to maturing, but because we are the social animals that Aristotle said we are, our relationsips with others can be the most powerful generator of healthy growth. However, we have to be vulnerable to and educable in such relationships.

7. "A lot can go wrong while growing up, but I have a self-regulating, psychic gyroscope that can help me grow healthily, if I can read its messages accurately and learn how to go with it in the direction toward which it is pointing."

8. "I don't have to be a permanent prisoner of what has gotten me to where I am now. Though it may take a lot of work, as Billie and the Millers have shown me, I can continue to grow despite my past. There's always hope."

Yes, mature persons are hopeful; they have the psychic resources to alter their environment or themselves more effectively. Less mature persons don't. But even the most discouraged, messed-up person can still hope. One of the study's brightest men had been an alcoholic for nine years; he went down and down until he joined the homeless existing under a bridge. I don't fully understand why, but one day he picked himself up to begin the long climb to where he is now: happily living with his lover, economically flourishing, and vocationally satisfied.

George Vaillant, studying how Harvard alumni changed over the years, pithily, and wisely too, said that "the things that go right in our lives do predict future successes and the events that go wrong in our lives do not forever damn us."[1] Billie, the Millers, and the remaining men and women of the study would qualify his advice by "*if* we are mature and androgynous." That *if* is crucial.

I have three of my own reflections that may be helpful.

9.   "A traumatic childhood, crippling handicap, or severe stress is *not* necessary to grow up healthily."

Gail Sheehy, an early popularizer of research on adult development, declared that a stormy childhood was necessary to learn how to cope with adversity and so succeed.[2] She relied on the few studies at the time that had followed children into adulthood. Children who experienced a lot of stress *but learned how to grow from it* — I'd suggest because they were more mature and had a richer variety of androgynous strengths upon which to draw — turned out to be more self-directing and confident adults than children who serenely sailed through life from one advantage to another.[3] Why? The pubertal boy who fails to sprout apace with his friends, does not make the basketball shots as easily, and is mystified about why his friends talk so much about girls must find other ways to establish his competence among his peers. An unattractive, moody, unpredictable girl who struggles with her emotionality and relationships with other girls and boys must learn to develop alternative ways to get along with herself and others. Billie, Andy, and Marty are sterling examples of Sheehy's claim.

Sheehy's prescription for success is certainly not the right medicine for everyone, however. Being abused by an alcoholic parent or losing the use of a leg is not essential to learn how to develop the character necessary to succeed. My study of successful persons tells us just the opposite. Those most able to cope with the problems of living came, as Vaillant said, from favorable homes and had nontraumatic childhoods and Bill Cosby-like TV fathers.

10.   "While individuals walk seemingly idiosyncratic and diverse paths to maturing, their trek can be described similarly."

The paths lead to minds and characters (interpersonal skills, values, and self-concepts) that are more reflectively aware, other-centered, well integrated, stable, and autonomous. They lead in the same direction for persons of any age, sex, and cultural background, when they are free to follow their inner gyroscopes — their equilibrating principles.

11. "The model of maturing identifies the critical strengths of Freud's concept of 'ego,' which mediates how effectively we adapt to both internal and external provocations."

Though both maturity and androgyny contribute to success, they are not the same. Mature men and women are reliably androgynous, or, if you like, androgynous persons are highly likely to be mature. However, maturity is not equivalent to or exactly the same as androgyny. You cannot clone mature persons and then call them androgynous. While you would recognize some of the same strengths in mature and in androgynous persons, they would still be recognizably different. An androgynous male might be quite masculine in his athletic and competitive skills and typically feminine in his warmth and gullibility but not be mature. Though maturity and androgyny go more or less together, as they did for Billie and Andy, they won't always for others, as they didn't for Marty. Remember that she scored much higher on androgyny than she did on maturity.

Maturity and androgyny generally go more together for women than they do for men. If you are a mature woman, your partner, friend, and colleague would rate you as very androgynous (A10). In their eyes, you would be seen as typically feminine, especially in your interpersonal relationships where strengths like your understanding, sensitivity to others' feelings, and compassion would be obvious. They would also think of you as masculine, though to a lesser extent, because of your autonomous strengths, such as self-reliance, decisiveness, and willingness to stand up for your beliefs.

On the other hand, if you are a mature man, you would not be seen quite so clearly by your peers as androgynous, though you would be thought of as typically masculine because of your assertiveness, decisiveness, and risk-taking strengths. Mature men don't have to be macho. They are neither more nor less competitive, aggressive, dominant, or self-sufficient than less mature men. Acting like a fighting cock may prove your masculinity to some impressionable hens but says nothing about how mature you are.

Much to my surprise, and theoretical discomfort, if you are quite a mature man, your peers do not see you as any more sensitive to others, sympathetic, and understanding than if you are quite an immature one. So just as stereotypic macho strengths are irrelevant to a man's maturity, so are typical feminine interpersonal ones. The model of maturity predicts otherwise about interpersonal strengths. If I use other measures of the men's maturity not derived from the model (A13e), however, then men judged by their peers to be mature are also judged to be more sympathetic, understanding, and so forth (A10a).

Exploring the relation of maturity to androgyny is a prelude to how I will now try to tease out of the individual lives of 105 men and women the strengths essential to succeed and be happy. What do Billie, Andy, and Marty share in common that helps us understand our own and others' successes and happinesses? The ways they have walked their paths are not typical, though, as I've said, what is "typical" anymore I'm not sure. However, the dilemmas that they faced include adapting to the changing meanings of femaleness and maleness and of women's and men's adult roles, creating more stable but truly egalitarian families, resolving the conflicts between familial and vocational demands, and discovering new ways to grow more healthily. What mind and character do we need to adapt successfully in such a world?

9

Becoming a
Successful Marital Partner

Despite the excruciating turmoil of many contemporary families, men and women still rank their marital and parental roles to be their most important sources of satisfaction, even more than sexual and occupational ones. I found this to be true for the forty-year-olds I studied; Robert Sears also found it to be true for sixty-year-olds,[1] as have more recent studies of young adults.

Given the importance of a happy family life, the question to ask has to be, "What personal strengths are necessary to succeed in our family roles?" The question was much easier to answer in the early half of the century than it is today. Then, society defined our roles and status more clearly and firmly, and how well we adjusted to the demands measured our success.

I remember my grandparents' golden wedding celebration, where they were toasted for their marital success. Five years later, my seventy-seven-year-old grandmother confided shortly before she died, "I've lived with your grandfather fifty-five years and for more than fifty of them I wanted to get a divorce but I never had the courage. No one has ever known. Thankfully, he never has." He lived to be ninety-four and never knew. Divorce would have been a devastating personal disgrace; it still is for many. Marital researchers of the day would have selected both my grandparents to be exemplars of success.

I also remember when our ethnic and religious status were

life-and-death issues. They still are, of course, in some parts of America and in other countries. Whites could not legally marry blacks in some states. Whites married whites; Catholic blacks married Catholic blacks; Jews married Jews. I remember when I and a handful of other non-Jewish friends were the only persons sitting on a Jewish friend's side of the church because her family boycotted her marriage to, of all persons, a most respectable and wealthy high Episcopalian.

Society's laws and expectations about how we should fulfill our roles are becoming less commanding; some have just withered away. The Census Bureau now counts cohabiting unmarried couples; more couples don't get a marriage license until their first child arrives; married women retain their family names; some churches marry gays; pregnant girls no longer must hide in Florence Crittenden homes; bastards are no longer called bastards; a minority of American children are now raised in traditional nuclear families; the majority of children will spend some part of their growing-up years with only one parent; divorce has lost its stigma.

How do we identify who is and who is not a "good family member" nowadays? I tripped on the meaning of "marital" partner. Society's definition of marriage as a legal relationship no longer fits several million American couples — more now define their relationship only in personal, not legal, terms. Several of the study's middle-aged men called themselves "married" though they could not legally deduct their "wives" for income tax purposes. A gay man complained that several marriage items were sexist, and he edited them to fit his "marriage." He will be angry when he reads that I have included the unmarried "married" men but not him in the married subgroup that I shall tell you about. It is not that his relationship was not a loving commitment; it had continued for nine years when I saw him and his lover. But I wanted to stay as close as possible to the definition of marriage of researchers who had not had to deal with its changed meanings.

The changing meanings of "marital partner," even of "parent," reflect a much more fundamental change in how we think about successful intimate relationships. The largest national survey of Americans' mental health, which originated in the mid-fifties and was repeated twenty years later,[2] found that over the study's twenty-year period there had been "a diminution of role standards as the basis for defining adjustment; . . . increased focus on self-expressiveness and self-direction in social life; . . . a shift in concern from social organizational integration to interpersonal intimacy."[3]

Andy and Marty mirrored quite well these changing cultural definitions of successful familial relationships. Rather than continue to adjust to societal norms about what a good marital partner and parent should be, they mellowed the traditional ones. Marty freed herself from what society, and she, had once thought a good wife should do: keep the house spotless and the family fed with prize apple pies; pick everyone up without complaining and follow her husband to Buffalo and then Great Falls; and raise healthy, happy, successful children. Andy assumed 50 percent of the parenting responsibility, even though his colleagues sometimes resented his absence to be home with the children. Marty created a more self-directed and fulfilling life for herself as a lawyer. Andy learned how to balance better his masculine strengths with more typical feminine ones, such as sensitivity to Marty's and the children's needs. After years of painful labor, they had created a mutually fulfilling and intimate family life by the time I saw them. I was delighted that their tests and peers identified them to be the most successful couple to describe at this time in our evolving society, because of their being at the edge of an advancing cultural change in relationships.

Our neat societal and research boxes and previous ideas and findings are getting messed up. Our changing ideas about ourselves are altering our definition of who is a "good marital partner" and may be making some earlier studies of what predicts marital success obsolescent.

When our customs and institutions no longer support our traditional roles, then our personal resources become more critical determinants of our success. To adapt to increased freedom demands greater maturity. The *marital* balance between adjustment and self-fulfillment has shifted for many from adjusting to what a wife and husband are "supposed" to do to fulfilling primarily our individual needs. Because our character thereby becomes more instrumental to how successfully we adapt as partners, researchers must explore our individual personalities much more deeply for clues to success than they have done to date.

Identifying Maritally Successful Persons

Today, we must ask other questions and create new methods to understand marital success. Since the methods I used to identify who is and who is not successful define what I mean by "success," I must briefly describe the existing ones I used and those I had to create to measure comprehensively the participants' personal meanings of marital success. More technical information may be found in the Appendix.

I did not ignore traditional ways of defining marital success. In addition to items used in earlier studies,[4] I used a survey that measured marital adjustment — one indication of success — based on findings about intact and divorced marriages: Happily adjusted partners agree about their religious values, argue less frequently about money or parents-in-law, frequently hug and kiss each other, and do twenty-eight other things that are as interesting (A7).

Andy and Marty have told us, however, that we cannot ignore the *personal* meanings that partners attribute to marital success. Remember that Marty felt she was a good but not an excellent partner, because she believed it important to fulfill her own needs as well. Let's assume that you are a participant in the study and I want to know what you and your partner mean by the term *good marital partner*. I would ask you to list six personal qualities you had learned from your marriage that contributed most to your fulfillment and happiness. I then would ask you to rate how much of each quality you and your partner had demonstrated in the marriage. By weighting and adding your ratings for your six criteria, I could roughly measure *your* view, not just mine or other researchers', about how successfully you and your partner had created a good marital relationship.

I have not yet thoroughly canvassed how good a marital partner you are. I don't know what your partner thinks. You may

think that you are a good spouse; your partner may not. Karl
and Jeannie Baker tell us why I must find out what your spouse
thinks. Karl, a consulting civil enginer, traveled abroad about
six months every year, while Jeannie remained home to care
for their two adolescent girls. He described his marriage in warm
and happy terms and himself as a most successful husband, parent, and lover; Jeannie definitely did not. Listening to each
describe their marriage, I thought they must be bigamists — I
couldn't recognize each from the other's description. Jeannie told
me that she was thinking of leaving Karl; after all, he had been
leaving her for years. Karl had no inkling of the surprise she
was preparing for him.

The most stringent question I can ask about your marital success is "What are your personality traits that contribute to your
partner's happiness?" To answer it, I rely on the study's unique
strength of having exactly the same in-depth personality information about each partner. I find out how happily married you
and your partner are and then what it is about each of you that
contributes to that happiness. As I said earlier, using others'
judgments — a partner's, friend's, and colleague's — enables me
to escape the weakness of those studies of adults that rely solely on
the participants' own reports. What would we discover, for example, about the character of successful partners studying only Karl?

I also want to know how well you measure up as a marital
partner, not just from your view of what a good marital partner is like, but *from your partner's view as well.* After all, your happiness also depends on your hopes and expectations for the marriage. You may feel a scrappy argument quickens your blood
and enlivens your placid relationship; your partner may dread
the spat. Or a hasty good-bye peck on your partner's cheek each
morning seems quite adequate to you; your partner takes it as
a sign you don't really love her. So I would ask each of you to
rate how much you had demonstrated the qualities that contributed to marital success that *your* partner had spontaneously
reported were most important to marital success.

You might protest, "Not fair, she's biased and hysterical besides" or "He's so blind to what goes on between us he might
just as well answer everything randomly." Okay. That can hap-

pen. Using different ways to define your marital success enables me to check to see if they agree with each other. Reassuringly, they did for the group. The individual members of the couples identified more often than not most of the same six attributes of a marriage and agreed about how much each demonstrated them in the relationship. Furthermore, relying on the results of 105 men and women dilutes the distorting effects of a hysterical or blind partner as well as unintended errors, like misinterpreting the instructions.

This mechanical way of ordering your success may offend you, but it is the only way to protect you from my biases. I could have taken the simpler and more delightful Maslowian approach and just relied on my intuitive impressions to rank the group from most to least maritally successful. Some of you might accept my judgments as fair and accurate, but I guarantee you others wouldn't. And I wouldn't, either.

I have gone into these technical details at this point because I took a similar multiassessment approach to identify who succeeded and failed in other adult roles. My use of self-reports and peer evaluations, ratings and established test and questionnaire procedures, and other means to identify who succeeded and who didn't increases, I hope, your confidence in the results. It does mine.

Character Strengths Needed for the Ideal Marriage

The study's men and women spontaneously identified a rich number of personal strengths, many of them attributes of maturity, that are necessary to create a happy and fulfilling marital relationship (A4b).

- Love and trust
- Interpersonal communicative skills, such as shared feelings, understanding, and sensitivity to a partner's needs
- Shared interests and responsibilities, such as common work and sexual compatibility
- Loyalty and commitment to the relationship, such as making time available for one another

- Sense of humor and other personal strengths, such as cheerfulness, self-confidence, and optimism
- Commitment to honesty and fairness

As the marital balance tips away from adjusting to society's expectations and toward fulfilling our individual needs, the character strengths needed to maintain a marriage become more necessary. Adjusting to the societal expectation that we grin and bear each other "until death do us part" no longer keeps modern couples together—only our character does. When I saw the men in their early thirties, about 5 percent of those who had married had divorced; in their mid-forties, 28 percent, and five years later 36 percent. Most of the men did not know or could not tell me why their marriages had failed. The easy reasons were the obvious ones that researchers had identified: arguments about money, children, and sex, or, in Andy's words, "incompatibility."

Their wives knew the reasons for marriage failure, however. They unfailingly zeroed in on the critical character trait, like poets, who are sometimes far ahead of the rest of us in their insights into our human condition. Robert Frost told us his thoughts on gender differences and their effect on marriage in his poem *Home Burial.* A mother is sharply lamenting her husband's muteness about the death of their child. He has just asked why he can't say how he feels.

> *"Not you! . . . I don't know rightly whether any man*
> *   can."*
> *"There's something I should like to ask you, dear."*
> *"You don't know how to ask it."*
> *   "Help me, then. . . ."*
> *"My words are nearly always an offence.*
> *I don't know how to speak of anything*
> *So as to please you. But I might be taught. . . ."*
> *"You can't because you don't know how to speak.*
> *If you had any feelings, you that dug*
> *With your own hand—how could you?—his little*
> *   grave;*

> *. . . And talk about your everyday concerns. "*
> *. . . "I can repeat the very words you were saying:*
> *'Three foggy mornings and one rainy day*
> *Will rot the best birch fence a man can build.'*
> *Think of it, talk like that at such a time!*
> *What had how long it takes a birch to rot*
> *To do with what was in the darkened parlor.*
> *You* couldn't *care! . . ."*

The father poignantly speaks for many of the men: "I don't know how to speak of anything/So as to please you." The mother speaks for many of the women: "You *couldn't* care!" But he does care, in his way. His "best birch," his child, has rotted. Frost captures what we now know, that women and men often speak in different tongues. Recent studies have confirmed these differences.[5]

The men and women were like those two proverbial ships in the night silently passing each other by, each only occasionally understanding the flashing code of the other. The couples could not communicate *in each other's language.* Like one of Marty's tapes, they told me over and over, "He's like a computer." "He's afraid of his feelings." "I've lived with him for ten years and I still don't know what he feels." "He comes home exhausted at night and just grunts, while hiding behind his paper, when I ask him about his day."

He: My words are nearly always an offense . . .

She: You can't (speak) because you don't know how to speak.

While we may not have much control over whom we "fall in love with," we can deepen our trust in our relationship by learning how to communicate our needs and feelings more openly and honestly. Andy reminds us that a marriage that lasts nowadays doesn't fall in our laps, like manna out of the heavens. It requires continuous work to learn how to speak to each other throughout our lives.

The Character of Happily Married Men and Women

We are now ready to answer two questions: the one that most researchers ask, "What are men and women who are happily married *actually* like?" and a rarely explored second and more stringent one, "What is the character of men and women whose partners are happily married?" Four themes describe men and women who report that they are happily married. None will surprise you; they confirm the findings of other researchers.

The first theme is that maritally happy men and women are also *competent* and satisfied parents, sexual partners, and marital partners. Competence in one role goes with competence in others because our interpersonally determined adult roles require similar strengths. Glance back at the list of saintly virtues essential for a happy marriage. Strengths like communication skills, commitment, sense of humor, self-confidence, and honesty are just as necessary to be a good parent, lover, and colleague at work.

Of course, there are exceptions. Bill Spaulding was one. He built a successful marketing consulting firm, was chief executive officer, and was respected, though not loved, by his colleagues for his forceful leadership. He learned how to make the "tough" decisions, like firing two key associates, friends of his, who had helped him create his firm twelve years earlier. Nevertheless, his wife rated him to be a dismal failure not only on her but also on his own criteria of the strengths necessary to create a happy marital relationship and be a competent father. He was rated the next-to-worst husband and father of the study (A4b). He saw himself to be much more successful. He succeeded in his work because he had a president's power to make others adjust to him. However, his aggressive entrepreneurial strengths that contributed to his firm's success got in the way of being a good husband. His wife wasn't about to kowtow to his dictates, once the feminists told her that she had her own right to happiness. He was vocationally successful to the public, maritally unsuccessful to his wife. Trouble obviously loomed over the horizon.

The second not-unexpected theme that describes the character of maritally successful persons is that they are *psychologically mature.* Other researchers, studying marriages that have endured for years, report similar results. Persons whose marriages have lasted are more self-confident and psychologically healthy[6]; they are also more affectionate, warm, and cheerful than those whose marriages have failed.[7]

A third not-unexpected strength of the maritally successful man and woman is that they are *androgynous,* and most salient is their interpersonal femininity (A10a). A few other researchers report that men satisfied with their wives' companionship are more feminine; women satisfied with their husbands' are more masculine.[8] To appreciate and enjoy being with a partner of the opposite sex, each must share some of the other's interpersonal strengths. If you are a man, do you enjoy talking with your wife about your feelings and relationship; if you are a woman, do you enjoy competitive games and really try to beat him at Scrabble and tennis? How do we understand and anticipate another's needs if we don't share to some degree the other's strengths? If we aren't maturely other-centered, we relate as an outsider, not an insider, to the other's personal world, so our partner never feels really understood. Many women felt that way about their partners: "He supports me but he doesn't understand me." One clue to Bill Spaulding's marital failure was that his peers rated him to be the seventh most masculine but fifth least feminine man of the study. He had not developed the interpersonal strengths necessary to enter inside his wife's world and respond empathically to her needs.

Bruce Jackson, one of the study's two unrepentant male chauvinists, illustrates why so many contemporary couples are in trouble. He is a typical macho male whose wife eventually got fed up. He had been laid off as a division manager of an electrical equipment company and was looking for another job when I saw him and June. She found his constant presence at home to be unbearable. Perhaps because he was hiding how severely he had been hurt by being fired, he was even more imposingly authoritarian and dominating than I remembered him. He rudely interrupted June, squelched and dismissed every one of her opinions, and refused to help her set the table when asked.

When their children tried to stand up to him, she loyally backed him up and went along with his ideas. (June confided to me that their oldest son, Tim, forced to go to a college not of his choosing, had dropped out and was living on the streets of New York. She hadn't told Bruce.) She also told me how much she still loved Bruce.

Three years later I got a call from Bruce, who had found another, less well-paying job in the meantime. He was desperate, lost, confused. He kept repeating, "She's left me. She's left me. After twenty-five years of marriage. She's left me. We had such a good marriage. She's gone. I have nothing left." He had absolutely no insight into how his steamroller personality had so squashed June that to survive she had to get out from under his physical presence. It is a tribute to Bruce's resiliency that he sought counseling, much to my surprise, and tamed his overbearingness enough to encourage June to return. But he since seems to have lost his spirit and vitality; he even looks defeated.

Finally, and again not unexpectedly, maritally successful men and women are *happy,* more so than those who feel that their marriages are more precarious or are failing. "Obviously," you'll say. But what is intriguing is that they had been happier and more competent and productive at every stage of their lives since their teens, which suggests that the roots of happy marriages reach back at least into our adolescent character (A4a). We prepare to succeed maritally long before marriage has even become an idea to romanticize or be scared about.

The Character of Men and Women Whose Partners Are Maritally Happy

My most rigorous test of the character necessary to create an enduring intimate relationship with another was to ask, "What is the character of men and women whose partners are happy and fulfilled?" What is an Andy like who makes a Marty say, "I feel wonderful. I have such a supportive and loving partner. I have not just a safe place but a very real and honest relationship . . . that makes my marriage an 'exceptionally happy' one." And what is a Marty like who makes an Andy rate the likelihood very high that his happy marriage will continue until his death (A4j)?

Two themes stand out about the character of husbands and wives who make their partners happy about their relationship (A7). The first is that singularly macho "Marlboro men," like Bill Spaulding and Bruce Jackson, are *not* likely to have contented wives and that interpersonally feminine and adaptable wives will most likely have happy husbands.[9] The second theme is that women who make their spouses happy must have almost three times as many virtues as men who make theirs happy (A10). Apparently, being a wife is much more demanding than being a husband. When I told Harriet about this result, she said, "So what's new?" It was new to me, though.

Interpersonally Feminine Men and Women Have Happy Marital Partners. If you are a man, the odds are long that your partner is happily content to live with you if you can honestly answer "yes" to each of these questions. Why not really reassure or disturb yourself by rating just how good a marital partner you are or would be if you are now single. Using a five-point rating scale, give yourself a 5 for each question you unhesitantly (honestly) agree with, a 4 if you hesitate momentarily, and so on until you must give yourself a 1 when you almost draw a blank.

First and foremost, are you an *adaptable, cooperative,* and *yielding* person? According to my unbiased neutered computer, women want to feel that their partners are responsive, open, and don't stubbornly resist and reflexively say "no" to their ideas.

Can you give several examples of how you've been *sensitive* to her needs and desires within the past two days? If you answered "yes," then cite several. If you have to scramble for a minute or two, then don't rate yourself higher than a 2.

Next, are you a *nonjudgmental* and *self-accepting* person and so more able to accept your partner's frailties and gaffs? If you unequivocally rate yourself a 5, then beware that your great strength doesn't disguise Roger's fatal weakness. He was so self-accepting that he infuriated Beth — she sensed that layers and layers of narcissism hid his flickering soul. Such self-contentment really makes saviors angry.

Because interpersonal harmony is so central to women's own self-worth, it is not surprising that maritally happy ones have husbands whose character helps maintain that harmony: flexible, yielding, sensitive to their needs. Their husbands definitely do not aggressively impose themselves on their wives, as I observed Bill Spaulding and Bruce Jackson do with their wives when I stayed with them (A10).

We men need provocations like rating ourselves on five-point scales to make us reflect about our relationships; women don't. They more frequently ask themselves such questions. They have known for eons that their nurturing strengths are necessary to keep men happily married to them. The research only confirms that knowledge, but in spades.

If you are a woman whose husband is happily married, then you are seen by your peers as *interpersonally feminine*, but also virtuous in innumerable other ways as well. How *warm, lovable, compassionate,* and *loyal* are you? Men value these virtues highly — in you. You also need to be *cheerfully, not moaningly, adaptable,* too. A sour and complaining wife grates on a man. Your husband doesn't have to be playful for you to be happy, but you sure must be if he is to be happy. Since men are not very expressive, particularly of their childish and affectionate selves, do successful wives have to be *playful* to help their spouses be more emotionally spontaneous? If you want to be maritally successful, you cannot be wishy-washy: You must be able to make decisions that are true to your character. And then there are twenty other angelic virtues you must have to make your partner happy — so my unbiased computer insists.[10]

Women Must Be More Virtuous to Have Happy Marital Partners. The second principal theme intrigued me. Why must women have so many more virtues, particularly interpersonal ones, than men to make their partners happy? Their tenderness, compassion, warmth, loyalty, and flexibility are critical to their husbands' marital happiness (A7). Without hesitation, Harriet interpreted the theme to mean that women have to be much more adaptable in a marriage than men. Rather humbling. My hunch is that since women's identity is so emotionally organized around their relationships, sometimes at their own expense, they are more fluid and no, not adaptable, but yes, more adjustable to the quirks and demands of their husbands. Both Billie and Marty spent years as nurturing wives adjusting to their spouses. That has been the historical definition of the role "the little woman" had to play: the self-sacrificing handmaid that Marty rebelled against so furiously.

If you are like Marty or younger than the middle-aged men and women I'm describing, you may be troubled and questioning yourself—or the validity of these findings for you or your generation. I too am uncertain. Roger tells me that younger women are forward, assertive, and aggressive. They more openly initiate contacts, even sexual ones, with men; they pay their own way, propose marriage to men, and initiate divorce more frequently. The study's middle-aged women said they had learned from their daughters what they could have been like. As women become more typically masculine, will they retain their femininity? Billie and Marty did, but then they had been socialized for years to be nurturers. Will younger males be as happily married in the future to more assertive and less accommodating females? What is going to happen to those males — still the majority—who have been raised to expect women to go along with them, keep peace in the family, and adjust to their needs?

Are you upset that the more successful partners are more interpersonally feminine than the less successful ones? All that that means is that they had been rated by their peers to have interpersonal strengths typical of women. Those who failed as partners were not judged to be warm, affectionate, and sympathetic. This does not mean that some successful partners were not also self-reliant, ambitious, and strong individualists, but the judges did not *consistently* describe the successful ones to be like that. Such masculine strengths are not necessary to be good marital partners. One good partner might be ambitious, for example; another might not be. At least ambition is not shared in common by persons who succeed maritally.

Stereotypic "macho males," like Bruce Jackson and Bill Spaulding, who have not developed interpersonal strengths such as empathy, are not coming out very well in their intimacy relations with others. The stereotypic feminine female is coming out well, but will she succeed as well in the future as she becomes more typically masculine? What will happen to marriage in the future?

Why Marry in the Future?

When asked what marriages will be like in the future, I can make the following guesses:

- They are going to be more "rocky."
- Women will not be as accommodating.
- Males will not change rapidly enough to develop the interpersonal skills modern women want.
- Because men need women more than women need men and men are less skilled in creating interpersonal supports, more men will suffer emotional isolation and loneliness.

One of the most important questions to ask as we think of the twenty-first-century family is the one I asked about Andy and Marty. Why would either want to get back together again? Because the women's movement affected so many of the study's women, some, like Marty, in dramatic ways, I shall narrow my question to one, which women here and abroad understand and nod in agreement to and to which men bewilderedly mutter, "What a stupid question." If you are a male, why would a young female these days ever want to marry, settle down with, and stay married to you all her life?

Any relationship as problematic as that between a man and a woman who don't use each other's language very well must fulfill many different needs to endure. When one need is frustrated, other, more fulfilled ones hold the couple together for the long haul.

What do I mean? Consider sex. Middle-aged men and women both want sex 2.6 times a week; when both work, however, they are washed out—not infrequently these days at different times. And now that women are less accommodating to men's timing, the couple probably is up for sex only on Sunday mornings. That leaves 1.6 orgasms unaccounted for. That's quite a lot of itchy horniness to carry around the next week. Ergo, frustration. If sex is the core of the marriage, what do you predict will happen? I agree. The couple had better have other needs they can mutually satisfy or your prediction will become a foregone certainty.

When I ask women why they stay married to men, they tell me instantly. At least five bonds (security, children, status, sex, and intimacy) have historically held them to the same men for a lifetime — and the length of women's lifetimes has almost doubled since the early 1900s, which can make living with men much more boring that it used to be. (That is Margaret Mead's comment, not mine.) Now only one bond (intimacy) holds modern marriages together, which is why they are so fragile and will remain so far into the twenty-first century.

Marriage Was Security. First in importance worldwide was that marriage provided the financial security necessary for a woman to have a family. She "needed to be taken care of," and a man learned to need to take care of her. No longer. As more women inch their way toward earning as much as men, security will become an ancient reason for marrying, or remaining married when a couple faces rough times.

Marriage Was Children. Second in importance worldwide was that marriage provided the opportunity to have children. Childless couples used to lose status; certainly an unmarried pregnant girl did. Hawthorne put Hester into a stockade. "Bastards" were pejoratively just that. No longer do these problems occur in many sections of the United States, as well as in some European countries. The 20 percent (or now more) of single female-headed American families reminds women that males are only necessary to provide the first impetus. Fifty percent of women in the Los Angeles area (where most societal trends begin) told the Institute for Social Science Research that they would consider having a child without a partner "if they were childless and approaching the end of their child-bearing years."[11] In the twenty-first century, sperm banks and sterile needles will take care of the necessary impetus and provide women much greater

choices about which genes to pass on. Since many men have
not been educated to be competent fathers or are seldom home
anyway, some women even now feel that males are obsolescent
as fathers.

Marriage Was Status. Probably third in importance for centuries was that marriage satisfied a woman's and her parents'
need for status or social acceptability. I remember when an unmarried woman was called "old maid" or "spinster." Parents of
spinsters also lost status and didn't talk about their unmarried
daughters. I don't know the origin of dowries, but surely some
parents used them to bribe someone, anyone, to marry their
daughters. No longer. Increasingly, in the United States and
other countries, an unmarried woman does not lose status when
she reaches thirty or forty. It has become her choice. Nor does
a divorced woman nowadays lose status in many communities.
Furthermore, as women get equal opportunities to achieve in
different vocations, whether as coal miners or lawyers, heads
of Fortune 500 companies or taxi drivers, a husband's vocation
no longer has to be her route to status in the community. In
fact, the time is here when some men, like Margaret Thatcher's
husband, get their status from their wives.

Marriage Was Legal Sex. Fourth, from society's view, marriage has been expected to resolve all of the frustrations that
complicate male-female sexual relations. Ready accessibility to
a sexual partner simplified much of living, left energy available
for other societal purposes, and ensured some continuity in the
caretakers of children who might appear one day. No longer.
In many regions of the United States, as has been true in France
for years, a single woman can have a relatively unfettered though
discreet and legal sex life and not be punished by her community. Husbands are becoming obsolescent for sexual satisfaction.

Marriage Is Intimacy. The only reason left for many women
to marry is to have an enduring intimate or companionate and
loving friendship with a man. But the meaning of intimacy for
women is vastly different from that for men, and women now

demand intimacy on their terms. The best friends of most women in the study were other women. The best friends of most men were their wives. For women almost everywhere I have been, an intimate friend is someone with whom to share one's feelings about one's self, others, and the relationship itself. No "bottom line" or conclusion must be reached when women talk, as it must more frequently when men talk. For women, one meaning of a conversation is in the moment of being-in-relationship, not just in its content. Men talk more at others and women with them. From the women's view of intimacy, few of their husbands had an intimate friend.

For most American men, intimacy means sex, so they can't use the word "intimate" in talking about their male friends. The men did not think of themselves as having "intimate" friendships—a good male friend is one with whom one plays poker, drinks, and watches the Tigers on TV.

So my next question is, "If women increasingly will marry men primarily for companionship, what qualities will men need to be able to establish enduringly intimate relations with women?" Women know. Men will need to develop those feminine interpersonal strengths that I found make a woman happy in her marriage: empathy, understanding, compassion, sensitivity to others' needs. These are just the strengths that Marty felt Andy had been developing under her rigorous tutelage. Everything I have learned about male-female differences tells me that generally males are not very mature in these typically feminine ways, and other researchers and popular writers agree.[12] When speaking about these issues, I say to women, "Be careful about leaving your partner; you most likely will not find a better one." The women look glum; the men smile for the first time and clap.

Some women despair, thinking that men are constitutionally built to be aggressively dominating and authoritarian antediluvians, but I'm more hopeful. American males are beginning to adapt. I think of the typical well-defended bastion of male virtue: a "macho" boy's school I visited where teachers, parents, and trustees agreed that the school was athletic, competitive, masculine, ambitious, aggressive, traditional, and conventional. The school's teachers as well as students described the "typical boy" similarly. So where is the hope? In their wishes that the typical boy were different. The majority of the male faculty wished that its students were more considerate, caring, and sensitive to the feelings of others — typical feminine strengths. The boys agreed with the faculty in their wishes. Though not much has changed at the school since, at least the wish is there. Until parents and educators raise boys to be more interpersonally mature, to learn how to bring their feelings out of their black holes and label them, to speak more intimately, hope for the future of American families risks being stillborn.

If you are a male, have you also asked why you would stay married to the same woman for fifty years? Because I haven't heard younger males ask themselves this question as insistently as females have, I am less certain about their answer. I doubt that security or status is an issue for younger males. To marry to have children is not as biologically compelling a reason for men as for women. Younger males are not really that concerned about passing on the family name or property or expecting their children to provide for them in their old age. Staying married "for the children's sake" is no longer as persuasive a reason as it used to be when the primary marital relationship goes sour. Sex will always remain an insistent reason to marry and stay married, at least until desire and potency begin to wane, but our increased freedom to satisfy that in almost any way we wish without guilt reduces its marital adhesive power. I think we men still want our partners to take care of us: bake those special apple pies, wash and iron our shirts, create an attractive, relaxing home, hoveringly anticipate our other needs, and be a gracious hostess for our business colleagues. What's left? We want to have a loving lifelong companion to whom we feel deeply committed. Do men have the feminine, interpersonal character to fulfill that need?

You may feel I have minimized the meaning of children to fathers. Perhaps. I don't have evidence about younger men's needs for children; I do about older men's. I turn now to the second of our three basic familial roles to ask what character strengths are necessary to feel fulfilled as a parent.

10

Successful Parenting:
Making the Commitment

When I married I just assumed I would be a father; it was no big deal; everyone became parents, if they could. I also had no idea whatsoever how demanding being a father was going to be, even in those days when women stayed home to be mothers without as many complaints. When I recall my first public talk to my son's nursery school parents, I realized I must have felt overwhelmed by how many virtues I lacked as a father. I titled it "Parenthood: The First Requirement for Sainthood."

Raising youngsters today demands much more of adults. Not knowing how to prepare them for a more uncertain future, deciding who is going to take care of them, and keeping our sanity while struggling to help them cope with sex, drugs, and our divorces make parenting infinitely more troubling and challenging. No wonder thoughtful adults now pause years to agonize about whether to become parents.

In spite of these uncertainties and disturbing demands, adults in their thirties and forties still value being good parents. They rate their parental role to be more important than any other except their marital role. Although Veroff's national survey found that adults in the 1970s valued being a parent as much as adults in the 1950s had, it also found that college-educated men had become less satisfied being fathers in the intervening twenty years. Apparently more men have become less emotionally fulfilled in their relationships, not only with their children but

137

also with their colleagues at work,[1] and possibly with their partners, if they too are working.

More young persons, like Roger, may choose not to become parents in the future. When I ask why, they tell me, "I'm scared to have kids. I wouldn't know what to do when they cry," or "I don't want to go through what my parents went through with me," or "I'm too selfish to give up what I want to do and be a slave to kids." Obviously, I am not talking about unwed teenage mothers who deliberately seek to have a "cuddly baby doll" to call their own, and the few boys who want to keep their pleasure's unanticipated consequences.

Modern parents feel that they don't know how to raise a child. They are right; no instinct tells them how to change diapers, help their baby sleep through the night, or make their kids share their favorite toys with their friends. The truism that even as basic a maternal skill as nursing is instinctual is just false. Harriet compared mothers who successfully breast-fed their first baby with those who did not. The successful mothers differed from the unsuccessful ones in only one major way: They had access to accurate information about how to breast-feed, which suggests that we must learn such skills to become competent parents.[2]

Marty and Andy tell us, moreover, that the fundamental issue is not the "mechanics" of parenting, like learning how to train a child to use the potty or deciding who is to take the children to school today. They could not settle these issues until they had resolved what parenthood meant to each of them. Andy only learned in his late thirties that he enjoyed being a father and had the character strengths to be a good one.

Identifying Successful Parents

As soon as I asked about the character of successful parents, I stumbled on the question, "How do I identify who succeeds as a parent?" How would you rank yourself and your friends in terms of parental success? The easy way is to ask parents to rate how much they feel fulfilled as a parent—the topic of this chapter (A9). However, to enjoy being a parent, to feel fulfilled, does not necessarily mean we are a competent one. The more difficult way is to measure how competent a parent is. But what does "competent" mean when talking about raising children? As in all complex human roles, *parental competence* has several different meanings.[3]

We may have all of those ideal qualities that saintly parents reputedly have. Like what? Well, the audit of the women's and men's six criteria of the qualities they had learned made a good parent produced sixty-three strengths (A4b). If you are a parent, don't despair, for I can boil them down to eight basic ones. In rough declining order of importance, they are

- Patience and other personality traits like sense of humor, high energy, self-confidence, and calmness
- A loving, affectionate attitude
- The ability to create a predictable environment for children that is consistent, firm, and fair
- Emotionally communicative skills like listening, understanding, openness, and empathy
- Respect for a child's individuality
- Playful involvement with and enjoyment of children
- Acting like a teacher who has expectations and goals for raising a child
- Taking a problem-solving attitude toward child-rearing and using such skills to help a child learn how to adapt

If I had had this list of virtues when planning the study, I could have designed measures to assess them and so order the men and women in terms of their "saintliness." Instead, I defined parental competence as I had marital success (A4b,c; A21). The easiest ways were to ask the parents to rate how competent they and their partners were as parents overall and then rate themselves and their partners on the six attributes that defined a successful parent.

The most stringent way would be to discover how the study's children turned out as adults. How many years later? And how can we figure out who was responsible for what? Mother? Father? Neither? Grandmother? The day-care center? "Sesame Street"? Bruce Springsteen? Bill Cosby? But even he, TV's "perfect" father and best-selling author about how to be a good parent, might not be that influential: One of his daughters was a drug addict and had been estranged from him for years.

Besides, I might not be here in 2010 A.D. when most of the children would have married, become parents, and settled into their work. What to do? I turned to two other ways to examine parental competence. The first asked the parents to rate each of their children over twelve years of age on fifty traits of maturity and adaptability. The second asked them to describe their own parents. I could then ferret out what the parents were like of the men and women whose success, health, and happiness I had actually measured.

I shall tell you now about the character of parents who enjoy being parents and find parenthood to be fulfilling, although I must postpone telling you about the character of *competent* parents until I track down the familial, adolescent, and other historical reasons why the men and women turned out as they did. Sorry, but my mortality has gotten in the way of a scientifically rigorous and tidily logical summary of the successful parent.

The Character of Women and Men Who Enjoy Being Parents

Do adults who feel fulfilled as parents share similar strengths? Can we really talk about *the* character of *the* satisfied and fulfilled parent? My answer is "probably 'Yes' for mothers, but probably 'No' for fathers."

Mothers and fathers who are satisfied with being parents in the rating of thirty different attributes of parenting (such as the amount of time demanded or the amount of growth they have experienced as parents) succeed in their principal adult roles and are mature and happy persons (A9). They are judged by their spouses to be competent parents and adapt well to the strains and difficulties of their other roles (A4c). Their maturity means that they have the strengths to adapt well to varied demands. For example, a good father must be aware of his child's and his own needs and be able to take his child's view (even while figuring out a new strategy to get him to eat his spinach).

Parents like Billie who know that they can cope with whatever may arise feel good about themselves, so it is not surprising that parents who enjoy being parents also feel good about themselves (A9; A13f).

Because almost no shared or common character strengths describe *both* the fulfilled mother *and* father, being a parent most likely means something different to women than to men. If you are a mother who really enjoys and feels fulfilled raising children, your peers will probably be impressed by your openness to change. They won't see you as a "stuck-in-a-rut" person; instead, they'll rate you to be sensitively responsive to your child, willing to try anything that might help him or her grow up healthily. They will also believe that you are an emotional person who has numerous feminine interpersonal strengths, like warmth, compassion, cheerfulness, and loyalty. The computer-drawn portrait of the fulfilled mother mirrors the character I associate with Norman Rockwell's famous *Saturday Evening Post* cover of a maternal mother in her kitchen baking what I always recall to be an apple pie. If you are a man looking for a partner who really enjoys children, look for her.

However, if you are a woman who wants a partner who will truly enjoy children, you will have to rely much more on your intuition than on what I found. Males who turn out to enjoy being fathers later in life come in many different packages that have almost no common colors, shapes, and wrappings. It's as if no "father character," no strong core of traits, is necessary to feel satisfied as a father. There are a few traits, however, which I never anticipated. The man who enjoys being a father is more adventurous, willing to take realistic risks, and, like the satisfied mother, is not stuck in a rut.

These traits of the fulfilled father made me feel better about myself as a parent. If you knew my son, you'd know why. He has really tested my adventurousness and risk-taking character. I never anticipated that when he was thirty-two he would decide to "play for one or two more years" before "settling down." After he bought a twenty-five-foot Vertue sailboat and taught himself how to sail and navigate by the sun and stars, he called us from Juneau, Alaska, where he had been working, to tell us, rather off-handedly, that he planned to sail around the world alone for several years. If you are a parent, you may empathically understand my reaction to what I called his "extended vacation." I asked him, "What if you don't arrive in Auckland when you plan? What should we do?" "Oh, just forget about me." Well! Easy to say when you've never been a parent. He's taught me that the riskiest thing a person can do is to become a parent. Could this be another reason why today's youth may be more leery about having kids?

So if fathers who enjoy being fathers are adventurous risk takers, and not stuck in ruts, then that makes me a satisfied father — except for the realistic part. I risked sailing with him from Tahiti to Bora Bora: forty-two hours to go 110 miles by his reckoning, battering huge waves head-on to my eyes while lying flat on the heaving deck, gripping the gunnels, as if my life depended upon it — which it did — as the tumultuous waves swept over the heeling cabin; apprehensively watching him dance around the deck, changing sails, and tying up ropes; wondering if Harriet would lose both of us on this trip; and upchucking despite Dramamine and my vow not to. I proudly discovered my son on that trip: his self-taught competence and serene self-confidence. But *realistically* adventurous? I didn't tell him that I swore if ever I got back on ground I'd never sail again. Instead, I'd be more sane and hike with him on land.

I did twenty months later. This time he chose Sri Lanka, which was in the midst of its brutalizing civil war. For a day we dodged trees felled to block the roads, saw generators knocked out so that large areas were plunged into darkness, and avoided buses and trains that were systematically being blown up or whose operators were being shot. If not on sea or land, then maybe in the air next time. How about free-fall parachuting with him over Kenya? (He insists I exaggerate both on sea and land; but it's how I felt.)

But the results of the study puzzled me. Why weren't satisfied fathers more sympathetic, warm, playful, and a host of other good things as well? Why weren't they like Andy? Why is a male's personality seemingly so irrelevant for enjoying kids? To discover what being a parent meant to men and women, I turned to my studies of the meaning of work. Work can be either a job to get done or a career to be called to and live — the historic religious meaning of "vocation." If you have a strong Number 1 Self, you may sense what being "called" means. If not, then think of Marty, called to be a feminist. She has a mission, a commitment, to do what she is meant to do, to have a consuming goal or way of life that focuses her best talents and energies for some transcendent purpose. (I sometimes think my son's calling is to be another Columbus or Neil Armstrong — an adventurer challenging destiny.)

Might not we talk similarly about parenthood? We could view parenting as our *job* and therefore be concerned about how much time and energy we spend on our children. We could believe that parents should be paid by the government. When the children reach late adolescence tell them, as Billie's father told her, to leave home, and never visit them as adults, as her father never did. Or we could view parenting as our *calling* and as our route to self-fulfillment, providing us the opportunity to continue growing and fulfilling some of our strongest needs. Harriet feels this way. She dropped her appointments, even our special weekend together, to drive four hours to be with our daughter and Benjamin when his temperature reached 102 degrees. She couldn't resist the siren of her emerging grandmotherly calling.

So why did satisfaction with being a father seem so irrelevant to the men's personalities? Of the thirty attributes of parenthood about which we can be satisfied, eight measure how much parenting is fulfilling, including meeting our strongest needs, utilizing our best talents, being central to our identity and compatible with our personality — signs that parenting isn't just an impersonal job but is deeply meaningful to us. For mothers, six of the eight items predicted their overall satisfaction with being a parent; women who are the classic mothers really enjoy being mothers. For fathers, only two items contributed as much to their fulfillment. Could this difference mean that a man's paternal role and strengths are peripheral to his identity and personality? American boys are not raised to think of themselves as fathers or develop the strengths necessary to be good ones.

How does this difference in the meaning of parenting show

up practically? If dad comes home tired one cold night wanting some fun in bed before going to sleep and the baby in the next room cries, what happens? Mom immediately loses her desire and feels compelled to leave their warm bed to go comfort her baby. Dad, impelled otherwise, irritatingly tells her to wait a minute or two. She may oblige but guess what she's thinking of? Or if a child is sick, who frets and feels called to stay home to take care of it? Of course, fatherhood can be a calling, motherhood a job; but the odds are long that it will not be men but women like Marty who will more sharply feel divided between taking care of their children and making the committee meeting.

When I talk of motherhood being a calling rather than a job, women know immediately what I mean. As a test of whether you have a gut feeling for what a calling is, why not try to identify other signs than those I'll list that show that a mother views her role as a job rather than a calling? See if you and your partner agree, for if you don't you could have a lot of arguments if you have a child.

A woman for whom being a mother is a job

- Complains constantly about how much time her children take
- Leaves her child to watch TV much of the time
- Gets bored when reading her child to sleep at night
- Looks forward to vacations without the children, whom she parks at grandmother's
- Makes no special effort to be home when the children return from school
- Nags her husband when he doesn't take over when there's a problem

It is not the occurrence of one or two such signs that tells us that our parenting is a job rather than a calling. Parents need to get away together or be alone to keep their own special interests alive. Mothers who must work can't be home when their children return from school. And they may be too tired to read patiently McCloskey's *Time of Wonder* for the eighth time before bedtime. Our underlying attitude, however, creates a pattern of numerous signs that parenting is a job, not a calling, and today's perceptive kids know the difference. Risk asking them which of their friends' parents is a "natural," really enjoys kids, and what they do or what they are like that gives them that idea. Or the easier question: "What are parents like, what do they do, that gives you the idea that they really are not caught up and excited about being parents?"

I now believe that the meaning of being a parent, like that of being a breadwinner, differs for the typical woman and man. Although their meanings may be converging in the younger generation, these differences still cause much argument and conflict between fathers and mothers.

If you are a woman, you may think I am sexist but I must raise the question, even if it offends you: How much does a woman's biology compel her emotional commitment to her child? I believe it does much more for her than a man's does for him. We are learning how mother and child become emotionally bonded. Researchers have not yet asked what the emotional effects are of feeling life in one's womb for months. They now know, though, that the fetus learns to recognize its mother's voice in utero, which may be nature's way of preparing for a recipro- cally strong maternal-infant bonding. The consequence of such bonding creates a more intense identity conflict for career women than for men: Few career mothers do not suffer a conflict be- tween their calling to be a good mother and their desire to be a good worker.[4]

Marty has told us just how painful the conflict can be. She was less satisfied with every item indexing parental "calling" than she was with every comparable item indexing vocational "call- ing." Being a top feminist lawyer fulfilled her more than being a good mother. She told us who her Number 1 Self was when she spontaneously said, "I can be successful in my work and feel good about myself and have some of that rub off on the family relationships." She did not say, "I can be successful in my family relationships and have some of that rub off on my work."

Andy enjoyed being a father more than Marty did being a mother. She sensed this, mentioning several times how "relieved" she was that he enjoyed being a father. That he so enjoyed it and was such a good father made her feel less guilty. But Andy also felt more fulfilled by his work than by fatherhood.

What about mothers and fathers in the twenty-first century? My hunch is that more will struggle with the issues, as Marty and Andy have, and will follow in their footsteps. Like Andy, younger males will still view their vocations as their Number 1 Selves. They may enjoy their children more than their own fathers did, for whom being a father was a Number 3 or 4 Self. However, when their last child has grown up and left home, they will most likely still judge their parental role to have been more important and satisfying than their vocational one, as I and others have found seems to happen.[5]

Now that women are more free to choose what they want to be, I expect more will choose not to have children. They will not lose status or others' respect, though they may not escape the regretful comments of their own mothers who would like to have grandchildren to mother again. More of those who do choose to have children will view being a mother as a calling, which bodes well for their children's future healthy growth and success. I am much less sanguine about those teenage mothers and fathers who have not chosen or have chosen unwisely. The rate of unwed teenage pregnancies will most likely not decline until society, through its schools, educates children more wisely about sex, babies, and their development.

The question is, "How do we resurrect in our society the idea that parenthood should be a calling?" We can encourage greater commitment to parenthood by appealing to today's value of becoming more self-actualized and fulfilled. Both fathers and mothers grow more healthily than childless adults do. The evidence is dramatically clear that the study's fathers became more mature during their twenties and thirties than the nonfathers.[6] Being a mother was one of the top three important determinants of the women's maturing in their thirties and forties. Children disturb us, provoke us, educate us, and tell us much about who we are; they make us more caring and less selfish; they prod us to grow up. If being a parent is more than just a job, children capture our hearts and bring much joy.

To grow up to succeed as a marital partner and parent depends upon our character, maturity, and feminine interpersonal strengths. Andy's and Marty's persistent and painful labor shows us that it is not easy to change our character but that it can be done. They show us that we can create happier, more fulfilling marriages and learn to enjoy being parents. Though most of us would like simple "self-help" books to teach us how to argue more constructively with our partners or deal with a stubborn two-year-old, in the long run no technique works unless it reflects our character — our attitudes, values, and ways of getting along with others.

Can we make the same comments about who succeeds as a lover? Is a good lover more than just a sexual technician?

11

Finding
Sexual Fulfillment

Tom Wolfe, the best-selling author, claims that Americans of the eighties were less proccupied about sex than those in the seventies. (If so, do you think it is because sex comes so easy nowadays, almost like a McDonald's hamburger?) When interviewed on NBC's *Today Show* about what he had learned from a tour publicizing a new book, he replied that Americans of the eighties were more obsessed with the acts and lives of the rich. Other writers aren't quite so sure. NBC's *L.A. Law* appealed because, as one journalist said, "They all drive BMWs and have affairs." Afternoon soap operas qualify for X ratings. My local video rental store has more sex couplings on tape in its curtained off back room than computer scams, bank robberies, and Wall Street shenanigans combined. Grocery store paperback stands would erotically charge the Rip Van Winkles of the world, though not those of us sated by that graphic barrage. They still sell, however. We are fascinated by the indiscreet antics of our politicians, preachers, and movie actors, just as the English are about those of their royal family.

Is sex as important to us as pop writers and advertisers obviously still believe? Important, yes. As Marty says, "It's the way I play." But consumingly important, no. The adults I surveyed ranked it ninth in importance, though men reliably ranked sexual fulfillment to be more important than women did. Except for those living in California, however, the men and women

I studied didn't consider sexual fulfillment to be one of their top priorities. Sex was more important to those who weren't getting much—like the study's few restlessly roaming men. Though not *the* top priority that Freud assumed, sex still excites us. Advertisers know that. They will continue to find ways to use our dreams of being the ultimate lovers to sell silky lingerie, scanty briefs, Calvin Klein's perfume, Obsession, and sleek Toyota coupes. Are they right about how to reach that pinnacle of lustful hope? Suggestive sexy stimulants? *Playboy* centerfolds? Kamasutran techniques? They obviously work for those who continue to buy them, but in the long run it is *character* rather than sexual accoutrements and techniques that makes us the ideal lover.

Attributes of Sexually Fulfilling Relationships

The list below may seem old-fashioned to you if you believe that all a successful lover does is hop in and out of a different bed every night seeking burning, laser-like lovings. But these qualities turn out to contribute most to a sexually fulfilling *relationship* (A4b). In declining order of importance, the men and women said that the ideal lover

- Is loving, tender, and considerate
- Accepts his or her own sexual and sensuous needs
- Is patient and self-confident and has a sense of humor
- Shares his or her feelings openly and honestly
- Is sensitive to and skillful in fulfilling the partner's sexual needs
- Is uninhibitedly imaginative and playfully experimental in bed
- Is in good physical health and has lots of energy

With the exception of Andy's health, these qualities describe his and Marty's sexual relationship. Their extensive experience in workshops on sexuality prepared them more than most to accept and integrate their diffuse sexual needs into their love for each other. They didn't need the Kamasutra or "how to have multiple orgasm" books. I asked Marty what sex meant to her since she and Andy had gotten back together again. She replied, "I'm now enjoying sex more than I ever have. I enjoy the variety of it. I don't feel I have to have it daily, even weekly. I don't think it's the central part of my life. But it is the way I play."

Men found no topic more difficult to talk about than what sex meant to them, how their feelings about it had changed since their early thirties, and how sex had affected their growth (A21). The women felt much more comfortable and were more articulate by far in describing their feelings about sex. I think women's magazines and their special friendships had better prepared them for my questions. The men talked more about sex than sexuality; the women spoke more about sexuality than sex. Despite their education, almost all seemed to be quite naive about the meanings of sex, even Marty and Andy, the most sexually sophisticated and knowledgeable couple of the group. Marty said, "I realize now that I just never asked for what I wanted. It seems simple now. I just expected myself to be an expert right away and I never got what I wanted and so blamed Andy and all men."

Andy, the most articulately knowledgeable of the men, added, "I never had permission to explore my sexual fantasies or feel comfortable and understand the male part of my sexual being. So in a sense I was intellectually informed but emotionally and spiritually naive, unsophisticated, and unaware of the gigantic area that so profoundly influences so many aspects of our behavior and our roles and interactions, whether in bed or at work." He then continued to distinguish between sex and sexuality, a confusion that blocked many couples' mutual sexual fulfillment. For men, sex was sex; for women, sex was sexuality. Neither really understood the other's meanings.

> There is an enormous difference here between sex and sexuality. Sex refers more to genital and physical pleasure that has its ultimate end in intercourse or sexual release. Sexuality is a much broader concept that involves how one feels about one's self, a sense of personal identity, one's physical image, knowing how to sexually relate to other people of

conned men and women into believing that w
as lusty as men.

However, the men and women did differ
plexing — even provocatively significant — way.
frequently a man has sex tells us almost nothin
except that he will be happily married (A7),
a good husband (A4b), and comfortably share
others (A8). But how athletic he is sexually w
about his happiness, maturity, and personality
masculinity. A male can have a lot of sex ar
or unhappy, mature or immature, and mascu
a male myth that having a lot of sex is a sign o

But how much sex a woman has *does* tell us
her. Although her partner will think she's gr
good wife (A4b), she won't necessarily feel he
as great as her husband does (A7). She'll tend
ture; she definitely will be more assertive, agg
tive, ambitious, and self-reliant — all typical
(A10) — than the woman who has much less

I didn't expect these differences between men
report having a lot of sex and so am not sure
them. After all, women can have sex even if
cited or don't enjoy it. Men are more vulner
to be excited enough to have an erection. They
ate sex if it is not enjoyable — one reason few
degree of their sexual enjoyment less than ecsta
words, "glorious." I would have thought that me
ily excitable and initiated frequent sex wou
character traits. The results say not true.

So I next asked what couples and then women a
enjoy sex. The couples continue through the ye
attracted to each other and are good lovers. T
their feelings and needs about sex and other fe
partners, and so can be spontaneously playful in
of each other's needs, they both feel good about
One couple, who enjoyed sex fives time a wee
they couldn't have sex *every* day. Middle age is
ing up on such greedy adolescents. Men and w
sex also make good spouses, according to their

both sexes and ages, and understanding all of the
dimensions of sexual relationships that have to do
with giving and receiving, communicating and caring: all of the ways of expressing one's self sexually
that have nothing to do with genital activity — ways
like massages that release all of the senses.

I asked Andy, "How have you changed in your own sexual
behavior?" He replied, "I've learned how important it is to pay
attention to what Marty needs, wants, both in terms of genital
sex and just in feeling nurtured and loved and respected. I've
also learned to become much more comfortable discussing my
own sexuality in large groups to which I speak."

Identifying Sexually Successful Men and Women

Other than inventing new ways to torture another human
being, I can't think of anything we do that over the centuries
has so excited our imagination as how to enjoy sex. Obviously
"sexual success" means different things. One male meaning can
be found in adolescent (and middle-age, too) fantasies of being
a debonair Casanova, Don Juan, or modern James Bond "pil-
lowing" — that marvelous Japanese term — a different woman every night. After knocking out the furious husband who bursts
into the bedroom to discover our betrayal, we escape out the
open window to catch a hovering helicopter's swinging rope to
fly us to the arms of the next night's temptress. Ah!

The number of conquests is still the measure of success for
young bucks. Why else do they use words like "score" to brag
about their adventures? Males admire the guy who has scored
with twenty-eight different women; they wonder about the masculinity of the man who has scored with only one or two.

I was not up to asking how many different partners the men
had scored with in their lifetimes, let alone in the past month.
(Actually, compared to Kinsey's "norms," the men and women
were almost impeccable examples of faithfulness.) So I opted
to explore three different increasingly more rigorous indices of
sexual success. The first measured what Andy meant by "sex":

sheer amount of enjoyable sex. The seco
what he meant by "sexuality." The secon
how mutually considerate, faithful, and
relationship with one's partner was; the t
ter of what I call the "good lover": the
feels fulfilled in a mutually compatible

The Character of Sexually Successf

I was surprised to learn that the cha
sary to enjoy a lot of sex and create a se
tionship differ for men and women. App
any character at all to enjoy sex. Wom
kind of character to enjoy having a lot of
to have mutually compatible sex. But bot
more of the same character to be good l

Success as Having Frequent Enjoyab
"performance" definition of sexual succe
ings a person has each week or month. I
portant enough to study, and writers f
to extol. By this standard, the men an
progressively and dismally less successfu
"honeymoon" years. But they are not a
decades ago. The decline is steeper the
and the study's men and women were hi
early thirties the men reported having s
times a month; regretfully, in their mid
a month. Their wives agreed in their es
women wished that they could have alm
(A4e).

Men and women who had a lot of s
it more than those who had little and
be better lovers as well as all-around mc
Given what I now view to be a myth, th
of the pre-eighties era were not really i
delighted to write that the women didr
in every measure that I had of desire, ple
fulness, and excitement. Our repressiv

Enjoying sex, like having it frequently, however, is more closely intertwined with a woman's personality than it is with a man's. Women who say they enjoy sex are seen by their peers to be sensuous Carmens: assertive, forceful, aggressive, decisive, competitive, and strong but playfully affectionate individualists.[2] They share no feminine character traits in common. Men who enjoy a lot of sex share nothing at all in common.

Fulfillment in a Mutually Compatible Sexual Relationship. Sex keeps its hold on us for decades. It can be addictively enjoyable. We savor the memory of a "good lovin'"; we think of a certain caress; we feel good about an intense attraction; we enjoy a wildly playful romp. But more is involved in enjoying sex, especially in long-term relationships. Masters and Johnson, the premier researchers of the sexual laboratory, told us years ago that those "glorious" and rapturous times in bed really depend more on our character than on our techniques.[3] Four themes summarize their detailed clinical findings about couples who greatly enjoy sex: psychological maturity (for example, self-esteem, stable sense of self); interpersonal maturity, especially understanding the feelings of the other; mutuality in values and responsiveness to the other's needs; and marital satisfaction that results from creating an alive and enduring relationship.[4]

They were talking about what I call marital sexual compatibility or mutuality, or what Andy meant by "sexuality"—a more rigorous standard of *success,* I think, than just having a lot of sex or one-night stands, as enjoyable as they may be. I defined sexual mutuality by how enjoyable, considerate, well mated, and faithful the men and women believed their sexual relationship to be (A4e).

When the men were in their early thirties, their degree of sexual mutuality, rather than the amount of "glorious" rhapsodic sex, turned out to be as miraculously revealing of their personalities as a Rorschach inkblot and Tarot cardreading. The men who had more faithful, mutually enjoyable sexual relationships were more mature; they had closer, happier marriages; and they had fulfilled their other adult roles more competently. Jumping in and out of bed with a different person every month or two, casually playing around with others, and splitting when the rose wilted and the wine was gone did not describe the successful, happy, and mature thirty-three-year-old men. Marty and Andy only discovered that when in their late thirties. Sticking it out, working through their conflicts, and making an enduring commitment not only reflected but also nurtured their maturity.[5]

That I found the same pattern of results for *both* the men and women when they were middle-aged suggests that marital sexual compatibility reflects some stable underlying character strengths. Those who had been faithful, considerate, and sexually compatible with their partners in middle age had been happier and more productive since adolescence (A4a). They were also more happily married and competent in fulfilling their adult roles (A4c), as well as more emotionally mature (A12).

However, men who had created mutually compatible relationships and had not strayed did not share any distinctive or specific personality traits according to their peers. The successful women did; their peers saw them to be loyal, conscientiously reliable, ethical persons of great integrity. Apparently, in women sexual faithfulness and mutuality are grounded in and buttressed by a strongly ethical personality, again revealing how well integrated sexuality is with a woman's character.

The study has taught me several important lessons, some unexpected, about the character of men and women who are sexually successful as I have defined success so far.

Men and women who think of themselves as faithful and considerate and who enjoy a mutually compatible relationship are competent, mature, and happy. They have learned how to adapt to one of our most impetuously demanding necessities in ways that bring not just immediate pleasure but longer-term happiness in a faithful relationship with another. That challenge requires maturity, which also enables them to become competent in their other roles.

Some Reflections About Differences
Between Men and Women

What are we to make of the consistent results so far that sex means something different to a man than to a woman? Is sex for a male really just a restless appendage for eliminating tension, needing only to be soothed, devoid of interpersonal meaning and so peripheral to more enduring personality traits and values? Is his erection only an Ollie North cannon running loose on the street, not integrated with or securely anchored to more stable personality qualities? To use Andy's distinction, is sex just sex for men? Many women and mythology say, "yes," and the results of the study agree. Sex does seem to be quite peripheral to a man's basic character. He doesn't even need to be forceful, aggressive, and competitive to enjoy sex. Despite widespread myths to the contrary, he doesn't have to be a James Bond — reassuringly!

For men, only when sex approaches what Andy described as sexuality and is embedded within a compatible mutual relationship do personality strengths, particularly those that make up maturity, begin to contribute to success. Any kind of man can have a lot of enjoyable sex. But only mature ones can establish a mutually respectful, enjoyable, and faithful relationship. Roaming James Bonds are to devoted husbands like Andy as sex is to sexuality. Do Casanovian pursuits of nightly adventures to bolster some macho ideal signal immaturity and an inability to make a loving commitment?

Typical feminine interpersonal strengths, which contribute so much to a man's marital success, don't stand out as essential to his feeling good about sex. This is true even for men who enjoy sex in a mutually fulfilling and compatible relationship. For males, sex as orgasm seems to be easily divorced from sexuality, even from intimacy. When I ask audiences what "intimacy" means to men, women answer immediately, "sex." No man has yet *publicly* disputed the women's equation to talk of intimacy as sexuality the way Andy did.

The separation of sex from sexuality, perhaps more a biologically given fact about men than most women would like to believe, explains why some men prowl sexually. Support anonymous prostitutes. Value so casually "being on the make." Date-even gang-rape. Act as if "No!" is "Yes." Use sex to take, not to give. "Make out," lose interest, and then drop out. Feel little remorse or guilt. Or not understand why their wives feel that "playing around" betrays their relationship.

One last question. Apart from biological reasons, why do males typically isolate sex from sexuality's intimacy meanings? Could it be that sex is much safer for men than sexuality? Intimacy requires vulnerability, dependency, and willingness to yield and abandon our self-control. Ian Fleming, James Bond's creator, tells us just how dangerous intimacy is in *Her Majesty's Secret Service,* the first and last time James falls tenderly in love and marries. Remember what happens when he leaves the church with his bride? Blowfield shoots her. The movie ends with James tenderly cradling his dead bride in his arms, hiding his eyes (tears?) from the camera. In this scene, Bond gives the depressing message to millions of males about what sexuality could be. The name "Bond" must equal sex, not intimacy; it can hurt.

For women, sex has a different meaning. Enjoying sex draws upon a woman's character in a way that it doesn't for a man. A woman who has a lot of sex and enjoys it thoroughly typically has many masculine traits like assertiveness and self-reliance but not necessarily any feminine interpersonal ones. Or conversely, a woman who has little sex and doesn't particularly enjoy it is not described by others in masculine terms. Neither woman, however, is more or less feminine than the other. A woman apparently does not have to be sensitive and empathic to enjoy or not enjoy sex. *Remember my cautionary warning?* Because sexually fulfilled women don't share in common any typical feminine attributes does not mean that some are not feminine. Also remember that all of us have both masculine and feminine characteristics.

However, when sex becomes more integrated in a mutually reciprocal and intimate relationship, then a woman's masculine attributes recede into the background as loyal commitment and other ethical strengths become necessary to sustain a faithful relationship.

Do you think that these male and female differences in the meaning of sex and sexuality reflect lingering cultural values that sex and its enjoyment should be more the province of males than females? Demure, modestly feminine Daphnes aren't supposed to be sexual; seductively assertive, strong, but feminine Carmens are. As women become more like Marty — less willing

to subjugate their needs to those of men and more insistent on
pursuing their own fulfillment — will we begin to see many more
actively seductive Carmens on college campuses and main
streets? Roger says, "Yes." He claims that the last four women
he has gone to bed with initiated the invitation. The chances are
good that sexuality may become sex for more women in the future.

Are masculine, assertive, forceful, and competitive women
better lovers from a man's point of view? Perhaps for a week
or a month. But what about living with a Carmen for a lifetime? Would women really want to spend a lifetime in bed with
the James Bonds of the world? For the study's answer to that,
let's turn to the third and most stringent sign of success — the
good lover.

The Good Lover

I have only told you about how women and men view their
own sexual pleasure and relationships. Now, I ask the more
demanding questions that I also asked about marital success.
"What are men like *whose partners believe that they are sexually com-*
patible, considerate, and faithful to each other? What is an Andy like
who makes a Marty feel that they have an enjoyable and mutually compatible relationship?" Apparently, for a male to be a
good lover, he must be yielding, cooperative, and sensitive to
his partner's need. He definitely should *not* be assertive, aggressive, and dominant. So much for the purely macho John Waynes
and James Bonds of the past.

"What are women like *whose partners enjoy sex and believe that*
they have a mutually compatible relationship? What is a Marty like
who makes an Andy really enjoy sex, want a lot of it, and feel
that they are sexually compatible?" They are more typically feminine: compassionate, sympathetic, sensitive to a man's needs,
tender, warm, affectionate, gentle, and loyal. Women who are
superb lovers do *not* share one masculine trait in common.
Remember the qualifying comment that I just made. An individual woman, like Marty, may be quite masculine but to be
a good lover she must be affectionate, sensitive to pleasing Andy,
and so on. Her masculinity has to be mellowed, in other words,
by feminine interpersonal traits. Men who want to have a sex-

ually compatible marriage ought, perhaps, to marry the firm's typically feminine secretary rather than the typically masculine executive vice-president, unless she is also quite feminine interpersonally.

What a Catch-22 conflict for contemporary women! To enjoy sex they probably should be quite masculine, but such qualities may well turn off men unless they also come across as feminine interpersonally. The only way they can have their cake and eat it too is to be androgynous. Does this idea ring true for you?

Again, given the changing character of younger males and females, a host of questions arise about what sex will mean in the future. As males learn how to get along with and enjoy more aggressive women, will they still need loyal, affectionate, sensitive ones with whom to enjoy sex and create a faithful and compatible relationship? Are younger males becoming more like Andy? By coming to terms with their own passive-feminine character, will they no longer be as defensive or uptight with more actively initiating and assertive women like Marty?

But what a growing survival problem for traditional men like Bill Spaulding, the tough marketing firm president but failed family man, Bruce Jackson, the authoritarian executive who squashed his family, and the Great Santini of the book and movie of the same name who treated his family like fledgling marines at boot camp. Are they in danger of becoming the macho sexual dinosaurs of the future, facing extinction? To survive, will they have to learn not only how to relate to more assertive and strong women but also how to become more interpersonally sensitive if their wives are to feel fulfilled sexually? If they don't grow up in these ways, with whom will they have sex in the future? I can't see them settling into an enduring marital relationship with the emerging modern woman.

I believe sex will remain as imperious for most men; it will be a long time before it will be well integrated with their sexuality. For many, Andy's path will not be an easy one to learn how to take.

I also wonder if the more sexually initiating and assertive women of the younger generation will discover that they don't need sensitive, caring, considerate men to really enjoy sex and to have an enduring sexually compatible relationship. If women follow men's path and segregate sex from sexuality, will they adopt the kind of impersonal and transient sexual behavior so typical of males for centuries? Marty didn't; her femaleness saw to that. But maybe younger women have now gone past the Martys who were their leaders a decade ago.

Our traditional meanings of maleness and femaleness are increasingly maladaptive. We know that when Bill Cosby's book on being a father becomes a best seller and a woman was at one time the chief security officer on "Star Trek"'s *Enterprise.* If a Bruce Jackson can get in touch with a quieter, softer, yielding side, perhaps he will feel more comfortable with a more initiating, assertive June. Maybe as women integrate more typical masculine strengths into their personalities, they'll stand up to the Bill Spauldings of the world and even enjoy sex with them for a lifetime.

Understanding "sexual success" is, always has been, and probably always will be a complicated though tantalizing quest. What have we learned so far?

First, sexual success has several different meanings. It can mean enjoying a lot of sex. It can mean having a mutually faithful sexual relationship with another. It can mean being a good lover who makes his or her partner feel well mated in a faithful, considerate, and enjoyable sexual relationship.

Second, women who have frequent sex that they enjoy are typically masculine. Men who enjoy and have a lot of sex share no common personality traits.

Third, women who enjoy sex as integral to a reciprocally mutual relationship are mature, loyal, ethical people of integrity. Men who create sexually compatible relationships are also mature, but not necessarily any more or less masculine or feminine than men who don't.

Fourth, good lovers, particularly women, who are considerate, faithful, and create mutually enjoyable sexual relationships are interpersonally feminine. How masculine they may be is *irrelevant* to how good a lover they will be. Men who are good lovers share some feminine interpersonal strengths, such as being yielding and cooperative. They definitely are not aggressively dominant.

Are the same traits needed for our same-sex friendships?

12

Succeeding as
a Friend

Roger, my spokesperson for the generations behind the one I
studied, insists that men, "when they're serious and not trying
to appear macho," really desire friendships with other men like
those that women have with other women. He may be right.
Nevertheless, the men were more inept in their friendships than
the women, so I shall focus primarily on describing their relationships with other men.

Four themes describe the men's and women's friendships with
their own sex: men and women do not differ in what they want
in their intimate friendships; men and women differ in the quality of their same-sex relationships; those who have intimate
friends are androgynous, especially interpersonally feminine;
and men's and women's ability to make intimate friendships
doesn't consistently tell us much about their other successes or
maturity (A4f).

The Ideal Friend

Above all else, men and women wanted friends with whom
they could be vulnerable, trusting, self-disclosing, and mutually affectionate and loving. They also wished that they could
be with each other more frequently than they were able to be
to share their mutual interests and activities; however, spending a great deal more time with each other, while desirable, was

161

not as important. They preferred to keep in touch primarily by phone; few wrote more than several letters a year to their friends. Almost all did not want any erotic feelings to complicate their relationships.

Male and Female Differences in Quality of Friendships

Widely held opinions that men and women differ in the quality of their same-sex friendships are true. The study's results are too clear to need more than a bare-bone summary. Compared to men, women

- Believe it is more important to have a close friend
- Feel more fulfilled in their friendships and so less lonely
- Are more intimate with and closer to their friends
- Are more open and self-disclosing in their relationships
- Feel more affectionate and loving toward their friends
- Feel more comfortable sharing their greatest insecurities, failures, and feelings about their own parents

Of twenty different personal topics that friends can share with each other, men feel most comfortable sharing their feelings about their successes, good times, hopes, conflicts at work, and children. If at all possible, they will avoid talking about their dreams, sexual needs, socially unacceptable desires, finances, insecurities, and failures.

Why are American male friendships so unexpressive and emotionally thin? Traveling in Asia and the Mideast always reminds me of how American males rein in their feelings and guard their inner selves in their relationships with each other. Turkish, Indian, and Nepalese friends walk arm-in-arm, hold hands, and lean on and hug each other publicly; Chinese male friendships are known for their depth and loyalty.[1] When I compared American with Turkish and Italian friendships, American young men felt more discomfort and anxiety expressing most of the qualities that describe an ideal friend.[2] Many American men resist reaching out to give emotionally to another, particularly support, affection, and love; one man spoke for many when he ruefully remarked, "I don't know how to tell a man that I like him and would like to be his friend." Some men of the study felt that sharing their feelings even with their partners was unmasculine and a sign of weakness that they equated with effeminacy. A few men had never hugged their wives away from their beds; a few had never told them that they loved them; a few had never given their wives a birthday present or spontaneously brought them a special gift or called them in the middle of the day to let them know that they had been thinking of them.

For at least 200 years, American society has not valued enduring, same-sex, intimate adult friendships (especially between males) as highly as other societies. Tocqueville told us this was true of early nineteenth-century American males. He observed them "always considering themselves as standing alone, and they are apt to imagine that their whole destiny is in their own hands."[3] Speaking of the effect of democracy on an American male, he said that it "separates his contemporaries from him; it throws him back forever upon himself alone and threatens in the end to confine him entirely within the solitude of his own heart."[4]

The lonesome American cowboy still remains a romantic hero. Strong, alone, self-contained Clint Eastwoods and John Waynes restlessly moving on from one adventure to another are enduring motifs of the American male psyche. Robert Redford and Paul Newman's friendship in *Butch Cassidy and the Sundance Kid* tells us that more modern Americans wish their cowboy heroes were not so lonesome. Their inseparable friendship was sealed by shared activities — robbing banks, visiting prostitutes together, loving the same woman, traveling to Bolivia and dying there together — but they did not talk openly about themselves with each other. Not until they faced capture and death did Butch admit to Sundance that he had never fired his gun to kill a man.

I can bring nineteenth-century American males up-to-date with these modern vignettes. A ten-year-old fourth grade boy began his poem, "I'm a space man, a great man, a high paid man, and lone"; he went on to talk about all the themes that have described the typical American male as a brave, heroic, adventurous explorer, and concluded with "circling . . . around the moon and seeing every distant star."

And by my son's ambition to circle the earth alone in his twenty-five-foot Vertue sailboat.

And by a national survey that reported that fewer than 25 percent of American adult males said that they had a close friend; when asked what "close friend" meant, they said sharing similar activities, like participating in sports, playing cards, drinking, and talking about women.[5]

And by Stuart Miller's three-year odyssey, almost a calling, in search of what he called a "true male friendship." Interviewing hundreds of American and European men in their thirties and forties about their male friendships, he wrote a poignantly sad book, one of whose chapters, "The Death of Intimacy in Our Times," captured what he discovered: Few men felt they had a deep friendship with another. Miller himself never created one either; he questioned why he failed in his book's last paragraph. "This reflexive cringing from all true engagement is a curious emotion. Probably it is part of human nature, the instinct of self-preservation asserting itself, a deep suspicion of involvement with others, of involvement with anyone outside of myself. A reaction known even to our most ancient poets. To meet such fears, only courage will do." He concludes by quoting Pindar's prayer, "Oh Gods! Let me have the strength and the courage to love my friends!"[6]

And by the "close friendship" of the study's Martin Brown which was not what it seemed. Martin talked warmly and animatedly about his "close" friend with whom he had had long "personal philosophical talks" for the past several years. His wife, a social worker sensitive to such relationships, had been worried about how alone he had been ever since she had known him, but now she was happy that he had found, in her words, a "soul mate." When interviewed about his friendships, Martin replied, somewhat disconsolately, "I've noticed what I do with my close friends over the years is I tend to lean on them to get enough support. Sometimes I push them to do more for me than what they want to do. They then set limits and after that I find I'm not as good friends with them. Now, for the first time in my life I have had a really close friend for several years. We talk and talk about the most personal things."

When I wrote his "close friend" to get his view of Martin and their "friendship," however, he returned the materials uncompleted with this comment: "I can't complete the enclosed ratings. I don't feel I know him very well. We have talked several times about my work; he usually just listens. I know almost nothing about him. Sorry."

In describing his friendships that had persisted, Martin was the study's fourth most alone and friendless man. No wonder just a few sporadic long talks with another man had given him the feeling of "closeness" which his wife had interpreted from her feminine perspective to mean a deeply intimate and self-revealing relationship.

Martin's "close friendship" is an exaggerated caricature of the persisting friendships that many of the men claimed. Few had what their wives would call a close friend. Predictably, after I had concluded the interviews and was talking with the couple about the study, the women, more curious than the men, would ask their husbands whom they had selected as their closest male friend for me to secure information from. With few exceptions, the women's impulsive reaction was, "You call him a close friend? He's just a speaking acquaintance." Only 22 percent of the men, one of whom was Martin, claimed that they had a very close friend.

The Androgynous Character of Successful Friends

You've probably already anticipated the character of the men and women who create close friendships with others (A26c). The character of a close friend is that of a good marital partner. The men and women who created intimate friendships — as they and their friends rated them — were androgynous. Their peers also described them to be cheerful, emotionally stable persons who cared for and were sensitive to others' needs. They accepted and felt in good control of themselves. No wonder they so trusted themselves to be playful and risk trying new things. Their commonly shared portrait makes a lot of sense. Friends don't have to appear what they aren't with each other, even when their guard is down, as when they are playful.

The other character strengths that described good friends were more clearly etched for the men than for the women. The men who made good friends were more typically feminine in every interpersonal strength on which their peers rated them: from being affectionate, understanding, and sympathetic to being loyal, warm, and yielding. While also seen as masculine—athletic, decisive, and leaders—the successful friends did not share in common one of the more typical macho traits, such as competitiveness, aggressiveness, dominance, or forcefulness, which can potentially divide and separate, if a friendship is not bonded by other strengths. The Andy Millers rather than the Bill Spauldings and Bruce Jacksons of the study had close male friends.

I remain uncertain how well I have examined the question of who succeeds as a friend. The meaning of success in male friendships may be more complex than my measures have captured. Since male friendships have not been well researched, particularly of men of different social classes and educational backgrounds, I cannot check how applicable the study's findings are. They do not describe Butch Cassidy and the Sundance Kid's friendship. I can't guess how they would have answered questions about the attributes of an ideal friendship and rated theirs. The movie makes it clear, however, that their macho strengths cemented their friendship; perhaps this is true of men today.

Apparently, men need many more strengths than women to succeed in their friendships. Remember that women who had happy husbands had many more virtuous qualities than men who had happy wives; women had to be more adjustable to keep the marriage going. I'd make the same interpretation about males who succeed in creating intimate male friendships. Good male friends are seen by their peers to have about three times more virtues than good female friends are seen by theirs to have. Since men are not raised to be proficient in intimate relationships—to be accepting, to yield, to cooperate, to soothe hurt feelings, and to bolster friends' good feelings about themselves—numerous strengths are necessary to sustain a close relationship over time with another male who may not have perfected such strengths.

What Success in Friendship Predicts About a Person

The last of the four themes — succeeding as a friend tells us little else about a person — stumbled over some methodological problems that confuse its interpretation. The problems provide some insights whose implications we need to reflect about. The women and their friends generally viewed their friendships as either very intimate or perfect — only 15 percent of the women rated their close friendships as less than quite close. Their best friends also inclined toward rating the women as perfect on the different attributes of an ideal friend. (Maybe most women are paragons of the ideal close friend, but they sure did not talk that way in the interviews. About 20 percent of the women had trouble giving me the name of a close friend even though only 15 percent had rated their friendships less than close. Could it be women believe women should have close friends and so rated them to be such, even though when asked some could not name one? Could it be that the women's friends did not want to hurt their feelings by rating them less than perfect, even though they had been assured that I would never let their friends know of their ratings? The women's results may not be discriminating enough to separate out the most from the least successful friend. This part of the study should be redone.)

Something else is not right about the study when Martin rates his friendship to be more intimate than Andy does his. For American males, words like "intimate" and "close" carry too many mixed meanings. Homophobic reactions to these words may cause some to undervalue the intimacy of their friendships.

Regardless of how I measured the men's and women's success as good friends, I could not get the consistent results that I have for other kinds of success. If you are willing to accept slightly higher odds that the findings may be due to chance, then the character of *both* men and women who succeed as friends becomes quite clear. The closer you feel your same-sex friendships are, the more likely your colleagues will rate you to be well adapted vocationally. Your partner will be happy that he or she married you, your closest friend will say that you excel on the six attributes you feel describe a close friendship, and everyone will rate you to be ethical and typically feminine in the way you get along with others.

That a man's maturity, which consistently predicts so many adult successes, does not predict well the quality of his friendships troubles me. Perhaps because the men's images of friendship were so diverse — more like juicy oranges for Andy, nuts for Bill Spaulding, and cauliflowers for Martin — my computer was confused.

However, women who have close and intimate friends with whom they share their personal feelings about almost everything under the sun are indeed more psychologically mature. Furthermore, women who succeed as friends are likely to also be competent and happy wives, mothers, and lovers. So a woman's intimate relationships with other women predict better than a man's her maturity and success in her other personal relationships.

I have completed the discussion in this part about intimacy in our marital, parental, sexual, and personal relationships. We are now ready to step back from each role's details to understand the character strengths that men and women who succeed in their familial relationships share in common. What are the irreducible attributes that men and women need to succeed in *all* of their familial roles — as marital partners, parents, and lovers?

13

Fulfilling
Personal Relationships

Numerous researchers have studied persons who succeeded maritally *or* parentally *or* sexually. I don't know of any who have asked about the most basic character strengths that describe men and women who succeed in *all* of their familial roles. The most similar studies, the Berkeley IGS and Harvard ones, did not focus in as much depth on the meaning of marital and parental success; they ignored sexual relationships. What can I tell you about familial paragons like Andy and disasters like Bruce Jackson who succeeded and failed as partners, parents, *and* lovers (A27)?

The Character of Men and Women
Who Succeed in Familial Roles

Successful partners, parents, and lovers are happy, competent in their other adult roles, open and nondefensive in their intimate relationships, ethically sensitive and idealistic, androgynous, typically feminine in their interpersonal skills, and quite mature. Nurture these strengths in yourself and your children if you value success in familial roles.

Persons Who Succeed in Familial Roles Are Happy and Fulfilled. Men and women who succeed as marital partners, lovers, and parents say they are happy and fulfilled. Their closest friends and colleagues who know them best *outside* of their marriages agree (A11). The person who is happy at home is likely to be so with friends and colleagues. Common sense tells us this is not always so. How can one be happy when Scrooge is our boss, piranhas our colleagues, and Brutus our friend? But the finding does suggest that the strengths that make for happiness in our intimate relationships also contribute to happiness in other relationships and roles. Billie and the Millers illustrate this truth. They, their friends, and their colleagues agreed that they were happy and fulfilled persons.

Success in One Role Predicts Success in Others. As we shall see over and over again, how well we adapt (not adjust) to the demands of one role reflects how we succeed in other roles. Immature persons who are not well integrated play roles, act like a bit of someone here and a piece of another there. Their successes are erratic—here today and gone tomorrow. Mature persons act out of wholeness with integrity. They use the strengths learned earlier as peers or later as parents or marital partners in their other relationships at work and elsewhere because the strengths are autonomously fixed in their minds and characters.

Marty knew this deeply human truth when she spontaneously said, "But as a quite good wife I can be successful in my work and feel good about myself and have some of that rub off on the family relationships." Marty and Andy fulfilled their other roles better than at least two-thirds of the study's other men and women. To make a good marriage requires the same maturing strengths that it takes to be a good parent or worker.

Persons Who Succeed in Familial Roles Are Open and Nondefensive. Successful partners, lovers, and parents are comfortable sharing their most personal needs, fears, and hopes with at least a few others (A8). Such openness is indispensable for creating a good marriage, even in expressing what may seem a trivial irritation to the other, such as telling your partner you don't appreciate the stringy hair she leaves in the washbasin after cutting it. Or telling your partner you don't like how he starts berating your parents for letting your drunken brother return home once more. Or telling your partner what sexually turns you on or off. Unspoken frustrations accumulate and gnaw at a relationship; a partner does not know how either to adjust or to adapt. Sharing your vulnerability with a partner in nonthreatening ways will, over time, encourage greater trust and openness and help you both to mature. More open persons are more mature.

Andy rated himself to be more comfortable sharing a variety of intimate feelings with Marty than she felt she could be with him (A8). She did not feel completely free to talk with him about her discouraged and insecure feelings or about her bodily troubles. Like most partners, neither felt fully at ease talking about their angry and socially unacceptable sexual feelings, even though they had been more open than any other couple in talking about such feelings with me.

Persons Who Succeed in Familial Roles Are Ethically Sensitive and Idealistic. Honesty, integrity, and compassion, among other virtues, are character traits that we call ethical. Our ethics help us get along with others (A31). Although ethical strengths did not saliently emerge when we analyzed the character needed to succeed in each role separately, they clearly do when we step back to examine who generally succeeds in their familial roles. A good marital partner, parent, and lover must be ethical and principled. Will our marriage survive and our children trust us if we lie, act selfishly, and don't care about others? Probably not, because we most risk revealing our real selves in our emotionally intimate relationships. To deceive others absorbs a lot of energy, requires continued self-monitoring, and creates hidden personal strain and suspicion that aggravate the normal conflicts that all intimate relationships experience.

Andy and Marty each judged the other, as did their peers, to be ethical persons. Deeply principled, both courageously stood up for what they believed. Marty's calling to work for healthier sexual roles spurred her to share her experiences with others in this book, even though she knows my apprehension that you may severely judge and condemn her.

Persons Who Succeed in Familial Roles Are Androgynous. Obviously, the more diverse and numerous strengths that we have, the more likely we can successfully fulfill our different roles. Our familial and friendship roles require interpersonal strengths that typically describe women. Although it is not an earth-shaking result that good marital partners, parents, lovers, and friends are interpersonally feminine, this is the first time that good evidence supports those who have advocated a more androgynous society.

Successful husbands, fathers, and lovers, as well as close friends, don't share any stereotypic masculine strengths in common. Assertiveness, aggressiveness, forcefulness, dominance, competitiveness, and self-sufficiency are either irrelevant to familial success or they can get in its way. Success as a hard-driving executive may not mean success as a marital partner or lover, unless one has also developed a warmer side to one's character—or unless one's wife is a statistical exception.

That traditionally defined female traits powerfully contribute to strong families and typical male strengths do not has forced me to think differently about how we raise males in the United States. Expecting them to be assertive, competitive, and self-sufficient, but not to be also empathic, caring, and sensitive to others' feelings, is to prepare them to be dangerously obsolescent in their future relationships with modern women. We are at risk as a healthy society if we don't alter our meanings of maleness to develop the strengths necessary to create healthier families and a sounder, kinder, and gentler America in the future.

Why do American males so unrepentantly fear to appear to be emotional, demonstratively affectionate, sensitive to others' needs, gentle, and yielding? Why do we label such feminine interpersonal strengths in a male as wimpy, weak, sissy, gay? When the peers of men who succeed as partners, parents, and lovers rate them to excel on 85 percent of Bem's twenty feminine traits and when our society tells its males to be otherwise, no wonder contemporary families are falling apart.

Of the reasons why, the research unequivocally rejects one as true: Because a man has such interpersonal strengths does not mean he is not a vigorously virile male. The successful partner, father, and lover is masculine, self-confident, self-reliant, independent, and respected for standing up courageously for his beliefs. Roger was right when he wrote me, "Because the person I see in the mirror is OK, I can be gentle and giving to others. I can expose my heart. That's something all the tough-guys in the movies aren't tough enough to do!"

Good Partners, Parents, and Lovers Are Psychologically Mature. The model of maturity identifies the primary strengths necessary to cope with the day-to-day stresses of living. Living closely with "foreign-speaking" partners, growing children, and aging lovers for many years inevitably provokes argument and strain. So it is not surprising that mature men and women competently adapt better to their familial roles than do immature men and women.

Brief Summary of Successful Familial and Friendship Relationships

I now highlight what may be most helpful to remember from the chapters about our relationships.

- Success as a spouse, parent, lover, and close friend has many different and complicated meanings. We must be clear about what kind of success we want if we wish to achieve it.
- Men and women who succeed in their familial roles are competent, mature, and happy persons. They're open, ethical, and generally androgynous.
- Success in one familial role predicts success in others. This is not 100 percent true, but occurs frequently enough to suggest that a core set of strengths contributes to our success.
- To succeed, we should make the development of mature and feminine interpersonal strengths a high priority. For the most part, typical masculine strengths do not contribute to marital happiness, parental fulfillment, intimate same-sex friendships, and sexual satisfaction, except for women who enjoy frequent sex. Masculine strengths may actually get in the way of creating a happy marriage unless they are integrated with feminine interpersonal ones like sensitivity to and understanding of the needs of one's partner.

- Some intimacy relationships may have different meanings to women than to men. Being a mother is more integrative of and central to the character of a woman than being a father is for a man. Sex seems to be more peripheral to the personality of a man than it is to that of a woman (at least to a contemporary middle-aged woman). For both women and men, however, when sex is integrated with their relationships, feminine interpersonal strengths describe the successful lovers' character.

- Men and women desire similar kinds of intimate friendships, but women are more successful in forming them. Just as men have become less satisfied with their relationships with their colleagues and (for college-educated men) their children in the past decades, I expect that more men will feel unfulfilled in their relationships with their partners and close friends in the future. As in the familial role, to approach their hopes for an intimate relationship, men need to risk becoming more interpersonally feminine and not let their typical strengths — aggressiveness, competitiveness, and dominance, which are appropriate in other roles — take over.

Billie, Andy, and Marty have taught us that to grow up healthily takes hard work. There is no quick fix, no shortcut, no amount of money that guarantees success and happiness. Ultimately, we make our own success and happiness because they are determined and limited by our character. Working to develop a more mature and androgynous character is where we must begin.

We will encounter many of these same themes as we now examine the character of men and women who succeed vocationally. But we will also discover that typical masculine strengths emerge to the fore as the critical character strengths necessary to succeed in our work. Androgynous men and women, however, can succeed in both their interpersonal and vocational roles.

Part Three _____

Succeeding
at Work

14

Jane Allen:
She Knew What She Wanted

What is the first word that comes to mind when I say, "success"? Is it money? It is for many Americans who dream of high-paying jobs, making it big, and becoming millionaires by their early thirties. Surveys of today's teenagers suggest that even a million may not be enough. Some want to be billionaires; 72.6 percent, the highest number found in the last two decades, say their primary reason for going to college is to learn the skills to make a lot of money.[1]

Vocational success means many different things: doing well in our work, making a great discovery, pioneering a new fashion, being regarded by our colleagues as outstanding, getting a promotion, achieving responsibility and power, having a job everyone envies, enjoying work, and, like Marty, finding our Number 1 Self in the work to which we feel called.

Just because we succeed in one of these ways does not mean we therefore succeed in the others. Do you know that half of today's lawyers are in their thirties or younger and that 45 percent of them are bored and discontented with law?[2] Why? Drawn to law because of the income, status, and power they thought it promised, they have discovered that they really don't enjoy their work. Remember Dave Corcoran, the well-adjusted lawyer I told you about. He was extraordinarily competent, respected, and wealthy, but unfulfilled. Another man of the study is a playwright but has to grub around to get enough money to survive. A woman is a creative research scientist who has published countless articles, is internationally recognized, yet dreads going to the lab each morning because, as she wrote me recently, "Doug, I hope my children learn early what will make them happy; I still don't know what I want to be." She's now forty-eight. I found no relation between how much money the men and women made and their satisfaction with their work. My surgeon discovered that for himself in his mid-fifties. He charges $3,000 for an hour's operating time; yet he told me that he hated his work and wished he could retire.

Some persons succeed in creating a vocation that integrates their interest and talents in a calling that they enjoy, do well in, achieve respect for, and earn more than enough in. They have everything. Jane Allen is such a person. After Billie and Marty, she scored highest on a combined measure of income, judged leadership, and her and her colleague's satisfaction with her vocational success — the four measures of success I shall use to identify the character strengths needed to succeed vocationally (A28). As you read about Jane, try to figure out why she succeeded so magnificently.

Jane fulfills the classic American entrepreneurial tradition. When she was twenty-nine, she started her own business distributing sporting supplies and equipment to schools and community groups. She did not fit my stereotype of a successful businesswoman selling sports equipment. Instead, I met a slender, subduedly warm, sensitively responsive, attractive brunette with a fiercely determined passion to make it on her own. She worked hard to fulfill her big dream.

Her first words in the interview were, "I started and couldn't stop. I created a monster; it kept growing and growing. I started with $600 of my own money. Four years later I am distributing nationally, have a paid staff of ten, am grossing over a million dollars a year, have just started my own advertising agency and a monthly newspaper which I edit. I now have a full-time art and graphic staff. It's a drive I can't really explain. Such a hunger to succeed. I have had a taste of success and will never let go of it."

When asked what goals she would like to fulfill before she

died, Jane immediately replied, "to build a multimillion-dollar business," which she was certain she would succeed in doing — and which she has done since I interviewed her. "I always wanted to succeed in life. My biggest dream has always been to be a millionaire. Not to marry one but to make it myself. I feel I have to do it by myself. When little I had no one to depend upon. I never would ask anybody for anything. I'd starve first." Jane indeed married a millionaire, lived in a spacious mansion that had a huge swimming pool, sauna, jacuzzi, and all of the other signs of opulence, including morning and afternoon "nannies" to take care of her three children.

But how had Jane made it on her own? She started by rebelliously defying her tyranically abusing mother, who tried to control her every movement when she became a teenager. When she was fifteen, Jane fled home permanently, dropped out of tenth grade ("I couldn't sit still long enough to bother with the books"), married a twenty-seven-year-old man, became pregnant seven months later, and vowed to herself to divorce him when she reached legal age, which she did. Supporting herself and her daughter, she did so well in sales that she won numerous sales campaigns. When she was twenty-two she met Vince, her future husband. Several years later, while she was inspecting a store with him that he was buying, a robber entered. In the fracas that resulted, the robber killed a customer and shot her, temporarily paralyzing her right leg. This accident was a turning point in her life. "Before the accident I had always been very moody, malcontent, unhappy. My mother had never allowed me to have a good friend, to even laugh, to totally enjoy myself. I had to go into therapy because I was reliving the accident day and night. After therapy, it was all of a sudden . . . everything suddenly snapped. My whole life changed. I was able to like myself, which I couldn't do before. After that I could pursue my career. For the first time I really feel very happy with my life."

When asked what she felt the sources of her drive to succeed were, she said her mother, but in what she called a "perverse, bull-headed" way. Her mother was an exceptionally strong, dominating, and authoritarian woman. "To deal with her, I had to be strong too. Otherwise, I'd be in an insane asylum today. I always felt as if I had been adopted. Though I felt much closer to my father. I loved him and wanted to be like him, probably because we were so temperamentally similar. But I never felt they were my real parents. I don't mean I felt rejected. I just felt I had to depend upon myself."

Another source of her hunger to succeed was envy. At the age of seven, she visited an aunt's beautiful home and immediately made up her mind that this was the way she wanted to live. "I have always envied people that had things. . . . I've always wanted to make enough money to help other people." About the same time, she decided she wanted to become a doctor, not just to help other people, a motive she still has, but also because it was a "tremendous status symbol . . . the ultimate one. I would want to be the best; I'd probably have to be a surgeon. I'd still like to be a physician."

I asked, "Would you want to go back to school and begin that career? You are still young and money is no problem."

"No way," Jane said. "It would be a waste of time and energy. I don't now feel that I could do it."

"What about nursing?"

"No! I couldn't work under the doctors. I'd end up taking a scalpel to them. It would be denigrating. Doctors are very chauvinistic. I could be a doctor but I couldn't work with one."

A third source of her urge to be in charge of her own life was the women's movement, whose themes had preoccupied her in therapy. Like Billie and Marty, she had learned how to get in touch with her more assertive self. "I have become a stronger person. I can understand what the feminists are talking about. Now if I think something is wrong, I speak out, like when the bank first refused me a loan because I was a woman. My business had made me a little harder, tougher, less feminine. It's like, 'Welcome to the real world.'" To succeed in such a world, she had found that she had had to become "almost brutal." Imagine a feminine-appearing young woman doing the following to survive in a competitive, male-dominated business.

> Intimidation is the rule of the day in my business.
> I had no idea of how rough New Yorkers could be.

They are street-wise and very coy. They understand
only one type of language and that is toughness.
When I first started out, they would say "Yes," and
a month later I still had not received my supplies.
So I drove a truck up there, parked in their doorway, and said I wasn't going to leave until I got
what I wanted. I have never had any more trouble. They'll chew you up if you let them. A man
has authority with other men. A woman has to earn
it their way. I'm no longer gullible. I don't take any
nonsense. I have a backbone now.

I felt her singular clarity about what she wanted was critical
to her success. By the age of thirty-three, she was well along
the way to becoming a millionaire; she had become a respected
leader of status in the local business community; she loved her
work, which her colleagues felt suited her very well.

And what of her marriage and family? When I saw her, she
was happily married, felt very supported by her husband, and
felt fulfilled as a parent. "The whole realm . . . the whole picture is finally together . . . the whole puzzle completed." She was
one of the three happiest persons of the study. Her peers agreed
that she was happy and fulfilled.

Attributes of Vocational Success

I don't know if Jane's story inspires or discourages you. It
can inspire us because she is another example, like Billie, Andy,
and Marty, of a strong person who had the talent and character — especially dogged determination and willpower — to overcome some incredible handicaps to achieve her dreams. Her
story can also discourage us. Our natural tendency is to compare ourselves with successful persons and feel down, particularly if we've had no real handicaps to blame for our inertia or
middling success. I hope you keep in mind that I am describing persons identified by objective means to be exceptional exemplars of what it takes to grow up to succeed. As I draw the
group portrait of the vocationally successful person, keep either
yourself or Jane in mind so you will have a real-life person on
whom to drape the statistical results.

Just as I had for their familial roles and friendships, I asked the men and women to tell me what they had learned were the six most important strengths that contributed to their success as engineers, journalists, accountants, and teachers (A4b). In rough declining order of citation, their audit included the following:

- Adaptive intelligence skills, such as analytical and organizational abilities and good judgment
- Motivational commitment to work hard
- Understanding and managing interpersonal relationships
- Communication skills, such as empathy
- Disciplined knowledge and competence
- Caring concern for and patience with others
- Adaptive work attitudes and habits: reliability, objectivity, and decisiveness
- Imaginative perspective
- Mature sense of self: self-confidence, mental health
- Ethical sense

An imposing list of virtues is required to succeed. Intellectual skills, disciplined knowledge, and competence now come into their own, but not at the expense of character strengths like working hard, empathy, caring, decisiveness, understanding, and ethical sense.

Today's youth, singularly motivated to get the "big buck," know the importance of intellectual skills and knowledge for their future success. However, few speak as if they know how important their character will be to their success. Maybe you will find James Ferguson's comments to a National 4-H Congress useful. Since he is chairman of General Foods, is rich, and probably enjoys his work, he should be credible.

> The future is not going to be a comfortable time for people who cannot adapt and be flexible, or who don't have imagination and a willingness to take some risks.
> I'm disturbed by the trend these days—all too

prevalent, in my view — of young people to narrow their sights too early, and to tailor their education or their career planning or their interests to one narrow specialty. Because it stifles that capacity to grow and change. Whether you go to college or not — stay as broad as you can, as long as you can! Because business fundamentally is a matter of relations among human beings. Success in business means successfully dealing with and motivating people. And the higher a person goes in most companies, the less important it is that he or she have facts, figures, and specific expertise. And the more important it is that he or she have flexibility, inventiveness, judgment and the capacity to deal with change, and with other people.

Specific vocations not only require specialized knowledge and competence but other strengths as well. Consider physicians. According to one observer, the most critical qualities they need to adapt to the stresses of modern medicine and be effective healers are psychological maturity, social competence, and the willpower to moderate their aggressively competitive Type A personalities![3]

Character of Vocationally Successful Men and Women

If you are a literary soul or humanist, interested in stories about individuals, you may think me foolish to try to find out what bond traders, poets, and computer designers have in common that makes them successful. I ordered the men and the women in terms of their overall vocational success (A28) to learn if successful persons are similar, regardless of their specific occupations. They are. As dissimilar as a biological researcher like Andy and a real estate developer like Jim or a feminist lawyer like Marty and a business entrepreneur like Jane are on the surface, they are alike in ways that you will recognize from the character of the person who succeeds in familial roles.

Vocationally successful persons are happy, succeed in their

other adult roles, and are strongly androgynous, particularly masculine. The computer-drawn portrait fits Jane to a tee. You may be asking, "Why is psychological maturity missing?" Well, it wasn't for the men and was only partially visible for the women when I defined their success by their income, judged leadership strengths, and colleague- and self-rated vocational adaptation. When I relied on my most reliable measure, self-rated satisfaction, or adaptation, I found that both vocationally successful men and women are mature.[4] That the women's results are somewhat inconsistent is the first of several clues that the meaning of vocational success is ambiguous, even conflictive, for some.

Vocationally Successful Men and Women Are Happy and Fulfilled. Like successful marital partners, parents, and lovers, vocationally successful men and women are happier and more satisfied with their lives in general than less successful persons are.

"So what's new?" you may be muttering again. What's new and theoretically important is that they had been productive and happy persons at *every* phase of their post-teenage lives (A4a). The roots of mid-life vocational, just as of familial, success go far back, at least into our adolescence. This result again signals how crucial enduring personality strengths, already visible by adolescence, are to later adult vocational success. The same strengths that enabled Jane to flee home when she was in tenth grade enabled her to become a successful sales manager in her early twenties and an entrepreneur by her early thirties.

Character, not a guardian angel, luck, or "contacts," is the route to success and happiness. Again you'll say, "Obvious!" But many don't live their lives as if that truth is known. Roger angrily has told me of the number of his affluent students who waste their growing-up years dozing in school, drugging their minds, and partying and sexing away their energies. To begin to succeed, they need a Reverend Jesse Jackson-type old-fashioned sermon to spark them to seize their talents and energies and develop their minds, learn to enjoy hard work, do well even if bored by dull courses, and learn while young how to get along with others. The research says his sermon is right on track.

Vocationally Successful Men and Women Succeed in Other Adult Roles. Competence in one demanding, complex role nurtures and confirms competence in other challenging roles. Vocationally successful men and women are also good spouses, parents, and citizens. Remember that Vaillant found the same thing for his Harvard graduates.[5]

As in every generalization based on the lives of diverse persons, exceptions occur that we should keep in mind. So while Billie, Marty, Andy, and Jane fit the finding, Bill Spaulding, the founder and CEO of his own marketing firm, did not. He was more vocationally successful than 90 percent of the other men, but his marriage was heading toward the abyss; his wife saw him as a failed husband and father.

Vocationally Successful Men and Women Are Androgynous, Particularly Masculine. Vocationally successful men and women are typically masculine. The judges described both as self-sufficient, ambitious, and as having strong personalities. Assertive, forceful, and aggressive, they made decisions easily and willingly took on competitive risks. They functioned well under stress. Because of their tough skins, criticism and rebuff did not devastate them. But they were also seen as affectionate, the most prominent warm trait about which the judges agreed. Remember that persons can be androgynous, but given the way I scored for it they can tilt more toward either masculinity or femininity. To score high in androgyny, they must also have an ample amount of the opposite sex's less developed strengths.

Can we now say that strongly masculine men like Bill Spaulding, the CEO of his own firm, and Bruce Jackson, the fired electronics engineer whose wife left him, can finally come into their own? Well, not quite. *Both* masculine *and* feminine strengths contribute to vocational success for men and women. Overbearing dominance, unchecked competitiveness, and driving ambition may eventually destroy a person, as former Wall Street inside traders discovered. The equilibrating principle warns us that one-sided excess destroys itself unless moderated by other compensating strengths. The audit of necessary vocational strengths and those James Ferguson also talked about included interpersonal skills like caring, understanding, and empathy.

The idealized, computer-drawn portrait doesn't fit any particular person, of course. Andy was seen as only moderately competitive; Billie and Marty were only moderately aggressive. But the rest of the portrait did fit them and Jane quite well, though each had more interpersonal feminine strengths than the group portrait had. Jane's colleague saw her to be a compassionate and sympathetic boss.

Jane's dream was not just to be rich. She became rich when she married Vince. No, she wanted to become a millionaire on her own — the old-fashioned American way. She became an entrepreneur in order to earn it herself. What is the character of people like Jane? The next chapter focuses on two of her successes: making a lot of money and exercising entrepreneurial leadership.

15

Earning It
the Old-Fashioned Way

Americans have long believed that anyone who worked hard, was enterprising, and did his best would not just survive but could fulfill his dreams — even become a millionaire, and thus happy. Such virtues may no longer be in fashion for those of us who look for the shortcuts to wealth and status. Tom Wolfe, the best-selling author about sex and greed, may be right after all. We are fascinated by those who "make it big" and how they did it: the outlandish salaries of Wall Street junk bond dealers, Donald Trump's eight-story yacht and the $100,000 a year he spent for its flowers, the planet's eighty-nine male and three female billionaires that *Forbes* editors have located. While it takes a billion dollars for real status nowadays, I think most of us would agree with Jane. A million or two would do. So we buy our daily lottery ticket, play the slots at Las Vegas, and keep pasting those stickers on American Family Publishers' ten-million-dollar sweepstake certificates.

Though wistfully envious of the instantly rich and powerful, many Americans still hold onto some old-fashioned values. We agree in ranking a happy marriage, parental competence, and vocational satisfaction far ahead of wealth, leadership, and power. Until this past decade, even teenagers ranked their goals similarly.[1] Entrepreneurial owners of small businesses, like Jane, say they value other goals more than they do money. Most important to them is the quality of their product and service.

They next value the freedom to make their own decisions, flexibility, self-reliance, good customer relations, and only then, a lot of money.[2]

Of course what we say and what we do are not always the same. I playfully test parents about their *real* priorities by asking, "How much money would you sell your children for? Twenty, thirty, or three hundred million dollars? Some really pause and consider their price. One frustrated parent didn't. She burst out that some days she'd like to donate them to charity.

Until we win the big one, most of us must be content to survive "the old-fashioned way." What are men and women like who work hard to do a good job, earn a lot of money, and hold positions of power? Though making a lot of money and succeeding as a leader draw upon similar masculine strengths, other differences suggest that I discuss them separately. Let's see why Jane succeeded in these two ways.

The Character of Men and Women
Who Make High Incomes

Do people who earn a lot of money have any character traits in common? The answer varies from "probably" to "possibly," depending upon how we go about finding out. The answer is "probably" if we ask strangers in a quick telephone survey to tell us about their marriages, sex lives, and vocational satisfactions; it is "possibly" if we examine in more depth the psychological meaning of money with a person we have known for years. Because telephone or door-step surveys can ask thousands of persons, but in-depth studies like mine can examine only a few, I am not confident how true my results are that seem to contradict those of much larger surveys. My findings do, however, provoke some disturbing questions to pursue further.

What do quick surveys say about men and women who succeed financially? Veroff's national survey in the seventies found that regardless of *their sex, age, and education,* "people with high incomes (1) report greater present happiness and higher future morale; (2) less often say they have felt as if they might have a nervous breakdown; (3) have a positive orientation toward and see fewer restrictions in marriage; (4) report greater happiness in their own marriages; (5) report greater job satisfaction; and (6) list fewer symptoms of ill health."[3] We know how debilitating and devastating poverty can be. And we all know how good we feel when we have enough money to live without excessive worry. The most recent American telephone survey on stress reports that "the more money you make, the less stress you report."[4]

Isn't the meaning of money more complicated? Does it make sense to say that highly paid executives feel less stressed than millions of lower-paid teachers? Are lower-income people really less happy, healthy, and satisfied with their work than physicians frightened by malpractice suits, middle managers apprehensive about being fired, and rock stars narcotizing and overdosing themselves? Is Ivan Boesky, the mid-eighties' Wall Street inside trader and apostle of greed, really right, as such surveys hint, to insist that "greed is healthy. You can be greedy and still feel good about yourself,"[5] even if you, like him, end up in a federal pen and are prohibited from ever practicing your calling again at your former scope? Does earning a lot of money really forestall a nervous breakdown and divorce?

Baruch's survey of middle-aged women does not contradict the tenor of Veroff's. Women who earned good incomes reported that they were happy, were sexually fulfilled, were satisfied with themselves as parents, and coped better.[6] I'm not so sure, however, that contemporary married mothers who work and earn a lot of money have it all. We cannot yet conclude, moreover, that high incomes produce greater happiness, health, and more successful marriages. They may. But it may be more accurate to say that the character strengths necessary to create a happy marriage and healthier way of life also contribute to earning more money. Let's see what other studies tell us about the meaning of money for those who are above the poverty line.

Those few, such as myself and the IGS researchers, who have studied men and women in much more depth have not found the same clearcut meanings about financial success. Men and women who make a lot of money are similar in only *one* way: They are singularly masculine, primarily because they are leaders who enjoy using power. Because of our societal fascination about money and the minimal amount of research about the character necessary to earn it, I list the common character traits the research identified to describe high-earning men and women. How many of these traits do you have?

Men	*Women*
Fulfilling potential	Enjoying exercising power
Competitive	Acting as leaders
Being viewed as authorities	Being viewed as authorities
Energetic	Lacking loyalty
Respected by others	Having feelings not easily hurt
Acting as leaders	Lacking gentleness
Functioning well under stress	Self-confident
Having deep interests	Aggressive
Self-accepting	Predictable
Aggressive	Competitive
Ambitious	Ambitious
Having leadership abilities	Dominant
Seven other primarily masculine ones	

If you want your children to earn a lot of money, the results are clear. At least raise them to be typical males. Certainly don't raise your daughters to be loyal, gentle, and tender skinned — women, as well as men, who earn a lot of money are aggressive, competitive, ambitious, and dominant leaders. Of course, your children may turn out to be statistical exceptions. But beware. If they don't also develop feminine interpersonal strengths, be prepared that they may race through marital turnstiles, enjoy innumerable nightly playmates, and be unwilling to give you any grandchildren.

Although men and women who make a lot of money have similar characters, their incomes predict different things about them. Knowing a man's income tells us some interesting and important things about how happy and successful he is in his other roles; knowing a woman's income tells us nothing else about her. This is another sign that vocational success may mean something different to men than to women.

How much a man earns does make a difference to his happiness, depending upon how long he has worked. When the men were in their early thirties, their earned income didn't predict much of anything else about them. Those who made more money were neither happier, more maritally or sexually satisfied, better parents, nor even more satisfied with their vocations (A6).

However, by their mid-forties, men who earned a lot were more satisfied with their salaries, judged to be fulfilled and happy persons, and involved as concerned citizens in their communities. They were not better husbands, lovers, fathers, or friends. Though judged by their colleagues to be well-adapted vocationally, they were only barely more satisfied with their work than the men who earned much less (A6). The IGS longitudinal study also found little relation between income and vocational satisfaction until men reached their late forties.[7] Might earned income be a better indicator of how well we have used our talents to adapt after we have reached more responsible job levels?

What do women's incomes tell us other than that they are judged to be leaders who enjoy using power and so are quite masculine? Nothing! Women who earn a lot of money are no more satisfied with their work than women who earn a lot less. A female bank president enjoys her work no more than a third grade teacher. Nor do their colleagues believe they are more vocationally fulfilled and happy in their jobs (A26). Making a lot of money doesn't make them any happier or more satisfied or maritally happy or better parents or better lovers to their partners (in either their own or others' eyes) or more mature, doesn't raise their self-esteem, and on and on. It is as if the amount of money a woman earns is irrelevant to her values, general competence, maturity, mental health, and personality (except to her masculinity). Remember, though, you may be the statistical exception.

These nonfindings blatantly contradict Baruch's survey results. How can mine possibly be true? Jane would surely disagree with them. Harriet also. She feels very good about being able to earn money, though I don't think her basic self-esteem has changed as a result of what she earns. I also find the results hard to believe. Common sense tells us that earning and having money can make us feel independent and good about ourselves and give us a feeling of control over our lives. One woman asked, "How do you think I feel when I must ask my husband for money to buy him his birthday present?" Another told me, "My mother left me a little inheritance. It's been a lifesaver. I've always been able to do things I want to do. Before I got my current job, it helped me feel that I was my own person."

So let's return to Baruch's and my seemingly contradictory results. Because they can be reconciled at a more fundamental level, I'm inclined to accept her findings, rather than mine, that women who earn a lot enjoy sex, are happy, and cope better. Why? Women who make more money are typically so masculine that their aggressiveness, need for power, competitiveness, and other traits work against feminine ones like loyalty and gentleness. Both Baruch and I found that women who enjoyed frequent sex were also almost exclusively masculine, and I'll show you later that women who are happy and cope well also have some masculine traits. Such consistency in the character traits that undergird earning power, sexual enjoyment, happiness, and coping ability is persuasive and lends more credibility to Baruch's than to my findings.

However, women who make a lot of money are not likely to be better spouses, more fulfilled mothers, or better lovers than women who earn a lot less — unless they, like Jane, are androgynous. Not even Baruch reports that they make better marital partners to their husbands. Good marital partners, mothers, and lovers do *not* share in common the strong masculine character of women who make a lot of money. More typically feminine, they are compassionate, warm, trusting, cheerful, emotional, sympathetic, and loyal. Not one of these traits is shared *in common* by women who make a lot of money. Some traits, such as loyalty and gentleness, actually work against earning a lot of money. Could it be that Baruch's working women claimed that they were satisfied with their parental role to justify to a stranger — and to themselves — their career commitment?

Remember, though, my earlier warnings about how to interpret the findings I report. High-earning women who are androgynous and so interpersonally feminine can be superb spouses, mothers, and lovers; both Billie and Marty have shown us that. Keep in mind that I'm reporting the strengths that are necessary to make a lot of money in our type of society. Most of the strengths do *not* preclude possessing the feminine interpersonal ones necessary for familial success. The modern woman's dilemma, so acute in Marty, is how to integrate both. Because few women succeeded in both their vocational and familial lives, William James's insight may be correct that we can have only one Number 1 Self, not three. Women like Billie may prove James wrong psychologically; we still have much to learn about the meaning of being an achieving mother who brings home a lot of bread to her partner.

That women who earn a lot of money are more masculine provokes another sobering thought. Women make less money and occupy fewer positions of high responsibility where they can make more money than men. They are the backbone of the low-paying nurturing professions of teaching and nursing. It is fashionable to assert that the income disparity between men and women reflects discrimination (which is true), unequal access to the "old boy network" (also true), and games played by men's rules on their turf (also true). But the results suggest another more telling reason. Many women may find the path to comparable pay to be too foreign to them, given the ways that their character has been shaped. Researchers may discover that interpersonally feminine women grow weary of the daily competitive and aggressive struggle of which Jane spoke. It requires masculine strengths not readily available or palatable to many.

Joan was such a woman. The study's most feminine woman, she was an artist of considerable talent. Her home overflowed with paintings that even my untrained eye could see were exceptional.

"Joan, why are you hoarding so many good paintings in your apartment?"

"I know I should take them to show at different galleries. But I just can't seem to get myself to do it. It's just that . . . well, I'm just not aggressive enough. I've never been. Anyway, they're not good enough. They couldn't compete with what I've seen. Besides, I'd feel devastated if none were sold."

Not having developed self-confidence, assertiveness, competitiveness, and a tough skin means that her talent, like that of Emily Dickinson, will never receive the recognition and rewards that it deserves while she lives. Unfortunately, Joan is not poor enough to be driven into the street to show her work. Fortunately, her more assertive daughter will inherit the bonanza.

These results may trouble you because they go against more palatable survey findings. Not until researchers go beyond quick telephone or doorstep surveys to dig more deeply into the psychological meanings of money will we better understand how important it is to our fulfillment, happiness, and health.

Given the media's, yuppies', and current youths' preoccupation with wealth as *the* measure of a person's worth, I'm concerned that it may distort our and our children's healthy growth. I must tell you a story about a six-year-old. I did not believe it until I verified it with the head of one of our country's most prestigious schools. While interviewing Bobby for admission to the school's first grade, he asked him why he wanted to come to the academy. Soberly and without hesitation, Bobby said, "Because it is a top school and will help me get into Harvard so I can become a doctor and make a lot of money." What a somber vision of one's future to have at the age of six.

What a tragically amusing caricature of our American obsession with money — so close to the "vision" many young adults have of their lives. Why else have so many become lawyers during the past decade and then become bored by their early thirties? Why do so many business school graduates want to work on Wall Street? And why have a few landed in jail by their early thirties? What is every commission's solution to our looming catastrophic teacher shortage in the next five years? What do we need more of to solve all of our societal problems?

Money!

Is that *the* route to a healthier Number 1 Self and society? The study's men and women say "no" very loudly. Of course, money helps; if spent to nurture character maturation, it could help many a great deal. But we must go beyond thinking it is *the* way to health and happiness. It is *a* way, but probably not the most effective.

Character of Men and Women
Judged to Be Good Leaders

Holding a position of leadership and responsibility and having power to control our work and that of others is another related sign of vocational success. I can't tell you much about the character you need to succeed this way—I had too small and diverse a group. It did not make much sense to compare the leadership success of an opera singer and a movie actress with that of a superb entrepreneur like Jane or an academic professional like Andy. Besides, hundreds of other researchers have studied many different leaders much more thoroughly than I could possibly do.

So I settled on two other ways of understanding the character of successful leaders. I identified the men and women who had leadership strengths from the personality ratings of the three judges who knew them best, even though they may not have had the opportunity to demonstrate them vocationally (A10b). Then I identified those who had been most involved as leaders in their communities. Although different occupations may not provide the same opportunity to demonstrate leadership, community roles, which everyone can volunteer for, and elected professional roles do. I postpone discussing the character of successful community and professional leaders until later.

If you want to succeed as a leader, what strengths should you develop? The best research has been done on successful managers. Although managerial and leadership success are not identical, particularly in political roles (as Ronald Reagan demonstrated), the research yields some glimpses into the variety of strengths necessary to fulfill positions of high responsibility well.

Before she "died," Ma Bell conducted the longest, most intensive, and most authoritative study of male managers yet completed. In rough declining order of importance, the following traits contributed most to subsequent managerial success.[8]

- Oral communication skills
- Human relations skills
- Desire for responsibility

- Ability to function well under stress
- Tolerance of uncertainty
- Organizing and planning skills
- High energy
- Creativity
- Wide range of interests
- Behavior flexibility
- Inner work standards

Similar strengths will be critical to managerial success in the twenty-first century, according to those who think that far ahead. Effective managerial leaders in fifteen or twenty years will need to speak and write well, understand persons and the culture in which they will work, and be empathic, creative, and flexible.[9]

Apparently, male and female leaders do not differ markedly in their personalities, according to one of the few studies I have found that compared male and female entrepreneurs like Jane.[10] My results agreed, but the strengths that contribute to leadership may be more central to men's than to women's identity at this time in history. I was surprised that the judged leadership strengths did not predict more than they did for *both* men and women. Those judged to be good leaders were idealistically involved in their communities, earned good incomes, and were definitely androgynous, though much more masculine than feminine. Both the male and female leaders possessed almost every typical male attribute: strong personality, dominance, forcefulness, aggressiveness, competitiveness, and ambition.

Not surprisingly, effective leaders of others must also have interpersonal skills; but unexpectedly, the judges rated the male leaders to have many more interpersonal skills than the women. The female leaders had not completely escaped their feminine history, however. They were warm, emotional, and, provocatively, flatterable! The Iron Lady, Margaret Thatcher, is an obvious exception. She could probably lead Britain until she died if, as many Brits, and especially Scots and Welsh, wished, she were more warmly compassionate, occasionally flappable, and minimally receptive to some flattery—but remained strong and forceful.

Men and women leaders shared few other strengths in common. Their peers see leadership strengths more frequently in men than in women, probably because so many typical masculine traits are associated with leadership as I measured it. Just as women needed more strengths to fulfill their traditional marital role well, so men need more character strengths to be good leaders, traditionally the province of males. At least at this time in women's development, their judged leadership strengths just don't predict much of anything else about them. Men's do.

Male leaders are mature and feel fulfilled by their work, which they view as their calling. Their interpersonal strengths contribute to being good friends and colleagues as well as being happily married. Generally, leaders are seen by others to be happy and fulfilled; they themselves report that they have been productive and happy since college, which again suggests that leadership, like other competences, is rooted in our developing character; it is not just a haphazard emergent.

Leaders whose masculine character strengths are so dominant that they exclude interpersonal strengths like warmth and understanding can have two vulnerable Achilles' heels. Remember Bill Spaulding, who built his own marketing consulting firm from scratch? I had to warn him in an awkward and tense postinterview session that his future success both as a CEO and as a spouse-father might be in more jeopardy than I felt he realized.

Among his peers, he ranked near the top in masculine character traits like the leadership, forcefulness, and competitiveness that he had used so well to build his multimillion-dollar firm. His vulnerability came not from such strengths in themselves but from their singular severity. They were not integrated with the strong people skills to which James Ferguson referred in his talk to the 4-H teenagers. His three peers rated him to be one of the five *least* feminine men of the study, and, more crucially, in the bottom 15 percent in quality of people skills like sensitivity, understanding, and sympathy. He could brusquely fire his two close co-founders without one sleepless night. Decisiveness not integrated with sensitivity can push a leader to self-destruct. Although he was one of the study's most vocationally satisfied and competent men, his colleague and his wife, who knew how good a CEO he was, rated him barely above average in vocational fulfillment.

His success as a husband and parent was his other Achilles' heel — at least as his troubled and unhappy wife viewed it. On each of her six criteria of what made a good marital partner and parent, she rated him to be one of the study's two worst spouses and fathers. He saw himself to be a much better husband and father: affectionate, sympathetic, understanding, and compassionate.

Inaccurate self-perceptions of this magnitude made him vulnerable to failure in any activity whose success depended upon understanding his interpersonal strengths. The dangerous gap between his and others' views of his strengths could have made him resist my warnings. Fortunately, he heard one, as he mused, "I wonder if that's why headhunters have refused to suggest me for the presidency of a large firm that has been looking for someone with my expertise and experience." He was more skittish about talking as humbly about his family life, however.

That's all I can say about the character of persons likely to wield power and influence successfully. I have not studied leaders of nurturing professions, such as principals, social service administrators, or deans of students. I assume they would tilt toward the interpersonally feminine and not be so typically masculine.

Jane's personality fit quite well the statistical portrait of the entrepreneurial woman who makes a lot of money. But she also succeeded in creating a calling that she enjoyed, so let's turn now to understand why.

16

Making Work a Calling, Not Just a Job

For most of us, a *healthy* Number 1 Self needs to be more than just making a lot of money and exercising power. Accumulating evidence tells us that our compulsive pursuit of money, our extravagant consumption, this past decade has not made us any happier or more satisfied with our lives. A *Psychology Today* article recently cited evidence that men and women in their thirties actually feel much more dissatisfied and defeated than older ones.[1] Can it really be so that *ten* times more baby-boomers are depressed than people in my Depression-wracked generation? Since the mid-fifties, the suicide rate among adolescents has increased continuously; in a 1987 national survey, 18 percent of girls and 11 percent of boys reported they had attempted suicide.[2] Can this really be true? Drug addiction, alcoholism, and crime never seem to abate, only to become more pervasive. Japan and Germany are also wealthy countries. But a recent Gallup poll found that of sixteen different peoples, the Japanese were the least satisfied with their lives and only ten percent of Germans claimed to be very happy.[3] Isn't it a peculiarly American, Japanese, and German paradox that the citizens of the three wealthiest countries on our planet are so discontented?

The equilibrating principle may be catching up with us. The young lawyers who are bored may be learning that they shouldn't have gone into law just for its money, status, and power. The young, instant yuppies on Wall Street now fleeing their well-paid jobs are saying, according to the *Wall Street Journal*, that their life of long hours and pressures interferes with their social and family lives and, in Bob Dylan's words, "strangles up" their minds.[4] Though one out of three teachers say they will leave teaching in the next few years because it doesn't pay much, my studies show that a more fundamental reason is that they feel they can't continue to grow and reach their felt level of capability.[5] Preoccupation with money can thus obscure deeper reasons for our vocational discontent, which we may not be able to express clearly even to ourselves. My studies convince me that once a person's basic survival needs are met, persons who make a lot of money are no more likely to be satisfied with their jobs than persons who make less. Satisfaction with one's salary, when it is enough to live reasonably well on, contributes little to vocational satisfaction.

Why? What have we forgotten about what makes a healthy and happy vocational self?

I recently asked students what the religious meaning of "vocation" is. They didn't know. When I said "calling," they looked at me blankly, as if they had never heard the word. (One smart guy yelled out, "a cat in heat." I looked at him blankly. The students went wild. But I looked it up later; he was right. Is it a sign of the times to think of a vocation as a transitory urge rather than a commitment?) Anyway, they are not exceptional. A recent commentary on changing American attitudes declared that we adults have substituted money and power for our lost historic understanding of work as a "calling." Work has now become just a job to get money and status.[6]

A "calling" is a way of life, formerly a divine summons, "what one was meant to be," that in religious terms leads to committing one's self to some transcendent purpose, like Marty to feminism. Remember the scandal of Mary Elizabeth Cunningham? A Phi Beta Kappa, a graduate of Wellesley College and then Harvard Business School, she became executive assistant to William Agee, president of Bendix, and then shortly afterward his lover, though both were married to other partners, and shortly after that, a young vice-president of the company, and shortly after being forced out of Bendix, an executive vice-president of Seagram & Sons. Surely she was a woman who succeeded financially, and held responsible leadership positions of great status and power. She learned, however, that her work had been a job, not a calling. In her words, it was a job, not "what I was always meant to do." She left her job and began her calling by founding a nonprofit organization that helps young women get through their pregnancies and create viable lives for their futures. She says of her calling, "It's like arms have just enfolded you, like a religion."[7]

What do we know about persons for whom their work is not just a "job" but has deep personal meaning and gives their lives significance? They are much happier, have higher vocational morale (A6), and are more mature. Their work intrinsically expresses their most important values, talents, and character strengths. From studying hundreds of professional groups, I have found that the most powerful contributor to vocational adaptation, high morale, and happiness is satisfaction with those attributes of our work listed below on the left-hand side; the least powerful contributor to our vocational success is satisfaction with those on the right-hand side,[8] a result also found by other researchers of vocational satisfaction.[9] Why not rate your own satisfaction with each of the items below.

Most Contributory	*Least Contributory*
Self-fulfillment secured from work	Salary received
Opportunity to achieve at our potential level of ability	Our competence for our work
Opportunity to continue growth most of our working life	Amount of energy our job requires
Work utilizes our best potentials	Amount of time our work demands
Work meets our strongest needs	Our relations with colleagues
Way of life associated with our work	Effects of our work on our family life
	Status and prestige of our work

Billie, Andy, Marty, and Jane had found their calling. Though Jane told me that she had always wanted to be a millionaire, her calling was not just to make money. She wanted to create a new company, a "monster" that grew and grew, reflecting her own expanding sense of self, dedicated to giving the quality of service to others that her earlier dreams of being a physician had expressed. That's what she was proud of, not just that she had more money to spend on a bigger swimming pool and larger house. She not only was more satisfied than most of the other women with the left-hand items indexing fulfillment, but her colleague gave her the highest ratings on every one of them. Remember I felt that Marty's calling was to be a feminist lawyer rather than a mother? She was more satisfied with every one of the left-hand items as a lawyer than she was with comparable items as a mother.

Why does satisfaction with the left-hand items contribute so much to overall vocational satisfaction or morale? Because the satisfactions contribute to our fulfillment and meaning as persons. When our work fulfills our strongest needs, then money, the clock, even the needs of our families, become less immediate. Absorbed in our work, which is really play for some, we don't notice that it is time to eat; we tap into energies unfettered by doubts about or resistances to our work; we don't care if others think that we are odd. The result is that we don't feel as unhappy about our salaries or the amount of time we put in. Our morale soars much higher than that of the person who watches the clock, worries about his status, and dreams about his next raise. The best protection against "burnout" is to be called to our work.[10]

To feel that our work fulfills our needs, provides our talents their full scope, and channels our deepest interests is deeply intrinsic, generic, to being human. Remarkably, the same meaning of vocation occurs in fifth graders in Saudi Arabia, eighth graders in Tokyo, and college students in New Jersey.[11] No wonder maturity so consistently predicts who will be more vocationally satisfied, when satisfaction so closely depends upon feeling fulfilled and growing in our own work. It is the more mature person who risks seeking new ways to grow; it is the less mature one who seeks only the security and signs of the known. We don't grow if we fear to risk, even our income and status. Billie, Andy, Marty, and Jane knew that existential truth. Many of today's youth, including six-year-old Bobby aspiring to go to Harvard, young M.B.A.s pursuing the fast track, and the rest who believe that money buys fulfillment, have yet to know that truth.

Of course, satisfaction with the right-hand items, such as our competence, relations with colleagues, and salaries, contributes to feeling good about our work. But they are more peripheral. At best they enable us to fulfill our basic needs and grow through our work. If we are highly competent in a task we don't believe is central to our needs and talents, then satisfaction about our competence is not going to increase our satisfaction with other aspects of our work. Our relations with our colleagues are not unimportant; they provide the emotional working conditions, climate, and models that in turn can enhance our own growth and so our sense of fulfillment.[12] An adequate salary can free us from preoccupations that divert our energies, rather than concentrate them on work.

We cannot reason ourselves into a calling or commitment. It emerges out of our character as we get ourselves more and more maturely together. Many years of tracking how men and women grow to succeed and become happy confirm over and over how much of what we achieve is only the *visible* projection of our less visible maturing character. That is also why we cannot buy success and happiness.

The Character of Vocationally Well-Adapted Men and Women

What are men and women like who really enjoy their day-to-day work and create that optimal balance between adjusting to their vocation's demands and fulfilling their needs and talents?

Men and women who enjoy their work are similar in some predictable ways, but most perplexing to me, *not* in others. We have seen earlier that being a mother is more integrated with a woman's personality than being a father is with a man's. Similarly, being a breadwinner is more integrated with a man's personality than it is with a woman's. I shall just cite how men and women who are pleased with their work are alike and then explore in more detail how they differ in their meaning of vocation, at least at this moment in women's evolution as women.

Men and women who enjoy their work resemble those who succeed in their familial roles (A6). They are more mature than those who are dissatisfied with their work. Their colleagues rate them to be better adapted to their vocations. They are also happier and have been since their teenage years.

To answer a question you may be asking, "No, the men and women did not differ reliably in overall satisfaction with their work." Whether they were researchers, designers, or singers, the men and women did not differ either in how well they had adjusted to their work or how much they felt fulfilled by it. Though not satisfied with their jobs' demands on their time and energy, for example, they did not differ in their degree of dissatisfaction. Similarly, the men and women were moderately satisfied that their jobs fulfilled their strongest needs and provided them with the opportunities to use the full range of their talents; they also did not disagree about how fulfilling their work was (A6).

However, the study produced two reliable differences between men's and women's meaning of vocation. Men who adapted well to their work differed from women who also adapted well by succeeding in more of their other roles; they were also more *androgynous,* particularly more masculine. A middle-aged man's vocational satisfaction predicts his success in his other roles; a middle-aged woman's does not. Middle-aged men who feel good about their work are happily married, sexually fulfilled, satisfied fathers, and generally more competent in their other adult roles. Andy was a vocationally successful leader in his field of biological research, but also, in the words of Marty, a "supportive and loving . . . strong and caring partner." He also was one of the top 10 percent of successful fathers. Or to phrase this important finding differently, men like Bruce Jackson, the laid-off electrical division manager, who have trouble at work are likely to also have trouble at home with their wives and their children, as he did.

That I had secured these same findings when studying the men in their early thirties tells us how stable they are. George Vaillant, studying Harvard middle-aged men, found a similar pattern, which suggests that adapting successfully to quite different, demanding roles is due to stable, underlying character strengths that describe psychological maturity.[13]

Men and women who are satisfied with their careers also differ in their personalities. The men are typically masculine. Strong, self-sufficient, and confident, they function well under stress. They impress their peers as being energetic, assertive and independent, in control, and ambitiously willing to take risks. They make decisions easily and defend them readily. Are they the typical cigar-chewing businessmen pictured in late night TV movies? No. Aggressiveness, dominance, forcefulness, and competitiveness — the core of the macho male — are not commonly shared traits of men satisfied with their work. Try acting like Bruce Jackson when working for IBM, AT&T, or your local hospital and see how far you would get. The men happy in their work are also androgynous, which means that their maleness is mellowed by feminine interpersonal strengths like understanding others. Their masculinity is more visible, however.

Because men satisfied with their work share so many similar character strengths (their peers reliably agreed in describing them on more than a third of the 100 traits that they rated), they are easily bonded into an unspoken fraternity or brotherhood. If the successful scholars, journalists, and engineers accidentally met at Heath's bar one evening, they would immediately feel comfortable with each other. They would intuitively understand each other's "deals," conflicts with the IRS, exasperating colleagues, and partners' complaints. Not just shared experience but common personality strengths cement the "old boy network," which may be one reason why women feel like outsiders or emotional strangers to men's groups. Women who feel excluded from the office lunch group or the late afternoon "beer gang" may be deliberately ignored, but there may be deeper reasons. They may not give off the same vibes, express themselves similarly, share the same unspoken experiences that had earlier formed the men's character, or appreciate the meaning of male competitive bragging, backslapping, and playful punching, and on and on. The men's shared character bonds them in unconscious but simpatico ways. Jane, with her entrepreneurial character and experience of the rough-and-tumble business world, might feel more comfortable if the men didn't exclude her for other reasons. Marty might also feel more comfortable, if she could check her passionate feminist distrust that men who succeed do so on the backs of submissive women.

On the other hand, a woman's work apparently means something different to her than a man's does to him.[14] Remember that I am describing what is more likely to be the case for many, but not all, women, and this may be truer of middle-aged than younger women these days. While a man's success and happiness as a worker, spouse, and parent go together, the study suggests that a woman's vocational satisfaction does *not* predict success in the other areas of her life. Few married mothers with careers in the study felt really happy, fulfilled, and, most critically nowadays, guiltless. Billie, Marty, and Jane were exceptions, but then the tests identified them to be exceptional: Billie because she had the adaptive strengths to be one of those rare superwomen; Marty, because she had redefined for herself what a good wife and mother were to be, had made her career her primary calling, and had a husband like Andy who accepted being an equal parent; Jane because her driving ambition to create a multimillion-dollar firm was her primary calling. She had always worked, had money to secure help with the children, and had a supportive, casual, even laid-back husband, quite proud of her achievement. Jane said that she would have been in severe conflict if he had felt otherwise.

Why can husbands succeed in their work, marriages, *and* families so much more easily than their wives? Why is it more probable that in a two-career marriage, the vocationally satisfied husband will more successfully balance his roles than his vocationally satisfied wife will hers? It was no mystery to Marty, who had fought that battle. Men still have only one calling—their work—and two jobs—their marriages and parenthood. Neither they nor others, until recently, expected as much of them as husbands and fathers. We can feel more easily satisfied doing well in a job than a calling. Men focus their energies and talents on making it, "getting ahead," not on developing the strengths needed to be better husbands and fathers. The maturity of the vocationally satisfied man also makes it easier for him to juggle his work and the competing demands of his wife and children.

Nowadays, women want three callings—children, marriage, and work—three co-equal Number 1 Selves. They focus on their relationships with their husbands, children, children's teachers, grocery clerk, in-laws, friends, neighbors, and everyone else whom they meet and must smile at, please, and adjust to. And if they are working, they must also focus their talents on "getting along," let alone "ahead." That is why, for example, women must have more varied strengths than a man to make a marriage work. I think Marty would go on to say that a woman's nurturing identity, so deeply imprinted in her psyche, emotionally hears the cry of her baby before that of any other person, even of her husband. She also is more aware of those at work who need her. Juggling three callings is inherently conflictive. Remember William James's quote about not being able to be a tone-poet, saint, and bon vivant living "in the same tenement of clay." Except for those rare persons like Billie, something has to give.

Alice Matthews was fighting—and losing—the battle of balancing three careers. She was a mother of a three-year-old boy and a six-year-old girl. As a pediatric physician on the staff of a major teaching hospital, she did not fully control her hours; she depended upon Jerry, her husband, who was a social worker, to adjust his schedule to fit hers. Like Andy, he had a deep egalitarian commitment, and he willingly altered his work so he could take the children to school every morning, make dinner, and generally be available when Alice couldn't be. But as he ruefully said, "I've come to feel that there is a special bond between a mother and her children; when they really hurt, they reach out to Alice. There's little I can do at such times." Though they had resolved the logistical problems, like having help, Alice admitted that she always felt torn when she left for the hospital before her daughter had left for school or came home late at night after Jerry had put the children to bed. She could barely hold back her tears when she talked of how she had to walk out on those mornings when the children were hurting. And how guilty she felt that Jerry was taking the full brunt of her career, even though he had never complained.

On the basis of Alice's psychological tests, she and I felt that the personal cost for her mental health of juggling three callings was too high and might actually work against filling any of them successfully. She had known this inwardly but had not wanted to admit it to herself. I said to her, "I'm going to say three words. Don't hesitate. Just pick one of the three: career, children, Jerry."

"Children," she instantly replied.

She heard the question. She heard what her calling was to be. When Alice finally faced that truth, her inner clouds evaporated and she accepted compromises about her work and her relationship with Jerry more serenely.

Billie had heard "problem solver," which included career, wife, and mother. Marty and Jane had heard "career": Marty to be a feminist, Jane to make a million as a creative entrepreneur. When push comes to shove, a calling means hearing one voice louder than others and following it as long as we are called. We then must make room as best we can for the other voices without guilt. Marty and Jane show some of the ways it can be done. In the long run, unless one is like Billie, trying to have three careers risks paying some damaging emotional costs.

Women may view their careers differently than men for another reason. We have learned that women who feel good about their work are, like the men, mature. However, these successful women, unlike their male counterparts, do not share any specific personality traits in common. For women, feeling good about their careers apparently does not arise from the shared childhood and adolescent experiences that create a common socializing experience for males in American culture. So if the women who were satisfied with their careers got together at Heath's bar to talk about their work, they'd feel more like strangers to each other than the men would. Not feeling similar vibes or having shared growing-up work experiences or thinking similarly when solving problems, they'd feel more strain around each other and notice how diverse rather than how similar they were.

They would, for example, have more trouble than the men agreeing about forming a Rotarian group or deciding to have a night out on the town together as a group. They would really come together, however, if they talked about their children and husbands.

A simpler reason may explain why women who feel good about their vocations share so few common strengths. For men, their vocations are their identities, and they have been since they were three when their fathers asked them what they wanted to be when they grew up: a space man, a fireman, a football player, like their daddies. For women, their vocations may or may not be at the core of their identities. Some women worked because their husbands expected them to; others were in fields that they didn't like but didn't know what they might prefer; some, even professionals like Alice, were reluctantly torn and ambivalent about succeeding too well; and some, like Jane, felt consumed to succeed. A number were satisfied just to "muddle along" because their work was not that important to them to expect more of it. Just as the men's different meanings of friendship may have obscured discovering many commonly shared character strengths, so women's diverse meanings of vocation may have clouded finding any shared character strengths among women satisfied with their work.

Understanding why men and women succeed is never as simple as surveys and my kind of statistical analyses suggest. I wondered if women whose vocational identities were similar to their traditional nurturing ones might not share more common character strengths. I was right. Both male and female elementary and secondary school teachers who view their work as a calling that they enjoy describe themselves differently than those who are dissatisfied with their jobs.[15] They are reliably more androgynous, and, as I expected, their interpersonal femininity is most pronounced in the satisfied female teachers. Compared with women who are less satisfied with teaching, they are reliably more sensitive to others' needs, more compassionate, more understanding, and so on. The nurturing demands of fields like teaching, social work, nursing, and other historically feminine vocations are good examples of how the special demands of different professions can override some of the more general character strengths required to succeed vocationally.

Jane succeeded not only in earning a lot of money, being a superb entrepreneurial leader, and creating a satisfying calling but also in being judged by her colleague to adjust well to the demands of her entrepreneurial role and fulfill her own needs and talents at the same time. Since I had extensive evaluations from Jane's and the others' colleagues about how well they adapted to the special demands of their work, I could ask, "Do men and women who colleagues believe are vocationally successful share similar character strengths?" (A26).

Colleagues' Beliefs About Vocationally Successful Men and Women

What our colleagues believe to be the critical strengths necessary for us to succeed has important practical consequences. Obviously, we need to know what special strengths our colleagues expect us to have. Individual organizations and vocations have their own peculiar criteria for success. Some colleges expect their faculty to do research of international distinction; others are thankful if they do any at all. Some expect superior teaching; many only expect few student complaints. As a teacher, I know that most students are remarkably oblivious of the mind and character strengths they need to do well not just in school but in their future adult roles as well. I also know that most faculty are remarkably adept at obscuring what strengths students need to do well in their classrooms.

Sometimes we and our colleagues agree that we are successful, as the study showed is most often the case. However, sometimes we disagree, bruisingly so. We may feel good about our work as a minister, teacher, or manager; our parishioners, students, or bosses may not. All of us know the results of such differences: deep hurts, wounded pride, appeals, fights, lawsuits.

Women feel they have suffered another practical consequence. They have argued for years that they must meet different and higher standards of success than men in order to reap the same rewards. I asked, "Is the deck called 'success' stacked against women? Do they have to outdo men, as Jane and other women claim?"

The study also enabled me to ask if there are *general* character strengths necessary to succeed in our colleagues' eyes that cut across different high-level vocations. Men and women whom colleagues rate to be well adapted vocationally are more satisfied with their vocations and more psychologically mature than those they rate to be poorly adjusted and unfulfilled in their work. Their peers rate them to be also highly ethical (A31) and androgynous. Successful men and women have healthy doses of both sex's typical strengths. As the list below shows, in the eyes of the women's colleagues (two-thirds of whom were women), successful women are masculine but not unredeemably so; their decisiveness, self-sufficiency, assertiveness, and competitiveness must be tempered by feminine strengths like compassion.[16] Successful men are warm and (not listed below) loyal, gentle, yielding, affectionate, and eager to soothe hurt feelings; they are *not* wimps. Intriguingly, in their colleagues' eyes, successful males do not have to fulfill the American stereotype that to succeed they must be forceful, aggressive, competitive, and dominant. Do their colleagues find such typical macho males, like Bruce Jackson, too irritatingly abrasive to work with?

You may be weary reading another list of the strengths you need to succeed, but it provokes more fundamental questions about the meaning of success for men and women. If you want to find out how well you stack up against those whom colleagues think highly of, rate yourself on my infamous five-point scales for each of the following strengths. I list here only the ten most important ones and in the notes the more prominent remaining ones.[17]

The character traits of women and men judged to be most successful by their colleagues follow, in rough declining order of importance.

Women	*Men*
Fulfilling their potential	Being viewed as authorities
Honest	Adaptable

Decisive	Energetic
Self-sufficient	Respected
Feminine	In control of their lives
Open and self-disclosing	Purposeful
Self-confident	Warm
Assertive	Accepting of their way of life
Competitive	Realistic in their judgments
Compassionate	Having leadership ability
	Twenty-one other traits, primarily interpersonal feminine ones

The complete list tells me three things. First, success from our colleagues' point of view requires a number of varied character strengths, regardless of whether one is an actress, college admissions director, or founder of an electronics firm. If I had listed the other reliably judged strengths, I would have mentioned numerous interpersonal ones, particularly for the men.

Second, in the eyes of the vocational world, successful men are seen to have quite a few more strengths than successful women. Their colleagues reliably rated them to share almost a third of the 100 personality strengths they rated; the women's colleagues only 18 percent. Is this because a man's Number 1 Self has always been anchored to his vocation? Only recently have more women's identities been expanding to include vocational success, which provides them with the opportunity, the playing field, so to speak, to develop their latent strengths. We saw a comparable finding for women who succeeded maritally, who had to have so many more strengths. The results may reflect centuries of developing the character appropriate to our traditional sexual roles.

Third, surprising to me, successful men and women share *few* common strengths, even though they both are more androgynous, particularly feminine. Clearly, for men to succeed they must be respected as strong, purposeful leaders who give the impression that they are in control. But they had also better come across to their colleagues as loyal, gentle, even lovable and caring. The evidence is consistent. The men whose colleagues believe are really fulfilled and competent in their work are interpersonally feminine; most typical masculine attributes are more or less irrelevant to their judged success.

Women may be right when they sense that they are held to different standards of success than men, though from these findings I cannot say the standards are more rigorous. Women cannot shake hands limply either, but their firmness and decisiveness must be noticeably integrated with their femininity. If you are a woman and ask me for a prescription about how to succeed in your colleagues' eyes, I will say, "Be assertively competitive but 'lightly' so. Be cheerful, caring, and understanding. But don't swear. Leave the 'damns' and 'shits' at home." (Please don't think me sexist for reporting what may be the reality of a currently sexist work world.) However, some women, like Jane, feel they must outdo men if they are to succeed. Jane said of her work that it had made her "a little harder, tougher, less feminine. . . . A man has authority with other men. A woman has to earn it their way. I'm no longer gullible. I don't take any nonsense. I have a backbone now."

Do women who are viewed by others as successful vocationally really believe as Jane did that they must "earn it" the men's way? Yes. Without question! The successful women, as judged by their colleagues, described themselves on the 100 personality items to be sternly masculine and autonomous. Just the persons who would drive a truck to New York and barricade their supplier's loading platform: self-sufficient, decisive, self-reliant, in control of themselves, assertive, and willing to stand up for their strong convictions.[18] From their view, they shared only two warmer feminine traits: tenderness and other-centeredness. The judges, however, also saw them to be compassionate, open persons sensitive to the needs of others. Jane saw herself as strong, decisive, and autonomous but not as sympathetic, compassionate, and sensitive to the needs of others. Her colleague agreed that she was a strong and forceful leader, but he also saw her as compassionate, sympathetic, understanding, and sensitive to the needs of others.

We have seen that men who feel good about their work are more typically masculine than men who are judged by their colleagues to be successful. And now we see that women whose

colleagues see them as successful describe themselves to be masculine though their colleagues have a much mellower view of
them. Could it be that ambitious men and women are blinded
by the American myth that success demands they be typically
competitive, aggressive, dominant, and forceful? Could it be
that men and women eager "to prove themselves" and "be a great
success" push themselves in what they believe to be the successful male way to win, when in their colleagues' eyes it is important to be also interpersonally gracious and mature?

Does the discrepancy suggest that the career woman may not
have created a healthy integrated identity yet? In searching for
a mature identity, she may exaggerate or overdevelop her more
"masculine" and autonomous qualities, suppress her potential
"feminine" interpersonal strengths, and so risk not achieving
vocational success in her colleagues' eyes. Jane apparently had
avoided this trap. She succeeded in making a lot of money, being a good leader, enjoying her work, *and* being viewed as a
success by her colleague.

It is now time for another capsule of the principal results I
hope you will agree are important to remember. Given the
conflict many feel about succeeding in their vocational and intimacy relationships, I shall conclude this part with some reflections about their relationship.

17

Reflections on Vocation and Intimacy

When speaking of vocational success, we must be clear about what we mean by "success." Different kinds, such as a good income, leadership, and our or others' satisfaction with our vocational adaptation, do not always go together. Just because your colleague makes more money than you does not mean she enjoys her work more. When we succeed in all of these different ways, as Jane Allen had, we are likely to be more competent in our other adult roles, happier, and more androgynous (though more masculine than feminine) than persons who do not succeed in as many ways in their work.

To succeed in any specific vocational way requires much more than sheer talent; success depends upon many rich and varied character strengths. Maturity contributes in a major way to vocational success, though more for men than women. Androgynous strengths also contribute to our success. More masculine ones contribute most to making a lot of money and being a leader; more feminine interpersonal ones contribute to our colleagues' rating us to be well adapted vocationally.

Our income tells little about us. How much a good income contributes to our happiness, familial success, and health is debatable. Anonymous, brief surveys of heterogeneous groups of persons suggest it goes along with many good things in living: better health, less stress, happier marriages, and greater job satisfaction. In-depth longitudinal studies suggest, however, that income may not be such an elixir. At least for professionals and managers, income provides no clue about how much they like their work.

To become leaders, both boys and girls need to nurture androgynous character strengths, again especially masculine ones, but both must also develop feminine interpersonal skills. The character necessary to be a leader seems to be more integral to a male's than a female's historic character. A male's potential leadership strengths are better integrated with his adult maturity and so competence in other areas of his life.

When our work is a calling, we enjoy work more than if it is just a job. Work is a calling when it integrates our deepest needs and best talents and provides us the opportunity to continue to grow throughout our lives.

Vocationally happy men and women are mature, because they have the maturity to create satisfying vocations for themselves. For males, vocational satisfaction is more clearly and closely integrated with other aspects of their personalities and competence than it is for females — at least at this moment in women's history. Women's vocational satisfaction seems to be more ambiguous and less central to their identities as females. Men satisfied with their work are viewed by their peers to be typically masculine; women similarly satisfied are neither more nor less masculine or feminine than women dissatisfied with their work. Typical feminine interpersonal strengths contribute more, however, to personal fulfillment in women's traditional vocations, such as teaching.

Men and women whose colleagues believe that they are fulfilled and competent enjoy their work, are highly ethical, and are androgynous. They also are judged to be typically feminine in their interpersonal relationships, which may make them easier to get along with. Whereas a man's masculinity is irrelevant to his colleague's vote about his vocational fulfillment, a woman's isn't. Women who have integrated their masculinity with their interpersonal skills will be viewed by their colleagues as more vocationally well adapted.

For most couples, familial and vocational success are difficult to achieve at the same time. Surveys confirm Roger's belief that more men are beginning to distrust exclusive commitment to vocational success when it is so focused on money. As some of the study's men also said, their fathers' singular focus on achieving damaged their healthy growth and familial success. If true, the change in values may reflect a societal equilibrating principle hard at work preparing the groundwork for a generational change in values.

If men wish to mellow their Number 1 vocational Selves and become better marital partners, parents, and friends, they will have to grow beyond the typical masculine strengths necessary to make a lot of money and achieve leadership positions. Otherwise, vocational success of almost any variety that is too tied to masculine strengths will lead to familial, even vocational, failure, as Bill Spaulding, the CEO of his marketing consulting firm, risked.

I am troubled that not *one* of the typical masculine traits necessary for a woman to succeed vocationally contributes to how good a wife, lover, and mother she is. Some of the study's most unhappy husbands had wives who had succeeded in their vocations after I had interviewed them in their early thirties. Their wives had become so absorbed, self-sufficient, emotionally distant, and self-assertive that their husbands, while proud and respectful of their success, felt that their marriages and sex lives had dried up and died. Some men are now experiencing what wives have felt for centuries and until recently been unable to escape.

With the exception of Billie, the Millers, Jane, and a few others, most men and women had not resolved conflicts between their intimacy and vocational needs. Andy's and Marty's painfully strenuous labor to create a mutually fulfilling resolution offers hope that the conflict between career and intimacy can be resolved. They show us that to successfully integrate intimacy and vocational success within an enduring marriage will require that men and women be much more androgynously mature in the future than has been necessary in the past.

Clearly defined sexual roles within a family can have both healthy and unhealthy consequences. Specialization of role and of the underlying character that supports it, like breadwinning

men needing masculine strengths and child-raising women needing feminine strengths, makes for efficiency, creates a mutual
dependency that can make the family a more stable unit, and
provides the opportunity to develop high expertise in the role.
But such role clarity, when excessively proscriptive, can have
unhealthy effects, as the feminists have rightly charged, on both
men and women. The effects are aggravated when a society
segregates and limits the development of what it defines as inappropriate contrasexual potentials.

On the other hand, abandoning role specialization to be expert in both familial and vocational roles can cause severe stress
as well. Strain will be most acute in those who have not developed the opposite sex's strengths required to succeed in its historic
domain of competence. A family of two self-sufficient familial
and vocational experts is potentially unstable, since either can
separate more easily and still survive. The instability latent in
two-career families can be moderated by the development of
a reciprocally mutual need for each other, a need whose fulfillment is given priority by each partner. Achieving this requires
considerable maturity since the relationship will need to be re-
created continuously.

If you value for yourself or your children growing up in ways
that best prepare you or them for the varied demands of the
future, I don't think you have a choice. You should value becoming more mature and androgynous. Society will have to help
you educate children more maturely and provide the cultural
climate that values androgyny more than it does masculinity
or femininity alone. If you are a parent or teacher, don't raise
boys to be so masculine and girls so feminine that they make
fun of or suppress strengths popularly attributed to the opposite sex. They will need them for their own future success, health,
and happiness.

Living involves much more than just intimacy and vocational
success. Adults rank religious-ethical ideals, health, and happiness higher than sexual satisfaction and wealth. So I turn now
to the theme of fostering other-centeredness and well-being.
Maturing means growing beyond ourselves and our immediate self-centered interests. As religions have taught us, the road

to fulfillment and happiness leads away from narcissism toward other-centered transcendent goals and ideals. So I shall begin the next chapter by telling you about Harry Barnett and the character of men and women who contribute selflessly to their communities. Harry, one of the study's five most contributing citizens, will also show us that we don't have to overcome a crippling handicap or have destructive parents to mature and become a successful and happy person. He is what you may have been asking for: a recognizably "normal" but highly successful and happy person.

Part Four——————————————

Enhancing Other-Centeredness and Well-Being

18

Harry Barnett:
A Model Citizen

We can succeed not only as good family members, friends, and workers but also as citizens of our community, nation, and planet. As we mature we begin to extend the self's boundaries, so spontaneously and beautifully expressed by the father I quoted in Chapter Three who said, "I approach selflessness with my child more than I do at any other time. . . . I'm also now more concerned for people other than myself. You become oblivious to yourself . . . your self really drops out of your own thinking."

Growing up means, among many other things, becoming more caring and empathically other-centered, developing altruistic values, and emotionally understanding that though each of us is unique, each of us is also like everyone else. It means integrating more self-centering identities, like "I'm a Californian," or "I'm an American," or even "I'm a twentieth-century male or female" with more universal other-centering ones, like "I'm a citizen of this planet," or "I'm a Greek of Plato's time," or "I'm a crew member of 'Star Trek's *Enterprise.*" It means feeling part of a historical procession of humans and of an expanding community whose current and future welfare takes precedence over our own selfish interests and whose well-being we assume responsibility for nurturing. More immediately, it means being a contributing and responsible citizen in our larger community.

Harry Barnett is such a person. He has devoted much of his life to helping others and his community but without sacrificing

223

his family or career. He is a sterling example of the contributing citizen, which the adults I surveyed ranked eighth in importance, ahead of sexual fulfillment, same-sex friendships, leadership-power, and wealth. After introducing Harry, I shall compare him with the computer-drawn portrait of the citizen who voluntarily contributes to his or her community.

According to the objective multiple tests and peer judgments, the same that I used to select Billie, the Millers, and Jane, Harry Barnett is the study's most all-around successful and happy man who *also* is a devoted citizen. Harry is not the perfect husband, ideal lover, best father, most satisfied breadwinner, or most ethical idealist. He also is not the happiest and most fulfilled, most mature, and most androgynous man either. But if you knew all sixty-five men and I asked you to select the two or three who most successfully fulfilled *all* of their major adult roles, including their way of reaching out beyond themselves and immediate family to serve others, I think you would select Harry to be one of them.

Harry had not changed much since I had seen him thirteen years earlier: a little heavier, a little less hair, a little grayer — not unexpected for a forty-four-year-old. His stocky five-feet-ten-inch frame vibrated with his typical energy; I caught my breath keeping up with him as we raced to his new Jaguar, which he was mighty proud of. On the way to his elegant but simple home, spaciously surrounded by acres of privacy, he invited me to go flying with him. (I took a dip in his pool, instead.) He found flying his own plane relaxing and used it to visit some of the more distant nursing homes that he owned. He relied on his wife, Eloise, a physician in internal medicine at the local hospital, for advice about medical policies — and politics.

He told me during the first minutes of our interview that after our last visit he had been asked to assist running a large metropolitan nursing home where there had been "a real vacuum of leadership." Once inside he found

> an incredible array of different groups to try to pull together. A very defensive and inadequate nursing staff. An incompetent administrative staff. A medical staff that was worn out with very low self-

esteem. Just a babble. I can be decisive. I'm a fairly strong personality and leader and I had their respect because I can be diplomatic and work with a variety of people. But some of the staff couldn't even speak English.

Well, I can set priorities, see what needs to be done, and do it. I had a vision of what could be done. I'm a much better idea person than one who likes to follow up on the nitty gritty details. Anyway, I soon discovered the home wasn't what I had been told it was. It was dying from lack of community support. So against a fair amount of pressure and some threatened abuse, I took on the City Council to force it to give more support to the home or close it down. It closed it down.

But I learned a lot about my administrative skills. And since then I have bought into eight nursing homes, am president of our corporation, and am becoming increasingly involved at the state level in legislative policy.

Later in the interview I asked, "What are your strongest convictions, the sources of your energy?" Harry said, "I have a high sense of trying to do right by my fellow man. I have a deep concern for the needs and rights of others. I have a deep concern for the rightness and wrongness of things. The morality of a situation."

Harry and Eloise had been happily married twenty-three years and had two adolescent children, an older son, Rusty, and younger daughter, Sally. His kinetic energy in his vocation and community activities—he was president of the Chamber of Commerce, served on several boards, and had received state recognition for his contributions—did not carry over into his relationship with Eloise. I asked her what the best things were about her marriage and what one thing she wished that she could change about Harry. Without hesitating, she said, "Our companionship, closeness, affection, and children. But I want him to be more compulsive about getting things done."

Surprised, I asked, "Compulsive? You mean about his work?"

Eloise replied, "No. Here. He doesn't get things done around here. He assumes I'll do them. He is very organized and he is very relaxed. He doesn't run a compulsively organized business the way some people do. He's very effective [deep sigh, almost of resignation]. But if only . . . he's very patient and very flexible. No . . . not flexible but very willing to go along with what I want if I take the lead. He's a very good father, concerned about the children." On her criteria of what made a good parent, she rated Harry to be higher than she on patience, consistency, self-confidence, and loving; she saw herself as more unselfish.

When asked how much he enjoyed being a parent, Harry checked "Nearly always," and to the question of whether he had ever wished that he could be free from a parent's responsibilities, he replied, "No." His fondest wish to see fulfilled before he died was "to see my children happy and successful."

"Why?" I asked. Harry answered,

> I suppose because of a deep feeling that I have about the kids. The sense of their worth and ability and the tremendous obligation I feel to provide what it takes for them to use their abilities. We both feel very lucky to have two very bright and able kids. . . . I think what would probably blow my computer most would be if . . . it's my selfish side . . . for them not to be successful and happy. That would be one of the hardest things for me to be able to cope with. Gets back to those feelings of their potential worth. How much that means to me. I'd feel a certain personal loss and responsibility.

This is Harry: a strong, solid, all-around successful man committed to serving others.

To learn what it was about Harry that was also true of successful community leaders more generally, another judge and I agreed in ordering the men's and women's increasing community involvement from 1 to 8. We defined it by how consistently they had volunteered to work for nonpaying community and professional groups in the past decade; their level of responsible activities assumed; the number of different community and professional activities served; and local or national recognition for their contributions (A4g).

Twenty percent of the men and 25 percent of the women, including Jane Allen, had not volunteered to serve others or been elected to a leadership position in their communities or professions within the preceding ten years. Andy and Billie scored about average: Andy scored 4 for, among other things, his political campaign and civil rights activities; Billie got a 5 for her election to national conferences and her city's mayoral commission on the handicapped; Marty received a 7 for her work with the peace and civil rights movements, NOW, and other extensive feminist activities. Harry was rated an 8 — one of the five most involved in their communities and professions. Another one of the five had received a prestigious national award for extraordinary service; another had been chairman of numerous nonprofit community boards and a United Fund drive as well as a faithful participant in local school and church activities.

The computer-drawn portrait of exemplary contributing citizens, like Harry, pictured four themes: They tended to enjoy being parents; they competently fulfilled their other adult roles; they were judged to be ethically sensitive, optimistic, idealistic, and principled leaders; and they were androgynous, particularly masculine (though the contributing women were also seen as interpersonally skilled, given their loyalty, compassion, and sympathy).

Doesn't this portrait of the person who contributes to others make sense to you? Might not the seeds of wanting to contribute to our community sprout first in caring for our immediate families? Enjoying being a parent — one of the more demanding and selfless roles an adult assumes — reflects and nurtures an other-centered and giving character. With such a character, it is not that big a step to want to give to our larger family — our community. Erikson calls this the stage of generativity in our lives and claims that it contributes to our adult maturing.[1] I found also that men who became fathers continued to mature more than married men who remained childless.[2]

It is also not surprising that those who contribute to their communities have the coping strengths plus extra energy and time to initiate other activities and take on other responsibilities. Harry is a fine example. He not only knew how to manage and get things done but he radiated energy — lots of it. Remember that energy available for new interests and commitments is a visible sign of a person's maturity — Harry was more mature than 85 percent of the other men. He had the character resources to succeed in his principal adult roles.

Those who select persons for responsible positions know intuitively to note how they have extended themselves into their communities. Clarke Williams, CEO of Century Telephone Enterprises, said, in speaking of the persons he prefers to hire, that being a good citizen is a "very good sign of character. . . . If you hire someone whose head is in the sand on the outside, you'll probably find that his head is in the sand on the inside." He is reaffirming a principal finding of the study: We carry our competence and success from one role to another because they manifest our underlying character.

To give our time and energy so generously to others must certainly be nourishingly renewed by enduring idealistic commitments and hopes that we can make a difference. Harry's colleague gave him top scores for his ethical sense and commitment to ideals and principles. Harry also told us this when he said that he had a "high sense of trying to do right by my fellow man" and "deep concern" for "the morality of a situation."

The androgynous and masculine character of male and female community leaders is predictable. You could infer from my description of Harry that he was androgynous, scoring higher than all but 15 percent of the study's men. His androgyny was due more to his feminine interpersonal skills, however, than to his masculine ones (the judges rated him to have more interpersonal skills than six out of ten of the other men).

The research has amply showed us that men and women who succeed in the traditional roles that historically have been their principal responsibility share a defined and coherent character. Women whose partners were maritally happy had many shared strengths; their husbands did not. Men most satisfied with their vocations also shared many strengths among themselves; the women did not.

Community leadership roles have been the province of males for centuries, so it is not remarkable that the male community leaders shared almost three times more strengths in common than the female leaders did.[3] They were happy and fulfilled and had been so since adolescence. (This was not true of the women who contributed a great deal.) Harry was the second most consistently happy and productive man of the group; he had functioned at the same high level of mood and achievement ever since he graduated from college. Men like Harry, who are deeply and responsibly involved in their communities, are mature, particularly in their stability and autonomy. They are energetic, self-confident, decisive, calm, self-controlled, and resilient. They also accurately understand themselves (A13a). Indispensable to a good leader is the ability to understand empathically how others see them. The men but not the women community leaders excelled in this strength (A13b). Overall, the men who contribute to others are healthier, both mentally and physically, than men whose heads are "in the sand" (A29).

As I said earlier, I had not anticipated how pervasively traditional sexual roles shape our character and contribute to our success in so many areas of our lives. I might not have been so surprised by this result if I had been a woman. Feminists have told us that persons who are in a subordinate or oppressed position, as women have been since Eve, are more sensitive to how their prescribed roles affect their behavior.[4] I don't know if and how the changing sexual roles of women will affect their historic feminine character and their future community leadership opportunities. Will studies of successful middle-aged women thirty years hence fail to replicate some of the differences I have found? Or will women's historical character limit how successfully they will adapt to the changing demands of their adult roles? Young women now think about work and careers and wrestle with what their Number 1, 2, and 3 Selves will be much earlier than their mothers ever did (some perhaps never did). More now begin their adult years as breadwinners rather than as mothers. Will they develop as clear and defined a masculine-

type character as men? Or will they come up against some biologically and historically rooted feminine character traits and
needs that tell them that their calling is to be a mother? Or as
we move into a tighter and tighter interdependent vocational
and political world, will their interpersonal skills become more
necessary and open the door for a new type of vocational person to step through? Community and public leadership positions are now much more available to women, even in rural
downeast Maine, where women are tax assessors and town
"selectmen." Will women leaders begin to develop a more sharply
defined and shared character that in turn will facilitate their further movement into such positions?

One of the stronger shared strengths of both men and women
who voluntarily serve others is a deep and principled ethical
sense, grounded on a religious commitment for some, though
not for Harry. The next chapter explores what the study's men
and women tell us about the character of religious and ethical
persons.

19

Religious and
Virtuous Individuals

Both religion and virtue have lost their centrality in American culture and political life in the past decades. Religion has become secularized for many, even profaned by our TV evangelists. "Virtue" has become another one of those old-fashioned words, like "calling" and, increasingly, "sin," "salvation," and "grace," that adolescents tell me they've never heard of. Does a religious faith still contribute to success, health, and happiness as early Americans believed? Does old-fashioned virtue still pay off in the long run, as religion has promised, in this day of Wall Street greed, political chicanery, Irangate deceptions, congressional meanness, and on and on?

Religion Is for God, Not Success and Happiness

I have been wondering lately what is left for religion to give us. Religion's symbols used to provide hope. I am not sure they still do for more and more Americans — they did for only a few of the study's men and women. I am sometimes asked, "Is a religious faith necessary to be healthy and happy?" Because the topic had not been thoroughly researched, I used to reply, "I don't know." Now, I have a glimmer that the answer is, "Traditional religious faith is not necessary to be healthy and happy, but it sure helps some."

We do not know what we should about the question because

researchers do not agree about how to measure "religious faith."
I will avoid that theological quagmire; I remember the discussions I once had as the research consultant to the former Academy of Religion and Mental Health. Although we were sympathetic to religion's potential to enhance our well-being, neither
I nor the other researchers of the time could agree on any *one*
measure of religion's rich meanings.[1]

Years of studies have shown that conventional signs of religiosity, such as attending church, reciting prayers, reading the
Bible, signing pledge cards, and reaffirming a statement of faith,
tell little about a person's well-being or personality. The practicing devout may be just as serene, healthy, and fulfilled as
the nonpracticing believer, agnostic, or atheist — or just as tor-
tured, wracked by doubts, and insane. At this moment, I am
mindful of what Job's trial taught us about God. Job was a good
man, of great rectitude, devoted to God. With God's consent,
Satan inflicted every imaginable suffering, pain, and disaster
on Job to test the depth of his faith in God. Despite Job's la-
ments about why he was being punished so cruelly, he did not
abandon God. Though God eventually "gave Job twice as much
as he had before," even a life of 140 years, Job teaches me that
we go to church, read the Bible, and pray to know God better,
not to receive a jigger of healthiness or a fix of happiness. God
can't be bribed by our goodness.

Just how religious were the men and women? Was religion
a source of hope to them? Were the more religious men and
women happier and healthier persons? A widely used test of
a person's values (A15), as well as numerous questionnaire and
interview items (A4h), showed them not to be traditionally religious or to rely on religion for hope. Though the women were
reliably more religious than the men, both valued traditional
religious beliefs and institutions less than, say, the life of the
mind, beauty, the marketplace, or service to others. When they
entered college, the men had been as religious as their typical
seventeen-year-old peers; but whatever the cause, by their early
thirties, they had become reliably less so than when they were
teenagers.

By their mid-forties, few in the interview spontaneously cited
religion to be a source of hope as Table 19.1 shows.

Table 19.1. Attitudes Toward Religion.

	% of Men	% of Women
Religion is my main source of hope and energy.	8	15
Religion provides a reason to live these days.	2	10
Religion sustains my hope.	22	29
My strongest convictions are religious.	5	15

Religion provided sustenance to a few. Betty, who led daily Bible study groups, reminds us how nourishing a religious belief can be to our hope. When asked, "What is your primary source of hope?" she responded simply, "I know that all things that touch my life come from the hand of God, so there is a purpose in everything we face and in all of our relationships with people."

Jim Pryor, imprisoned for his anthropological filming indiscretions, was the second most religious man and most religiously articulate person of the 105 men and women. He replied to the following questions:

What are your main sources of hope?
I know inwardly that feelings of despair are merely self-illusions. . . . It is as if God is constantly going into hiding. "Can you find me? When you find me you will experience the warmest embrace imaginable because my nature is a loving one."

Why live in days of such despair?
The blessing of life is its opportunity for adventure and discovery, and the very involvement in this process of creation and discovery is . . . to feel one is making a contribution to a movement that has unlimited meaning and value.

Do religion or other beliefs sustain hope for you?
To the extent to which one unburdens one's self of all ordinary religious, political, social hopes and beliefs, one will come into touch with reality that is so fundamental that it cannot be shaken by any opinion or result. Real value is imperishable and

immaculate, complete, full, and absolutely hopeful and trustworthy. . . . Ordinary beliefs in fact
keep you asleep.

What are your strongest convictions?
There is an intelligence that includes my own and
uses my own that far surpasses anything personal
of my own. It has absolute power and is absolutely
beneficent with respect to my life and the welfare
of the entire cosmos. I need only cooperate with
this higher force and my welfare and happiness are
assured.

Do you have any doubts why he adapted so serenely to his
five years in a federal prison and became the leader of his fellow inmates? So religion, as history has shown us for centuries,
can aid individuals to transcend desolation and sorrow and
ground them to an absolute and beneficent source of hope.

When I turned to the entire group of men and women for
insights about religion, success, and happiness, I had to conclude that religion is for devotion to some transcendent purpose or god, not for success and happiness. Are traditionally
religious, church-going, and devout persons more successful than
the nonreligious? No. More healthy and happy? No. Do they
share any common familial or parental traits? Practically none.

Nevertheless, the few results provide some tantalizing ideas
to ponder. The differences between the more and less religious
individuals' personalities affirm religion's potential hope. Religious women and men are seen by their peers to be virtuous,
idealistic, and understanding persons of strong convictions. The
religious women are judged to be mature (A13e), self-confident,
optimistic, reflective persons who, like Betty, stand up for and
defend their beliefs without apology. The religious men are more
feminine, especially in their interpersonal skills. Like Jim Pryor,
the religious man is loved by others who view him as gentle,
sensitive to their needs, and eager to soothe their hurt feelings.

The last tantalizing hint about traditionally religious persons
is that for the only time in the study, a positive adult outcome

may be rooted in an unfavorable family background (A1a). The hints are few but consistent. The religious men's and women's fathers had been either remote and withdrawn or absorbed in themselves; the men, in particular, reported that they had needed their fathers to depend upon. Had God become the father they desired but never had when younger?

The answer to the question about religion's contribution to our health and happiness is: "Traditional religious beliefs and commitments contribute to some individuals' well-being; they are *not* necessary to succeed and be healthy and happy." The answer did not surprise me. Other researchers of religion's contribution to our well-being had alerted me to its probability.[2] The peccadillos of the TV evangelists Bakker and Swaggart remind us that professed faith and practice not rooted in and consistently integrated with our character can even destroy us.

I pursued the question by exploring religion's handmaiden: virtue.

Virtue Pays Off

For many, religion's meaning is found not in what we profess but in how we actually live ethical and therefore virtuous lives committed to transcendent values or ideals. The study's religious women and men, like Betty and Jim, were highly ethical, but the ethically committed ones, like Billie, the Millers, and Harry, were not necessarily religious. When asked about the strongest convictions that gave them hope and energy, more than a third described *only* a humanistic ethical ideal that valued goodness in others and their responsibility to nurture it and to create a better society.

- I want to turn out strong, moral, hopeful children.
- I believe in the essential goodness of human beings.
- I am not here just for myself; I draw my vitality by being helpful and valuable to others.
- I conduct a personal continuing inquiry into the meaning of life and the ultimate good of society and how to achieve it.

- The world can be improved and everyone must join in to make it a better place.
- I have faith in you and me.

I can make five fairly firm assertions about virtuous persons.

First, sensitivity to ethical issues and holding ideals are highly valued by most as essential to living.

Second, measuring who is and who is not virtuous is a more troublesome procedure than I anticipated, and its result may explain why we know so little about the character of ethical persons.

Third, virtuous men and women are indeed more successful, happy, and healthy than unethical ones. Unquestionably, old-fashioned virtue does pay off in most of the good things of life.

Fourth, ethics and ideals are rooted in our character, particularly the strengths typical of other-centered, stable, and autonomous persons.

Fifth, it may be easier for women than men to be virtuous because virtue is rooted in feminine interpersonal strengths.

Ethical Qualities Are Highly Valued. Americans highly value being ethical and idealistic despite ceaselessly appearing examples of unethical and cynical behavior: the dishonest gaminess of political TV ads, daily revelations of premier companies like Unisys and General Electric bilking the Defense Department, illustrious senators on "the take," and surveys reporting that the majority of California high school students cheat and don't care if others do.[3]

Ethical ideals ranked fifth in importance in my informal survey of several thousand adults. When I ask teachers to name the five most important strengths their students need to be effective adults in the future, they always include honesty and integrity. The study's men and women spontaneously identified the virtues necessary to succeed in their principal adult roles, values that religions have advocated for centuries: honesty, compassion, integrity, dedication, and commitment.

When we study a group of exceptionally good and effective

men and women, we discover that their peers rate them to be
honest, deeply ethical, and principled persons of high integrity.
Their colleagues rate their integrity and ethical practices to be
the most distinctive of thirty vocational strengths. With the exception of Jim Pryor and one man who had been in jail overnight for an alcoholic binge, none had been troubled by the law.

Measuring Ethical Character Is Ambiguous. How we measure an attribute is the only meaning researchers can attach to
it. Because of the confusion about what "ethical" means, I must
tell you how I ordered the men and women from most to least
in ethical maturity. As you know, I have not been content with
research that relies solely on self-reports about one's effectiveness and does not go out into the "real world" to get independent measures of how persons actually function. Well, for the
first time in the study, the "real world" let me down. Not only
did the judges not agree among themselves, but the men's and
women's descriptions of their honesty, for example, did not agree
well with those of their peers.[4] Why? I thought of Jesus' comments about hypocrites and then of the Swaggarts and Bakkers.
Their TV viewers would have rated them to be most righteous
and upright exemplars of honesty, integrity, and principled commitment, but both knew differently. Or consider James Wright,
the deposed speaker of the House. He told us he had not done
anything illegal or "unethical"; he had not intended to skirt the
House's ethical rules. Remember Edwin Meese, Reagan's chief
of staff and later head of the Justice Department, who also
vigorously insisted that he had not done anything illegal or unethical when he assisted in getting a friend of his a lucrative
government contract. Others claimed that Wright and Meese
had. What did others see that Wright and Meese didn't see?
Or what did Wright and Meese see that most of us didn't see?

The lessons are several. Any study of ethical persons cannot
ignore their own view of their moral maturity, nor can it dismiss the views of others. It must also be clear in its definition
of the meaning of "ethical."

How could such issues be untangled to measure objectively
who was and was not virtuous? To clarify what I wanted to mea-

sure, I used the model of maturity's guidelines about value maturity described in Chapter Three. Mature persons are aware of
their values, which are other-centered, integrated, stable, and
autonomous (A14). These strengths predispose us to be honest,
compassionate persons of integrity who courageously stand up
for principled commitments and ideals.[5] Think of Harry courageously fighting the city council to support the city's nursing
home. Think of Marty fighting for her feminist beliefs. I combined measures of the participants' own ratings of their value
maturity with their peers' ratings of their honesty, depth of ethical
sense, and so on to get a measure of their overall virtue (A31).

Virtue Brings Success, Health, and Happiness. Are ethically
mature, idealistically committed men and women successful,
healthy, and happy? Are those who said about their strongest
convictions "I don't have any," "I really don't know," "I like to
use power and enjoy while here," "I am motivated by dollars
to be successful," and "I believe only in myself" less healthy and
happy than those who affirmed the worth of others and the desire
to help them and create a better world?

The answer is "yes." Virtue pays off royally in success, health,
and happiness.

Virtuous men and women succeed in all of their principal
adult roles. They are good marital partners, competently fulfilling all of their various marital responsibilities, and they feel
fulfilled as parents. They are also good lovers, both by their own
and their partners' signs of a good lover. The virtuous men and
women are also comfortable openly sharing almost anything with
their close friends (A8). Finally, they are mature, physically and
emotionally healthy persons. No wonder they are happy and
fulfilled and seen by their peers to be living a full and satisfying
life. If I had taken a slightly less rigorous stance about what
results I would accept as probably true, I would also have said
that virtuous men and women are rated to be great friends by
their friends (A26), are responsibly and extensively involved in
serving their communities (A4g), and have mature children
(A17). Virtuous men are also vocationally well adapted and
viewed as such by their colleagues. But this is not true of virtu-

ous women, probably because the meaning of work differed so much among them.

Regardless of how I measured "virtue," it is clear that it does *not* bring higher incomes—just good health, happiness, and self-fulfillment in the long run (A29).

It is no mystery why being a virtuous person pays off in success and happiness. How do you feel if your lover or children are dishonest, duplicitous, untrustworthy, and selfish? Or if you had a colleague who cheated, lacked integrity, was sociopathic, and stabbed you in the back? Or if you have a friend who is too morally insensitive to know when he is transgressing? Unethical people just create a great deal of pain and misery for others and eventually for themselves. They must always be on guard to protect themselves from discovery or suffer the pain and misery that guilt provokes. I do not recommend Reverend Dimsdale as a model to live by if you rank happiness and health as high priorities for your life.

Virtue Is Rooted in Our Character. Our ideals spring out of our character. So do our ethics. Virtue is not a pleasing garment to put on and take off at will—it is part of us. The men and women recognized this truism when they spontaneously described what kept them going on down days: "There is something internal to my character," "I am not the pessimistic type," "I am an eternal optimist," "I have a tremendous amount of energy I have not yet begun to tap." They sensed what I found.

Perhaps you would like to match yourself against the more outstanding traits that virtuous men and women share in common. If you are virtuous, you are, above all else, psychologically mature. You are a cheerful optimist, hopeful, decisive, energetic, and reliable. Your peers also see you as sympathetic, tender, open, and loyal. Intriguingly, and perhaps because of your self-confidence, you seek out new experiences and are willing to playfully take risks to continue growing.

Some character strengths appear more visibly in virtuous men than women or in women than men. If you are a virtuous man, you are cooperative, gentle, understanding, and sensitive to other persons' needs. Because you feel in control of yourself, others see you as calm and not easily upset by stress. If you are a virtuous woman, you are an autonomous individual, willing to learn new things and stand up for what you believe.

So hope — having ideals, principles, and ethical maturity — is firmly rooted in our personality, especially in feminine interpersonal strengths for both men and women and also some masculine ones for women. Again, just as we saw for successful men and women, each virtuous person has developed the strengths typical of the opposite sex.

Virtue May Be Easier for Women Than Men. Have you ever wondered why it is males who usually get into trouble from kindergarten on? Why are our jails packed with about 85 percent males and only 15 percent females? Who more often bribes, fights, steals, rapes, and whores around? Will the ratio of males to females who get into trouble change as women get an equal opportunity to bribe and sleep around? I am sure there is no one simplistic answer to my question. But I have three clues that suggest it may be easier for the typical woman to be virtuous.

Clue number 1 is that virtuous men (and women, too) are clearly understanding, sensitive to others' needs, sympathetic, and have all the other interpersonal strengths that typically describe women. Jim Pryor's friends and colleagues gave him top scores for being an ethical person; he ranked fourth among the sixty-five men in understanding, sensitivity to others' needs, and other similar interpersonal strengths. Since men are often not raised to have such feminine interpersonal traits, they may have to work harder to be virtuous.

Clue number 2 is that the men's peers saw them as a group to be reliably less sympathetic, compassionate, sensitive to another's needs, understanding, and so on than the women's peers rated the women to be. Do virtues like honesty, integrity, and a deep ethical sense grow out of the more "feminine" quality of our relationships with others? If so, then women may be more predisposed with the character to be virtuous.

Clue number 3 is that the men thought of themselves (and

their colleagues agreed) as less ethical and idealistic than the women rated themselves to be. I wondered if this might be because "real" men find "ethics" irrelevant to their principal identities. Somewhat playfully, I created a macho index that combined the judges' ratings of the core attributes of the historical American male, as Tocqueville described him 175 years ago: forceful, self-sufficient, dominant, masculine, aggressive, and competitive. The answer to my question is "yes." The macho male may or may not be very ethical; his maleness does not contribute anything to being ethical. (Incidentally, macho males succeed in only two ways: They are perceived by their peers to be leaders who enjoy using power and making a lot of money. Aren't these the areas that virtue seems to be most egregiously lacking in these days?)

So could it be that being virtuous comes easier to women than to men because, for whatever biosocial reasons, they are more attuned to their relationships with others? Do men have to work harder to develop, if not their consciences, the values that will govern their relationships with others? Are males of other cultures, like the Balinese, who are raised to be gentle, kind, and sensitive, as ethical and idealistic as females of those cultures? I don't know.

You may now be asking what some implications are of the result that the well-spring of virtue is a person's character. Three come to mind immediately.

Only if transcendent religious beliefs, like a belief in God, are deeply internalized in virtuous ways of getting along with others will they contribute much to our success, health, and happiness. Signing a pledge card just won't do it, unless we have ethical characters already.

Second, if you wish to raise your children or educate students to be virtuous, do not settle on a sermon, morning prayer, or flag salute. Instead, create a home, school, and classroom that enhance the maturation of character, especially the kind of interpersonal strengths that apparently support virtue.

Third, if George Bush had been serious about wanting a "kinder and gentler" nation, then he should have selected women, like his wife Barbara, to be his vice-president, secretary of war, and a majority of other cabinet positions.

We have seen that men and women who succeed in their adult roles and are virtuous are happy and healthy persons. The book's next three chapters directly examine the character of persons' health and happiness, which are adults' two most highly valued goals.

20

A Toast to
Good Health and Happiness

Chapter One previewed five themes that course through the lives of actualized and successful men and women. I have focused on four so far: their generalized competence in living, psychological maturity, androgyny (particularly their feminine interpersonal skills), and virtue. Although I have alluded to the fifth theme, health and happiness, only now are we ready to examine it systematically. Recall that Maslow likened us to multifaceted crystals. We have concluded examining our principal facets, such as our roles as partners, lovers, and citizens. Although each facet has its special character, it also reflects the crystal's principal organizing properties. As I begin to examine the state of the crystal itself, you can probably anticipate what the men and women will tell us about their well-being. The chapter summarizes what I have learned about the state of the whole person.

The adults who ranked the twelve values that you also ranked in Chapter One prized happiness and good health most highly. The study's men and women also valued happiness and health highly, even more for their children than for themselves. Of the ten wishes I asked Marty to list that she wanted to fulfill before she died, her first was, "to have raised healthy, happy, strong kids." Andy, after maintaining his "good health until the end" and a "good relationship with Marty," wrote, "to see my children grow into mature adults." Billie's answer was, "My children can do whatever they want to do." Jane's was, "to see my

243

children successful." And Harry wrote, "to see my children happy and successful." Their wishes remind me of our American right to life and the liberty to pursue happiness.

But what are good health and happiness? How do we tell who is healthy and happy and how to achieve these results? These are more slippery and subjective questions to ask than "Who is a successful parent, lover, or physician?" At least I can eventually find out objectively how the men's and women's children turn out, count how many lovings they have each month, and ask their colleagues to rate their competence.

Physicians and psychologists — philosophers too — trip over the meaning of good health and happiness. Rather than talking of health, physicians describe symptoms of its absence. Rather than talking about mental health, psychologists talk about the absence of symptoms of mental illness. The National Institute of Mental *Health* should be called the National Institute of Mental *Illness*, if its budget priorities are a clue to what it means by "health." Ironically, some researchers speak of "positive mental health," as if "mental health" doesn't mean "mental *health*." Others prefer *well-being*,[1] the term I use to include both physical and mental (or psychological) health and happiness. Have you noticed that I have equated maturing with growing healthily? Because others do not accept my equation, I do not include my test of dimensional maturity in the measure of well-being (A29). Actually, the study showed that for all practical purposes, well-being and psychological maturity are the same.

Although professionals dispute what health means technically, you and I know when we feel good. We know when we're not up to par, even if physicians can't find anything wrong with us. We know if we are better or worse than we were last week or year. I can no longer race up even a few steps without pausing to catch my breath. I could, if I wanted, even plot my changing physical health from my doctor's annual cholesterol count, blood pressure readings, and dismal weight record. But I leave that up to him. We know how to improve our health. We know what smoking does to us. We struggle to eat less fat and more fiber and make our lives less stressful. We know we should assert our willpower, though most of us have trouble finding it.

Self-fulfillment and happiness are something else altogether. They are much more elusive to pin down and know what to do about than our physical, even mental, health. Only I know that I *really* feel happy or fulfilled — and sometimes I don't even know how happy I have been until I look backward in time. Climbing four thousand steps one unforgettable late afternoon on Nepal's Annapurna trail was excruciating. "Never again," I told myself. In retrospect it was a necessary element of an inexpressibly glorious, fulfilling experience. Now, I plan to go back to take an even more arduous trek.

Others who know us well feel our vibes and can tell how happy we are.[2] I gave up long ago trying to fool Harriet about how I feel. She knows when I am down. Think of someone you know well. Would you really have trouble rating how happy he or she is? Maybe you would if you used a 100-point scale, but I doubt that you would if you used the 5- or 7-point scales national surveys have used.

As Americans, we are guaranteed the right to pursue happiness — but how? Some students I know think getting money, partying three nights every weekend, and having frequent sex is the way. A mother wrote me recently she was really going to be happy when her teenager left for college. Another told me that finding Jesus made her happy. I move my winter office to Key West to escape cold feet and hands that had made me gloomy for years.

Are these the ways to happiness? To anticipate what the research told me, "no." The pursuit of happiness is not by way of seeking pleasure but by way of developing our characters. A golden parachute, a Ferrari, cocaine, or a cellar of vintage wines may give us pleasure but not happiness if we don't have the character that predisposes us to enjoy our pleasures or be happy. The signers of the Declaration of Independence should have guaranteed us "life, liberty, and the opportunity to develop a mature character," not "the pursuit of happiness," too often translated to be "the pursuit of money." My amended guarantee is not a fighting or elegant slogan, but it is much more accurate psychologically.

Because the study produced so much information about well-being, or health and happiness, I shall ruthlessly simplify what I tell you about it. After mentioning in a sentence or two how I ordered the men's and women's well-being, I shall highlight what a person's well-being predicts. Then I will describe the character of healthy and happy men and women.

Identifying Healthy and Happy Persons

So that I did not inflict my biases on the results by prejudging who were the study's healthier and happier persons, I assessed their well-being as comprehensively and objectively as possible.[3] I combined their self- and judge-ratings and measures of their physical and mental health and happiness in a way that allowed me to rank the women and men in their overall well-being[4] (A29). Among the women, Billie ranked first, Jane sixth, and Marty only seventh of the forty women, probably because she was undergoing the turmoil of therapy when I saw her. Among the men, Harry ranked fourth in overall well-being. Andy ranked third in mental health and happiness, after I had excluded the measure of his physical health because of the re-emergence of his earlier symptoms.

What Does a Person's Well-Being Predict?

Physically healthy men and women are mentally healthy.
Mentally healthy men and women are also physically healthy.
Body and spirit are really inseparable, a truism doctors of past years who used to see us in our homes knew in their bones. Specialized physicians who run us through their offices, concentrating *only* on our incontinent bladders or wavering hearts, don't seem to understand this truism.
Happy persons are physically and mentally healthy. Energy for living is not drained into preoccupations about constipation and ringing ears, or obsessive worries about children and paralyzing hangups about performing sexually in bed. Of course, unhealthy persons can transcend their bodily pains to experience serenity, perhaps even happiness. Andy's maturity enabled him to accept and adapt to his crippled leg and become one of

the happier men of the group. Good physical and mental health, however, makes it easier to create a happy life for one's self. Feeling happy may improve our health — both bodily and mentally.

Just as virtue pays off, so does well-being. Healthy and happy men and women *succeed in all of their familial roles.* They and their partners agree about their competence. They are maritally happy, successful and sexually compatible lovers, and fulfilled parents, possibly because they are open and self-disclosing. Their children are also mature for their age (A17). It is not surprising that good health and a happy disposition contribute to how well we succeed, particularly in our familial roles. Imagine playing vigorously in bed with our lover or hiking and camping with our children in between asthma attacks and arthritic pains, and unpredictable attacks of diarrhea. Living with a hypochondriac or ceaselessly suffering person can be wearying and discouraging. Or even worse, living with a morose grouch who sees every rising sun as his last can darken every day. They do provide one solace, however. They force us to find the stuff of which saints are made.

Success also contributes to good health and happiness. It strengthens our feelings of competence, self-confidence, and maturity. We feel good about ourselves and what we have done and can do. That warm glow must just do something good to our blood flow, endorphins, immune system — and spirit.

Men and women who are physically and psychologically healthy and happy have been *happy and productive persons throughout their adult lives,* which again suggests that our happiness is deeply rooted in our character. Adolescents living fully, productively, and happily are more likely to turn out to be happier when they are middle-aged than adolescents unhappily limping along on three instead of four physical and psychic cylinders.

The same principle holds true for men and women in their sixties. Sears found that those happy with their current lives were more mature and productive when adolescents.[5] We can buy pleasures like yachts and BMWs. But we can't buy happiness, unless we have the character that predisposes us to be happy while enjoying our pleasures.

The relation of well-being to vocational success is questionable

because of male and female differences. Men who succeed vocationally — regardless of how we define their success — are healthier
and happier than men who fail. This is *not* true for women who
succeed. Just because a woman earns a lot of money, holds a
major leadership position, or enjoys her work does not mean
that she is either physically healthy or happy. These differences
are even sharper when we examine the mental health of vocationally successful men and women. Vocational success or lack
of it apparently does not affect a woman's mental health.

That a woman's traditional familial role but *not* her work outside of the home predicts her well-being may trouble you. It
does me. I would like to believe that men and women can move
healthily and happily into each other's traditional roles. So I
am predisposed to reject the finding as a fluke, especially because it contradicts some surveys that find that working women
declare they are healthier and happier than nonworking women
do.[6] The finding may also be a fluke because the meaning of
"vocation" to contemporary women is so ambiguous. Or it may
well be that when women's work is a calling, as for Marty, vocational success does contribute to their well-being.

Nevertheless, the relation between a woman's well-being and
her vocation is too important and timely an issue to ignore the
possibility that full-time work may be irrelevant to her well-
being. If work outside of the home is not a reliable source of
a woman's well-being, what happens to her future health and
happiness if her traditional sources of well-being — her familial
competence and fulfillment — are diluted or only partially tapped?
Will her well-being actually decline as her intimacy relationships become less intense and less fulfilling? A number of the
study's working women struggled with just that question. Remember Alice Matthews, the pediatric physician, torn between
her career's and her children's demands and guilt about relying
on her husband so much? Others felt that their friends were slip-
ping away and bemoaned the "thinness" of their emotional and
social lives. Is success in traditional nurturing fields like teaching and nursing an easier route to well-being for feminine women? As younger women organize their identities increasingly
around career rather than intimacy roles, will their route to well-

being become more like that of men's? If so, how healthy and happy will they be in their middle and later years?

Until someone follows today's adolescent girls into middle age, we will not know if my results are due more to biological constraints or to generational differences produced by societal values about what femaleness should be.

The Character of Healthy and Happy Persons

Healthy and happy men and women are mature and androgynous. They are well integrated, stable (though not rigid), and autonomous persons, as well as optimistic, growing persons.[7] Their peers respect them for fulfilling their potentials. Such persons so accept themselves that they can freely share their feelings with others. Their self-control engenders a positive emotional attitude about living. In the language of the psychoanalyst, they have great ego strength: the strength to control their own talents, make their own decisions, and direct their own growth. Like Billie and Harry, they are in charge, "on top," of themselves.

If you teach or are interested in education, you will appreciate that the character of persons who are healthy and happy is remarkably similar to that of liberally educated men and women. Educational philosophers like Cardinal Newman, Dewey, and Whitehead assert that a liberal education should produce more autonomous persons in command of themselves and their talents. Van Doren beautifully captures the maturing character that a real education produces when he writes: "As a ruler, he has first ordered (self-integration) his own soul. As the ruled, he likewise orders his soul. . . . For without autonomy, he cannot find the center in himself (stable self) from which in fact emanate the very generosity and lawfulness, the respect for others that is a form of respect for himself, necessary to the operation of society (other-centered self)."[8]

I have been impressed by how frequently strengths like willingness to risk climbing out of our personal ruts to try new things, optimism, and feeling in control of ourselves contribute to our success and well-being. These strengths are not peculiar to my study. Similar ones contribute to recovering from debilitating illnesses,[9] as Andy demonstrated in his dogged persistence to adapt to the loss of his leg. If you asked me to prescribe how you can grow up to succeed and be happy, I'd include the following advice:

- Don't ever give in to the temptation to remain mired where you are.
- Believe you can grow up.
- Assert your will to change yourself.
- Learn how to make your mind and character work for, not against, you.
- Think "Billie, Harry, Andy, Marty, and Jane" the next time you feel stuck in your rut.

Although the characters of healthy and happy persons are similar, they are not identical, so I will describe each only briefly. Since the strengths that describe well-being are more clearly seen in the character of mentally healthy and happy persons than of physically healthy ones, I shall postpone telling you more about physically healthy men and women until the next chapter. You may find the descriptions of mentally healthy and happy persons repetitious and dense; however, I include them for those, particularly mental health professionals, who want to know the core strengths necessary to have a strong ego or be psychologically healthy.

Character of Mentally Healthy Persons. I know of no studies by other researchers of adult mental health that provide such a pure, coherent, and convincing picture of its essence.[10] Mentally healthy men and women share not only the core strengths of well-being but also several additional mature ones. Maturely stable and autonomous persons are not only the decisive, self-determining, growing persons I just described, but they are also energetic, self-confident, and self-reliant. They have a strong sense of themselves, so are not easily hurt by others' barbs and attacks. Harry's peers agreed that he was a good example. Most conspicuously, he was predictable, open to new ideas, not stuck in a rut, and dealt cheerfully and calmly with the stresses of his high-powered administrative life, as Eloise spontaneously also told me in her interview.

Mentally healthy persons are also androgynous. Healthy men are typically feminine in the way they relate to others. Harry, for example, was loved by others, probably because of his warmth, cooperativeness, and sensitivity to their needs. Andy was seen by Marty, his friend, and a colleague to be quite sensitive to and considerate of the needs of others.

Mentally healthy women are typically masculine in their stronger sense of themselves that enables them to be courageous individualists. They stand up for their beliefs and ideals to maintain their integrity, regardless of what others think of them. They don't try to please others if that violates their integrity. Again, think of Marty, Jane, and Billie. Marty's integrity was a major strength, and she was also widely known for her courage in publicly asserting her beliefs. Jane's courage was also judged to be one of her principal strengths. Think of what it took to confront tough New York sports suppliers by refusing to move her truck from in front of their warehouse door. And think of the grit, even toughness, that Billie needed not just to survive but to achieve what she did, as when she put herself through medical school.

Character of Happy Persons. Happy men and women are similar. In addition to the traits I have already mentioned about their well-being, they are also *adaptable, well-integrated,* and, like mentally healthy persons, *stable* and *autonomous.* Their stability is seen in their cheerfulness, emotional steadiness, and predictability; their autonomy shows in their self-control and decisiveness. Happy men, like mentally healthy ones, are also typically feminine in their interpersonal strengths; they are sensitive to the needs of others, gentle, affectionate, and understanding of others. But happy women may or may not be masculine or feminine. Just as we have seen earlier that androgynous men and women succeed in their various adult roles, so we now see again that they turn out to be mentally healthy and, for men, happy as well.[11]

I began by lamenting how elusive the meanings of health and

happiness have been. Adults are right to highly value well-being, for it predicts so many good things in life. By identifying the core character traits of healthy and happy persons, we now know where to begin to improve our well-being and so increase the odds that we will succeed in our adult roles. We also now know that the character of mentally healthy and happy men and women is generally similar. When growing up, men and women need to keep their eyes on becoming better integrated, stable, and autonomous. In addition, men also must work on becoming more interpersonally mature, women on developing more maturely autonomous self-concepts.

Though we now have a sturdier understanding of men's and women's mental health and happiness, we do not yet know much about their physical health. The differences puzzled me for months and require a chapter to themselves.

21

Male and Female Paths
to Physical Health

The meaning of men's and women's well-being is remarkably similar, but the meanings of a man's body apparently differ from a woman's.[1] Men's physical and mental health are almost one-of-a-piece; they are rooted in similar character strengths. Women's are not. Although women's mental health is inextricably meshed with numerous character traits, their physical health is not. Physically healthy men differ from unhealthy men in their personalities; physically healthy women do *not* differ from unhealthy women in theirs. What do such differences in the meanings of men's and women's bodies tell us about maleness and femaleness?

Men's Physical Health

Physically healthy men succeed more consistently in most of their adult roles than unhealthy men. They are better husbands and lovers, have more sexually compatible and faithful relationships, are fulfilled fathers, satisfied breadwinners, better leaders, and contribute more to their communities as citizens.[2] They may or may not make good friends. Their maturity is seen most clearly in their stability; they are calm, not moody or easily hurt by criticism, and so they are predictable.

Physically unhealthy men are, among other things, indecisive pessimists, not in control of their lives; not motivated to

253

strike out on different paths, they are rigidly stuck in deep ruts. Their lack of confidence robs them of the courage to risk altering their life styles, even taking decisive steps to deal with their poor health. They don't see themselves (nor do those who know them best see them) as having the motivation or skills necessary to cope with their poor health.

We and doctors responsible for our health should not ignore our character, particularly the traits I just listed. They could be keys to improving our long-term physical health. Educating a man how to plan, experiment with, get more control of, and feel more optimistic about what he can do with his way of life may more effectively prevent a stroke than prescribing a daily aspirin.

Since my visit, Jane's husband, Vince, had had cancer. She called to complain bitterly. "He's not doing anything to alter the way he lives. He says 'What's the use?' He resists every suggestion I make about changing his diet. He won't even tell me how he feels about cancer. I think he's given up. I think he's suicidal."

Having known Vince for thirty years and being concerned about him, I asked, "Can I do anything?"

"Well, would you try? But I don't think anyone can reach him."

I tried. She was right. Only his physician could possibly help, but my hunch was not for the long haul, if he prescribed only drugs and ignored Vince's character.

Women's Physical Health

Women's physical health predicted little else about them. Healthy women are good marital partners and have mature children, but that is all. Similarly, healthy women share only a few character strengths in common. Their peers agree that they are predictable and warm women fulfilling their potential. Again, that is all. Incidentally, the portrait confirms that drawn by the IGS staff conducting the principal longitudinal study of adult women.[3] They too found few traits that physically healthy women shared in common.

Male and Female Differences in Physical Health

To understand these male and female differences, I examined how the men and women actually differed in their physical health. Several converging findings suggest that a woman's body means something different to her than a man's does to him.

The women reported many more specific signs of bodily dysfunction than the men did (A5b), but, strangely, neither they nor their peers rated them less physically healthy (A5a). How could this be? They worried more about their bodies and more frequently rated themselves tired, tearful, and constipated. They reported more headaches, nipple pains, heart palpitations, cold hands and feet, as well as reduced concentration. Neither the women's ages nor menopausal status accounted for their bodily inefficiencies. *But* reporting signs that their bodies did not work well (A5b) did *not* predict their overall physical health or symptoms of mental distress (A5a, A2).

The men's reports did.

I puzzled about this difference for months. I asked myself, "Why may women's physical health be less well integrated with their personalities? Why do women report signs of bodily distress but neither they nor their peers rate them to be less healthy than men?" Two hypotheses provoke intriguing ideas about the meaning of femaleness and maleness: (1) Women's shared menstrual cycles shape the meaning of their bodies differently than men's erections do theirs. (2) Women's and men's bodies make it easier to grow up in different ways: for women, in other-centeredness; for men, in stability and autonomy.

Menstruation and its panoply of physical symptoms are not signs of "sickness" for which women are responsible. From adolescence to middle age, menstruation reminds them every twenty-eight days that they can create babies. They learn to accept — even celebrate, as Marty did — their biological cycles and accompanying distress as inherent to their femaleness. Women may learn how to become sensitive to their bodies' periodic messages of rich and varied feelings that can so affect their relationships and thus learn the language of their feelings in a way that most men do not. They also learn how to go with and not fight their bodies' temporary inefficiencies and claims upon their attention and energy. Their tears, irritability, and moodiness do not signal personal weakness for which they are responsible, as such reactions might for "stiff-upper-lipped" American males.

Moreover, men experience no similar *periodic* reminders of their bodies, varied subtle feelings, and vulnerability. Their bodies hover for months at the periphery of their awareness like fleeting indistinct shadows. Men take their bodies' reliability and efficiency for granted—until their stamina begins to fail when they can no longer clamber up 4,000 Himalayan steps without interminable pauses or swim the fifty laps they did only several years ago. No prods recurrently turn men inward to enrich their inner worlds, feeling language, and awareness of how their bodies affect their relations with others. To men, something that goes wrong can become a big deal. A symptom becomes a personal, not a gender, issue of their responsibility, so their bodies and physical health become spurs or challenges to cope with. They consequently become intertwined with idiosyncratic coping personality traits.

For example, those men who believe they must be real "men," and not simpering crybabies, learn to deny their bodies' messages of pain. Clamping their teeth together, suppressing pain, plugging ahead regardless, they make the committee meeting or play all four quarters. That's real "character." When last visiting my physician, I overheard him "order" a desperate wife to get her husband out of his committee meeting and to the nearest hospital's emergency room immediately. He had awakened with the left side of his face paralyzed; it had returned almost to normal before he manfully left for the office, ignoring his wife's protests that anything was really wrong. My doctor thought he had had a possible stroke and might have a more massive one any moment.

Women also know their bodies differently in another important way. Because they share hundreds of similar gender-related menstrual experiences from puberty to menopause, they regularly and empathically reexperience their common biological identity with each other. They become more sensitive to, understand, and accept each other's temporary inefficiencies, moods, and tears. Marty emotionally "knew" her periods biologically bonded her to her sisters.

Men experience no comparable periodic bodily reminders of their biological commonality and vulnerability, but they have shared one biological similarity while growing up: puberty and its most prominent enduring problematic outcome — heightened erectile responsiveness. Until I read Richard Handy's description of his impotence and its effects, I had not known how erections' richly varied meanings could contribute to a man's identity and influence his relationships. How boys learn to cope with their embarrassingly unpredictable and visible erections apparently can etch even more deeply their competitive, dominating, controlling, and inhibiting interpersonal styles.[4]

Effects of the Body on Maturing

Our bodily changes produce psychic effects, some we may not yet know of, that fashion the different meanings that females and males attribute to their bodies' health. One particular effect, however, helps me make sense of the differences in the women's and men's test results. A girl's predictable menstrual periods may not spur her to develop as individualistic and autonomous a self as a boy's unpredictable erections may. Her individuality is periodically tugged by and partially reabsorbed into a commonly shared menstrual experience which she cannot control and therefore must learn to *adjust* to and accept, or as Marty learned to do, *adapt* to and celebrate. Gender similarities can override more individualistic meanings of her body. May this not be a reinforcing biological reason for women's alleged "communality"[5] and salient other-centered maturation? May this not also be why so many of the women's bodily signs of dysfunction did not predict their individual physical health? Also, in spite of such signs, neither the women themselves nor their peers rated the women to be less physically healthy than the men and their peers rated the men to be.

Whereas most women learn to yield resignedly to their bodies' given cycles as signs of being nurturing females, men learn to control and *use* their bodies as signs of being achieving males. Handy claims that the essential unpredictability of pubertal boys' visible erections, so responsive to any strong stimulation, makes their drive to control their public appearance and associated emotional arousal or excitement more urgent. He shows how erections acquire, as a result, many diverse and individualizing meanings, including excitement, sexual desire, emotional control, competitiveness, dominance, and aggressiveness.[6]

Learning to deal with such meanings draws on individual personality strengths, most important, the ability to control one's body as well as the threats to that control, such as women or other sources of excitement. Seeking to master unpredictability rather than to yield to predictability leads to greater individuality and so stability and autonomy. Obviously other reasons than just learning to control their erections contribute to men's use of their bodies to control and achieve. However, erections' unpredictability provides an "athletic playing field," so to speak, for reinforcing self-command and then testing and stabilizing it in all of the thrill-seeking ways adolescent males do. Their bodily route, more likely than girls', leads to greater individuality. Their bodies become more fused and integrated with their personalities and, as a result, their bodies' health becomes a better predictor of their personality than women's health does.

I shall provoke you further. You may think that I underestimate how women learn to use their bodies to get what they want. Many societies expect girls to learn how to enhance their bodies' attractiveness to please males and so confirm their femininity—and desirability. Boys also mold and groom their hair, squeeze their pimples, and build their muscles. Yet historically, have not girls' bodily routes to growing up been more proscribed by their role of adjusting to boys' expectations than boys' bodily routes adjusting to girls' expectations? Males rather than female types of bodily competence lead to a more stable sense of self independent of the opinions of others. That the men's physical health but not the women's predicted many adaptive coping strengths is consistent with the gist of my argument.

Given the changes in the meaning of being a woman, I hesitate to claim that the study's middle-aged women's results, at least as I have interpreted them, may still apply to younger women who have grown up in a different cultural era. As girls participate more actively in team sports, test themselves against boys in Little League, and survive marine boot camp, some women's physical health may acquire more masculine meanings in the future.

I have now completed telling you about the character of men and women who achieve the twelve goals that you ranked in Chapter One. Roger suggested that I give you a summary capsule of what he calls "zingers" about growing beyond ourselves and enhancing our well-being before telling you about parents, school experiences, and other determinants of our adult success.

22

Ten Facts About
Other-Centeredness and Well-Being

You may think the following "zingers" are only common sense platitudes that you would read in any popular magazine. But I think they are more than just personal opinions whose merit we must take on faith. They are firmly supported now by objective evidence. The evidence makes them *believable* zingers for me, rather than only obvious platitudes. Do any of these prescriptions zing for you?

Zinger #1: To increase your odds of succeeding and becoming a happy adult, begin by selecting a "normal" family. Evidence? Harry Barnett. He had one mother and one father, enjoyed being a child rather than becoming a premature parent at the age of five, had two legs with which to play tackle football in high school, and didn't run away from home in order to protect his sanity.

Zinger #2: To become a good citizen and community leader, learn to enjoy helping children grow up, develop the skills of being a competent adult, get hold of some ideals and principles, and become androgynous. Evidence? Harry and the computer's portrait of men and women who voluntarily contribute to their communities.

Zinger #3: Hold onto your religious faith for spiritual, not material, reasons. Evidence? Religious persons are no more successful, physically or mentally healthy, or happy than nonreligious persons, but a religious faith may contribute to an individual's health and happiness; it is just not essential.

Zinger #4: Be virtuous; it pays off in corporal rewards in the long run. Evidence? Honest, compassionate, principled men and women who have integrity and a deep ethical commitment have all the good things that religions have always promised us: success, health, and happiness. Religions have wisely not promised that virtuous people will be wealthy; they may or may not be. Money does not necessarily come with blessedness.

Zinger #5: To have good physical health, pay attention to your mental health. To have good mental health, don't neglect your physical health. Evidence? The study clearly shows that they go together empirically, as wise persons have known for centuries.

Zinger #6: To succeed in most adult roles and be happy, learn how to create a mentally healthy life. Evidence? By most measures of familial success, mentally healthy men and women are better marital and sexual partners, as well as more fulfilled and competent parents, who raise their children to be mature. Both are more mature, particularly in their open and nondefensive relationships. Mentally healthy men are also well adapted vocationally and involved in community activities. Mentally healthy women have close friendships with other women.

Zinger #7: To become mentally healthy, learn how to become more stable, autonomous, and androgynous. Evidence? A convincing core group of strengths describes the mentally healthy woman and man. More than intellectual and even interpersonal strengths, mentally healthy persons have strongly grounded and independent selves. They are self-determining, self-reliant, self-confident, resilient persons. Mentally healthy men are interpersonally feminine. Mentally healthy women are typically masculine, though not macho, in their individualism and willingness to defend what they believe.

Zinger #8: To succeed and be happy, keep in good physical shape, particularly if a male. Evidence? Men in good physical health consistently succeed in more areas of living than men in poor health. Though the study's men and women did not differ in their overall physical health, a healthy body may mean something different to a woman than to a man. Her menstrual periods may sensitize her to her body's changing moods and provide a biologically shared identity with other women that men only experience through shared achievements.

Zinger #9: To be happy, work hard to become more mature. Evidence? Happy men and women share many similar character strengths. They are well integrated, stable, and autonomous persons. Happiness is the payoff for becoming more mature.

Zinger #10: To become virtuous and enhance your well-being, develop a mature and androgynous character. Evidence? The most consistently prominent traits of virtuous men and women, as well as the biggest contributors to their well-being, are their maturity and androgyny.

The prescriptions may sound like variations on the same theme. They generally are. Though altered in emphasis and limited by our traditional sexual roles, the prescriptions reflect the underlying structure of the effectively functioning individual. Some prescriptions may not sound "new" and don't violate your common sense, and this reassures me about the validity of the study's methods and the generalizability of its results. What zings for me is that the ten zingers are now more firmly grounded in scientific research, not just opinion and bias. They suggest which common sense ideas may more likely be true.

I turn now to the book's last part, "Paths to Adult Success and Well-Being." Which parents contribute most to their children's adult success and happiness? What do a school's academic grades and test scores predict about how its students turn out? What adolescent strengths best predict adult success and happiness? How do men and women grow during adulthood and what causes their growth?

Part Five _____

Paths to
Adult Success and Well-Being

23

Harry Barnett:
A Loving, Democratic, Firm Parent

I now risk disappointing you as I dig for the early roots that nourish adult success and happiness. I frustrated Roger. He wanted "forty-nine specific steps" he could take *now* to grow up, such as telling himself how good a lover he is ten times a night for thirty consecutive nights, or strengthening his self-confidence by listing every example of how much control he really has over his life, beginning with, "I decide when to get out of bed each morning" or "I can shower when I want." If the thousands of books about how to enjoy sex, raise children, and outwit Wall Street really work, why are we not better off by now? You know my answer. The key is not a technique but a change in our character. The men and women have told us the character necessary to succeed and be happy. What should be the first of the forty-nine steps? Become clear about what we want. The second step? Decide the character we then need to develop. The third? Develop a strategy of action to alter our ways of behaving. And the fourth?

Margaret Mead once wisely said, "A clear understanding of a problem prefigures its lines of solution." Research has begun to clarify the significant influences that contribute to enduring changes in our character. Knowing the character of parents whose children grow up to succeed can suggest steps we might take to raise our own more wisely.

Right off, I can tell you that the causes of how we mature

265

or go wrong are much more complicated than the Bible's answer: Eating an apple does not account for why we are what we are, as I hope you now know from my attempt to understand why Billie, the Millers, and Jane succeeded. Genetic, hormonal, and prenatal experiences, parental personalities, personal strengths, schools, peers, and cultural expectations, among others, steer and push us to grow up.

Psychologists dispute how much each affects maturing. Some even insist that what we or our parents were like when we were younger is irrelevant to how we act today. Thirty-five years of observing how and why my children and other adults develop tell me differently. Our basic character is far more historical than it is contemporary. I returned to my high school class's forty-seventh reunion. Though I had seen only two former classmates since graduation, I recognized most from their personalities, despite their brown blemishes, gray hairs, and dumpy figures. John was just as stuffy and ramrod-stiff as ever; Charlotte was as appealingly flirtatious; Bill was as ponderously dull; Winfred was as aggressively witty and sarcastic. Others charitably saw me as just as talkative and quizzical as I had been in Miss Kirk's English class. My study confirmed over and over that remarkable personality stability and continuity are more the rule than the exception. Bend a spruce sprig when it is little and watch how that "bentness" shapes how it imperceptibly turns to the sun over the years.

When I try to figure out why our kids are the adults that they are, I immediately see that they have inherited a few quirks of their parents — even grandparents. Harriet says my son forcefully and impatiently punches his computer's keys as I do. He also writes some of his letters similarly — and as illegibly. Studies of identical twins confirm that temperamental traits like aggressiveness, sociability, and emotionality have a major genetic component.[1] So it is not inconceivable that our genetic histories predispose us to develop some character strengths more than others, such as those necessary to succeed as leaders or lovers, or to become mature or even ethical.

We know most about the influence of parents. Parts of them become part of us; we carry them with us through the years in many guises. Sometimes at the most inopportune moment, for example, when we are angry at our kids, our parents pop out in our tone of voice and impulsive "no" to their provocations — even long after the children have left home to become parents themselves.

What are parents like who raise children to be good partners, lovers, and contributing citizens? I again ask the question from Chapter Ten: What is the character of competent parents?

They are loving.

They are democratic.

They have firm expectations of their children.

These are the parental keys to how children turn out,[2] keys that do not come only from the study's statistical results but also emerge out of hundreds of other studies about how children grow.

Feeling loved gives us the security to explore and risk. If we fear to risk, we don't discover anything new about ourselves or our world. Being loved also provides us with the model of how to love others. Feeling unloved and rejected can devastate us. Charles Dickens wrote in *Dombey and Son:* "For not an orphan in the wide world can be so deserted as the child who is an outcast from a living parent's love."

Feeling that we are genuinely listened to and respected affirms our sense of worth and autonomy. Parents who are not democratic, who walk roughshod over our needs and temperament, can squash our individuality and self-confidence.

Knowing that our parents flexibly but firmly expect us to behave in certain ways gives us predictable guidelines that encourage us to control and guide our efforts and talents by ourselves. Parents who too quickly give in to our screams can aggravate our petulent self-centeredness and dilute our will to persist and learn how to cope.

The character of parents influences how children act and turn out far more than their child-rearing techniques do. Two parents may restrict TV to only Saturday mornings, but that technique's effects may radically differ. One child may feel he is being punished by a rejecting and hostile parent; another may not. The first becomes sullen and sour or resistant and negativistic;

the other complains and argues but does not become withdrawn or hostile.

To identify the specific character we need to be a competent parent, we first must identify who is more or less competent. Chapter Ten told us we can identify a competent parent in several ways. I have mentioned the audit of the women's and men's reflections about the strengths they learned a good parent had (A4b). Remember the list of eight saintly core strengths that began with patience and ended with a problem-solving attitude about child-rearing?

If we order parents by their own and their partners' ratings of their competence as parents[3] (A4c) and examine what distinguishes them, the outline of a "competent parent character" begins to emerge. Both competent mothers and fathers share similar feminine interpersonal strengths. For example, the more competent father was like Andy; he was less assertive and dominant but more understanding, gentle, sensitive, even soft-spoken, than the less competent one.

I felt that a more stringent index of parental competence might be children's emotional maturity and adaptability (A17). Competent parents do not mess up their children's emotional growth and adaptability as readily. Emotionally stable, physically and mentally healthy, and happy mothers raise mature children. They are also loved by others, conscientious, open to trying new things, and so can fulfill their potential more than mothers whose children are less mature. The fathers of mature children are also mentally healthy, mature, open, warm, not overly demanding but decisive and adventurous risk takers. Vaillant similarly found that the fathers of mature Harvard graduates were mentally healthy and warm men.[4]

My most demanding index of parental competence was how children turn out as *adults*. Since I didn't have the patience (and years) to wait around until the men's and women's children had grown up, I did the next best thing. Each participant rated his or her familial home and each parent on attributes researchers had found describe favorable homes and competent parents[5] (A1a).

To illustrate the parents whose kids turn out well, I shall tell you more about Harry and then his parents. Although I had not reviewed his family background before selecting him, when I did study it I was delighted how closely it fit the computer's portrait of the family from which successful adults come.

Harry's loving, democratic, and firm attitude toward his children came out clearly in the interviews. He had said that his "fondest wish to fulfill before I die is to see my children happy and successful . . . I suppose because of a deep feeling that I have about the kids. The sense of their worth and ability and the tremendous obligation I feel to provide what it takes for them to use their abilities . . . it's my selfish side . . . for them not to be successful and happy . . . I'd feel a certain personal loss and responsibility."

To my question, "What are you trying to do about fulfilling such hopes?" he unhesitatingly replied, "Our approach has been to try to set as good examples as we can, to give them a standard to at least have as a reference. And to provide what direction we can and the responsibility. It is a tough line to draw when we have the money and yet we want them to have some feeling of responsibility for what they have."

The depth of Harry's feelings for his children and his felt responsibility for them emerged also in the picture and story he projected onto the same blank card to which Marty had given her story about playing with children.

> Here we see a man in a plane, flying through the clouds with a dog and one of his children. They are off where they can see no other human or any sign of civilization. The father and child are enjoying the solitude and isolation, and the ability to talk and communicate with each other without any interruption from anyone else around. Very happy and a very deep feeling for each other. I see it as a break from the usual more hectic existence. It is a rare opportunity for them to be together and enjoy each other, their dog, and nature all around them.

In the interviews, Harry kept returning to Rusty, then fourteen. Sally, his youngest, "doesn't do much wrong and is a fan-
tastically good student and so it is easy to ignore her needs."
But Rusty was something different.

> He's a real problem. He's been very challenging.
> Very strong, decisive but somewhat insecure. Be-
> ing the first child, his unpleasantness here in the
> home reverberates down to Sally. Rusty is caught
> between his insecurity and push to be independent
> and rebel against us. And he's so outspoken and
> aggressive.
>
> We have sought counseling about him and learned
> that in our attempt to have an open communica-
> tive relation with him we may have blurred the
> generational boundaries. He really rakes Eloise over
> the coals. It has been a hard time for her. He "ma-
> tured" early and when thirteen wanted to try his
> wings. We didn't think it was time yet. Well! We
> got into these huge spiraling conflicts. Nothing got
> accomplished. All of our ideas went up into smoke.
>
> It's a tough time for kids. Drugs, alcohol, sex.
> Just their safety. And the tremendous peer pres-
> sures that Rusty is under.
>
> It's a tough time for parents too. And the school
> didn't help. Tough, rigid, unforgiving. Several
> faculty had been in the marines. Their discipline
> had no love, no warmth. Made everything worse.

I felt some hurt in Harry about Rusty's orneriness. Maybe
he had forgotten that he too had rebelled against his father. I
interpreted Rusty's rebellious thrust to independence to be a predictable and healthy effort to become his own person, particularly given how decisive and strong Harry and Eloise were. I
counseled patience, of which Harry claimed he had little. Harry
admitted later that he and Eloise were perfectionists and may
have been too tough in their demands, which they had not made
with much "finesse." Both parents saw themselves as "tough disciplinarians." Harry told me:

I think parenting is the most demanding, challenging, frustrating job one can do, if you really are critical and sit back and think, "What could I have done better?" Virtually impossible to be perfect. It is so . . . it requires you to be objective about things which you can't be because you are so enmeshed in them yourself. It is so much easier to be understanding with those you are not so close to. So many demands and challenges that are always changing. You just have to walk that thin line between too much and too little.

Amen!

Harry was a loving father, as Eloise told me. He also valued and respected his children's talents and individuality and accepted responsibility for helping them to fulfill them. However, as he told us when he said "it's my selfish side," he was aware that his hope that they would succeed and be happy was *his* wish and might not be theirs. He also held them to firm expectations. Like most parents, however, he was challenged to walk that thin line between holding them to his expectations and being either too authoritarian or too permissive in ways that might blur legitimate generational boundaries.

Being a loving, democratic, but firm parent to today's adolescents is, as Harry said, the most demanding and frustrating job we can have. As the opportunities for them to go astray have multiplied in the past decades, parents since the mid-fifties have enjoyed being parents less. But not Harry: He made being a good father a genuine commitment. His loving, respectful, and firm attitudes sustained him as he explored how to be one. (Harry's story tells us, though, that even good parents can have troubled children and be baffled about how to assist them to grow up healthily.)

Eloise and Harry are now happy about how their children have been growing. They described Rusty and Sally at the end of the study to be quite mature, ranking above two-thirds of the study's other children (A17). Rusty has since gotten himself more together — Harry told me last year that he had gone

to Earlham College where he did quite well. He feels that they
are now good friends.

How might Harry's parents have influenced his attitudes and
values about parenting (A1a)? Harry felt that his parents loved
and respected each other; they demonstratively and affection-
ately showed each other their love. They also accepted and enjoyed their parental role. Because his parents had had clear
values and expectations, the atmosphere of Harry's childhood
home had been consistent and predictable. Speaking for Eloise
as well, he said, "Our parents were disciplinarians; they both
were pretty tough. We had to work for things, obey certain rules.
We had our curfews and expectations. Eloise and I are trying
to have a more open communication, more give and take, be
more willing to listen than our parents were with us."

Both his mother and father had been in good physical and
mental health. He recalls them as active, energetic, affirming
persons not absorbed in their own lives but interested in their
children's. Feeling close to and loving them, he respected and
valued them both (though his father more) as role models. He
could count on them. Actively concerned about his development,
particularly his intellectual growth, they made themselves available when he needed help; both helped him with his homework.
He never felt that they rejected him. His mother, with whom
he felt more temperamentally compatible, was a warm and emotionally expressive person. His father, more stern, even authoritarian, held him to higher disciplinary expectations against
which Harry stubbornly rebelled.

If you are a parent and want prescription number 38 about
how to be a good one, then say these magical words ten times
before breakfast every day until your last child leaves home:
Be loving, democratic, but firm with the children today. And then try
to be like that. I would prescribe the same for teachers or others
who want youngsters to grow up healthily.

The next two chapters describe the computer-drawn mothers
and fathers whose children grow up to succeed and be happy.
We will discover many of the characteristics of Harry's parents
and of Harry himself in them.

24

Mothers of Children
Who Grow Up to Succeed

The study produced three messages about competent parents whose children succeed in their intimate, vocational, and citizenship roles and who are healthy and happy (A29).

Competent parents create a home whose climate is loving, democratic, and firm.

- The home is loving because successful men and women recall their childhood homes to have been warm, demonstratively affectionate, and, most important, accepting, not rejecting, of them.
- The climate is democratic because they feel that neither parent was excessively dominant or authoritarian and each listened to and respected them.
- There were clear, firm values because their parents agreed about their values, such as creating an intellectually and culturally stimulating home and expecting academic achievement and ethical relationships with others.

Mothers and fathers contribute to how well their children function as adults but in different ways.

- Mothers influence much more their children's future success in their intimacy relationships.[1]

- Fathers contribute more to their sons' early vocational and citizenship success and to their daughters' continuing vocational success.
- Neither contributes much to their adult children's friendships, ethical sense, and well-being; but when they do, mothers influence their sons' ethical character and fathers' their sons' mental health more than either do their daughters' ethical character and well-being. Neither directly contributes to their children's later happiness.

Successful adults feel good about their parents and rate them to be mature. Only vocationally successful daughters express ambivalence about their parents. Unsuccessful adults don't feel good about their parents. They believe that their immature parents created unhappy childhood homes for them.

Trying to distill the essence of the study's many rich findings about the men's and women's families to make these few points may make a syrup that's sweet to your taste, but at what price? Subtlety, fineness, depth? I am not sure just how much detail you might like. To help you take quite a bit, I will be slightly more formal. This chapter organizes the mothers' contributions to their children's familial, vocational, and community success, as well as, briefly, their ethical growth and well-being. The next chapter will discuss the fathers' contributions. You can then skip more easily to the sections that most interest you.

Mothers of Children Who Succeed as Marital Partners, Lovers, and Parents

Daughters Who Succeed in Familial Relationships. A woman trying to balance her graduate work with her work and children said of her mother, "Everything I know about relating to my children I learned from my mother. I just brought it up to date in some ways. All I learned about how to respect my kids, how to talk with them, confront them, demand respect and integrity from them . . . it all comes from a certain tone of love and firmness that was so much my mother. It's a tone that is a big part of me, and I can pass it on."

The evidence overwhelmingly confirms her judgment: Mothers can greatly influence their daughters' future familial relationships. Daughters who, as adults, create successful intimate relationships had warm, affectionate, and outgoing mothers who were emotionally involved with others. Open to sharing personal secrets and feelings with their daughters, their mothers maturely and clearly affirmed their values that their daughters should achieve academically, be ethical persons, and create warm and loving relationships with others. They were neither rigid nor dogmatic nor long-suffering and defeated martyrs. As a consequence, the successful daughters respected and loved their mothers and wanted very much to be like them. Identifying with mothers so mature in caring and communicative strengths was a major reason why the women succeeded as wives, mothers, and lovers.

Some prescriptions for mothers who want their daughters to enjoy fulfilling and intimate relationships with their adult partners and children might be:

- Talk very openly and freely with your partner in front of your adolescent daughter about what you think and feel.
- Expect that she develop loving and caring relationships with others.
- Be sure that she clearly understands where you stand, particularly about how she should get along with others.

Sue Schwartz was one of the study's three most fulfilled and competent working mothers, as well as one of the most happily married women whose best friends gave her an almost perfect score for being a close friend. Sue loved being a mother; she never had had the desire to be freed of her responsibility for her children, who she said had never created any problems for her. Her husband agreed with her judgment. Their two children were the fourth most mature and healthy of the group.

Sue's mother modeled the computer's portrait of the ideal mother. Sue replied to my question, "For what are you most grateful about your mother?" (A4i): "For her example. Many ways. Not everything because she wasn't perfect. She did everything she thought best to be a mother. She made mistakes because she was so overzealous as a mother. Too unselfish in many cases; that's what I am not grateful for. She loved to teach us things; she loved to love us. She had no favorites; she loved all four of us."

Is it any wonder she rated her feelings toward her mother as warm, close, and understanding and spontaneously replied "loved each other a great deal" to the incomplete sentence, "My mother and I . . . " and "When she thought of her mother . . . she smiled with affection."

The woman who failed in her intimate familial roles came from a home that had few of these strengths. Her mother was more self-absorbed, cold, even hostile, severely disciplining, and didn't give as lovingly of herself or as openly and freely as mothers like Sue's did. Such mothers tended to provoke their daughters to resist and rebel stubbornly against them.

Sons Who Succeed in Familial Relationships. I also have no doubts about who contributes most to boys who grow up to create close intimacy relationships with their partners and children.

Their mothers!

Men who create happy marriages and mutually fulfilling sexual relationships, and who are good fathers, have had mothers whose mental health was excellent when they were growing up.[2] Their mothers were outgoing and emotionally involved with others. Though accepting their sons, they held them to high expectations, particularly academic, but not in ways that eroded their sons' basically good feelings about them. By being demonstratively affectionate within the home and creating close and loving relationships with their sons, they helped them learn how to relate intimately within the family.

Harry's mother fits most of this picture more than Andy's. He felt close to, respected, and loved his mother who, a warm and affectionate woman, had devoted herself to others, including him and his education. To Harry, however, she had not walked that thin line very well of balancing respect for his needs and ideas and her own too firm ones about how to raise him.

Andy did not feel what Fromm called "unconditional love"

or acceptance from his mother. She loved him, so he felt, for his achievement, not for himself. Perhaps, however, because he didn't feel that she squelched or rejected him, he was able, with some therapy and support, to eventually learn how as a male to create a fulfilling intimate relationship with Marty and his children.

Men who did *not* succeed in their primary intimacy relationships felt rejected by their mothers when young. They in turn did not love their mothers, who they recalled were distant, authoritarian, dominating, even hostile. We have seen that success in our intimate roles requires typical feminine interpersonal strengths. Growing up with a rejecting, cold, or hostile mother may propel a boy to reject his own feminine interpersonal potentials and to overdevelop masculine traits in order to assert his own independent identity. Bruce Jackson illustrates the effects of a coldly rejecting mother. He failed maritally because he needed June to be the mother he never had, but a mother whom he could tyranically control the way his mother had controlled him.

The results are convincing and consistent. Mothers whose sons later become good marital partners, parents, and lovers are loving, accepting women who respect their sons' individuality but who expect them to fulfill their high expectations.

Mothers of Children Who Succeed Vocationally

Daughters Who Succeed Vocationally. Not unexpectedly, the women's mothers contributed much less to their girls' vocational success than their fathers did (A28). Women who succeeded in their work came from favorable home environments and had mature parents. But there were exceptions. Women who were leaders and earned a lot of money had mothers whom their daughters described as tense and physically and mentally unhealthy. They possessed few qualities, in other words, that would inspire a daughter to emulate them as models, and so over time they became less and less relevant persons in their daughters' emotional histories.

Both Marty and Jane described their mothers in this way.

They and some others frequently expressed hostility, certainly disappointment, about their mothers in the interviews. One told me, "My mother could have been so much more than what she had become — just a housewife and mother." Their mothers had not provided them with a model of how to resolve the conflicts that many successful women now feel between their careers, family responsibilities, and personal needs.

The research provides, however, some hopeful clues about what women like Sue need to juggle successfully their careers and familial roles. Much depends not just on how adaptable their husbands are but also upon the strengths they can draw from their childhood homes and the maturity of their mothers. Working women who are fulfilled and competent mothers come from different homes than working women who do *not* successfully fulfill their maternal role. When they were young, they had favorable parental relationships and warm and caring, not tense, angry, and conflictual home atmospheres. Their mothers and fathers had enjoyed being parents and welcomed being actively involved in their daughters' education. They had respected, loved, and been openly affectionate with each other. Able to talk openly and freely with each other about their feelings, they could agree about how to raise their children, and so had created a consistent, calm, and nondivisive home atmosphere.

You may be asking at this point, "What happens to the girl whose mother works when she's a young child?" I would say, "Having an absent working mother may not in and of itself be as important as having a *maternal* working mother and a nurturing father." I still would argue that a child needs a loving, democratic, and consistently firm parental presence — whether paternal or maternal — to mature and succeed. A mother who remains at home and who views her maternal role as a job and emotionally rejects it could destroy her daughter's later healthy identity as a mother; a mother who works outside of the home who values and enjoys being a mother probably won't.

Sons Who Succeed Vocationally. Mothers directly contributed little to their sons' vocational success. The extent of their contribution was that they were silently but positively present to

their successful sons and were recalled to have been self-affirm-
ing, actively involved in their sons' early education, and openly
sharing their feelings with them when younger.

Mothers Whose Children Are
Ethical and Mentally Healthy

You may be as incredulous as I, but the study's women agreed
about only a few prescriptions for raising daughters to be ethical and mentally healthy.[3] I can tell you very little about how
to raise either a daughter or son so they will be happy middle-
aged persons. And I have no inkling why—yet. It is another
piece of the puzzle I hope I can eventually fit into the emerging
portrait of the effective woman.

Daughters Who Are Ethical and Mentally Healthy. If you
asked me to prescribe for your daughter's ethical development
and mental health, the results would permit me to recommend
only the following.

- Be a model of an ethically concerned mother who encourages
  your daughter's ethical as well as intellectual growth.
- Do not be like Jane's mother—an authoritarian marine drill
  instructor.
- Talk openly and freely about your feelings and ideas with
  your partner and daughter when she's mature enough to understand.
- Urge your husband to teach her how to enjoy outdoor physical activities, like teaching her how to throw a football.

Sons Who Are Ethical and Mentally Healthy. If you and your
partner love and respect each other, enjoy being parents, and
have created a calm, consistent, and intellectually stimulating
home, you are well on the way to assisting your son to become
an ethically principled and healthy man.

If you are like the typical mother of highly ethical and mentally healthy men, he will remember you as an actively energetic mother who valued his intellectual development and helped

him with his homework. He may have stood his ground, argued with you, and may have even threatened to run away. But he would not have felt you were rejecting him; he would have felt close to you and still loved you. Just be sure, however, that you do not come across to him as dominating and controlling his father.

The Parental Roots of Adult Happiness

I could not trace the roots of the women's or men's happiness back to any parental trait, perhaps because I had no information about their parents' personalities when the men and women were children. Apparently, there is no cookbook recipe I can give mothers about how to raise their adolescent daughters and sons to guarantee that they will become happy middle-aged adults. Happy adults have had such diverse upbringings and parents that they share no common familial home or parental traits. The histories of the book's principal actors and actresses have already told us this. Billie had three unpredictable mothers. When she was five, Marty became the "mother" to her own inept mother and alcoholic father and their children. Jane was almost destroyed by an authoritarian and smothering mother. Andy felt his mother loved him only conditionally. Harry's mother lovingly held him to too severe expectations. But each became a happy and fulfilled adult.

As adults we are the primary agents of our own happiness; we cannot blame our parents for our unhappiness. Or as parents, like Harry, concerned about our children's future happiness, we can press no obvious buttons or pull levers that will *directly* contribute to our children's subsequent happiness. They will just have to work on their own to make their lives happy and fulfilling ones.

Again like me, you may be now saying, "Unbelievable. You mean that parents have no influence whatsoever on how happy their children will be as adults?" No. I don't think we can say that. Parents can affect their children's personality and so their mental health and happiness.[4] However, their direct impact on their middle-aged children can no longer be discerned, although they *indirectly* contribute to their children's later happiness by enabling them to mature in all of the ways that I have described earlier. For adults, maturity is a principal contributor to how successful and happy adolescents will become by middle age.

If you pushed me, I would agree that when an adult is still emotionally tied to parents and, like Marty, fighting to be free of their lingering presence, then maybe it is more difficult to make one's own happiness.

But the more mature we are, the more our happiness is in our own hands.

Whoever planned that children should have two parents was very wise. If a mother fails her child, a father may not. The next chapter reports the character of fathers who aid their children to succeed as adults.

25

Fathers of Children
Who Grow Up to Succeed

Generally, the fathers of middle-aged men and women who succeed as partners, parents, and lovers shared few common character traits. They did, however, as fathers of sons who succeeded vocationally in their early thirties, became community leaders, and were mentally healthy. Fathers contribute much more than their wives to their daughters' continuing vocational success but little to their adult mental health. Apparently, ethical and happy men and women did not have similar fathers when younger.

Fathers of Children Who Succeed as
Marital Partners, Lovers, and Parents

Sons Who Succeed in Familial Relationships. Fathers contribute little to their sons' subsequent success as marital partners, parents, and lovers (A27). Sons like Harry, who succeeded in their intimate relationships, had fathers who accepted them. Sons like Bruce Jackson, who failed in such relationships, had fathers who rejected them. Rejecting a son turns out to be the most demoralizing thing a father can do to his son. Feeling rejected by a distant, uninvolved father sows the seeds for later fractiousness, particularly an inclination to be stubborn and rebellious in one's relationships.

Perhaps you will be as uneasy as I am about results that seem to show how meagerly a father apparently contributes to his son's later intimacy relationships. Two types of evidence make me doubt my findings. Vaillant claims that fathers more than mothers help their sons to develop more mature relationships, which he feels is close to the heart of being a mentally healthy adult.[1] Although his and my results have dovetailed so well up to this point, I could not replicate his finding using any combination of methods to assess the men's interpersonal maturity.

The second evidence is purely observational and anecdotal. Our style of getting along with others can be planted in us very early by our parents. Two-year-old Georgie comes to mind. He was pointing out trucks, cows, and trees in his picture book as he slumped, cradled in my arm, on his living room couch while waiting for his father to come home to begin the interviews. When his father came in the door, Georgie immediately ran toward him with his arms outstretched to hug him. His father shook his hand instead. Georgie's mother told me that her husband had never hugged him or her, told her that he loved her, or remembered Georgie's or her birthdays. Such a model of intimacy! What interpersonal seeds was he sowing in Georgie? Which would sprout? Rather, which wouldn't?

I will always remember a five-year-old black boy in an inner-city school who came up to me scowling and with clenched fists as I walked past his kindergarten room at dismissal time.

"Get your dukes up. I'm going to fight you," he screamed.

Momentarily taken aback and thinking that he was being playful, I raised my fists. He wasn't being playful. He charged into me, flailing. Fortunately for me, at that moment his mother swept by, and, without breaking her step, swooped him up under her arm and sailed serenely off down the hall as he squiggled and squirmed, still screaming at me, "Get your dukes up. Get them up." I inwardly cried for him. Not just for his mortification but for his future. I could see a hurt, defiant "father" inside him urging him to put up his dukes to protect himself by attacking first all strange "whiteys" who were out to hurt him.

Why do fathers contribute so much less than mothers to their sons' intimacy relationships?[2] I draw some hunches from men's male friendships, which are scarcely intimate ones. Typical American male friendships are quite emotionally superficial, primarily social rather than personal. The fathers could not teach their sons about intimacy very well, for they themselves did not have the skills to be intimate with others. Like Andy, few of the men had been close to or good friends with their fathers, who were part of a generation, so man after man told me, that had only worked to fulfill its breadwinner duty.

How does a son learn the self-disclosing skills that intimacy requires if he has a father like Mark's? Mark's father was dying of colon cancer, just as Mark's grandfather had fifteen years earlier. He, like his father before him, never uttered a word about it and avoided all of Mark's determined efforts (as his grandfather had resisted his grandmother's) to talk about it. Be a man. Be strong and silent. Grin and bear it. But this is not a good father.

If fathers are unable to talk with their sons about how they feel, even about the most important of all topics, such as their impending deaths, how are sons to learn the skills of being intimate with their spouses, lovers, and own children? Being open, expressing feelings, and sharing experiences are some of the most precious gifts a father can give his son. He should allow his son to know him from the inside out.

When I asked the men what their greatest disappointment was about their fathers and later about how they wanted to raise their children, many told me that they regretted never *knowing* their fathers and that they wanted to be different with their own children. Harry's story about flying alone with one of his children and the dog captures what I heard over and over from the more competent fathers: They wanted to have a more intimate relation with their children. We have seen that such fathers are more mature and have more competent and mature children, so perhaps they are sowing seeds that will enable their sons to become more successful marital partners, parents, and lovers themselves.

Roger also believes the younger fathers he knows want to be more emotionally involved with their sons. He told me about John Lennon, an idol to millions, who seldom saw his first son, Julian. But during his final years, Lennon became a house-husband and retired from public life to be with his second son, Sean.

Harry's father was typical of those whose sons turned out successfully in their marital, parental, and sexual roles. Andy's father was less so, more because of his New England taciturnity than his active rejection of Andy. We'll never know just how much his father's reserve pushed Andy to self-consciously pursue support groups that encouraged him to be more emotionally expressive. But Andy felt very good when he first hugged his father, who so warmly responded that Andy looks forward to similar hugs when they meet. Moral? If you are a son, don't give up on your father. He may just need some loving prodding. (Bruce Jackson might need bulldozing.)

With only one exception, all of the men had grown up with fathers present in their homes. This is no longer the case for millions of boys, and I am frequently asked nowadays, "What about boys who grow up in single-parent families where no father is present? What happens to them?" Since no one has yet thoroughly studied how such boys turn out as adults, I answer, "I'm not sure." A few studies report that boys survive divorce much less well than girls, particularly if they subsequently live only with their mothers. They are more aggressive and less socially mature. Boys living only with their fathers are more mature, cooperative, and feel better about themselves.[3] However, no researcher of whom I am aware has followed such boys into adulthood to discover the character of either their mothers or fathers who have raised them to succeed.

What may be most important for a boy's future healthy growth may not be just having a man at home but a father who really wants, for example, to be a single parent for his son. He should be a competent but loving, interpersonally mature man who cares about and is actively involved in his son's development. Boys whose fathers are rejecting, emotionally inaccessible, distant, and cold may well be better off in the long run not to have them around.[4] To grow up with fathers like Bruce Jackson, who reject them and, worse yet, hostilely so, could undermine their future intimacy, social, and vocational success. Boys need to develop a sustained relationship with other males, like older brothers, friends, teachers, scout leaders, and grandfathers, who provide that loving, respectful, and firm presence so essential to healthy development and adult success.

Daughters Who Succeed in Familial Relationships. I also cannot say much about the fathers of women who grow up to be good wives, lovers, and parents. They had been emotionally present in their daughters' early lives but only quietly so, certainly in contrast to the overshadowing presence of their wives. They had not withdrawn from family disputes and arguments and had freely shared their feelings and ideas with their daughters. The girls' fathers had supported and encouraged them, particularly their physical and athletic activities. But they did not have the same emotionally involving and so enduring influential effects on their daughters' later familial success that their wives had had.

Sue described the typical father of the study's women when she answered my question, "What's your greatest disappointment about your father?"

"My father could never tell me he loved me or that I looked nice or pay me a compliment until three days before he died."

"What did he say?"

"Thank you, sweetheart. I'll never forget what you've done for me." Sue then said, "I nearly fainted. He leaned over and kissed my arm. That's the most wonderful thing that ever happened to me. I was so glad. It took forty years but I no longer feel bitter. He just really felt he could never tell me."

Fathers of Children Who Succeed
Vocationally and Are Good Citizens

Sons Who Succeed Vocationally and Contribute to Their Communities. Men who succeeded vocationally by their early thirties had fathers who were energetic and in excellent physical health. They had been available and accessible when their sons needed their help, for example, with their homework. Their sons also remembered their fathers as warm, affectionate, and loving men who made it clear that their sons should care for and love others in turn, as Harry described his father.

Sons who did *not* grow up to succeed in their work by their early thirties had fathers who had been authoritarian and severe disciplinarians when they were little. They had been excessively firm but scarcely democratic. As a result, their sons had felt rejected and stubbornly rebelled against their dads. Failing in college or being fired from a first job may be the only way some sons can safely get back at fathers who despotically squashed them when they were little tykes. Was this why Bruce Jackson's son dropped out of college and lived on New York City's streets? What a beautiful way of silently not fulfilling an overpowering father's high hopes without defying him openly.

Twelve years later, however, when the men were middle-aged, their fathers' contribution to their vocational success had become much less discernible, actually almost invisible. The only lingering quality that successful men reported about their fathers was their acceptance of and emotional involvement with them when young. The unsuccessful middle-aged men still felt rejected by their fathers. They probably will always feel that pain.

If we fathers wish to claim any credit for the vocational success (or lack of it) of our sons when they are in their early thirties, we may do so, but only modestly so. By the time they are middle-aged, we must suppress our pride (or regret) that we contributed to their success (or failure). They have made it or failed to make it largely on their own — our influence has become part of their history.

The fathers of men who responsibly contributed to their communities were similar to those of men who succeeded vocationally in their early thirties. They were warm and loving men who expected their sons to love and care for others also. They did not autocratically or severely discipline their sons. Not feeling squelched or rejected, their sons did not need to rebel stubbornly against them.

Daughters Who Succeed Vocationally. Fathers may have more enduring effects on their daughters' vocational success than mothers (A28), though neither seemed to influence their daughters' community involvement. The vocationally successful women identified with their fathers, whom they loved, felt close to, and respected as persons they wanted to be like. Warm and emotionally expressive, they valued their daughters' intellectual development, actively participated in educating them, and opened up the outside world to them. These paternal strengths provided the woman who succeeded in her work with a strong emotional core that undergirded the masculine identification necessary to succeed in traditional male-dominated fields.

Such fathers teach vocationally successful women how to "connect" with the more typically masculine work world.[5] They talk to their daughters about how to get a job, prepare for an interview, dress appropriately, get along with men and their bosses, deal with male ways of being critical and supportive, read the financial pages, ask for a raise, invest their money for income and capital gain, make alliances, and anticipate the changing office politics that make survival more likely the next time the pink slips are handed out. Jane said that she could never have succeeded if her husband had not taught her what her father had not about the business world. As more Janes and Martys enter the vocational world, perhaps they will begin to influence their own daughters' vocational success more visibly than their mothers had theirs.

We can now return to the puzzle that I reported in Chapters Fifteen and Sixteen: Why is the meaning of vocational success more ambiguous and conflictive for women than for men? Women like Jane, who are judged by their colleagues to be vocationally successful, are androgynous: decisive and competitive but also compassionate and sensitive to the needs of others. They take on qualities usually attributed to males, but without identifying totally with the male stereotype or believing that success comes only to the cutthroat. On the other hand, women who earn high incomes and are leaders are predominantly masculine: aggressive, competitive, and dominant.

Perhaps we can trace these personality differences back to different parental traits. Women judged by their colleagues to be fulfilled and competent have different parents, particularly fathers, than those judged to be less successful (A26). Their fathers are similar to those I just described more generally: respected, loved, and viewed as role models by their successful daughters. The fathers of the women who do not do well in their work are not loved and respected enough to emulate.

On the other hand, women who earn a lot of money and hold leadership positions have a unique relationship with both parents. They recall their mothers to have been tense and unhealthy persons; they do not attribute one shared positive trait to them.

Given the absence of a strong and positive maternal model, might such daughters have tried to become like their fathers, whom they respected and loved?

The fathers of high-income leaders are warm, affectionate, and value caring for and loving others. But when their daughters were younger, they firmly (and even sharply) held them to high expectations, actively spurred their academic achievement, and stringently disciplined them for failing. Their daughters reacted predictably — they ambivalently loved but rebelled against their fathers. I don't think that they abandoned their more masculine identification. Instead, they may have overemphasized it in order to please their demanding fathers. They also became stubbornly rebellious and may have learned how to convert their rebellion into an independent autonomy to fashion a nontraditional female career in a male vocational world. Apparently ambivalence toward a loved, respected, but demanding father is the cauldron from which aggressive, competitive, and rebellious energies can be drawn to make it in the typical world of money and power.

Marty's and Jane's fathers now begin to measure up a little more to the computer's portrait of the fathers of daughters who become leaders and earn high incomes. Both viewed their fathers to have been warmer, more emotionally expressive, and lovingly supportive than their mothers had been. No wonder they felt closer to and loved their fathers more than they did their mothers.

On the other hand, I could not detect any lingering paternal contribution to their daughters' involvement in the community. Perhaps the typical masculine strengths Chapter Fifteen identified to be necessary to succeed in the business and political worlds may be less useful in volunteer community activities.

Fathers of Mentally Healthy Sons and Daughters

Mentally Healthy Sons. Mentally healthy men rate their fathers to have a large number of strengths, the most general one being good mental and physical health.[6] The men felt close to and loved their fathers; they never felt rejected by them or the need to rebel against them. Mentally healthy men believed their fathers strongly supported the development of their talents; they helped them with their homework when they were in school. They also encouraged their sons' physical and athletic growth, as well as their independence. Their concern for and involvement in their sons' decisions grew out of affectionate respect, not out of an authoritarian desire to control. The mentally unhealthy men's fathers had been severe disciplinarians whom they had not respected when younger.

George Vaillant, studying how Harvard men grew into middle age, identified some similar and other causes of a man's poor mental health. "The antecedents of poor . . . midlife social adjustment at 50 were a cold childhood environment, mentally ill parents, poor adolescent social adjustment, prolonged maternal dependence, and being an only or oldest child."[7]

Mentally Healthy Daughters. Mentally healthy women do not recall many similar strengths in their fathers, as they also did not for their mothers. If you are the father of a daughter, you may not be able to do much directly to help her become a mentally healthy woman once she has reached her teens. Above all, however, do not withdraw defeatedly from any conflicts you may have with your partner and detach yourself emotionally from her or your daughter. Be emotionally present; better yet, invite her to play ball or golf with you. I had not anticipated how frequently successful and healthy women would describe fathers who encouraged them to participate in outdoor activities. Fathers may assist their daughters to learn how to connect with the world outside of the home in this way, enabling them to step more autonomously into it.

I have no idea if these generalized portraits will predict if today's adolescent boys and girls will succeed in their work by their middle age. Women's rapidly changing roles since the late sixties and early seventies are probably altering parents' long-term effects on their children's familial and vocational success in ways I cannot predict with much confidence.

Today's parents, particularly working mothers, occupy much less of a child's psychological space than they used to. Other influences can therefore affect how a child grows up healthily more directly than they used to. School is one. What does a child's school experience predict about how he or she will grow up to succeed?

26

School and Adult Success

When speaking with parents about what predicts how well their children will succeed when adults, I am asked without fail about academic grades and SAT scores. Despite my answer, some parents insist an A record and high SAT scores guarantee their children's future success. Some even threaten, bribe, or verbally flay their children to get better grades. One senior girl tearfully told me, "My mother ordered me to get all As this next grading period; she said she didn't care how I got them." Another said her parent paid her $100 for every A that she got. A junior claimed his parents told him that he was a failure because his SAT scores barely reached the average of college-going students.

My research and others' provide a different perspective about what schools predict about the future success of boys and girls of *above-average intelligence and school achievement* (note the emphasis). Some of the results, in a nutshell, are the following:

- School grades and achievement test scores predict moderately well which students will do well in school the next year; they do not predict well which students of average or above-average grades and test scores will succeed later in life.
- Scholastic aptitude (as shown in SAT scores) does not predict adult success.
- Intelligence, when more broadly defined than just scholastic aptitude, contributes to success, particularly occupational,

291

but less than many character strengths do. Scholastically talented youngsters therefore risk failing when adults if they do not develop the character strengths necessary to succeed.
- Failure to do well in school does not limit youths' future success *if* they have developed the character strengths necessary to succeed.
- Extracurricular participation is a school's best predictor of an adult's success.

If you are the parent of a child, I can almost feel your argumentative vibes at this moment. Remember, I confine my comments to capable college-going students; I have not studied how high school graduates and dropouts succeed later in life. However, others studying more varied students report similar results. You will just have to trust me. It is true.[1]

Of course schooling is important to the maturation of our minds and characters. I value academic and character excellence highly — too highly, some of my students believed. Why then the dismal results that suggest schools don't contribute much to success? It is because schooling produces many more liberally educating or maturing effects than teachers and tests measure. When studying how Haverford College helped its students become adults, for example, I discovered that, yes, it improved their minds, but it more profoundly altered their characters, an effect faculty's grades did not measure.[2]

Academic Grades Do Not Predict Adult Success

Since schools have no good measures of how liberally educated their students become, I had to rely on feeble ones like academic grades, achievement test scores, and other indices for clues about how well they prepared the men and women to be effective adults. Because the study's men were educated in the same college, and their grades meant the same thing, I can more reliably compare them than I can the women, who attended a variety of colleges with different standards of excellence. Though it may be true that a rose is a rose is a rose, it is not true that an A is an A is an A in three different colleges.

Within my bright group of men and women, college grades predicted little about their adult lives. C students were just as likely as A students to be happy and satisfied with their lives when middle-aged. They had just as happy marriages and close friends, were as good lovers and as competent parents, had as high incomes, were as involved in their communities, and were as ethical as A students.

How well had Andy and Harry achieved in school? Both had done well in high school. Andy's counselor had seen him as "serious-minded and hardworking with a high sense of responsibility"; Harry's saw him as "fundamentally serious and a responsible worker but also a playboy, very diversified in extracurricular activities, and just very outstanding." At Haverford, both of their undistinguished academic records did not predict their later success. Andy's solid B record was marred by only a few C's in ethics and eighteenth-century literature. It sparkled with a few A's in chemistry and poetry. Upon graduation, his adviser said that he had been a "fundamentally serious and responsible worker, well-balanced, most likable, superior person all-round" and rated his determination, intelligence, and originality to be good but his emotional stability and personality excellent. Harry's low B grade record also did not foretell his later vocational and community success. One of his two A's was in economics; two of his very low C's were in chemistry. His senior adviser wrote that he was a "sound and hardworking" man of "good character" and rated his emotional stability and determination to be excellent, his intelligence and personality good, but his originality only fair.

Are there no specific comforting findings for highly achieving persons? Yes, for the men I studied, but not for the women, whose academic grades predicted not one adult competence.[3] Not unexpectedly, the men who got high grades earned more fellowships and honors in graduate and professional schools and published more scholarly books. Those who knew them best in their mid-forties rated them to be vocationally competent and fulfilled, possibly because of their purposefulness, reliability, and self-control. But that is all.

Are you muttering, "Unbelievable. Something is wrong with

your study"? Well, I was not very happy either, recalling the thousands of hours I had apparently wasted grading hundreds of students' work. So I tracked down what researchers claimed grades and achievement tests predicted. I was dismayed by how few adult successes had been studied. Apart from the next year's achievement in similar academic fields, only vocational success, particularly income, eminence, and creativity, had been seriously studied. I was even more discouraged to discover that in those few studies academic grades predict achievement in the next year's courses quite well, in college not quite as well, in graduate school less well, and in the "real world" of adult success scarcely at all.

I can't resist telling you that as long as thirty years ago medical school admissions directors should have known that aptitude tests and premed grades only moderately predicted the grades of medical students in their first two years and predicted not one single measure of their clinical effectiveness in their third and fourth years.[4] Seventy percent of those who excel in their clinical work have *not* done well in their basic science courses, according to another study.[5]

I could go on and on, but the weight of the evidence now is that academic grades and honors only "marginally," in the words of one review, predict vocational success,[6] and only questionably predict income, eminence, and creativity. One reason for these dark results is that it is difficult to compare different adult achievements, whether grades from dissimilar colleges or success in diverse occupations. Consider income: How can we fairly compare the sweet honeydew melons of physicians and rock stars with the sour lemons of teachers and ministers?

Failure to do well in school, or even graduate, does not bar us from doing well later in life *if* we have the character strengths I have described. Jane has demonstrated that truth. Although she was a school dropout, Jane has shown unusual talent and creativity in her business — which promises to make her a bundle of money in the years ahead. (And remember how poorly Einstein did in school.)

Achievement Test and SAT Scores Do
Not Predict Adult Success

Achievement and aptitude tests do not predict adult success any better than academic grades. Teachers that I work with feel pressured by their students' apprehensions about tests, such as the English achievement tests, that colleges require. While such tests help some admissions directors, they predict little about their students' futures. Despite great variation in their scores, the English achievement test scores of the study's men barely contributed to their subsequent academic grades and did not predict one measure of adult competence. Andy scored in the 40 percent range and Harry in the 99 percent range nationally, but Andy, not Harry, has since written extensively, including a book. "Incredible," you say. I agree, but until someone else studies adults systematically for decades, this is the only evidence we have about how unimportant such tests are to a broad range of adult successes *for above-average students*.

Surely a student's scholastic aptitude, closely related to intelligence, must contribute something to his or her future success. Well, it does, but not quite what I had thought. Yes, the dreaded SAT scores predict freshman college grades, though not very well; fifteen and twenty-five years later, those high school juniors who scored high will be no more successful, healthy, or happy than those who scored average or even somewhat below. Sorry, my high-scoring SAT readers. How did Andy and Harry do? Not so well and very, very well. Andy's verbal and quantitative scores were slightly above those of the average student applying to colleges, but below the Haverford average. Harry's were much higher, almost perfect. He was in the 94 to 99 percent range, respectively, though his academic grades were below the average of his class.

The troubling finding is this: Fifteen- and sixteen-year-olds who score very high on the SAT, especially the quantitative reasoning section, will more likely than not be the *less* interpersonally mature, empathic, and self-confident thirty-three- and forty-five-year-olds. These are key strengths necessary to succeed.[7]

Harry is an exception and reminds us that my statistically based generalizations only tell us what is probable, not what is certain. If scholastic aptitude scores of above-average college students predict something positive later in life, Andy's, Harry's, and the scores of the entire group of men do not tell us what it is.

Not only students' academic grades and tests but also teachers' ratings of their intellectual capability do not predict success or happiness. However, the men whose professors rated them to be their most intellectually capable seniors were seen by their peers as ambitious, self-controlled, analytical, and possessing strong personalities twenty-five years later. But that also is all.

Since others have found similar results with more intellectually diverse groups, I now no longer question my findings as much.[8] I cautiously conclude that intellectual level makes an important contribution to certain kinds of adult success, primarily occupational, but within a bright group of adults, it contributes much less than many character strengths to almost any definition of success you and I may want to use.[9]

You are probably impatiently asking why some intellectually capable students may be at risk for failing—or not fulfilling their promise—as adults. One reason is that adult success depends upon many diverse strengths (particularly interpersonal); high intelligence can isolate a child from others when young. Again, I cannot resist citing a few studies. Quantitatively gifted pubertal boys and girls are impatient, sarcastic, argumentative, opinionated, and socially aloof—scarcely qualities that would attract their peers to want to be friends with them.[10] The study's quantitatively gifted men could not share their feelings with others; their peers rated them to be interpersonally immature. Others report that the most academically involved college student grows least in all other sectors of his personality.[11] At Harvard, writing "a senior honors thesis . . . tends to predict a decline in maturity of adaptation among men."[12]

May not the more clarifying question be, "What distinguishes those talented persons who fulfill their intellectual promise later in life from those who never do?" My results and those of the too few who have asked this question generally confirm those of Terman, the earliest and most distinguished researcher in the field. Those who fulfill their talents are emotionally stable, persistently motivated, purposeful, self-confident, and have stronger personalities.[13] These are the qualities of those who are more mature.

Extracurricular Participation Makes the Difference Later in Life

As a teacher all my professional life, I am humbled that not my grades, tests, and academic awards but students' depth of genuine involvement in extracurricular activities predicts best how well they will succeed in their adult years. Billie, Andy, Marty, and Harry participated extensively in athletic and other extracurricular activities and held major positions of leadership. Only Jane, estranged from her school and suppressed by her mother, didn't participate in extracurricular or community activities. Of the study's 105 men and women, those who had actively participated in their schools' co-curricular activities fulfilled their primary adult roles successfully and were generally mature.

Though other research evidence is sparse, it is consistent.[14] I feel I must justify your suffering trust in my judgment by this time, so I shall quote a summary of a major comparative study of diverse students' high school grades, scholastic aptitude tests, and extracurricular involvement. Grades and test scores were generally useless. Instead, "the best predictor of creativity in mature life was a person's performance, during youth, in independent, self-sustained ventures. Those youngsters who had many hobbies, interests, and jobs, or were active in extracurricular activities, were more likely to be successful in later life."[15]

Some who have heard these results blame their messenger — yours truly. As I said initially, schools produce many more maturing effects than we know or measure by our grades and tests. That is why a school or college degree, rather than the specific grades achieved or detailed information gained in tests, predicts more effectively some forms of subsequent success, such as managerial level achieved.[16]

Most studies of a school's long-term effects have researched only adolescents and young adults. The teenage years are potentially high-growth ones, when parental influence begins to diminish and youngsters begin to get more conscious control over their own growing up. What adolescent character predicts future adult success and happiness?

27

Adolescents Who Become Successful, Healthy, and Happy Adults

Billie Leighton's story reminds us how formative the adolescent years can be. It tells us that we can take ourselves by the scruff of our necks, shake ourselves up, will ourselves to take charge of our lives, and educate ourselves about how to grow up healthily. It is the time we can learn how to reflect on and understand ourselves more accurately and so self-consciously determine our purposes. Billie's willed program to become a healthy person began in her early teenage years when she used her "log" to learn how to problem solve the dilemmas her seven mothers and fathers provoked. I hope Billie's story reassured you that we are *not* condemned to eternal torment because our parents were screwed up or our teachers failed us.

Billie's story, as well as those of the book's other leads, raises the question of the character of the adolescent who becomes a successful, healthy, and happy middle-aged adult. What are the emergent critical strengths of that period to encourage, reward, and mention in those reference forms that ask us to predict how a youth will succeed in the future? If you are a parent of a teenager, what strengths should you *not* inadvertently step on and squash? If you are a student, what strengths should you cultivate and value, in spite of your academic grades and SAT scores?

My ideas about the youthful personality of successful adults come from ratings that the men and women made of what they were like when they were adolescents (A1b). They rated themselves

299

on fifty adolescent traits and specific activities that I and other researchers had earlier found predicted adult success and well-being. I hope you are asking the obvious question. Who can remember accurately ten to fifteen years later what one was like in high school, the time the men and many of the women described their teenage selves? Since I had numerous measures of what the men were actually like when they were sixteen and seventeen, I could determine that their memories were, in fact, reasonably accurate.[1] I had no reason to question the women's, particularly because the pattern of their results made so much sense.

Four themes emerged out of the men's and women's memories of their youthful personalities and activities.

1. Mature teenage girls and boys get the brass ring when they are adults.
2. A boy's adolescent personality predicts his adult success much more consistently than a girl's.
3. Boys and girls whose strengths are typical of their sex succeed in their traditional adult sexual roles, though androgynous youngsters may succeed even more.
4. A boy's personality predicts his well-being at middle age. A girl's does not.

Mature Boys and Girls Get the Brass Ring When Adults

Men and women who succeed in their adult roles and are ethical, healthy, and happy persons had been mature and successful teenagers. The findings are overwhelmingly consistent. Neither the successful men nor women shared one strikingly immature or unhealthy trait in common when teenagers. I rephrase this important result differently. Adults who fail their spouses, children, and bedpartners, who don't do well in their work or contribute to their communities, who are not ethical, or have poor health, or are unhappy predictably describe their adolescent personalities and activities in immature terms.

Billie Leighton and Harry Barnett stood out as all-around successful and competent adults as measured by objective tests.

They also were superb examples of the computer-drawn portrait of the adolescent who turned out most successfully. As a teenager Billie had been more mature, stable, and autonomous than 90 percent, 80 percent, and 98 percent respectively of the other women when they were adolescents. Harry also had been more mature, stable, and autonomous than 97 percent, 98 percent, and 98 percent of his peers had been as teenagers.

Do you understand again why I argue, as have many other liberal educators, that the proper goal of schooling is to enhance students' maturing, not their SAT scores? Just as healthy families produce successful adults, so healthy and mature adolescents become successful and happy adults.

Male but Not Female Adolescent Personalities Predict Adult Outcomes

Table 27.1 summarizes the percentage of the 50 personality traits that the men and women rated about their adolescent personalities that reliably predicted different adult outcomes. It raises perplexing questions about how boys and girls may develop differently, at least through adolescence.

Table 27.1. Percentage of Adolescent Traits That Predict Adult Outcomes.

Adult Outcome	For Men	For Women
Intimacy roles	16	10
Vocational success	42	4
Community citizenship	26	8
Ethical idealism	20	16
Well-being	30	4
Physical health	40	6
Mental health	34	6
Happiness	10	4

The table says that the men's vocational success could be predicted by 42 percent of their adolescent personality strengths but the women's by only 4 percent and that the men's well-being could be predicted by 30 percent but the women's by only 4 percent of the fifty adolescent traits I assessed.

Since the boys' personalities, but not the girls', powerfully predicted their success and well-being in middle-age, I list their most important adolescent strengths that predicted the largest number of adult outcomes.

- Optimistic attitude
- Emotional health
- Enjoyment of school
- Curiosity and interest in many different things
- Assumption of or election to leadership positions
- Knowledge of strengths and weaknesses
- Tough skins so they are not overly sensitive to peers' slights or disapproval

Do you remember that optimism was the second most noticeable strength of healthy and happy adults? As only a small but important example of the interwoven coherence of the study's findings, we now see that optimism also heads the list of adolescent strengths. It was the only one of the fifty youthful traits that predicted *every* adult male outcome. Optimism means hope. Developmentally, adolescents have the cognitive capacity to imagine alternative futures for themselves and for their society and so to hope. Rebellious East German, Korean, Burmese, and Chinese students demonstrating for democratic reforms remind us that adolescents are neurologically programmed to be optimists. What happens when a generation's hope is snuffed out by their "gerontocratic" Chinese elders in Tiananmen Square? Or when youngsters have lost hope in their country's future or think of suicide as a realistic solution to despair?[2] How successful and happy will hopeless young persons turn out to be when adults? The crisis of our schools is that too many kids no longer view them to be enablers of hope.

The table above also tells us that successful women shared few adolescent personality traits in common. Like the males, they had been leaders in their schools, but as is typical of females, they had been sympathetic and concerned about others' welfare and willing to share their feelings with them. That is about all. For all practical purposes, we cannot predict which teenage girl will turn out to succeed in most areas of her life ten to twenty years later.

You might say, as I did initially, that their reports of their adolescence just are not accurate. The principal reason that I do not agree that the women's sparse results are due to inadequate methods is that the IGS longitudinal researchers found the same thing. As I had done when the men were adolescents, they actually had measured a raft of personality strengths when their middle-aged women were in their teens. They too found that a girl's personality did not predict much about her later success or the career path, such as homemaker or paid job, that she took.[3] However, a girl's personality did predict her adult commitment to her work. When they were teenagers, the vocationally committed women had been anxious, defensive, self-conscious, hostile, and typically masculine. This pattern of adolescent traits might be inferred from the adult character of my study's vocationally successful women, but I could not confirm it directly. Finally, the IGS staff found that unmarried working women, but not married working women, had been more ambitious and achieving in their teenage years.[4] Again, this is about all the IGS study discovered.

The IGS researchers believe, as I do, that girls, traditionally oversocialized into their feminine familial roles, learn to adjust to the needs and demands of others at the expense of developing and asserting their individual strengths. Many of their youthful potentials remain dormant and so do not contribute to their adult success as saliently as men's do. Now that women initiate their careers and develop the necessary strengths to succeed earlier in their lives, their adolescent character may better predict their success in the future.

Stereotypic Adolescent Sexual Role Differences

Boys have been raised for centuries to succeed in their occupational roles and girls in their familial roles. Boys and girls who have developed by their mid- and late teens the strengths typical of their sex will more likely than not fulfill their traditional adult roles more successfully than boys and girls who haven't.

The Adolescent Character of Vocationally Successful Men.
Middle-aged men who succeeded vocationally had been stable
and autonomous adolescents. At that time of their lives, they
had known who they were, what they believed, and where they
were going. They had strong wills and could make their intellectual talents work for them, as in arguments with their peers.
Their feelings were not easily hurt by their peers' sarcastic put-
downs. Such strong boys not only had enjoyed school but also
had participated extensively in extracurricular activities, which
they had led; they generally had shared the interests typical of
boys, like having girlfriends. Vocationally successful men had
not been one-sided achieving adolescents, however. They also
had been interpersonally mature teenagers who empathically
understood others and their feelings about them. Friendly and
socially outgoing, they had felt at home with others and so did
not feel lonely or isolated.

In his teens, Harry had modeled every one of the specific
adolescent strengths of such vocationally successful men. He had
a strong will, shown in his good control of his talents; he was
purposeful, had strong beliefs, was emotionally stable and independent. Harry also had been more interpersonally mature
than his peers. He had good male friends, was "on time" in his
emerging female friendships, and felt at home in social groups.
He enjoyed school, participated in extracurricular activities, was
recognized as a leader by his peers, and generally had wide-
ranging interests. Harry, like the other vocationally successful
men, had his teenage act together. He had created a strong self,
according to Erikson's prescription for healthy male development.

The tenor of these results agrees with those of the IGS researchers. They found that more ambitious, dependable, intellectually effective, and interested adolescents, who were not self-
indulgent, achieved higher occupational levels by their forties.[5]
What do these results suggest about more willful and apathetic
boys, indulging themselves in drugs and sex, disliking school,
and chasing the fast buck at McDonald's to feed their thirsty
sports cars?

The adolescent roots of vocationally successful men are clear.

What were the adolescent roots of men who succeeded as partners, parents, and lovers? I could find no adolescent interpersonal skills that they had shared in common when young. It may be that adolescent males' principal developmental task is, as Erikson has proposed, to fashion their identities by achievement and mastery, which the vocationally successful men certainly had done as adolescents. The interpersonal skills necessary to be a good marital partner, parent, and lover may not, as he also suggested, become a primary developmental task for males until later. Men may need sustained exposure to the intimacy demands of their spouses and children to bring their latent interpersonal skills into prominence. Certainly this was the case for Andy and other men whose wives and, especially, children taught them how to become more maturely other-centered. Exceptions exist, of course. Harry was one. As a teenager he was more other-centered and interpersonally mature than 90 percent of the other men had been when adolescents.[6]

May not the findings reflect how the typical male *is* socialized but not how he *could* be by his teens? Studies of other men growing up at Haverford College showed that their interpersonal maturation ranked third in amount among the twenty outcomes that the model of maturing predicted would occur during their college years. Much of that maturation occurred as a consequence of learning how to get along with roommates and girlfriends as well as emotionally buying into the college's social honor system, which expected them to respect and consider others' rights.[7]

The Adolescent Character of Women Successful in Familial Roles. Women who succeeded in their intimacy roles shared when teenagers only the interpersonal strengths that later contributed to their marital, parental, and sexual success. As adolescents, they were concerned about and sympathetic with others; they forged close friendships with other girls, with whom they easily shared their feelings and were demonstratively affectionate. Of the few others who have studied female adolescents in depth, Douvan and Adelson believe that intimacy and not identity issues are the focal concern of their development.[8] Women

who later succeeded in their intimate relationships had successfully developed the necessary interpersonal skills by adolescence.

The data suggest that more androgynous teenagers, especially
girls, will succeed twenty years later in their major adult roles.
The successful women had been clearly more autonomous, independent girls, as Billie had been.[9] They, like Billie, had been
leaders, had participated extensively in extracurricular activities, and had many interests. For girls (boys as well), these
adolescent strengths also predicted responsible community involvement during their adult years.

Boys' but Not Girls' Character
Predicts Adult Mental Health

The table's most puzzling finding is not that men rather than
women who succeed in their work had more sharply defined
adolescent personalities. After all, males are brought up since
the age of three to think of their Number 1 Selves as achievers
and the primary earners of the family's bread. That the table
also shows that physically healthy men but not women shared
similar personality strengths when young also doesn't surprise
me. We have already seen that a woman's physical health is not
a good indicator of her character strengths.

But I was dumbfounded and then dismayed by the dramatic
finding that mentally healthy men agreed among themselves
about a large number of strengths that they had had in their
adolescent years and that mentally healthy women definitely did
not. If Freud had seen these results, he would have exclaimed,
"That's why women are mysteries. Their youth seems to have
nothing to do with their adulthood. Impossible. Psychoanaly-
sis has proved that the 'daughter is the mother of the adult
woman.'"

I cannot wish the results away as unreliable because I could
actually check what the adolescent character of the adult men
had been like. It was what the mentally healthy adult men had
described it to be. I had numerous measures of their mental
health when they were in college (such as judgments by peers,
coaches, and teachers and standard psychological tests).[10] Men-

tally healthy middle-aged men had also been mentally healthy young men (A32).

I told you in Chapter Twenty about well-being that the mentally healthy man's core strengths are his interpersonal other-centeredness, stability, and autonomy. The same adolescent strengths herald the adult man's mental health, which again confirms how deeply etched is a man's health in his enduring character predispositions. The principal adolescent strengths that contributed to a man's later mental health are reviewed in Table 27.2.

Table 27.2. Male Adolescent Character Indicators of Adult Mental Health.

Other-Centeredness	Stability	Autonomy
Empathically understood what others felt about him	Was not moody	Did not give in to others
Was friendly and social	Was predictable	Had good control over his talents
Did not feel lonely	Had a strong sense of purpose	Was not impulsive
Felt at home in social groups	Had strong beliefs	Was a leader

The healthy boy's other-centeredness, stability, and autonomy undergirded his enjoyment of school, optimism about his future, and emotional health — all outcomes of psychological maturity. No wonder such adolescents turn out to be healthy when middle-aged. These results are more consistent and firm than those of the few other researchers who have studied the adolescent roots of later adult psychological healthiness and maturity.[11] These are a boy's strengths that parents and teachers need to encourage and reward — not his SAT scores.

The remarkable coherence of the mentally healthy men's adolescent and adult character prevents me from dismissing the women's nonresults. So I accepted the finding that a teenage girl's character tells us little about how mentally healthy she will be twenty years later. I will pursue that mystery in Chapter Twenty-Nine, once I have marshaled all of the necessary evidence to make some reasonable guesses about what is going on in a girl's development.

I can say little about the adolescent roots of happiness — the other component of well-being. Just as our parents' characters and attitudes toward us do not seem to contribute directly to our adult happiness, neither do specific adolescent traits. We create our own happiness and develop our own character. Our childhood and parents contribute to forming that character, but they are not responsible for what we do with it as we move into our twenties, thirties, and forties.

As we also saw when unearthing the adolescent roots of vocational and familial success, *not one* unfavorable character attribute occurred in the collective adolescent history of the healthy and happy adult man or woman. We can amend and extend Vaillant's comment this way: "The things that go right in our lives do predict future success *and, for men in particular, well-being* [emphasis added] and the events that go wrong in our lives do not forever damn us."[12]

If you are a woman, I hope that you are not feeling neglected at this moment. The results just were not present about the adolescent roots of women's success and well-being. But in a paradoxical way, that nonresult proves to be most revealing about women's healthy growth. I shall explain why after I finish talking about how males mature from their early adult years into middle age.

28

Men Growing
into Mid-Life

I have told you about how our parents, schools, and adolescent personalities contribute to how we grow up as adults. Now, I shall mention a few results about how the men grew in their twenties and thirties and the principal reasons for that growth. Men's growth is much simpler to understand than women's during their adult years. Men's growth did not take any right-angled or surprising turns. The men's maturing path from the thirties into middle age remarkably resembled the one they had traveled in their twenties and early thirties. Nine of the ten principal changes that occurred then were the same most important ones that took place from their early thirties to their mid-forties. However, only about half of the *causes* of such growth were similar. Do different experiences at different times in our lives have similar maturing effects?

Before continuing you might reflect back to what you were like when you graduated from school and then what you are like now and try to identify how your mind and character, values, relationships with others, and view of yourself have changed. Then try to figure out what the principal causes of those changes were.

Before describing how the study's men grew from their twenties to their mid-forties, I must comment about the rate or timing of such changes. If you are an unmarried twenty- or thirty-year-old, you may report less growth than the study's men did about those years. Why? The study's men had settled down and committed themselves to their vocations and begun their marriages and families by their mid- and late twenties. Since the challenges of these commitments were the principal determinants of their growth, I'm not sure what will spark your continued growth if you are like Roger and have postponed assuming or don't plan to assume such commitments. Are today's younger generations as mature and healthy as earlier generations were when their age? Or will they turn out in the long run to be happier and healthier when middle-aged? By delaying making commitments, will they make more lasting and healthy ones by middle age?

Societal changes in timing are one reason I and others studying adult development over many years do not accept the idea that there are age-fixed stages or crises to growing up in the adult years. Maturing is continuous and similar from the twenties to middle age. However, the specific developmental tasks and level of maturity required to adapt to them fluctuate as a result of changing societal expectations about when it is "time" to marry or have children or settle down to earn a living. Career women, for example, who postpone having children until their mid- or late thirties face a different psychological task from women who have children in their late teens and early twenties. They need to be more sure of themselves and their priorities to avoid communicating resentment and rejection to a child whose need for their constant presence interferes with fulfilling their career aspirations.

Maturing in the Twenties and Early Thirties

The principal growths the study's men experienced from their early twenties to early thirties were increased awareness, integration, certainty of their identities, and caring for others. The principal causes of such maturing were their partners' personalities and their type of occupation (A23).

To illustrate the information I had about how the men's partners influenced their maturing, I have selected some typical quotes from their interviews when they were in their early thirties. To appreciate just how much loved ones can help us grow,

I shall first tell you what the men said of their premarital selves and then of their marital ones.

The men used similar words to describe what they were like before they settled down with their partners. "I was a hermit." "I found socializing difficult before I met her." "My dealings with others were harsh." "I was very crude as a bachelor." "I was a very closed and uncommunicative kind of person."

One man's wife-to-be really shook him up. "I was sitting in that chair over there and she said to me, 'Look, when are you going to stop this formal behavior and this aloofness and admit that we have a relationship?' That really blew my mind. Challenged my whole life and my way of relating to people. She dared to say, 'I can see through you.' A little female [a pre-women's movement comment] had dared to challenge my behavior and make me look at myself."

After living intimately with their partners for years, the men spoke quite differently about themselves. One man's comment is typical. It also strikes close to home to me, though Harriet isn't an accusing person at all. "She's leveled me a few times. Said that I'm not all I'm cracked up to be. Accused me of being dull and having a tunneled view of life because I work and do nothing else. Not that interesting a person. That taught me I'm missing out on things, like how flowers grow, how my son is growing." (Harriet would say "writing books and lecturing all of the time and missing out on how your grandsons are growing.")

I like this one. It shows how living closely with another can tell us what we are like and what we should be. "She has helped me to learn what I don't have to be. I don't have to be a perfectionist. I don't have to be deadly serious about everything I do. She has helped me to have fun, to laugh at myself. She has challenged me when I've been pompous or pedantic or petty. She's really made me feel that no matter what happens she will stand with me and by me and that gives me a great sense of security and confidence in what I do."

Do you now understand my comment about the effects of delayed timing? The longer some men postpone assuming the trials and joys of committing themselves to an enduring relationship, the harder time they will have getting over being crude, unsocial, uncommunicative hermits.

Maturing from the Thirties into the Mid-Forties

The men's and women's interviews in middle age about how they had changed since their early thirties were also scored for the model of maturing's categories. In rough declining order, they grew most in the following ways:

- Becoming more aware of themselves
- Thinking more relationally or integratively
- Becoming more other-centered in their relationships
- Stabilizing their self-concepts
- Integrating their self-concepts
- Becoming more aware of their values
- Stabilizing their values
- Developing more autonomous self-concepts

To make these abstract categories more meaningful, I shall translate each in turn into predictions I made to Roger, if he grew into middle age in these ways. Roger will continue to discover more about what is behind his partly closed mineshaft door. If he yields to Beth's wishes and has a child, I guarantee that he will discover how angry he can be when provoked. He will actively make more connections between the heroes of the American lit novels and the historical and social settings of the American history courses he teaches. If he stays with Beth, he most likely will become more caring and compassionate; if not and he restlessly continues going from one woman to the next, then I doubt that he will grow much in other-centeredness. He probably will settle even more firmly into his Number 1 Self by accepting and integrating the assertive maleness of his fighting dogs into his day-to-day relationships. He should become clearer about what he wants out of his life; he might even summon the determination to begin writing the historical novel he has been dillydallying about for years. And as he develops a more autonomous sense of self, he won't need to ask me how he can continue to grow up.

Causes of Maturing into Middle Age

What kinds of experiences contribute most to how a man grows into middle age? To find out, I used the same objective procedures I had developed to identify what attributes of school[1] or young adulthood produce maturing (or immaturing) changes.[2] Do you recall from my second interview with Billie Leighton how I gave her fifty different possible causes of change — such as her husband, her job's demands on her time, and the women's movement — and asked her to sort them in terms of their influence on the changes she had mentioned (A23)?

The principal prods to men's maturing into middle age are in declining order of influence:

- Type of occupation
- Personality of their partner
- Major changes in their work (for example, more responsibility)
- Role as husbands to their wives
- Being parents
- Receiving counseling
- Their children
- Physical and mental health
- Becoming middle-aged

Rather than describe the main maturing effects of each of these determinants, I will describe those that contribute most to men's becoming more insightful about themselves. Recall that they had grown most in their self-awareness from their early thirties to their mid-forties. The main cause of the men's *increased self-awareness* continued to be, as it had been in their twenties, their partners' personalities and their relationship with them. Beth will probably continue to provoke Roger to edge further through his mineshaft door, at least until he's forty-five. After that I don't know, since I have not followed the men into their fifties and sixties.

The next most influential spur to the men's increased self-insight was counseling. Recently, one of the study's men wrote me a postcard. His wife had told him two days before my visit seven years ago that she wanted to divorce him. He had angrily locked her out of their house several evenings before when she had come home later than he expected. Not expecting her to take that step, he was torn apart and paralyzed for five years before his misery reluctantly drove him into counseling. His card read, "Eight or nine sessions with the counselor were wonderful for me. I learned why I had done what I did. I'm extremely happy, and I hope to be married before the year's end."

The remaining principal causes that goaded the men to become more aware of themselves had a lot to do with growing older. Approaching middle age and their changing health began to tell them that they could not play as fast a tennis game as they used to. (Logging out my dead spruce trees tells me that if I am going to trek again in the Himalayas, I had better do it soon.) If middle age is still ahead of you, I can alert you about many other changes you may face, such as what your vocation's demands on your time and energy may do to you or what contributes most to developing more firm values and more autonomous personal relationships. But then growing up may be more interesting if you don't know what is in store for you.

The path that middle-aged women took from their early thirties to their forties is similar; I predict that women in their twenties and thirties are already treading it. Let's discover what growing up to be a woman means these days.

29

Women Growing into Mid-Life

Understanding how females grow up to succeed has been dogged by four seemingly inconsistent and unexpected findings. For me, the book remains incomplete until I make some sense of them. The results that have puzzled me most are

- Women's vocational satisfaction was consistently not related to or integrated well with their character.
- Women's physical health predicted little else about them.
- Mothers and fathers contributed so much more to their daughters' adult success than they did to their sons'.
- Parents and adolescent character contributed almost nothing to the women's adult mental health.

Three clues helped me frame a hypothesis to explain these diverse results:

1. The women's objective tests and peers identified three similar women, Billie, Marty, and Jane, to be among the more successful and happy ones of the study.
2. Stability and autonomy are the core strengths of mentally healthy and happy women, as they are for men.
3. Androgynous strengths are necessary to succeed and become mentally healthy.

My hypothesis is that women's maturing is more conflictive than men's. Their biology, parental enmeshment, and oversocialized feminine interpersonal strengths have blocked their healthy growth. Their equilibrating principle's potential for encouraging maturing is, one might say, put on hold.

If you are a woman, I hope that the hypothesis won't inflame you. Harriet doesn't like it. Her reaction was, "At least women are trying to grow. Men aren't." I'm not sure where that leaves me. Anyway, the hypothesis is the only one that makes sense of the women's findings for me. Other women already have proposed similar ideas, for which the study may now provide the scientific support. I shall briefly review the evidence and then describe in more detail how the women matured in their adult years and why.

Biological, Parental, and Interpersonal Constraints

Biological Constraints. Women but not men share similar recurring biological experiences, like menstruation, pregnancy, birth, and nursing, that strengthen and reaffirm a communizing rather than individualizing identity. The consequences of developing such an identity are numerous and pervasive: the development of interpersonal skills that further communal harmony, language that is sensitive to and articulates feelings, and values that conserve social rather than promote individualistic traits and roles. Too developed communizing strengths can block the development of individualizing potentials and so hinder maturing.

The suggestive evidence? The women's peers reliably rated them to be more interpersonally feminine than the men's peers rated the men to be. Women's bodily health and adolescent personalities did not predict much about them as adults, which suggests that gender and oversocialization into typical feminine roles because of common biological experiences may have suppressed or obscured their individual talents and needs.

Parental Enmeshment. Women but not men remain emotionally close to and enmeshed in their families of origin far into their adult years. They also look back to their mothers more than men. Worldwide, fathers do not expect their daughters to "get out on their own" as early and in the same way as their sons. They early model and expect their sons to roam, explore, climb trees, get drunk, gamble, race cars, and generally "get into trouble." Fathers also have a biological ally. After all, testosterone is an assertive, intruding, penetrating, risk-taking hormone. So boys are often goaded to learn how to cope, achieve, and master themselves on their own.

Girls are raised to stay home. The consequences of such enmeshment are, among other things, valuing security more than risk taking; reaffirming a prescribed identity rather than fashioning one's own; and, by not testing themselves against a rich variety of challenges, other than interpersonal, not discovering and expanding new interests and developing latent strengths, particularly initiating and asserting ones.

The suggestive evidence? Women satisfied with their vocations or serving their communities as leaders share few common character traits because they have not been raised to succeed in those ways. Parents continue to contribute more directly to their adult daughters' than to their sons' successes. Two reasons help explain why women continue to be more affected by their parents than men are.

First, women are reliably more sensitive and responsive to parental cues and expectations than men are (A4i). The women's parents occupied more of their daughters' emotional life space than they did of their sons', as the interviews and tests showed. The women reliably valued their parental (even parent-in-law) relationships more than their husbands did. They also did not feel as understood by or act as equals with both parents.

Like Marty and Jane, though not to the same pitch, the women felt divided and distressed by their mothers, around whom they still felt like children. More than the men, they felt that when they were younger their mothers had rejected them. Also, the women disagreed and argued with their mothers much more than the men did about almost every topic, most notably about sex and ethical-religious issues. When we are so emotional and unsettled about our relations with another, that person can

affect us in singularly enduring ways. In contrast to the men,
few of the study's women had "freed" themselves of their mothers:
not Billie, who at the age of forty-one still "wanted more" from
her dead mother; not Marty, who was still arguing internally
with her mother in therapy; not even Jane, who still simmered
and fumed about her mother, whom she wouldn't allow to visit
her grandchildren.

Second, the women's parents continued to influence their
daughters because they were in flux, unsure of their future, and
searching for a more comfortable identity. By their mid-forties,
the men, with only one exception, had themselves together, but
many of the women had not, except for a few like Billie, Marty,
Jane, and Sue. If we are unclear about our priorities and who
we are and want to be, we may be more vulnerable to continuing parental influences. When we are unsure of ourselves, have
not tested ourselves in many different ways and found our path,
we may reach back into and find support from our families. We
"call home" more frequently.

Oversocialized Interpersonal Strengths. I now raise some con-
troversial issues. Do not forget how much typical feminine interpersonal skills like compassion, sensitivity to another's feelings,
and understanding contribute to adult success. Carol Gilligan,
studying how adolescent girls make moral decisions, believes
that their interpersonal skills and values are *the* pinnacle, *the*
measuring rod, *the* summum bonum of female moral and personal growth.[1] The study's adult women resoundingly say otherwise. The core of their maturity and well-being is their stability
and autonomy, not their other-centeredness.

The equilibrating principle warns us that every outstanding
strength can be a potentially fatal weakness if it is not integrated
with other strengths. Scholastically talented but interpersonally
immature youth may never realize their talent later in life. Or
too self-sufficient autonomy, as occurs in men, not integrated
with other-centered interpersonal skills can produce an arro-
gant and self-centered narcissist who fails in his familial roles.

So also, too developed feminine interpersonal skills, as occurs in some women, can block continued growth. When such

potential strengths are not integrated with a strong and independent sense of self, they can produce a conforming adjustment but unhealthy adaptation. Women have always faced unhealthy trade-offs for adjusting. For years, researchers have consistently found that women are more depressed and have lower self-esteem and self-confidence than men.[2] The negative effects of being raised to be a woman who pleases and conforms to others' expectations are several: Interpersonal adjustment bars discovering potentials that might disrupt harmonious relationships; one's self-worth depends upon others' approval; and so maturing remains blocked and well-being elusive.

The suggestive evidence? The women's peers judged them to be more compassionate, sensitive, and understanding than the men's peers rated the men to be. Regardless of how I measured the women's and men's maturity, mental health, and happiness, their stability and autonomy consistently were at their center. Their feminine interpersonal strengths were not; they are necessary but not as critical to maturity and well-being.

Androgynous women and men are mature and healthy persons. Women's and men's mental health is predicted by their masculinity; not, however, by macho qualities like aggressiveness, competitiveness, and forcefulness, but by autonomous and stable strengths, like self-reliance, courage, decisiveness, and self-confidence. A psychology of women that ignores such strengths to overemphasize their historic interpersonal ones risks entrenching women's past psychic oppression even more and undermining their potential to be healthy and happy persons. The meaning of a woman's maturity and well-being has to be much more complex and multidimensional to be faithful to how she grows healthily.

As long as women fulfilled their traditional feminine roles, they could adjust successfully to being wives, mothers, and lovers, roles that their mothers had modeled and prepared them for. Those who wished to work could be satisfied in a limited number of nuturing vocations, for example, teaching. They did not have to modify their feminine identity in such jobs, for their interpersonal skills contributed to their vocational fulfillment. Until the late sixties, therefore, the values of the women's parents and their upbringing matched those needed to succeed in their traditional roles.

But the world changed in the late sixties in ways the women had not been prepared for. They discovered that they had been raised to play a social role that did not fit many of their talents and needs. They became enigmas to themselves because many could not discover who their "real" selves were. They did not feel strong inside themselves. They told me, "All I am is an empty eggshell." "I am a wife to my husband, a mother to my children, a daughter-in-law to my mother-in-law. I don't know who I am." Or, in the words of the unexcelled leader of the League of Women Voters and other community groups, whom I quoted earlier, "All I am is a collection of roles put together by a committee."

None had talked like that in the late sixties when they were in their late twenties and early thirties. Twelve years later the women told me that they had no strong sense of themselves. They had identified with their other-centered interpersonal roles at the expense of developing stable and autonomous selves.

I could not trace the roots of the women's mental health back to their parents or adolescent personalities because neither had prepared them to develop the strong autonomous selves that are the core of a mentally healthy woman. The study's nonresults mirrored the women's transitional steps away from identifying with a prescribed social role to fashioning a more centered and independent self.[3]

Growing Healthily into Middle Age

The intriguing question now becomes, "How did women, raised to be collections of roles, develop more mature personalities?" Billie, Marty, and Jane showed us how modern women may have to grow to become successful, happy, healthy, and distinctive women. Marty struggled for years to grow beyond her biological nurturing disposition, without denying it. All three had to separate emotionally from too intense involvement with their mothers and discover their more androgynous, particularly latent masculine, strengths. Each developed a defined stable and autonomous sense of herself that integrated her feminine other-centeredness into a healthier, more complete self.

Maturing from the Thirties into the Forties. The women grew in ways similar to those that the men did, but their leading edge was autonomy and stability while the men's was awareness, integration, and other-centeredness (A23). In rough declining order of importance, the women matured in the following ways:

- Developing more autonomous self-concepts
- Becoming more aware of themselves
- Stabilizing their self-concepts
- Developing a more other-centered view of themselves
- Integrating their cognitive skills
- Developing more other-centered relationships
- Integrating their views of themselves
- Integrating their values

The women grew most in altering their concepts of themselves as women; they became stronger, more independent, as shown by Billie, Marty, and Jane. I hazard the guess that as they developed more stable and autonomous identities, their mental health improved and they became happier.

Their pattern of growth reflects an irrepressible human urge toward wholeness and shows the equilibrating principle diligently at work in the lives of middle-aged women. The centuries-old view that women should be only accommodating homemakers and mothers had become too maladaptive and suppressive of their urge to wholeness. Though the feminist movement had been preparing us for such a revolutionary change for decades, the integration and consolidation of its values precipitously occurred only within the few years that passed between my meetings with the women.

Causes of Maturing into Middle Age. The most important determinants of the women's maturing had been, in declining order of their actual effects,

- Personality of their partners
- Role as partner to their spouses
- Being a parent
- Counseling
- Physical and mental health
- Their adolescent children's values and strivings for independence
- The women's movement

Marty's life vividly shows how most of these influences could affect a woman's development. Before analyzing the maturing effects of the women's movement, two deserve special comments. Two-thirds of the women had sought some form of counseling since I had seen them in the late sixties and early seventies. Although many wanted advice about specific family issues, a not inconsiderable number had entered long-term therapy because of depression and self-doubts. Analyses of their tests suggested that some were really grappling with their identities as women rather than with classical neurotic conflicts and symptoms. Their upbringing as females had turned out to be inappropriate for the roles that they and society now expected.

The older women felt most provoked by their teenage children, who were demanding the freedoms and opportunities that the women's movement had brought. As one mother told me, "I feel like my adolescent daughter trying to figure out what I want to do the rest of my life, particularly now as I see her leaving home in a few years. We're dealing with the same issues. It's scary."

I had no glimmers of the potentially radical effects of the women's movement upon the women's sense of self when I interviewed them in the late sixties. Twelve years later, it ranked seventh out of the fifty reasons that might have contributed to their growth in the meantime. Few women had *not* been affected by the movement. Eighty-five percent had been changed: 25 percent very dramatically, 28 percent moderately to considerably, and 32 percent somewhat. It affected most prominently the maturation of the women's self-concepts and values.

When we self-consciously seek to test and discover what we are and could be, we sometimes engage in what appear to be immature behaviors. So when women began to wrest control of their identities from men, who for centuries had told them how to act and what to become, they had to experiment to learn what identity would be most integrative for them. Very predictably, some, like Marty, plunged into exaggerated excesses, self-centered liaisons, and potentially self-destructive experiments. These transitional calamities can mask, however, great resilience and other undiscovered strengths that slowly begin to emerge in time.

Typical signs of how reasonably mature people find their way out of their "adolescent" identity experiments are liberation of energy, enhanced self-confidence, a more mature assertive autonomy, and heightened creativity. Marty, Jane, and Billie all followed such a path.

I best make sense of how the women matured as a result of their movement by using the model of maturing to provide five signposts of their growth. The first is that the women's movement made all of us more *aware* of the immature effects of women's historical sexual role. After I spoke on this theme at a women's conference, an anonymous woman, whom I only fleetingly saw, slipped the following poignant note into my coat pocket.

Personal Reflections

I am one of those women
Tossed and turned by various claims
Vacillating between feelings of confidence,
*   and fears of being discovered a "phony."*
Trying while at a National Conference
*   to "forget" my parental responsibilities*
*   but not being fully able to do so.*
Though my husband says he's glad to fill the gaps.
What's shaped my hesitation,
*   my ambiguities,*
*   my goals?*

While those may be strengths,
I experience them more often as limitations.
Where is the power I seek
    to claim my full personhood,
And what price will be paid
    if I am able to fully exercise that power?

She tells us what a "collection of roles" feels like. She, like other women, had become aware how much she had lived for others at the expense of developing her own "personhood," her own strong sense of self.

The next signpost along the maturing path was for the women to learn that their doubts and hesitations were not theirs alone. They became more *other-centered* in their concept of themselves by identifying with women throughout history. Marty got right to the nub of this phase, when she said of the women's movement, "It taught me that I have sisters, that there is a sisterhood and that a lot of pain that I was feeling was also shared by other women. Furthermore, that the reason for the pain was outside of myself."

"I'm not sure what you mean. Could you give me an example?" I asked.

Marty answered, "The pain of feeling trapped as a mother and wife. Other women were feeling that same type of trapped feeling. There was something historical about that. Women have felt that for a long time."

The third signpost that marked the maturing effects of the women's movement was the encouragement of women to get in touch with how they really felt and thought, which then became *integrated* into their views of themselves. I had not anticipated the number of women who talked of taking over the political and social views of their partners. They wanted to please and not provoke argument or disharmony; they also did not know what they thought. Joan, the artist and the most typically feminine homemaker in the study, said that the women's movement "gave me the courage to say what I am thinking is okay, a kind of validation. It's strange that a woman needs that validation. Just to be . . . just to think what she wants to. Just to think that what I had on my mind was okay to say."

What I heard women like Joan telling me was that they now had permisison to no longer be good little girls trying to please their parents. Again, Marty's path seemed typical. Achieving integration involved the struggle to free herself from being fused with her parental, particularly maternal, internal presences. She began to learn how to meet her mother as an independent but loving equal.

The last two signposts pointed to a growing certainty of a more firm, *stable* sense of self and to a feeling of being in control of their own decisions and acts and so more *autonomous.* These two themes ran through one interview after another, particularly those of the ten women whose views about themselves had been most influenced.

It was Jane Allen who forcefully insisted,

> My idea of who I am has totally changed.
> I like myself. I didn't before.
> I'm able to do anything if I set my mind to it.
> I'm self-confident. Much more aggressive, much more.
> I have always been aggressive, but I never knew the strength I really have.
> I feel more confident to say "no."
> I am not afraid to offend others any more.

Cynthia more quietly spoke for the other women who had traveled the same route.

> I am more independent and rely on my parents less.
> I don't need approval from other people now.
> I accept whatever I choose for myself.
> Just that I can take responsibility for myself without being a shadow of my parents.

Both had become their own persons.

From a historical viewpoint, some form of the women's movement was inevitable. From a practical viewpoint, exaggerated self-centeredness, broken marriages, and wounded children were, sadly, also inevitable. Any such extraordinarily fundamental shift in the meaning of femaleness demands a heavy price in suffering and hurt. How long such emotional damage will continue is unknown. Much depends on women's determination to continue growing, men's adaptability, and women's and men's success in working together to create healthier definitions of femaleness and maleness for themselves and their children. While many are now being grievously hurt, we must not forget that millions of women and other minorities have also been emotionally maimed for centuries because society has denied them the opportunity to grow healthily. Change always produces trade-offs.

Reactions of Men to Women's Maturing. Since the personal meanings of femaleness and maleness are so reciprocally intertwined, changing the meaning of femaleness presages changes in the meaning of maleness. Inevitably! So I return to men, especially those of the study. They have been struggling not just to adjust but to adapt to women's and their own needs to grow more healthily. Roger believes that increasing numbers of younger men are becoming more sensitive to women's needs and learning how to adapt to more assertive women. It is older men, more set in their traditional sexual role and benefiting from it, who suffer the effects of women's maturing more acutely.

How have middle-aged men reacted? They have adjusted more than they have adapted. Of the men I studied, 83 percent claimed that the women's movement had affected them, mostly their values and relations with their wives. While a respectable 32 percent said that the women's movement had also altered their concepts of themselves as men, its *actual* impact had been much more modest. Whereas the women's movement was the seventh most important cause of the women's maturing as they entered middle age, it ranked thirty-eighth out of the fifty causes for the men. They had adjusted but only grudgingly begun to adapt by actually altering their deepest beliefs and attitudes about their maleness. Just as Billie's and Marty's paths prefigured the route other women began to take, so Andy's and Harry's was the one that more men will begin to follow. They not only adjusted but also adapted.

You may feel that my hypotheses miss the mark, but I have not been able to think of others that make as much sense of the women's seemingly inconsistent findings. I feel there is enough truth in them to begin to bring this book to a close. I shall begin by offering some prescriptions about how to raise children to grow up to succeed and be happy. I shall end by telling you the hope for our society that the study's men and women have given me.

30

Ten Prescriptions for Building a Strong Family

Our parents, schooling, adolescent personalities, and experiences as adults are keys, but they are not the only contributors to growing up healthily and succeeding in achieving our goals. Peers, TV, church, our own children, luck, and other influences affect us too. Because a healthy family and parents are so vital, however, to a healthy society, I will take the role of a psychological Dr. Spock and give you my own "zingers," prescriptions for creating a strong family and raising healthy children.

I, Dr. Doug, prescribe the following for you and your partner:

1. Be loving, democratic, and firm parents. Enjoy raising your kids.

2. Love and respect and don't try to dominate each other. Share your feelings and ideas openly with each other and your kids — when they're ready. Create an intellectually and culturally stimulating home. Be a teacher to your kids. During meals, don't look at TV but talk about politics, budget deficits, the Burmese, and the Supreme Court. Define words. Explain. Value their minds. Teach them how to study and think about problems.

3. If you are a woman, stand up to your friends for your calling to be a mother. Remember that it is mothers who value typical feminine interpersonal skills, such as caring and relating to others ethically, who most directly help their daughters and sons succeed in their intimate relationships and become ethically principled adults.

4. If you are a father, never reject your kids, particularly your son, even if you do separate from your partner. Be actively involved in their lives; include your daughter as well as your son in camping and sports activities. Teach them both what it takes to survive outside the home. Help your daughter become as strong and autonomous a woman as you expect your son to be a self-confident and self-determining man. Don't put down either child for developing the traditional strengths of the other sex. Be available when they need you. Hug them every day and tell them how much you love them.

5. Value your children's work in school but not at the expense of their extracurricular and community activities. Encourage their leadership potentials. Above all, don't pay them for getting A's, and never even hint that they will be failures the rest of their lives if their SAT scores are undistinguished.

6. Remember that your kids' adolescence is a potentially high-growth time during which they can more firmly build on (or rebuild, if they have to) their foundation for becoming emotionally stable and autonomous adults. They will have to explore and test themselves in numerous ways. Keep in mind that successful, healthy, and happy adults are not stuck in ruts, are optimistic, and feel in control of their own lives. So raise your kids to take judicious risks, to hope, and to assume responsibility for their own maturing.

7. Remember that you can best help your kids grow healthily into adulthood by making their teenage years high-growth years for yourself and each other. Grow with them. They will "disequilibrate" you — either unthinkingly or deliberately — to test what you feel is important. They will test just how saintly you are. Be a firm but respectful and loving parent. You will need in abundance the greatest parental virtue: patience. The next most important virtue is sense of humor; the next, high energy; the next, calmness. And then there are fifty-nine others. Reread Chapters Ten and Twenty-Three about fulfilled and competent parents each Sabbath before you go to church or to your favorite quiet spot to meditate.

8. Keep growing healthily at least until you reach your mid-forties. (I can't be so dogmatic for later years, not having studied

what happens then. But if your thirty-two-year-old daughter decides to sail around the world alone in a twenty-five-foot Vertue sailboat, you will continue to be stretched to stay sane even into your sixties.) Be models to your children of how mature and healthy adults continue to grow. Help each other to continue to grow.

9. Be sensitive to how traditional sexual roles affect your children's maturing. Fulfilling them well during adolescence contributes to success in traditional adult roles. However, value and encourage those opposite-sex strengths that also contribute to future success and well-being. Remember that the process of maturing is the same for boys and girls, though each may need to develop more on some dimensions than others at different times in their lives. Help your girls to become more healthily autonomous and your boys to mature interpersonally in the stereotypic feminine ways during their teenage years.

10. Read Chapter Twenty-Two about growing beyond your selves. Remember that despite some help from our genetics, parents, schooling, spouses, and children, we still create our own success, mental health, and happiness. We are our own psychological Horatio Algers.

31

A Perspective on Hope

Readers of the book's earlier versions have urged me to sum up what the study has told me about how to grow healthily in our society and to bring a ray of hope for the future. Roger wrote, "Soar, and say what you believe it tells us today."

Perhaps it is the teacher in me, or the arrogance of age, but I have accepted their invitation to get on my soapbox to talk about three issues: what impels growing up healthily, why developing healthy identities is more perplexing today, and what our society can do to help today's children grow up to succeed.

What Impels Growing Up Healthily?

I have learned that we grow for many reasons, but if three of these are absent we begin to die psychologically. To grow, we must be in an *alive relationship* with others, whether as workers, partners, parents, or friends, even as communicants and believers in God. Erich Fromm taught me that also.

"Not just a 'relationship,' but an 'alive' one," he insisted. As a psychoanalyst, he participated actively in growing with his patients. "When I become bored in therapy, something is wrong. For growth to occur, our relationship must be alive."

"And the effects?" I asked.

"My best self-analysis comes from my work with patients when we are both alive in our relationship."

"I'm not sure I understand what you mean by 'alive.'"

"Waking up more and more to become aware of yourself, others, and the world around you. Becoming more excited."

The study's men and women have helped me understand Fromm's definition more precisely. Their greatest growth occurred when a trusting and accepting relationship encouraged their vulnerability and openness to the influence of a respected person they loved.

However, just being in an alive relationship is not enough; another impetus to grow must be present, a *basic drive*. Roger mentioned it, almost off-handedly, when he tried to explain why he had changed since he wrote, "It's time for me to grow up, but how?" He wrote, ". . . and something else. Something inside but I can't put it into words. Something else pushes me to keep growing . . . not give up." Carl Rogers, the founder of client-centered or nondirective therapy, believed we have an "inherent tendency" to grow wholly. I do, too. The equilibrating principle is its guardian and spokesperson. Fromm also believed that each of us has a "basic drive . . . to grow," though, he felt, we vary in its strength. Billie's drive to grow healthily was exceptional, as were Andy's and Marty's determination to make their marriage succeed, Jane's doggedness to "make it on her own," and Harry's devoted commitment to his family and community.

Our drive to grow varies for many reasons, including the genetic histories and biohormonal experiences that contribute to our restless vitality, even from the moment of birth. The drive to grow also goes hand in hand with the need for more alive relationships. Societal agents, such as families and schools, can subdue if not snuff out our drive to grow, as I see in so many of the schools I visit. In a nationally recognized school, 55 percent of the teachers described their students to be apathetic; 85 percent of the students believed that high school was boring; only 20 percent thought that their teachers were intellectually exciting. In another academically superb school, 65 percent of the teachers wished that they were more intellectually exciting persons themselves. Fromm tells us no real growth will occur in schools until we create more alive faculty and student relationships. I agree. We need to teach to bring our students and ourselves more and more alive, not to worry about their SAT and achievement test scores.

A third necessary impetus to growth is to have a vision of what we want to become. A hopeful vision of the future inspires us to grow up.

Why Developing Healthy Identities
Is So Perplexing Today

What is our vision of the future today? A woman in her late twenties reacted to what I had written about the "American paradox" in Chapter Sixteen—being so wealthy but so dissatisfied and depressed—by perceptively writing, "I think this goes deeper than money, though. What about mission? That's what Roger is looking for. Franz Vehrman said, 'It is the task of every generation to find a mission, fulfill or betray it.' Our generation has not found a mission so we feel we are betraying. What is worse is that we are betraying nothingness, emptiness, thus the existential crisis. . . . We have less personal day-to-day needs to worry about so we can afford to be depressed."

Or in the words of the author of Proverbs, "Where there is no vision, the people perish." The revised version speaks more directly to the American paradox: "Where there is no revelation, the people cast off self-restraint." We live for ourselves. We want things fast. We expect others—our parents, schools, government—to give us what we want. Not just today's students and young adults live for now, but my generation does too, and my mother's as well. Her wealthy friends even want their generation's catastrophic medical insurance to be paid for by their children and grandchildren. We want to enjoy now. I have a cocktail napkin that pictures five ice cream cones with the words, "Life is uncertain. Eat dessert first." We have been doing just that, and more of us now ask, "What's been the point of it all?"

Mission? Vision? Calling? Purpose? Number 1 Self? Each points to what we want to be and do with our lives. Our "existential crisis" is that we are freeing ourselves from traditional sources of meaning but don't now know what to do with that freedom.

Where did our meaning come from yesterday? Certainly from our need to survive. As a Depression child, I dug for clams on Long Island's beaches so my family could eat each evening. As a thirties youth, I worked for ten cents an hour to get money to buy my two weekly pleasures — one ice cream cone and the Saturday matinee. Survival dictates our view of the world, its possibilities, and so our choices. For most contemporary Americans, sheer day-to-day survival is no longer a determiner of meaning, but finding money for five ice cream cones — those unnecessary extras — is.

Work's meanings have expanded and so provided more freedom. It no longer rigidly commands as much of our lives as it did 100 years ago and still does in most other countries. It no longer consumes so much of our life space unless we decide to let it. American pubertal children worked long hours less than 100 years ago; children still do in Benares, India, weaving silk ten hours a day. The work day and week have shortened since World War II. We work fewer years of our lifetime; we can retire earlier. We can choose between many more types of jobs now. We are freer to change our work and create our own work environments. Our ties to our work are gradually coming more under our own control.

Our identity as a Catholic, Jew, or Methodist used to tell us how to act and what to believe. It still often does, but no longer as compellingly for more and more of us. Catholics have sex to enjoy, not just to produce babies. Most Jews no longer follow their dietary laws as strictly. Even some Methodists now drink wine. Beliefs about immortality, heaven, hell, and the devil are myths, not living options, for more and more of us. We are freeing ouselves from religion's traditional meanings.

Our identity as a Daughter of the American Revolution, a Mississippi black, a Massachusetts Kennedy, or a Vietnamese refugee used to tell us our status, what we could or should aspire to, what doors of opportunity were open to us. It still often does, but again in an increasingly diluted way for more and more of us. Membership in exclusive groups like the DAR no longer has the same clout. Skin color is slowly yielding its deadening grip on hope as competence becomes the way to fulfill the American dream. Our aristocratic dynasties linger on, but less and less prominently. Immigrant status no longer impedes success as firmly for those, like our Asian citizens, whose talent and hard work quickly unlock our educational and economic doors. We are slowly freeing ourselves from family, ethnic, social class, and national status as primary sources of meaning.

We are also modifying the influence of age and gender as sources of meaning. Our developmental age both limits and makes available opportunities for society to program meanings for us. Biological changes, such as the onset of puberty, menopause, and physical decline, powerfully affect our character and how we act. Their relative "fixity" means that aging's changes will continue to be a source of meaning.

Societies vary in how prescriptively they define the meanings of age. We tell our five-year-olds that they must take on the identity of a student — ready or not. Two decades ago we disapproved, even prohibited, the expression of sexuality, affection, and dependency between different age groups more than Italians and Turks did. Take affectionate relationships. Of the ninety-six different possible age and status ones that I surveyed, including an eighteen-year-old boy hugging and kissing a middle-aged woman, Italians approved expressing affection in six times more possible such relationships than Americans did; the Turks approved it in four times more. Americans approved erotic flirtatious activity only when the partners were similar in age.[1] Now we are less proscriptive about such relationships. We are securing more freedom to decide if and when we want to have sex, marry, and work. We don't have to marry by our mid-twenties or retire at sixty-five to be considered "normal."[2] Though age still determines many meanings for us, we can override its social constraints more acceptably nowadays.

Like our biological age, our identity as males and females will always be a source of meaning. Handy tells us gender shapes meaning by showing us how rooted maleness is in the rich meanings of a male's penis and erections.[3] Within whatever limits biology sets to the meanings of maleness and femaleness, all societies attribute other meanings to them. The study's women and men have shown how determining biosocial meanings of femininity and masculinity are to our health, success, and happiness. The post-sixties' revolutionary changes in sexual roles have freed women — more than men — from an oppressive sexism. While gender, and its associated meanings of maleness and femaleness, will always be a source of a person's identity, its commanding influence is diminishing — certainly for women worldwide. Women are becoming more free to create their own meanings of femaleness; eventually men will also be more free to redefine their maleness.

So we are freeing ourselves from traditionally prescribed and commanded sources of meaning. Freedom brings emptiness, nothingness, however, to those who have depended on prescribed work, religion, status, age, and sexual role for meaning. Remember what the study's women told us. "I'm only a collection of roles put together by a committee"; "I'm just an empty eggshell"; "I don't know who I am." Emptiness is so painful it drives us to eat five ice cream cones to fill it up, to seek therapy for our existential "crisis," to work compulsively. What do we do with our growing freedom from traditionally prescribed meanings? Only one answer suffices for the future: Create our own meanings.

The inescapable question becomes, "What are the personal strengths needed to create our own mission, vision, calling, purpose, Number 1 Self?" Whatever form our meaning takes — to be an Andy as a competent and fulfilled parent, a Harry volunteering as a citizen to create a healthier society, a Marty called to a feminist vision, a Billie transcending her traditional feminine identity to create her Number 1 Self as a problem solver, or a Jane gripped by the "monster" that she created — psychologically mature and androgynous strengths are indispensable to create a healthy, successful, and fulfilling way of life.

Religions have always provided us with visions of healthy growth. We can draw upon their symbols, as Fromm did with his Buddhist metaphor of waking up to become more aware, that articulates humans' accumulated wisdom of what it means to grow, to become more alive and whole persons. Research is beginning to verify and, I think, extend and project religions' historical insights into modern terms. Maslow preferred the term *self-actualization;* I prefer *psychological maturity.* Others use words like "authenticity" or "self-fulfillment." When men and women have the opportunity to grow healthily, become more mature, or be self-actualized, they grow similarly. They become more aware, other-centered, integrated, stable, and autonomous persons.

The study's men and women call us back to the verities of the past. Billie, Andy, Marty, Jane, and Harry have shown us just how contemporary and empowering out-of-fashion religious words such as "calling," "commitment," and "virtue" are to living a meaningful, healthy, successful, and happy life. They tell us that we do not have to endure nothingness; we do not have to be rudderless; we do not have to start from ground zero to create afresh a vision of healthy growth, authenticity, or self-actualization.

How to Help Today's Children Grow Up to Succeed

We do not grow up alone in a vacuum without help and guidance from others, particularly our families and schools when we are young. The study has confirmed and extended the findings of other researchers. A loving, democratic family that has strong values and expectations contributes greatly to a child's healthy growth and future success. Children not so blessed with such a family need not despair, however. Others — grandparents, partners, counselors — and their own personal strengths — a strong will, interpersonal skills, and optimism — bring hope.

Today's children do not have as many sources of hope available as yesterday's. Fragile and unstable families, missing parents, inaccessible grandparents, rotating caretakers, chaotic neighborhoods, among other potential sources, explain why teachers see more vulnerable children today. Teachers feel they must be parents more than teachers.

Schools are society's only remaining means to provide most youth with hope. They can empower them with the maturity to get command of themselves today to be able to create their own meanings tomorrow. They can also witness a vision of what a healthy society and better world could be like. Just as parents can continue to support and guide us after we have left home, so may teachers and schools. Following Haverford men for so many years has taught me that. When they were in their early thirties, the men selected Haverford College, primarily because of its Quaker religious philosophy, to be one of the nine most important causes of their growth since they had graduated twelve years earlier. Few of them had entered Haverford as Quakers. How could a school continue to influence its graduates so far into their adult lives? Because they had made its values of what a better world could be like their own. Its vision had become part of their character.[4]

The study tells me that the effort to improve our schools is failing because we have not asked the essential questions and so not used our resources as wisely as we might. The two core questions are, "What is a school of hope for today's youth?" and "How do we create a school of hope?"

What is a school of hope? It is a school that educates for maturity—human excellence, not just academic excellence. It does not naively believe that requiring more and more liberal arts courses, such as math, language, and history, necessarily produces such maturing effects. More likely, these courses produce boredom, even in our recognized academically achieving schools. Not until we teach our academic courses in ways to produce liberally educating effects will students begin to feel that they are getting command of themselves and so be able to create their own meanings, their own hope, for the future. And not until that happens will today's students see schools as places in which to grow and become more alive, not stagnate and die from irrelevance and boredom. Only then will students become mature—and their test scores improve.

A school of hope that consistently educates for maturity witnesses a vision of goodness that the study shows us pays off in future health, success, and happiness. Recall the metavalues that define a mature person: honesty, compassion, integrity, commitment, and courage. These values are intrinsic to the academic enterprise and pursuit of truth, to becoming liberally educated, as they are to every great religion's vision of wholeness.

How do we create schools of hope that help students and teachers become more mature in mind *and* character? Focusing only on one and excluding the other distorts healthy growth.

Research tells us that the school that generates hope has[5]

- A distinctive vision of its liberally educating goals that is widely shared by all members of the school and by the parents
- Adults that are as committed to the character as to the academic maturation of their students
- A leader whose primary role is to be the steward and articulator of its vision
- Teachers who empathically understand the interpersonal world of their students *as their students perceive it*
- Teachers and students for whom teaching and learning are a calling rather than a job and whose morale about their work is high
- Teachers and students who emotionally own not only the goals of the school but the means of implementing them within the school *and* the classroom
- Adults and students who have alive interpersonal relationships that are growth inducing for both (intellectually exciting, trusting, caring, adventurous)
- Adults and students who value risking together to discover more effective ways to achieve their goals, who are willing to hold themselves accountable for their success and failure, and who reflect about why their school and classroom climates and methods have not been as effective as they had hoped

As obvious as these and other attributes are that empower hope, I know no school that has gathered its adults and students together to implement them self-consciously and sytematically. Why? We fail to understand empathically what it means to be a young person today, how both youth and adults grow healthily, what steps must be taken to create a school of hope, and most important, what a school of hope is.

I hope you now understand why I have tentatively titled my next book *The Missing Vision: Educating for Hope,* which will speak to these failures and show how we can create schools of hope.

Now that our work together is completed, I shall end by soaring high to tell you what hope means to me.

Hope is the future alive in the present. Hope prefigures its own fulfillment. Hope disciplines. Without an *alive* hope, we cast off self-restraint and succumb to the seductions of the present: five ice cream cones, drugs, sex now, self-centered aimlessness, even death, as research tells us about so many youths today. "The (suicidal) adolescents we talked to groped for words to describe what they felt was a void in their lives—the lack of anything to stand for, of an altruistic goal."[6]

Without a shared hope, a society drifts, becomes paralyzed by special interests, falls apart into deceit and violence, and eventually perishes. The most serious threat to our future health, success, and happiness is the absence of individual and collective hope, that "void . . . lack of anything to stand for, of an altruistic goal." Nothingness. Emptiness. When I ask students about their symbols of hope, they answer with silence.

The book has been a search for hope—to prod us to learn from our mistakes; to provoke us to think about what we want to work toward and stand for; to identify the character we need, as Andy told us, to be the "large family flying together among the stars" in the future. The result will be not just to "see life on the planet continue," but also to be happy, to have stronger marriages and families, to better the lives of all children, to reclaim work as a calling, and to become more virtuous, contributing members of our planet.

Notes

Preface

1. See NAPS document #04793 for 98 pages of unpublished test, questionnaire, and interview items, as well as associated reliability statistical information. Refer to NAPS document #04798 for 28 pages of statistical results supporting the book's conclusions. Order from NAPS c/o Microfiche Publications, P.O. Box 3513, Grand Central Station, New York, N.Y. 10163–3513. Remit in advance, in U.S. dollars only, $31.15 for document #04793 and/or $10.15 for #04798 in photocopies or $4.00 for each document on microfiche. Outside the United States and Canada, add postage of $4.50 for the first 20 pages and $1.00 for each set of 10 pages of material thereafter for each document, or $1.50 for postage for each microfiche. This is not a multiauthored/multiarticle deposit.

Chapter One

1. Erikson, 1950.
2. James, 1890.
3. National surveys of adolescents (Bachman, 1987; Bachman & Johnston, 1979) and adults (Veroff, Douvan, & Kulka, 1981) report similar rankings. Values do change,

however, over decades. Bachman & Johnston report eighteen-year-olds in the seventies valued good marriages and
family life most and wealth and leadership least; Astin
(1988), however, reports eighteen-year-olds in the eighties valued vocational success and making money much
more; Veroff, Douvan, & Kulka found that American
adults valued self-fulfillment and interpersonal intimacy
more and marriage, parenthood, and religious activity less
than Americans did in the mid-fifties; Stark (1988) found
that workers in the eighties valued income more and career
advancement less than workers in the early seventies.

4. Gurin, Veroff, & Feld, 1960; Veroff, Douvan, & Kulka,
    1981.
5. Maslow, 1954, Ch. 12.
6. Psychologists dispute how to define and measure androg-
    yny. For a technical discussion of the concept, see Taylor
    & Hall (1982). To maximize the use of small samples, I
    defined androgyny as securing a high score when com-
    bining masculinity and femininity scores on Bem's scales
    (1974), a definition closer to that proposed by Spence,
    Helmreich, & Stapp (1975). Spence's and my method iden-
    tified the same women, all of whom scored above the
    group's mean on both masculinity and femininity and in
    total score. So few differences occurred between similarly
    defined men that I was satisfied that Spence's definition
    would produce results similar to those the book reports.

Chapter Two

1. Maslow, 1954.
2. Smith, 1973.
3. Bem, 1974.

Chapter Three

1. D. H. Heath (1977c, pp. 216–221) discusses the transcul-
    tural agreement about the value of psychological maturity.
2. I have argued that terms like "psychological health," "posi-

tive mental health," "emotional maturity," and "psychological maturity" are in fact synonymous, and I use them as such in this book. (See Heath, 1977c, Ch. 1.) Sanford (1962) has argued differently. The IGS researchers claim that psychological health comprehends but is not the same as social maturity (Brooks, 1981, p. 243); however, they use both terms atheoretically, which reflects the lack of any developmental theory ordering the selection of measures used in the IGS studies of mental health. I prefer the term "psychological maturity" because it can be theoretically grounded in developmental research and more clearly implies a continuous rather than a dichotomous attribute. Vaillant (1975) also assumes that "mental health" refers to a continuum and has proposed an alternative, empirically grounded model of healthiness organized around a developmental hierarchy of defensive strategies. For example, the most mature person uses mechanisms called altruism, humor, suppression, anticipation, and sublimation (1977). No empirical evidence yet exists about how similar and dissimilar his mentally healthy person is to my psychologically mature one.

3. D. H. Heath, 1977c.
4. Vaillant & McArthur, 1972.
5. D. H. Heath, 1978c.
6. D. H. Heath, 1977c.
7. Piaget, [1936] 1952.
8. D. H. Heath, 1978b.
9. D. H. Heath, 1977c.
10. Lowenberg, 1988.
11. Using the IGS data, Haan rejects stage theories of development to advocate a dimensional view similar to mine. Although the IGS studies were not guided by a comprehensive rationale, her findings about changes over time can be readily mapped into the model of maturing. As both men and women matured, they became more cognitively broad (cognitive integration) and efficient (cognitive stability); became more nurturant, giving to others, and self-extending (other-centeredness); acted with greater

integrity (value integration); and became more self-confident (self-concept stability) and self-directing (self-auton-
omy) and less conventional (value autonomy). We do not
know what other maturing effects may have occurred, since
the IGS researchers did not use a comprehensive model
of maturing to guide the selection of their assessment
procedures (Haan, 1981; Heath, 1980).

   Hare-Mustin & Marecek, apparently also unaware of
the research on maturity, have independently identified
autonomy for women to be a developmental growth (1986).

12.   D. H. Heath, 1977c.

Chapter Four

1.   Noble, 1987.
2.   See D. H. Heath (1983) for a summary of research on
     maturity and an extended discussion of theoretical issues
     in studying mental health.
3.   Gilligan claims that a developmental psychology of women
     may differ from that of men (1982). For example, the IGS
     studies found that male but not female adolescent psycho-
     logical health predicted subsequent adult psychological
     health (Peskin & Livson, 1981). Male and female adoles-
     cent identities were found to predict outcomes eighteen
     years later that differed for men from those for women
     (Kahn, Zimmerman, Csikszentmihalyi, & Getzels, 1985).
     Later I also report male and female differences in matur-
     ing. However, as I shall also show, confusing what seem
     to be phenotypic male and female differences with optimal
     psychological well-being, as Gilligan does, risks distort-
     ing our understanding of healthy growth. Peskin has con-
     cluded, as I also have, that a developmental theory based
     on phenotypic differences will lead nowhere (1973). Any
     adequate theory must propose underlying more genotypic
     developmental dimensions, which, I will also show, apply
     to both men and women. By not locating her ideas about
     female development within a more comprehensive model
     of healthy growth, Gilligan elevates only one dimension
     of health, other-centeredness, at the expense of a more con-

textual understanding of the complexity of the maturing process. I have illustrated elsewhere how phenotypic cultural differences have to be understood in terms of genotypic indices of maturing if we are not to be misled in interpreting the healthiness of the phenotypic differences (Heath, 1977c, pp. 192–200).

4. Brooks, 1981; Livson & Peskin, 1981.
5. Maslow, 1966, p. 125.
6. D. H. Heath, 1977c.
7. Erikson, 1950; Levinson, 1978.
8. Douvan & Adelson, 1966.
9. Neugarten & Neugarten (1987); the IGS researchers (Eichorn, Mussen, Clausen, Haan, & Honzik, 1981, Ch. 16), as well as Baruch, Barnett, & Rivers (1983), also found no evidence to support Levinson's claim that a mid-life crisis is either a normal developmental mid-life event or even a frequent one. See Rosenfeld & Stark (1987) for a summary evaluation.
10. Williams, 1986.

Chapter Five

1. Andy and Marty Miller would have ranked as the third most successful couple if I had included couples who were childless or whose wives had no paying job.

Chapter Six

1. Barron, 1955, 1963.

Chapter Seven

1. Werner & Smith, 1982.
2. Thomas & Chess, 1969.

Chapter Eight

1. Vaillant & Vaillant, 1981, p. 1438.
2. Sheehy, 1976.
3. Peskin, 1973.

Chapter Nine

1. Sears, 1977.
2. Gurin, Veroff, & Feld, 1960; Veroff, Douvan, & Kulka, 1981.
3. Veroff, Douvan, & Kulka, 1981, p. 529.
4. See A4b,c,d; A7; A8; A21; A23. Other scales from Kelly's marital study (1955) were used but not described in the Appendix. Spanier & Lewis (1980) review the extensive research on marriage since 1970.
5. Kohn, 1988. Maccoby (1990) summarizes similar and other gender differences.
6. Skolnick (1981) reports that the IGS study found only a few personality traits associated with marital satisfaction, for example, self-confidence for males and nurturance for females. However, achieving rather than feminine women were more happily married. She did not ask which traits described the men and women who made their partners maritally happy.
7. Kohn, 1987.
8. Kohn, 1987; Skolnick, 1981.
9. Baruch, Barnett, & Rivers report that cooperative, supportive, but not macho or "hard-working professional (men) in a high-status job" had happier wives (1983, p. 87).
10. Among other traits reliably describing women whose husbands are happily married are tenderness, optimism, feelings not easily hurt, sympathy, sensitivity to husband's needs, affection, loving children, conscientiousness, eagerness to learn new things, and not falling apart under stress.
11. *Wall Street Journal,* July 14, 1989, B1.
12. Block, J. D., 1980; Pleck & Sawyer, 1974.

Chapter Ten

1. Veroff, Douvan, and Kulka, 1981.
2. H. E. Heath, 1976.
3. D. H. Heath, 1976b, 1977b.
4. Stroud (1981) shows the complexity of the methodological issues to answer questions about a woman's career and familial satisfaction. One's stage of parenting, for exam-

ple, teen-agers still at home, meaning of "career," and educational level affect the intensity of conflict. Exclusive homemakers had the highest morale and self-esteem and were the most feminine, for example, warm, nurturing, and submissive, of the different categories of women studied. However, when she compared just the working and nonworking college-educated women, the former were more satisfied with their careers than the latter with their household roles. I could not confirm this finding. Working and nonworking college-educated women did not differ in any attribute: self- or judge-rated happiness and fulfillment, marital and parental satisfaction, self-, spouse-, or judge-rated competence in the principal roles of a married woman, and psychological maturity. In contrast to Stroud's overall results and mine, Baruch, Barnett, & Rivers, relying only on self-reports, found that working women reported higher self-esteem (1983).

5. Sears, 1977.
6. D. H. Heath, 1978c.

Chapter Eleven

1. Frequency of marital sexual relations does not inevitably decline in the first decade of marriage. I found that mutuality, shared values, and partner satisfaction with how well he or she fulfills the different roles of a spouse contribute to maintaining frequent sexual relations during this time.
2. Baruch, Barnett, & Rivers also found that masculine women enjoyed sex more (1983).
3. Masters & Johnson, 1975.
4. D. H. Heath, 1978a.
5. D. H. Heath, 1978b, 1979. Baruch, Barnett, & Rivers also report that sexually satisfied middle-aged women were more maritally happy (1983).

Chapter Twelve

1. Yeh & Chu, 1974.
2. D. H. Heath, 1977c.

3. Tocqueville, [1835] 1945, p. 105.
4. Tocqueville, [1835] 1945, p. 106.
5. Block, J. D., 1980.
6. Miller, S., 1983, pp. 197–198.

Chapter Fourteen

1. Astin, 1988.
2. Munneke & Bridger-Riley, 1981.
3. McCue, 1985.
4. Clausen (1981) and Vaillant (1978) also report that vocationally successful men are more mature than less vocationally successful men.
5. Vaillant (1975) reports that Harvard men in their late forties who had made a good career adaptation were also better adapted socially, had had stable, satisfying marriages, and were psychologically and physically healthier than those who had not made a good adaptation.

Chapter Fifteen

1. See Chapter One, note 3.
2. Gallante, 1988.
3. Veroff, Douvan, & Kulka, 1981, p. 391.
4. Poll on stress shows that money does offer many rewards. *Wall Street Journal,* May 5, 1989, p. B5D.
5. *The Miami Herald,* January 10, 1988.
6. Baruch, Barnett, & Rivers, 1983.
7. Clausen, 1981.
8. Bray, Campbell, & Grant, 1974.
9. Johnston & Associates, 1986.
10. Welsch & Young, 1981.

Chapter Sixteen

1. Seligman, 1988.
2. *Wall Street Journal,* May 22, 1989.
3. M. James reports that in the mid-1980s Americans, Danes,

and Swedes were most satisfied with their lives; he did not break down his results by age to be able to compare his results with researchers reporting depression in more younger adults.

4. Bennett, 1985.
5. D. H. Heath, 1981b.
6. Bellah, Madsen, Sullivan, Swidler, & Tipton, 1985.
7. Mehren, 1987.
8. The most and least contributory attributes to overall morale or vocational adaptation were determined by an item analysis of the VAS scores. That is, those attributes that contributed most correlated most highly with the VAS total score; those that contributed least correlated minimally with the total VAS score.
9. Clausen (1981), studying 100 men in the IGS groups, found that their most important job satisfactions were attributes intrinsic to their work, that is, job reflects their personal interests, permits use of abilities, and provides freedom to develop their own ideas. Satisfaction with income was not associated with job satisfaction in men in their early forties; it was for men in their late forties.
10. Perhaps the high disillusionment of lawyers with law, regardless of the size or location of their firms, is because their work contributed least to their self-fulfillment when compared to other needs like income (Leete, Francia, & Strawser, 1971). For middle-aged women, increased "challenge" to grow in their work is directly related to their well-being (Baruch, Barnett, & Rivers, 1983).
11. Two scales to measure student morale have been developed, modeled after the Vocational Adaptation Scale (A6): one for fifth to seventh graders; the other for older students, including college students.
12. Baruch, Barnett, & Rivers report similar findings for middle-aged working women (1983).
13. See Chapter Fourteen, note 5.
14. Stroud (1981) found that although working women and men had the same degree of intrinsic interest in their work, the women maintained more of a balance between their

work and family identities than the men did. The women less involved in their work were primarily emotionally committed to their families.

15. Female teachers reliably differ from male teachers in describing themselves as feminine, affectionate, sympathetic, sensitive to others' needs, understanding, compassionate, eager to soothe hurt feelings, warm, tender, gullible, and loving children. Male teachers reliably describe themselves as more masculine and athletic.

16. Stroud reports similar findings. Women committed to their work have a "complex personality organization in which stereotypically feminine characteristics such as warmth and insight . . . [are] integrated with stereotypically masculine ones such as rationality, independence, and ambition" (1981, p. 372). Executive women also have both masculine and feminine traits necessary for success (Morrison, White, & Van Velso, 1987).

17. Men rated by their colleagues to be well adapted vocationally were reliably rated by their peers to be interpersonally other-centered, trusting, affectionate, loyal, understanding, compassionate, eager to soothe others' hurt feelings, gentle, loved by others, and loving children, among other traits.

18. Baruch, Barnett, & Rivers also report that middle-aged women who are satisfied with their work describe themselves in more typical masculine terms (1983). However, I have found that type of occupation limits this conclusion. Women satisfied with typically feminine or nurturing professions, such as teaching, consistently describe themselves in feminine interpersonal and not masculine terms.

Chapter Eighteen

1. Erikson, 1950.
2. D. H. Heath, 1978c.
3. The men's and women's peers reliably judged the community leaders to share in common 33 percent and 13 per-

cent of the 100 personality strengths rated. In addition to those mentioned in the text, the male community leaders were rated by their peers to be self-reliant, adventurous, predictable, other-centered, trustful, reflective, and realistic and to have strong convictions, integrity, and courage, among other strengths.

4. Miller, J. B., 1976.

Chapter Nineteen

1. See Dittes (1971b) and Spilka, Hood, & Gorsuch (1985) for analyses of religion's meanings. Gorsuch (1984) critiques their measurement problems. Signs of religious devoutness, like frequency of church attendance, are quixotically related to well-being. Vaillant (1978) reports that frequent attenders have less happy marriages than infrequent ones; other researchers report that occasional attenders are more prejudiced and immature than non- or regular attenders (Dittes, 1971a; Spilka, Hood, & Gorsuch, 1985).

2. D. H. Heath, 1969; Becker, 1971.

3. Fallon (1986) reports that 73.5 percent of California high school students cheated, 75.3 percent said that they did not believe most of their peers cared if their classmates cheated, the incidence of cheating was much higher in the most academically oriented schools, and 42.4 percent said that there could be good reasons to cheat (196).

4. The participants' ratings of their ethical character only moderately correlated with their peers' combined rating, that is, .29 for the men and .49 for the women.

5. The theoretically constructed measure of value maturity reliably predicted the participants' ratings of their ethical traits like honesty and deep ethical commitment, but only the women's peers' ratings. The measure of value maturity (A14) included in A31 is highly correlated with psychological maturity, as measured by the PSQ (A12). It is derived from the same rationale, constructed similarly, and shares many of the same extensive validity correlates

found transculturally (Heath, 1977c). No other adequate measure of value maturity exists. Though Kohlberg's theory of moral stage development and the dimensional model of maturity share similar genotypic dimensions, for example, increasing moral judgment implies increasing value symbolization, other-centeredness, integration, and autonomy, Rest's objective measure of Kohlberg's stages is not related to psychological maturity (Miller & Moser, 1977).

Chapter Twenty

1. See D. H. Heath (1977c, 1983) and Seeman (1989) for a critique of health and similar concepts. The concept of well-being has been increasingly used in surveys that use only self-ratings about "feeling on top of the world" (Bradburn, 1969), or questions about degree of distress, frequency of worrying, happiness, and satisfaction with life (Campbell, 1981; Gurin, Veroff, & Feld, 1960; Veroff, Douvan, & Kulka, 1981). Baruch's study of the well-being of women is the most recent one comparable to mine. She defined well-being by three questions about happiness, satisfaction, and optimism, called Pleasure, and three scales measuring self-esteem, physical health, and feelings of self-control, called Mastery (Baruch, Barnett, & Rivers, 1983). I had included the same or similar scales of all of these items. I could *not* replicate her two-dimensional theory about well-being on either the women or men. Pleasure and Mastery were highly correlated, predicted the same personality and other measures of success, and correlated with my summary well-being score (A29) very highly, for example, .81 for men and .70 for the women. Although the extensive interpretations that Baruch, Barnett, & Rivers make of their results must be seriously questioned, the similarity of their actual results to mine reassuringly suggests that mine may have considerable generality.

2. The participants' and peers' ratings of their happiness and self-fulfillment were highly correlated. I focus on happi-

ness rather than self-fulfillment, which has been misunderstood by commentators who have confused a naive popular belief with its sophisticated psychological meanings (Heath, 1977c, Ch. 1). Recent attacks on self-fulfillment's proponents—Maslow and Carl Rogers—by sociologists (Bellah, Madsen, Sullivan, Swidler, & Tipton, 1985) and historians (Bloom, 1987) unfortunately should have made such a distinction and did not. They ignored the fundamental issue: What is the mature self, the topic of Chapter Three? Yankelovich, the pollster who probably knows more about the contemporary American character than anyone, believes a wiser popular understanding of self-fulfillment is emerging that begins to approach psychologists' more sophisticated meaning. He suggests that fulfillment is changing to mean establishing connections and commitments to others, nature, and more sacred/expressive goals. The new ethic recognizes that self-fulfillment requires that one mature in other-centeredness, as well as autonomy, making "commitments that endure over long periods of time and that the expressive and sacred domains can be realized only through a web of shared meanings that transcend the conception of the self as isolated physical object" (1981, p. 89).

3. See Chapter Three, note 2. Although I believe the model of maturity is the most comprehensively validated one now available for defining psychic well-being or mental health, I excluded its most valid measure, the PSQ (A12), from the summary index of mental health for the reason mentioned in the chapter. I could then determine if maturity, as theoretically defined, actually predicts mental health, which it did.

4. Judge ratings of the men's well-being have been highly reliable. Judge ratings at Phases 2, 3, and 4 reliably predict each other, reflecting the stability in well-being over decades. The men's own ratings reliably predicted judge ratings at each phase. Judge ratings of the women's well-being, however, were reliable only for the women's and their spouses' ratings of their happiness and physical and

psychological health. The women appeared the same to themselves as they appeared to their spouses; however, they did not agree with their closest friends or colleagues, who also did not agree between themselves about the women. Are women really three different people? It is not that judges cannot tell who is mature; it is more likely that a woman's identity is defined by her role competence, which may not reflect her intrapsychic integration and autonomy (Helson & Wink, 1987). IGS researchers have had trouble, as I have, sorting out for women stable personality traits from what they call "oversocialization" or what I call overdevelopment in other-centered maturing. Clearly, the issue of phenotypic and genotypic differences and its implication for understanding female development go far beyond this book, though I cannot ignore it when interpreting the meaning of success and happiness to women.

5. Sears, 1977.

6. Baruch, Barnett, & Rivers, 1983.

7. The summary is based on the seventy-item Personality (A10) and thirty-item SIQ (A13) scales. I first identified those shared traits the men *and* women had rated about themselves that reliably predicted their well-being. I next winnowed out those traits about which the men's *and* women's peers disagreed. The core strengths defining well-being, in rough declining order of importance, were: not being stuck in a rut, optimism, having control of own life, fulfilling potential, acceptance of self, open sharing of feelings, making decisions easily, being respected by others, and being self-sufficient.

8. Van Doren, 1943.

9. Eysenck, 1988.

10. The measure of mental health (A29b) is not completely independent of the peers' descriptions of the men and women. One of its six indices was the SIQ-judged total score based on twenty-six of the SIQ traits (A13).

11. Bayer, Whissell-Buechy, & Honzik, 1981; Eichorn, Mussen, Clausen, Haan, & Honzik, 1981, Ch. 16; Maas & Kuypers, 1974. Baruch, Barnett, & Rivers report that au-

tonomy in judgment is crucial to a middle-aged woman's well-being (1983).

Chapter Twenty-One

1. IGS researchers also found that a man's but not a woman's physical health was associated with personality traits. Generally, however, of all of their measures, physical health was least associated with other measures of adult personality and outcome (Eichorn, Mussen, Clausen, Haan, & Honzik, 1981). This is a much more substantial observation than what I can make, since the IGS staff had extensive measurements of the actual physical health of its participants, particularly in their early years.

2. House, Landis, and Umberson (1988) review the accumulating epidemiological and experimental cultural evidence to show that quantity and quality of social relationships predict physical health, more in men than women; they suggest that decreasing frequency of marital relations, voluntary community participation, and informal socializing may create increased health problems in the future.

3. Bayer, Whissell-Buechy, & Honzik, 1981.

4. Handy, 1988.

5. Bakan (1966) contrasts female "communality" with male "agency" to describe their sexual role differences.

6. Handy, 1988.

Chapter Twenty-Three

1. Goleman, 1986; Holden, 1987.

2. Overall favorable childhood environments, which include favorable father and mother relations, have been consistently found to contribute to the mental health of middle-aged men (Vaillant, 1974a,b) and women as well (Block, J., 1971).

3. The men and women did not agree in rating paternal competence; while they did agree about maternal competence, their agreement was not striking, which suggests that men

and women differ in how they view parental competence. I had found this to be so about the ratings secured when they were in their thirties (Heath, 1976b).

4. Vaillant (1978) reports that men who were good fathers had had warm relationships with their own fathers when young. Sears (1977) also reports that maritally unsuccessful men had been rejected by and were rebellious toward their fathers and mothers when young.

5. Longitudinal studies initiated in adolescence must rely on participants' recall of their familial and parental relationships when younger. When Vaillant & McArthur assert that "maturation makes liars of us all" (1972), they are questioning the reliability of such reports. I take a more pragmatic view. Adult decisions and behavior are influenced by what we *believe* about our earlier lives and parents. Because I have found great continuity in personality over the adult years, participants' descriptions of parents may well be applicable to their earlier lives. So retrospective descriptions of parental traits of parents when younger may still be useful. The most conservative interpretation of such descriptions is to say that, for example, persons who succeed in their familial roles reliably agree in attributing such and such trait to their parents; it is an inference I risk making to assume thereby that such a trait caused or contributed to their later familial success.

Chapter Twenty-Four

1. Youniss & Smollar (1985) agree. Mothers contribute to their children's mutuality skills, such as learning conversational and self-disclosing skills; fathers introduce their children to the vocational and societal world.

2. Vaillant also found that men who had unhealthy marriages had had unhealthy mothers who had continued to dominate them into adulthood (1978). He also reports that "home atmosphere (or mother/child relationship), high school adjustment, and father/child relationship, in that order, accounted for most of the statistical association be-

tween the childhood and object relations scores" (p. 17), which he had defined as having close friends, a stable marriage, and enjoyable relations with one's parents (1974b).

3. Peskin & Livson, 1981. See Kohlberg, LaCrosse, & Ricks (1972) for a trenchant assessment of the relative importance of different types of predictors of adult outcomes, particularly psychological health.

4. Shedler & Block's (1990) longitudinal study of children from the age of three to eighteen illustrates how parents' personality and behavior can affect for years their children's success in school, relationships, mental health, and happiness. For example, eighteen-year-old adolescents who used drugs frequently had been maladjusted and unhappy when they were seven and eleven also. When these adolescents were five, their mothers had been judged by psychologists to be cold, nonsupportive, insensitive to their needs, and excessively demanding. As Billie, Marty, and the study have told us, some of the eighteen-year-old drug users may learn how to leave their pathogenic mothers emotionally behind as other influences help them mature and so become happy and mentally healthy middle-aged adults.

Chapter Twenty-Five

1. Vaillant reports that for males good fathering more than good mothering, when rated in college, contributed more to subsequent mature interpersonal relations, which he found was central to good adult mental health (1978).

2. Vaillant, 1974b.

3. Buie, 1988.

4. Rejecting, cold, and inaccessible fathers reinforce a son's antisocial behavior, which in turn contributes to subsequent adult maladjustment (Kohlberg, LaCrosse, & Ricks, 1972).

5. Youniss & Smollar, 1985.

6. DeWinne, Overton, & Schneider, 1978; Werner & Smith, 1982.

7. Vaillant, 1978, p. 656.

Chapter Twenty-Six

1. Jennings & Nathan, 1977; Slack & Porter, 1980; Willingham, 1974.
2. D. H. Heath, 1968.
3. The women's grades were much less reliable, so their results may not be believable. It was not possible to check them against college records. Since the women had gone to so many different colleges of differing standards, grades in one college could not be compared to grades in another.
4. Kelly, 1957; Whitaker, Kelly, & Uhr, 1956.
5. Rhoads, Gallemore, Giantureo, & Osterhout, 1974.
6. Cohen reviewed 108 studies on the relation of grade point average to adult achievement and concluded that for all practical purposes college grades are not useful in predicting adult outcomes (1984). Using different criteria of adult achievement, for example, acceptance of responsibility, Lewis & Nelson (1983) report that grades made no contribution to such outcomes. They did find that males with high grades were less involved as adults in community activities. Finally, another review of all of the research since 1950 on academic predictors of adult outcomes like income, job satisfaction, and competence concluded that grades did not practically predict achievement in adult life (Samson, Graue, Weinstein, & Walberg, 1984). One reason academic grades do not predict much in studies that identify income or competence of a group composed of persons from many different schools is, of course, the lack of comparability of academic grades from one school to the next. That academic grades of the men in the study who came from one college also did not predict any adult outcome strengthens these other findings.
7. D. H. Heath, 1977a.
8. J. Block, 1971; Bray & Howard, 1978; Jennings & Nathan, 1977; Reinhold, 1970.
9. Wallach, 1972.
10. Haier & Denham, 1976. Eichorn, Hunt, & Honzik (1981) using the IGS data, found that high-IQ youngsters were

judged to be calm, dependable, overcontrolled in their sexual reactions, and socially aloof from their peers.

11. Astin, 1977.

12. Winter, McClelland, & Stewart, 1981, p. 132.

13. Terman, 1954.

14. Jennings & Nathan, 1977; Willingham, Young, & Morris, 1985; Office of Educational Research and Improvement, 1986.

15. Jennings & Nathan, 1977.

16. Bray & Howard, 1978.

Chapter Twenty-Seven

1. Livson & Peskin (1980) have carefully evaluated the reliability of retrospective ratings used in longitudinal studies. I checked the accuracy of the men's ratings three ways: First, when he was seventeen each youth had taken the MMPI (A2); second, when he was twenty, his peers, faculty, and coaches had rated his psychological maturity; and third, he also had taken the Rorschach, which assessed his mental health.

   The adult men's ratings of their adolescent personalities agreed with these three different measures of mental health secured fifteen to twenty years earlier. Boys more maladjusted on the MMPI when seventeen rated themselves when adults to have not functioned well under stress and to have been lonely, friendless, socially aloof, and emotionally unstable, many of the traits that their adolescent MMPI's had shown.

   Those twenty-year-olds whom the judges had rated to be psychologically mature and effective rated themselves when in their adult years to have been that way in college, that is, more mature on one-third of all of the positive adolescent traits I had measured. At twenty, they had been more autonomous, well integrated, and interpersonally mature.

   Finally, the adult men who had described themselves to have been mentally unhealthy when adolescents had

been in fact so clinically evaluated from their college Rorschachs. The men said that as teenagers they had been
very lonely, moody, insensitive to others, pessimistic, and
interpersonally immature, as well as unhappy with school.
Most of these traits consistently agreed with the kinds of
Rorschach clues judges had used at the time to assess their
mental health.

No comparable data were available to assess the reliability of the women's retrospective ratings. Rosenthal
claims that forty-year-old women recall their adolescence
less accurately than men do (1963). I return in Chapter
Twenty-Nine to argue that discontinuity in a girl's development may account for such findings. The study's women's ratings were very useful. In any case, the proof is
in the pudding. Do women's retrospective ratings of their
adolescence increase our understanding of why they turned
out as they did?

2. Otten, 1989a.
3. Bayer, Whissell-Buechy, & Honzik, 1981; Brooks, 1981;
    Peskin & Livson, 1981.
4. Stroud, 1981.
5. Clausen, 1981.
6. The IGS studies found that boys "who are nurturant and
    warm in early adolescence" are more socially mature in
    their forties (Brooks, 1981, p. 258).
7. D. H. Heath, 1968.
8. Douvan & Adelson, 1966.
9. IGS researchers agree. Self-confident, purposeful, and am-
    bitious girls turned out to be socially mature forty-year-
    old women (Brooks, 1981). That few adolescent traits
    predicted a woman's career success might be the result of
    unreliable retrospective female ratings, except that the IGS
    studies, using actual measures of adolescent personality,
    also found that adolescent traits did not predict adult out-
    comes for women as well as they did for men (Brooks,
    1981). Stroud found that no female adolescent traits pre-
    dicted the career path women eventually took, for exam-
    ple, homemaker, dual job-homemaker role. However,

women committed to their work, that is with a sense of calling, had as adolescents not conformed to traditional sexual roles. They had been anxious, defensive, self-conscious, hostile interpersonally, and more masculine in temperament. These results generally confirm mine. Married in contrast to unmarried working women had reliably less strong drives to achieve when young (Brooks, 1981).

10. See note 1.

11. Vaillant also found that psychological soundness rated by professional judges when the person was in college predicted absence of psychiatric symptoms, good relations with others, overall career success, as well as psychological and physical well-being when middle-aged (1974b). The IGS results are more equivocal. Adolescent social maturity (SM), assessed by Q sort items like good impulse control, dependability, and nurturance, predicted social maturity at middle age, defined by the CPI SM score (Brooks, 1981). Adolescent psychological health, indexed by clinician Q sorted items of ideal mental health, predicted middle-aged male but not female health. Because psychological health in early but *not* late adolescence predicted health at age thirty-one, but psychological health at thirty-one did *not* predict it at middle age (Livson & Peskin, 1967), Livson and Peskin say that our health is not a stable attribute (1981). Since their index of psychological health was based on opinions of therapists about the ideal healthy person rather than derived from actual studies of psychologically healthy and mature persons, the meaning of the IGS findings, as yet unreplicated using other methods and samples, remains moot. I found that psychological maturity in adolescence predicted psychological maturity in the early thirties, which in turn predicted maturity in the mid-forties. Bayer, Whissell-Buechy, & Honzik, using IGS data, report that adolescent personality traits, which I interpret to indicate psychological healthiness, predicted middle-aged men's physical health (1981); Thomas (1976, 1981); Vaillant (1979).

12. Vaillant & Vaillant, 1981, p. 1438.

Chapter Twenty-Eight

1. D. H. Heath, 1968.
2. D. H. Heath, 1977d, 1978c.
3. D. H. Heath, 1978c.

Chapter Twenty-Nine

1. See Chapter Four, note 3.
2. See Verbrugge (1982) for a thorough review of differences between men's and women's physical health and the contributions that their different social roles make to their health. Gove & Tudor review similar sex differences for mental illness (1973). The IGS and Vaillant studies have shown that physical and psychological health are closely related, so that differential illness rates for males and females may indirectly reflect difficulties in adjusting to one's social roles.
3. Maas & Kuypers (1974) report that the fathers of the IGS participants showed much greater continuity in life style from the age of thirty to seventy than the mothers did. As a result, earlier personal experiences and antecedents predicted the men's later behavior much more decisively than they did women's.

Chapter Thirty-One

1. Heath, 1977c.
2. Neugarten & Neugarten, 1987.
3. Handy, 1988.
4. D. H. Heath, 1976c.
5. D. H. Heath (1981) illustrates how some of the listed attributes of a school of hope can be objectively measured.
6. Giffin & Felsenthal, 1983.

Appendix

The Study of
Adult Development

Background Studies of Adults

Few studies have followed youths into their adult years. Gifted boys and girls have been studied by Terman (1954), Oden (1968), and more recently, with questionnaires, by Sears (1977). The Intergenerational Studies (IGS) of the Institute for Human Development, University of California at Berkeley, are the most well known and intensive. IGS combined three longitudinal studies: Macfarlane's guidance study, begun in 1928 on every third birth in Berkeley, totaling 248 babies (1938); Bayley's Berkeley Growth Study, begun in 1929 on 61 infants, focusing on intellectual growth (1940); and the H. E. Jones, M.S. Jones, & Stolz's Oakland Growth Study, begun in 1931 on 212 children ten to twelve years of age (Jones, 1940). Though the studies were not initially planned to continue throughout the life span, other researchers have maintained the studies and reported the results in Block (1971); Haan & Day (1974); Maas & Kuypers (1974); Eichorn, Mussen, Clausen, Haan, & Honzik (1981). Compared to the study I report, the IGS sample is larger, is more diverse, had available extensive child and adolescent observations, including physical health examinations, and had extensive professional resources.

The Grant study initiated more than forty years ago on well-functioning Harvard men (C. W. Heath, 1945) has been continued by Vaillant and reported in numerous publications since 1972. He also restudied Glueck & Glueck's original group of fourteen-year-old Boston youths (1943) when they were forty-seven (Vaillant & Vaillant, 1981). Other adult longitudinal studies have been done by Cox (1970), Golden, Mandel, Glueck, & others (1962), Super (1985), and Thomas (1976, 1981). The well-known Fels study has been reported to be following children into their adult years but its results are not yet available (Kagan & Moss, 1962).

Among others, Gould (1972, 1978), Levinson (1978), and Lowenthal, Thurnher, Chiriboga, and Associates (1975) have studied middle-aged persons but not longitudinally or as intensively. Neugarten and her colleagues pioneered studying how middle-aged persons develop into their older years (Neugarten & Associates, 1964). Sheehy's book, *Passages* (1976), drew heavily on these original researchers.

Other than IGS's studies of adult women, no other research has been reported that is as intensive. Helson & Moane have studied Mills College women at ages twenty-one, twenty-seven, and forty-three, relying primarily on several hours of self-reports (1987). Baruch, Barnett, & Rivers (1983) studied the well-being of 232 women representative of a Boston suburb, using a several-hour survey. It is the nonlongitudinal study of women that is the most similar to the one I report. Antonucci summarizes the extensive survey studies and other longitudinal studies of women in their middle years (1982).

The longitudinal study I report differs from previous ones. It has been more theoretically systematic, has used numerous repeated measures in precisely the same way over time, has been conducted by one person and so developed unusual rapport and participants' cooperation for longitudinal studies, and relied much more extensively on independent knowledgeable judges to assess adult effectiveness. Despite marked differences among the principal adult studies in their samples, procedures, and data analyses, the results of the longitudinal IGS, Vaillant, and my own studies generally converge, supporting each other. Baruch, Barnett, & Rivers and I used very similar measures; I was able to confirm about half of their findings. Since this book focuses on adult success and happiness, rather than on development from adolescence, I cite only selective findings from the adult development literature, primarily from the more similar IGS, Vaillant, and Baruch studies.

Purposes of Study

Adolescent and Early Adult Phases. The purpose is to understand the meaning of competence and psychological maturity, their course, and their causes through the early adult years.

Middle-Age Phase. The purpose is to understand the meanings of adult competence, successful adaptation, and happiness; each of their personality correlates; and familial and adolescent precursors.

Another purpose is to understand how men and women grow in their adult years, to test the principal hypotheses about adult development and their relation to male and female development, for example, adults go through age-specific stages, have big dreams for their futures, rely on mentors (Levinson, 1978); adults alter their time perspective (Neugarten, 1968); mid-life crises involve anticipations of mortality (Osherson, 1980); men become more feminine and women more masculine (Guttmann, 1975). These hypotheses are not specifically addressed in this book, which focuses instead on the meaning of adult success and its roots.

Plan

To study the meaning of competence and psychological maturity of college men, extensive personality information had been secured from all entering Haverford College freshmen during their first week (Phase 1) for five successive classes and of the study's men in their junior and senior years (Phase 2) (Heath, 1965). Because little was known about the development of adults, the study was resumed when the men were in their early thirties (Phase 3), at which time the men's partners completed extensive material about them, less about themselves; two-thirds volunteered to be interviewed about their spouses and relationship after the initiation of Phase 3 showed that many women wished to participate more actively. The women were invited to be full participants when the men were restudied in their mid-forties (Phase 4).

Phases 3 and 4 were organized by the model of maturing that

had emerged from Phases 1 and 2. Phases 3 and 4 were designed similarly. All tests and interviews have been administered by me, scored, and/or judged in precisely the same way to maintain comparability across the four phases.

Participants

Eighty men had originally been selected randomly or by eighteen diverse judges when they were juniors or seniors. The judges had been nominated by key leaders in the community and were selected in terms of ratings of how well they knew the upperclassmen. The nominated students, faculty, coaches, administrators, and counselors used sorting and other systematic procedures to identify and order men who were and were not adapting well to the college's social, athletic, extracurricular, ethical, and academic demands (Heath, 1965). Sixty-eight of the original eighty men completed Phase 3. They did not differ from those who had died, whom I was not able to locate, or those who did not wish to participate. Sixty-five men and forty of their wives or partners participated in Phase 4. Three men declined for personal reasons. A few wives declined because of strong feminist beliefs about men studying women; some could not participate because of career demands; the remaining declined for various reasons, the most frequent being that their marriages were in difficulty and they did not wish to discuss them.

At the time of Phase 4, eighteen men were separated or had been divorced; forty-two men still lived with their first wives. Five had never married. Four women had been divorced before marrying the study's men. At Phase 4, the men averaged forty-five in age, the women thirty-nine.

Eighty-six percent of the men and 90 percent of the women were parents. They averaged 2.4 children. The average age of the eldest was fifteen, though the children ranged in age from four months in utero to twenty-six years ex-utero. The fathers and mothers did not differ in either their overall or specific satisfactions with their parenting (A9). They were most satisfied with watching their children grow, their home's living conditions, and the social value of being a parent. They were most dissatisfied with the amount of time and energy that parenting required.

Vocationally, the men and working women did not differ in satisfaction with their adjustment or fulfillment (A6). The men earned much more than the women. Eleven of the women were not earning a regular income and were not included in the analyses of vocational satisfaction and competence. In the early eighties, the men ranged in income from $13,000 for some teachers to more than 25 percent, particularly lawyers and physicians, making between $100,000 and $350,000 annually. More than half of the women made less than $15,000; none made more than $40,000. I did not ask about inherited and other unearned income.

Methodological Assumptions

Personality must be studied intensively using many diverse measures that assess it at different levels of awareness. In Phases 3 and 4, each participant completed twelve to fourteen hours of self-report questionnaires; standard personality, semiprojective, and projective tests; behavioral tests of their dimensional maturity; and structured interviews. Wherever possible, interviews should be conducted in participants' homes to observe and participate in the family activities.

Tests of hypotheses, particularly about competence and maturity, must rely on different types of methods to confirm their reliability across varying "levels" of personality functioning.

The design of tests and interviews should be guided by a comprehensive theoretical rationale. A model of maturing, summarized in Chapter Three, provided such a rationale for the development of some measures, the administration, and the scoring of interviews.

Measures should be objective, scorable, and amenable to statistical analysis. Structured interview procedures were used to provide the participants the opportunity to define for themselves the critical issues before more focused questions were asked.

All participants should receive all tests and interviews in *precisely* the same or counterbalanced order, where necessary, to control for errors and enable statistical analyses and reliable comparisons.

Independent assessments by those most familiar with a person's competence and maturity are essential in any study of adult development. Phase 2 relied on teacher, dean, coach, and peer judgments; Phases 3 and 4 relied on extensive spouse, closest friend, and vocational or community colleague judgments to check the validity of the participants' self-reports and tests. Opposite-sex judgments were secured for unmarried participants.

Procedure and Methods for the Mid-Life Study, Phase 4

(References in the chapters to the Appendix's measures are preceded by "A," for example, A7 refers to the Marital Adjustment Scale described below.)

The procedures for Phases 1 and 2 have been described in Heath (1965); Phase 3 in technical articles, commencing in 1976, which are reported in the References. Phase 4's general procedures were similar to those of Phase 3. Unpublished individual measures deposited with NAPS are underlined.

I.   **Mailed battery of tests**
     A1.   Developmental History Questionnaire (DHQ), given midway between Phases 3 and 4 for the men and at Phase 4 for the women. The DHQ is a revised version of one developed by Olney & Peters (1979).
           a.   Participants rated seventy-two statements that assessed attributes about their childhood homes, parental personalities, and the relationships between their parents as well as those to themselves that researchers had reported contributed to positive adult outcomes. (Prior studies of adult outcomes, mentioned in the background above, as well as from Murphy & Moriarty, 1976; Siegelman, Block, Block, & von der Lippe, 1970; and Westley & Epstein, 1969, were the principal sources

used.) Scores indexing favorableness of over-all family-parental environment, maternal and paternal healthiness, and quality of relationships with each were constructed.

b. Participants also rated what they were like as adolescents on forty behaviors, drawn from the above-mentioned references, that indexed how mature they had been on each dimension defining growth of cognitive skills, relationships, values, and self-attitudes; for example, wide range of interests stood up against peer opinions, strong willpower, and close friends. Scores for overall adolescent maturity as well as for the components of the model of maturity described in Chapter Three were created. An additional ten items described other child-adolescent attributes found to contribute to adult success, for example, enjoyment of school, interests typical of own sex, optimism. The men's ratings of their adolescent maturity and mental health were validated against measures of their actual adolescent maturity and health, that is, judge ratings, MMPI, and Rorschach.

A2. Minnesota Multiphasic Personality Inventory (MMPI), also given at Phases 1 and 3. Though optional for Phase 4, fifty-six men and all of the women completed it. The MMPI consists of 566 items that produce a large number of scores. In the chapters, I refer to a total weighted score combining its eight basic scales indexing potential maladjustment, which covaries inversely with measures of psychological maturity. MMPI scores have not proved to be as powerfully predictive of adult adaptation as measures of maturity (Heath, 1977c). The California Psychological Inventory would have permitted me to compare the study's results directly to those of IGS. However, I con-

tinued to use the MMPI because it had been given
in Phase 1; I wanted to maintain continuity in tests
over time.

A3.   Strong Campbell Interest Inventory (SCI), given
at Phases 1 and 3. Though optional for Phase 4,
most men and all of the women took it. The SCI
measures temperamental similarity to successful
and happy men and women in various occupations.

II. **Mailed battery of questionnaires-tests upon return of
first set**

A4.   Personal History Questionnaire (PHQ). I describe
only those scales and items to which I refer in the
book; some items not now reported are described
in the chapters. Major tests and scales that were
included in the PHQ are described separately below in A5–11 and in A26 for partner ratings. Unless stated otherwise, questionnaires and tests
asked for ratings on five-point scales. Each participant created his or her own "time line" by listing in order for each five-year period the significant events that had occurred since graduation
from college.

a.   Stage productivity. Participant rated on a ten-
point scale degree of productivity, fulfillment,
and mood for each three-year period beginning with late adolescence, for example, early
twenties, mid-twenties, late twenties, to Phase
4. A total score summarized reported overall adult productivity-fulfillment. Scores for
each period could be compared with every
other period.

b.   Criteria of role competence. At the beginning
of each PHQ section about a new adult role,
the participants listed the six strengths most
critical to success in the role if they had played
it, for example, qualities important to make
a happy marriage, be a good lover, be a com-

petent parent. They then rated themselves and partners on each of the six attributes. Each partner also subsequently rated the other on the partner's own criteria of success. Scores were available about self- and partner-judged competence on one's own and on partner's criteria of role competence. A score indexing overall competence in the principal adult roles was used.

c. Self- and partner ratings of role competence, also secured in Phase 3. Each also rated overall competence in seven marital roles: spouse, parent, lover, breadwinner-homemaker, friend, community participant, and host or hostess. Scores for each and overall role competence were available. The items were taken from Kelly (1955).

d. Other indices of vocational success, including achievements, awards, and earned income (rated in terms of seven categories), were also secured.

e. Sexual behavior and relation. Items from Kelly's study of married couples (1955) had been used in Phase 3 and their results reported in Heath (1978a, 1978b, and 1979). They measured degree of enjoyment, consideration, frequency, faithfulness, and other aspects of sexual behavior. A marital sexual compatibility score combined ratings of self and partner sexual enjoyment, degree of sexual "matedness," consideration, and faithfulness (Heath, 1978b). Other items about sexual fulfillment and competence were included in Phase 4.

f. Nonmarital close friendships. In addition to listing and rating the six attributes necessary to be a close friend to another of the same sex, each participant rated forty-seven items describing number of close friends, frequency and types of contact, importance, degree of intimacy, and wished-for intimacy of friendship. Various indices about friendship were constructed from such items.

g. Community involvement. In addition to listing and rating the six most important strengths needed to be an effective community citizen, each participant listed his or her principal voluntary community responsibilities and contributions for the past ten to fifteen years. Two judges independently rated all participants' degree of community involvement by sorting their protocols into eight categories and then agreed upon a final community involvement score that reflected variety and duration of community activity, recognition, and responsibility elected to or assumed.

h. Religious involvement was measured by six items about frequency of church attendance, religious interest, belief, and degree of intrinsic religious motivation. The items were highly intercorrelated and satisfactorily predicted a total score of religiosity (A30) that also included a well-established scale of religious behavior and attitudes (A15).

i. Relationships with own parents. In addition to completing A1a, each participant rated sixty items describing relationships with mother and father. Topics included degree of warmth of relationship, frequency of contact, feelings of being understood and disagreement with, and quality of current relationship with each, as well as ratings of degree to which each parent was still "present" internally and influencing values and decisions. Other questions were asked in an interview (A21).

j. Goals for future. Each person rated the importance of commonly shared goals, spontaneously listed the ten specific goals he or she would most like to fulfill before dying, and then rated the likelihood of their achievement.

A5. Health was measured in several ways.

a. Self-, partner, friend-, and colleague-rated physical and mental health.

b. Self-rated bodily symptoms and change in past decade. Thirty-four items had been drawn from various sources that described symptoms of menopause (Neugarten, Wood, Kraines, & Loomis, 1968) and mid-life disturbance, for example, fatigue, pounding of heart, depression (Lear, 1973).

A6. Vocational Adaptation Scale (VAS), also used in Phase 3. Twenty-eight items measured degree of satisfaction about key sources of vocational adaptation. Vocational adjustment was measured by ratings of items like quality of work, salary, work conditions, time demands; vocational fulfillment was measured by items like job fulfills potentials, provides opportunity to live up to potentials and to grow rest of life. Scale has been widely used with teachers and administrators as well. VAS total score predicts a wide variety of personality and competence measures (Heath, 1976a, 1981b).

A7. Marital Adjustment Scale. Spanier's thirty-two-item scale includes every major attribute that researchers had found predicted a happy marital relationship, for example, degree of agreement about variety of decisions, frequency of discussing and working together. Three additional items were included. Items were weighted to yield a total marital adaptation score (1976). The scale correlated highly with numerous other PHQ items about the participants' marital adaptation as they, their partners, and closest friends rated them.

A8.   Interpersonal intimacy. Twenty personal self-revealing topics, for example, anger, dreams, failures, sexual wishes, were each rated by participant for degree of comfort when sharing with partner, mother, father, a child, and close friend. Weighting and summing the ratings provide a score measuring degree of openness of communicating about very personal issues with each person and a total score defining intimacy.

A9.   Parental Adaptation Scale (PAS). Dr. Harriet Heath created a thirty-item scale that included the twenty-eight VAS items, reinterpreted to apply to parents, that measured parental adaptation. Each parent rated satisfaction with parental adjustment (for example, recognition for parenting, energy demands), and fulfillment (for example, amount of growth experienced as a result of raising children, basic needs satisfied). A total score indexed parental adaptation, which I also refer to generally as satisfaction or fulfillment.

A10. Personality Scale. Included in the seventy-item scale were Bem's sixty items (1974), twenty of which measured masculinity, twenty femininity, and twenty buffer traits. Ten other personality traits not assessed by other tests of the study were included. Each participant and judge completed the scale about the participant. I modified Bem's scale to use five-point ratings and to define androgyny as the sum of the weighted scores for masculinity and femininity. Each person got a summary masculinity, femininity, and androgyny score. Though the concept of androgyny has provoked both theoretical and methodological arguments about its measurement (Spence, Helmreich, & Stapp, 1975; Taylor & Hall, 1982), most now agree that any person can be described in terms of both the masculine and feminine traits. The judges did, in fact, describe the men to be reliably more masculine than the women, for example, self-reliant, independent, analytic, self-sufficient, dominant, aggressive, and individualistic. They also identified the women to be more typically feminine than they described the men, for example, sensitive to others' needs, sympathetic, warm, and tender. An item analysis of the scale showed that femininity items like shy, flatterable, gullible, and childlike did not predict the total femininity score.

    a.   An interpersonal femininity score was constructed using ten of Bem's items, including affectionate, loyal, sympathetic, sensitive to others' needs, and loving children.

    b.   An index of leadership potential was constructed based on the participants' three judges' ratings of their leadership ability, leadership activities, enjoyment of exercising power, and being viewed as authorities.

A11. Happiness and fulfillment, also given in Phase 3. Each participant, partner, and closest friend rated the degree of participant's happiness on a three-point scale and degree of fulfillment and satisfaction with life on a seven-point scale. The items were taken from a national survey of mental health (Gurin, Veroff, & Feld, 1960); the men and women were similar in rated happiness and fulfillment to comparable representative Americans.

A12. Perceived Self Questionnaire (PSQ), also given in Phase 3. It is a fifty-item bipolar scale that measures the model of psychological maturity described in Chapter Three. A participant rates how true each item is on an eight-point scale. The PSQ was created for Phase 3, following the model's validation in Phase 2. It assesses the dimensional maturity, that is, awareness, other-centeredness, integration, stability, and autonomy, of a person's cognitive skills, male and female interpersonal relationships, values, and self-concept. Extensive evidence, including transcultural results, confirms its predictive validity for men; the current studies have now confirmed its validity for women as well (Heath, 1968, 1977c, and technical articles listed in the references).

A13.   Self-Image Questionnaire (SIQ), also given in Phases 2 and 3. It is a bipolar scale consisting of thirty traits reported by others to describe mature persons (Heath, 1965). However, research has since shown that only twenty-six were valid transculturally (Heath, 1977c). When given with different instructions, the SIQ behaviorally measures the dimensional maturity of the self-concept described in Chapter Three. Each participant, marital partner, friend, and colleague rated the participant on an eight-point scale for each of the thirty items. Combining its individual traits with the Personality Scale (A10) gave 100 key personality strengths rated by each participant and his or her three peers.

The SIQ yields a number of scores. The following are the ones cited in the book:

a.   Accuracy of self-awareness is measured by the degree of agreement between the average of the ratings of the three judges and of the participant for each item.

b.   Degree of other-centered empathy is measured by how accurately a participant predicts partner's and friend's (for Phase 4 only) ratings on each item. To economize on time, participant was not asked to also predict colleague ratings, which had been done in Phase 3.

c.   Degree of self-concept integration is measured by the degree of agreement between participants' ratings of selves and their *predicted* partners' and friends' ratings of them.

    d.   Stability of self-concept is measured by the degree of agreement between a participant's ratings about self and ratings he or she makes again about self four to six weeks later.

    e.   Judged maturity was measured by the weighted sum of the three judges' ratings of the twenty-six traits earlier found to predict psychological maturity.

    f.   Self-esteem was measured by the sum of the participant's ratings of the twenty-six traits indexing maturity.

SIQ scores correlate very highly with PSQ scores. Transcultural studies demonstrate that the SIQ, like the PSQ, scores powerfully predict many other indices of a person's competence and well-being. Because of the massive amount of information such scales provide, only a few selected results are reported in the chapters in order to not burden the general reader with technical detail.

A14.   Valuator Test (VAL), also given in Phase 3, is a fifteen-item bipolar eight-point scale designed to supplement the PSQ's measures of value maturity. The model of maturing provided the theoretical rationale for its construction. Its total score indexes the dimensional maturity of a person's values and was used primarily as one component of a measure of virtue.

A15.   Study of Values (SV), also given in Phases 1 and 3, measures a person's preferences for six different ways of life, that is, theoretical, economic, esthetic, political, social, and religious (Allport, Vernon, & Lindzey, 1960). Its religious score was used in the index of religiosity (A30).

A16.   Loevinger's Ego Development Scale was given to determine the relation of ego development to adult success and maturity (Loevinger, 1966; Loevinger & Wessler, 1970). The scale was reduced to thirty

items and modified to include items relevant to
middle age. The test consists of incomplete sentences that a person completes. The coded and
randomized men's and women's responses were
scored by an expert judge who had no knowledge
whatsoever of the study. Since level of ego development predicted almost no measure of success,
adaptation, maturity, or happiness, I do not refer
to it, except as a projective test revealing individual motives and wishes.

A17.   Parental ratings of each child's psychological
maturity and adaptability on the Developmental
History Questionnaire's fifty scales (A1b). Because
analysis of the results showed that the scales more
appropriately described older children, I secured
the average maturity score from both parents for
all of their children twelve years old or older. The
mothers and fathers agreed quite well about the
maturity of their children. Limited resources pre-
vented securing teacher judgments as had been
originally planned.

III. **First interview session, typically in the participant's
home**

A18.   Self-Image Questionnaire readministered, as also
in Phases 2 and 3, to measure the stability of the
self-concept (A13d).

A19.   Rorschach ink blots, administered in Phase 4 exactly as they had been given in Phases 2 and 3.
This complicated projective test provided insights
about defenses, modes of coping, intellectual
strengths, less conscious values and motives, and
relationships. Since Klopfer's scores had not proved
to be useful in the earlier phases or the transcultural studies of the model of maturity, I relied on
Holt's primary process and defense effectiveness
scores, which had proved to be more useful (Holt
& Havel, 1960). However, their validity has not
been sustained in the adult phases. So I relied on
the Rorschach primarily for the clinical insights

it provided about each participant and its power to illuminate the other test results that I summarized in my report about their results to each participant.

A20. Thematic Apperception Test cards 4, 10, 15, and 16 were used for insights about heterosexual relationships, male-female relationships, feelings about death, and unfulfilled wishes. It consists of pictures to which a person gives as imaginative a story as possible (Murray, 1943). The stories are used in the chapters to illustrate a person's personality.

A21. First structured interview was then given, recorded, and typed. The two-hour-plus interview focused on how a person had coped with different problems faced since Phase 3. Topics included principal achievements; failures; goals; hopes; and vocational, marital, parental, and friendship issues. Many items were taken from a national survey to be able to compare the group to a representative cohort (Gurin, Veroff, & Feld, 1960). The participants also rated themselves and their partners on the attributes the partners had previously identified to be essential to successfully fulfilling such roles.

IV. **Second interview session, typically the second day**

A22. Self-Image Questionnaire readministered, also in Phases 2 and 3.

a. Names and addresses of the closest friend and colleague most knowledgeable about participant's vocational or community activities were secured.

b. Each participant predicted as accurately as possible how the partner and friend would complete the SIQ about him or her (A13b).

A23. Second structured interview, also given in Phase 3. The taped interview secured objective scores about how the person had changed since Phase 3 and the principal determinants of the changes.

The method has been used to determine the maturing and immaturing effects of different aspects of college (Heath, 1968; 1976c), and parental (1978c) and vocational (1977d) roles. Since I refer in this book only to the determinants of the men's and women's growth in their thirties, I describe the method only briefly. After describing spontaneously how he or she had changed since Phase 3 in one of the model of maturity's four personality sectors — intellect, interpersonal relationships, values, and self-attitudes — each person sorted fifty cards listing a possible cause of such changes into five categories of their degree of influence. The fifty causes had been identified by independent judges and included ones like type of occupation, approaching middle age, and partner's personality. After next ranking the ten to twelve most influential causes, each person described specific examples of how the four most influential causes had affected him or her. The same procedure was repeated for each of the three remaining sectors. Their order of presentation was randomized across the group. Trained judges independently scored the typed interviews for the presence of dimensional maturing, relying on a revised manual earlier used for Phase 3. Objective scores about total amount of maturing and maturing in each area and on each dimension defining maturing were then obtained. The interview summary scores were validated against test measures of change.

A24. Sex-role interview, consisting of sixteen items, assessed changes in attitudes and behavior since Phase 3 was administered, recorded, and typed.

A25. An interpretive analysis of the psychological tests, as also in Phases 2 and 3 (focusing for the men on how they had changed since Phase 1), was given to each participant who requested it. All but one did. The analysis was prepared prior to visiting the participant; the Rorschach results were integrated with the Phase 2 and 3 ones for the men and the tests' results following the first interview. This was my way of expressing appreciation to the men and women for giving so much time so generously to the study. I also then made myself available for any counseling that they requested at the time or since, which about 10 percent of the men and women have done. I viewed the participants as colleagues understanding adult development, not as "subjects" to be observed and then forgotten in time of need. Perhaps because they knew their welfare has always taken precedence over the research, they have been extraordinarily cooperative and open about the most intimate aspects of their lives.

V. **Judge descriptions of participants secured**

A26.   Spouses or partners, closest friends, and colleagues were contacted, as in Phases 2 (close friends only) and 3. With only a few exceptions, all of the friends and colleagues assisted. Four wives refused, so other women completed the materials about the men. All judges rated the participant on the

a.   Personality Scale (A10)

b.   Self-Image Questionnaire (A13)

c.   Criteria identified by the participant to be critical to success in the role that the judge knew best, for example, friend-rated friendship criteria (A4b)

d.   Participant's physical and psychological health (A5)

The judges also rated other competences with which they were most familiar. The colleague and partner completed the Vocational Adaptation Scale about the participant (A6). The partner and friend rated the person's happiness and fulfillment (A11), as well as quality of relationships with different persons, for example spouse, children, parents. Marital partners completed a number of other scales, particularly about partners' marital, sexual, and parental competence (A4b,c).

Summary Scores and Statistical Analyses

Summary Scores. Composited z scores were used to combine the multitest indices of competence and well-being. Generally, each person's score on a specific index was converted into a z score, which in turn was averaged with other z indices of the same competence.

A27. Summary z score of familial success averaged the converted z scores indexing marital, familial, and sexual success. Marital indices included the amended Spanier's Marital Adjustment Scale (A7), a marital sexual compatibility score (A4e), Parental Adaptation Scale total score (A9), and self-rated competence on seven roles as a spouse (A4c) as well as on the six self-defined criteria defined to be necessary to be a good marital partner, parent, and lover (A4b).

A28. A summary z score of vocational success averaged the converted z scores for the total self- (A6) and colleague-rated (A26) Vocational Adaptation scores, earned income (A4d), and the average of the three judges' ratings about leadership from the Personality Scale (A10b).

A29. A summary z score of overall well-being averaged three z summary scores of physical health, six of mental health, and six of happiness-fulfillment. The combined physical, mental health, and happiness z scores contributed equally to the well-being score.

   a. The physical health score combined the self-rated and averaged judge-rated ratings of current physical health (A5a) with the bodily health total score (A5b).

b. The mental health score combined
1. SIQ-judged maturity (A13e)
2. SIQ measure of self-concept integration (A13c)
3. SIQ measure of the stability of self-concept (A13d)
4. Minnesota Multiphasic Personality Inventory total score (A2)
5. Self-ratings of psychological health (A5a)
6. Three judge ratings of psychological health (A5a, A26d)

Though assuming that the model of maturity comprehends what others mean by mental or psychological health, I did not want to impose that assumption on the measurement of mental health. I relied on behavioral indices, like the SIQ procedures, earlier found to be the most useful measures of mental health transculturally (Heath, 1977c), as well as judge ratings and standard psychological tests of mental health to snare as many different indices of mental health as possible.

I had planned to include Loevinger's Ego Development total score and Holt's Rorschach scores, which moderately correlated with each other. However, each predicted so few of the numerous measures of competence, adaptation, health, and happiness, as well as of the above-listed six measures of mental health, that their inclusion in the summary index would have severely attenuated the results.

c. The happiness score combined self-ratings of happiness and of fulfillment in one's life with the partner's and friend's ratings of the participant's happiness and fulfillment (A11). The self- and judge ratings for happiness and fulfillment were reliably intercorrelated as were the participants' and their peers' ratings.

A30. Summary score of religiosity was a z score that combined a z score for self-rated attributes of religious behavior and belief (A4h) and a z score of a test of religious values (A15).

A31. Summary score of virtue or value maturity (also referred to as ethical idealism) combined z scores for the participants' own self-ratings and the averaged judge ratings on the Personality Scale (A10) of each participant's virtue, for example, rated honesty, compassion, integrity, deep ethical sense, idealism, and courage (A10), and a z score for the Valuator total score (A14).

A32. Summary score of adolescent mental health in Phases 1 and 2 was a composited z score that combined a summary Rorschach clinical evaluation of mental health, the MMPI total score (A2), SIQ judged maturity (A13e), and SIQ self-esteem (A13f) (Heath, 1965). The summary index was highly correlated with Phase 3's measure of mental health (.55) and Phase 4's also (.40) (A29b).

Analyses and Reports of Significant Findings. All findings cited in the text are statistically significant or reliable at at least a .05 two-tailed probability level. When I refer to those few findings that approached significance, I use phrases like "tend to suggest." I relied primarily on Pearson r and Student t analyses. Given the purposes of this book, small samples, type of data secured, and previous experience with the instability of complex factorial and path analyses, I have resisted the temptation to make more refined or sophisticated analyses of subgroup results. While I forfeited subtlety and possible precision as a consequence, I had to simplify, rather than complicate even more than I already had, the presentation of complex technical material for the general reader.

References————————————————

Allport, G. W., Vernon, P. E., & Lindzey, G. *Study of Values. Manual of Directions.* Boston: Houghton Mifflin, 1960.

Antonucci, T. C. Longitudinal and cross-sectional data sources on women in the middle years. In J. Z. Giele (Ed.). *Women in the Middle Years.* New York: Wiley, 1982.

Astin, A. W. *Four Critical Years: Effects of College on Beliefs, Attitudes, and Knowledge.* San Francisco: Jossey-Bass, 1977.

Astin, A. W. *The American Freshman: National Norms for Fall 1987.* Cooperative Institutional Research Program. Los Angeles: Graduate School of Education, U.C.L.A., 1988.

Bachman, J. G. An eye on the future. *Psychology Today,* 1987, July, 6, 8.

Bachman, J. G. & Johnston, L. D. The freshmen, 1979. *Psychology Today,* 1979, September, 79–87.

Bakan, D. *The Duality of Human Experience.* Chicago: Rand McNally, 1966.

Barron, F. The disposition toward originality. *Journal of Abnormal and Social Psychology,* 1955, *51,* 478–485.

Barron, F. *Creativity and Psychological Health.* Princeton, NJ: Van Nostrand, 1963.

Baruch, G., Barnett, R., & Rivers, C. *Lifeprints.* New York: McGraw-Hill, 1983.

Bayer, L. M., Whissell-Buechy, E., & Honzik, M. P. Health in the middle years. In D. H. Eichorn, J. A. Clausen, N.

Haan, M. P. Honzik, & P. H. Mussen (Eds.). *Present and Past in Middle Life.* New York: Academic Press, 1981, Ch. 3.

Bayley, N. Mental growth in young children. *Yearbook of the National Society for the Study of Education,* 1940, *39,* Part II, 11–47.

Becker, R. J. Religion and psychological health. In M. P. Strommen (Ed.). *Research on Religious Development: A Comprehensive Handbook.* New York: Hawthorn Books, 1971, Ch. 10.

Bellah, R. N., Madsen, R., Sullivan, W. M., Swidler, A., & Tipton, S. M. *Habits of the Heart: Individualism and Commitment in American Life.* Berkeley, CA: University of California Press, 1985.

Bem, S. L. The measurement of psychological androgyny. *Journal of Consulting and Clinical Psychology,* 1974, *42,* 155–162.

Bennett, A. Some business grads learn to hate their glamorous Wall Street jobs. *Wall Street Journal,* 1985, December 18, 31.

Block, J. *Lives Through Time.* Berkeley, CA: Bancroft Books, 1971.

Block, J. D. *Friendship: How to Give It, How to Get It.* New York: Macmillan, 1980.

Bloom, A. D. *The Closing of the American Mind.* New York: Simon & Schuster, 1987.

Bradburn, N. M. *The Structure of Psychological Well-Being.* Chicago: Aldine, 1969.

Bray, D. W., Campbell, R. J., & Grant, D. L. *Formative Years in Business. A Long-Term AT&T Study of Managerial Lives.* New York: Wiley, 1974.

Bray, D. W. & Howard, A. Career success and life satisfactions of middle-aged managers. Paper presented at Fourth Vermont Conference on the Primary Prevention of Psychopathology, 1978, June 23.

Brooks, J. B. Social maturity in middle age and its developmental antecedents. In D. H. Eichorn, J. A. Clausen, N. Haan, M. P. Honzik, & P. H. Mussen (Eds.). *Present and Past in Middle Life.* New York: Academic Press, 1981, Ch. 10.

Buie, J. Divorce hurts boys more, studies show. *The APA Monitor,* 1988, January, p. 32.

Campbell, A. *The Sense of Well-Being in America: Recent Patterns and Trends.* New York: McGraw-Hill, 1981.

Cannon, W. B. *The Wisdom of the Body.* New York: Norton, 1939. (Originally published 1932.)

Clausen, J. A. Men's occupational careers in the middle years. In D. H. Eichorn, J. A. Clausen, N. Haan, M. P. Honzik, & P. H. Mussen (Eds.). *Present and Past in Middle Life.* New York: Academic Press, 1981, Ch. 13.

Cohen, P. D. College grades and adult achievement: A research synthesis. *Research in Higher Education,* 1984, *20,* 281–293.

Cox, R. D. *Youth into Maturity.* New York: Mental Health Materials Center, 1970.

DeWinne, R. F., Overton, T. D., & Schneider, L. J. Types produce types — especially fathers. *Journal of Vocational Behavior,* 1978, *12,* 140–144.

Dittes, J. E. Religion, prejudice, and personality. In M. P. Strommen (Ed.). *Research on Religious Development. A Comprehensive Handbook.* New York: Hawthorn Books, 1971a, Ch. 9.

Dittes, J. E. Two issues in measuring religion. In M. P. Strommen (Ed.). *Research on Religious Development. A Comprehensive Handbook.* New York: Hawthorn Books, 1971b, Ch. 3.

Douvan, E. & Adelson, J. *The Adolescent Experience.* New York: Wiley, 1966.

Eichorn, D. H., Clausen, J. A., Haan, N., Honzik, M. P., & Mussen, P. H. (Eds.). *Present and Past in Middle Life.* New York: Academic Press, 1981.

Eichorn, D. H., Hunt, J. V., & Honzik, M. P. Experience, personality, and IQ: Adolescence to middle age. In D. H. Eichorn, J. A. Clausen, N. Haan, M. P. Honzik, & P. H. Mussen (Eds.). *Present and Past in Middle Life.* New York: Academic Press, 1981, Ch. 4.

Eichorn, D. H., Mussen, P. H., Clausen, J. A., Haan, N., & Honzik, M. P. Overview. In D. H. Eichorn, J. A. Clausen, N. Haan, M. P. Honzik, & P. H. Mussen (Eds.). *Present and Past in Middle Life.* New York: Academic Press, 1981, Ch. 16.

Erikson, E. *Childhood and Society.* New York: Norton, 1950.

Eysenck, H. J. Health's character. *Psychology Today,* 1988, December, 27–35.

Fallon, M. "Success at any price": Cheating common, California survey finds. *Education Week,* 1986, April 30.

Ferguson, J. Untitled address. National 4-H Congress, Chicago, IL, 1983, November 30.

Gallante, S. P. Small business. *Wall Street Journal,* 1988, January 12, 39.

Giffin, M. E. & Felsenthal, C. *A Cry for Help.* Garden City, NY: Doubleday, 1983.

Gilligan, C. *In a Different Voice: Psychological Theory and Women's Development.* Cambridge, MA: Harvard University Press, 1982.

Glueck, S. & Glueck, E. *Criminal Careers in Retrospect.* New York: Commonwealth Fund, 1943.

Golden, J., Mandell, N., Glueck, B., and Feder, Z. A summary description of 50 "normal" white males. *American Journal of Psychiatry,* 1962, *119,* 48–56.

Goleman, D. Major personality study finds that traits are mostly inherited. *New York Times,* 1986, December 2, C3.

Gorsuch, R. L. The boon and bane of investigating religion. *American Psychologist,* 1984, March, 228–236.

Gould, R. L. The phases of adult life: A study in developmental psychology. *American Journal of Psychiatry,* 1972, *129,* 521–531.

Gould, R. L. *Transformations: Growth and Change in Adult Life.* New York: Simon & Schuster, 1978.

Gove, W. & Tudor, J. Adult sex roles and mental illness. *American Journal of Sociology,* 1973, *78,* 812–835.

Gurin, G., Veroff, J., & Feld, S. *Americans View Their Mental Health: A Nationwide Interview Survey; a Report to the Staff Director, Jack R. Ewalt.* New York: Basic Books, 1960.

Guttmann, D. Parenthood: A key to the comparative study of the life cycle. In N. Datun & L. H. Ginsberg (Eds.). *Life-Span Development Psychology.* New York: Academic Press, 1975.

Haan, N. Common dimensions of personality development: Early adolescence to middle life. In D. H. Eichorn, J. A. Clausen, N. Haan, M. P. Honzik, & P. H. Mussen (Eds.). *Present and Past in Middle Life.* New York: Academic Press, 1981.

Haan, N. & Day, D. A. longitudinal study of change and sameness in personality development: Adolescence to later adulthood. *International Journal of Aging and Human Development,* 1974, *5,* 11–39.

Haier, R. J. & Denham, S. A. A summary profile of the non-intellectual correlates of mathematical precocity in boys and girls. In D. P. Keating (Ed.). *Intellectual Talent: Research and Development.* Baltimore, MD: Johns Hopkins University Press, 1976, Ch. 11.

Handy, R. *Male Sexuality.* Buffalo, NY: Prometheus, 1988.

Hare-Mustin, R. T. & Marecek, J. Autonomy and gender: Some questions for therapists. *Psychotherapy,* 1986, *23,* 205–210.

Heath, C. W. *What People Are.* Cambridge, MA: Harvard University Press, 1945.

Heath, D. H. *Explorations of Maturity: Studies of Mature and Immature College Men.* New York: Appleton-Century-Crofts, 1965.

Heath, D. H. *Growing Up in College: Liberal Education and Maturity.* San Francisco: Jossey-Bass, 1968.

Heath, D. H. Secularization and maturity of religious beliefs. *Journal of Religion and Health,* 1969, 335–358.

Heath, D. H. *Humanizing Schools: New Directions, New Decisions.* Rochelle Park, NJ: Hayden Book Co., 1971.

Heath, D. H. Adolescent and adult predictors of vocational adaptation. *Journal of Vocational Behavior,* 1976a, *9,* 1–19.

Heath, D. H. Competent fathers: Their personalities and marriages. *Human Development,* 1976b, *19,* 26–39.

Heath, D. H. What the enduring effects of higher education tell us about a liberal education. *Journal of Higher Education,* 1976c, *47,* 173–190.

Heath, D. H. Academic predictors of adult maturity and competence. *Journal of Higher Education,* 1977a, *48,* 613–632.

Heath, D. H. Maternal competence, expectation, and involvement. *Journal of Genetic Psychology,* 1977b, *131,* 169–182.

Heath, D. H. *Maturity and Competence: A Transcultural View.* New York: Gardner Press (Halstead division of Wiley), 1977c.

Heath, D. H. Some possible effects of occupation on the maturing of professional men. *Journal of Vocational Behavior,* 1977d, *11,* 263–281.

Heath, D. H. Marital sexual enjoyment and frustration of professional men. *Archives of Sexual Behavior,* 1978a, *8,* 463–476.

Heath, D. H. Personality correlates of the marital sexual compatibility of professional men. *Journal of Sex and Marital Therapy,* 1978b, *4,* 67–82.

Heath, D. H. What meaning and effects does fatherhood have for the maturing of professional men? *Merrill-Palmer Quarterly,* 1978c, *24,* 265–278.

Heath, D. H. Marital sexuality and the psychological health of professional men. *Journal of Sex and Marital Therapy,* 1979, *5,* 103–116.

Heath, D. H. Wanted: A comprehensive model of healthy development. *Personnel and Guidance Journal,* 1980, *58,* 391–399.

Heath, D. H. A college's ethos: A neglected key to effectiveness and survival. *Liberal Education,* 1981a, *67,* 89–111.

Heath, D. H. *Faculty Burnout, Morale, and Vocational Adaptation.* Pamphlet. Boston: National Association of Independent Schools, 1981b, p. 33.

Heath, D. H. The maturing person. In G. Walsh & D. Shapiro (Eds). *Beyond Health and Normality.* New York: Van Nostrand Rinehold, 1983, 152–205, Ch. 6.

Heath, H. E. Determinants of parenting behavior: The effect of support and information on the breast feeding experience. Unpublished doctoral dissertation, Bryn Mawr College, 1976.

Helson, R. & Moane, G. Personality change in women from college to midlife. *Journal of Personality and Social Psychology,* 1987, *53,* 176–186.

Helson, R. & Wink, P. Two conceptions of maturity examined in the findings of a longitudinal study. *Journal of Personality and Social Psychology,* 1987, *53,* 531–541.

Holden, C. The genetics of personality. *Science,* 1987, 237, 598–601.

Holt, R. R. & Havel, J. A method for assessing primary and secondary process in the Rorschach. In M. A. Rickers-Ovsiankina (Ed.). *Rorschach Psychology.* New York: Wiley, 1960, Ch. 10.

House, J. S., Landis, K. R., & Umberson, D. Social relationships and health. *Science,* 1988, July 29, 241, 540–545.

James, M. Report of Gallup poll to Market Research Society's conference. Brighton, England.

James, W. *The Principles of Psychology.* New York: Henry Holt, 1890, Vol. 1, 309–310.

Jennings, W. & Nathan, J. Startling/disturbing research on school program effectiveness. *Phi Delta Kappan,* 1977, *58,* 568–572.

Johnston, J. S., Jr. & Associates. *Educating Managers: Executive Effectiveness Through Liberal Learning.* San Francisco: Jossey-Bass, 1986.

Jones, H. E. Educational research at the Institute of Child Welfare. *Journal of Educational Research,* 1940, *34,* 158–159.

Kagan, J. & Moss, H. A. *Birth to Maturity.* New York: Wiley, 1962.

Kahn, S., Zimmerman, G., Csikszentmihalyi, M., & Getzels, J. W. Relations between identity in young adulthood and intimacy at midlife. *Journal of Personality and Social Psychology,* 1985, *49,* 1316–1322.

Kelly, E. L. "Consistency of the adult personality." *American Psychologist,* 1955, *10,* 659–681.

Kelly, E. L. Multiple criteria of medical education and their implications for selection. In H. H. Tee & J. T. Cowles (Eds.). *The Appraisal of Applicants to Medical Schools.* Evanston, IL: Association of American Medical Colleges, 1957.

Kohlberg, L., LaCrosse, J., & Ricks, D. The predictability of adult mental health from childhood behavior. In B. B. Wolman (Ed.). *Manual of Child Psychopathology.* New York: McGraw-Hill, 1972, Ch. 42.

Kohn, A. Making the most of marriage. *Psychology Today,* 1987, December, 6–8.

Kohn, A. Girl talk, guy talk. *Psychology Today,* 1988, February, 65–66.

Lear, M. W. Is there a male menopause? *New York Times Magazine,* 1973, January 28, 10.

Leete, B. A., Francia, A. J., & Strawser, R. H. A look at lawyers' need satisfaction. *American Bar Association Journal,* 1971, *57,* 1193–1196.

Levinson, D. J. *The Seasons of a Man's Life.* New York: Knopf, 1978.

Lewis, J. & Nelson, I. The relationship between college grades and three factors of adult achievement. *Educational and Psychological Measurement,* 1983, *43,* 577–580.

Livson, N. & Peskin, H. Prediction of adult psychological health in a longitudinal study. *Journal of Abnormal Psychology,* 1967, *72,* 509–518.

Livson, N. & Peskin, H. Perspectives on adolescence from longitudinal research. In J. Adelson (Ed.). *Handbook of Adolescent Psychology.* New York: Wiley, 1980.

Livson, N. & Peskin, H. Psychological health at age 40: Prediction from adolescent personality. In D. H. Eichorn, J. A. Clausen, N. Haan, M. P. Honzik, & P. H. Mussen (Eds.). *Present and Past in Middle Life.* New York: Academic Press, 1981, Ch. 7.

Loevinger, J. The meaning and measurement of ego development. *American Psychologist,* 1966, *21,* 195–206.

Loevinger, J. & Wessler, R. *Measuring Ego Development: Construction and Use of a Sentence Completion Test.* San Francisco: Jossey-Bass, 1970, Vol. 1.

Lowenberg, P. Einstein in his youth. *Science,* 1988, *239,* 510–512.

Lowenthal, M. F., Thurnher, M., Chiriboga, D., and Associates. *Four Stages of Life: A Comparative Study of Women and Men Facing Transitions.* San Francisco: Jossey-Bass, 1975.

Maas, H. S. & Kuypers, J. A. *From Thirty to Seventy: A Forty-Year Longitudinal Study of Adult Life Styles and Personality.* San Francisco: Jossey-Bass, 1974.

Maccoby, E. E. Gender and relationships. A developmental account. *American Psychologist,* April 1990, 513–520.

McCue, J. D. Influence of medical and premedical education on important personal qualities of physicians. *The American Journal of Medicine,* 1985, *78,* 985–989.

Macfarlane, J. W. Studies in child guidance. I. Methodology of data collection and organization. *Monographs of the Society for Research in Child Development,* 1938, *3,* No. 6.

Maslow, A. H. *Motivation and Personality.* New York: Harper & Brothers, 1954.

Maslow, A. H. *The Psychology of Science: A Reconnaissance.* New York: Harper & Row, 1966.

Masters, W. H. & Johnson, V. E. *The Pleasure Bond: A New Look on Sexuality and Commitment.* Boston: Little, Brown, 1975.

Mehren, E. After scandal, she adopts her first ambition. *Los Angeles Times* Service, 1987, December.

Miller, J. B. *Toward a New Psychology of Women.* Boston: Beacon Press, 1976.

Miller, K. & Moser, G. Moral judgment, personality maturity, and perception of others. Unpublished senior thesis, Haverford College, 1977.

Miller, S. *Men and Friendship.* Boston, MA: Houghton Mifflin, 1983.

Morrison, A. M., White, R. P., & Van Velso, E. Executive women: Substance plus style. *Psychology Today,* 1987, August, 18–26.

Munneke, G. A. & Bridger-Riley, N. K. Singing those law office blues. *Barrister,* 1981, Fall, p. 10.

Murphy, L. & Moriarty, A. *Vulnerability, Coping and Growth.* New Haven, CT: Yale University Press, 1976.

Murray, H. A. *Thematic Apperception Test Manual.* Cambridge, MA: Harvard University Press, 1943.

Neugarten, B. L. The awareness of middle age. In B. L. Neugarten (Ed.). *Middle Age and Aging. A Reader in Social Psychology.* Chicago: University of Chicago Press, 1968, Ch. 10.

Neugarten, B. L. & Neugarten, D. A. The changing meanings of age. *Psychology Today,* 1987, May, 29–33.

Neugarten, B. L., Wood, V., Kraines, R. J., & Loomis, B. Women's attitudes toward the menopause. In B. L. Neugarten (Ed.). *Middle Age and Aging. A Reader in Social Psychology.* Chicago: University of Chicago Press, 1968, Ch. 21.

Neugarten, B. L. and Associates. *Personality in Middle and Late Life.* New York: Atherton Press, 1964.

Noble, K. D. Psychological health and the experience of transcendence. *The Counseling Psychologist,* 1987, *15,* 601–614.

Oden, M. H. The fulfillment of promise: 40 year follow-up of the Terman gifted group. *Genetic Psychological Monographs,* 1968, *77,* 3–93.

Office of Educational Research and Improvement. Extracurricular activity participants outperform other students. *Bulletin.* U.S. Department of Education, Center for Statistics, 1986, September, 1–7.

Olney, M. & Peters, R. Intelligence correlates and developmental antecedents of adult maturity and competence. Unpublished senior thesis, Haverford College, 1979.

Osherson, S. *Holding On or Letting Go: Men and Career Change at Midlife.* New York: Free Press, 1980.

Otten, A. L. Surveying teen-agers on health and behavior. *Wall Street Journal,* May 22, 1989a, p. B1.

Otten, A. L. UCLA looks at marriage California style. *Wall Street Journal,* July 14, 1989b, p. B1.

Peskin, H. Influence of the developmental schedule of puberty on learning and ego functioning. *Journal of Youth and Adolescence,* 1973, *2,* 273–290.

Peskin, H. & Livson, N. Uses of the past in adult psychological health. In D. H. Eichorn, J. A. Clausen, N. Haan, M. P. Honzik, & P. H. Mussen (Eds.). *Present and Past in Middle Life.* New York: Academic Press, 1981, Ch. 6.

Piaget, J. *The Origins of Intelligence in Children.* New York: International Universities Press, 1952. (Originally published 1936.)

Pleck, J. H. & Sawyer, J. (Eds.). *Men and Masculinity.* Englewood Cliffs, NJ: Prentice-Hall, 1974.

Reinhold, R. Harvard study calls emotional illness major cause of drop outs. *New York Times,* 1970, October 25.

Rhoads, J. M., Gallemore, J. L., Giantureo, D. T., & Osterhout, S. Motivation, medical admissions, and student performance. *Journal of Medical Education,* 1974, *49,* 1119–1127.

Rosenfeld, A. & Stark, E. The prime of our lives. *Psychology Today,* 1987, May, 62–72.

Rosenthal, I. Reliability of retrospective reports of adolescence. *Journal of Consulting Psychology,* 1963, *27,* 189–198.

Samson, G. E., Graue, M. E., Weinstein, T., & Walberg, H. J. Academic and occupational performance: A quantitative synthesis. *American Educational Research Journal,* 1984, *21,* 311–321.

Sanford, N. What is a normal personality? In J. Katz and others (Eds.). *Writers on Ethics: Classical and Contemporary.* Princeton, NJ: Van Nostrand, 1962.

Sears, R. R. Sources of life satisfaction of the Terman gifted men. *American Psychologist,* 1977, *32,* 119–129.

Seeman, J. Toward a model of positive health. *American Psychologist,* 1989, August, 1099–1109.

Seligman, M. E. P. Boomer blues. *Psychology Today,* 1988, October, 50–55.

Shedler, J. & Block, J. Adolescent drug use and psychological health. A longitudinal inquiry. *American Psychologist,* 1990, *45,* 612–630.

Sheehy, G. *Passages: Predictable Crises of Adult Life.* New York: Dutton, 1976.

Siegelman, E., Block, J., Block, J., & von der Lippe, A. Antecedents of optimal psychological adjustment. *Journal of Consulting and Clinical Psychology,* 1970, *35,* 283–289.

Skolnick, A. Married lives: Longitudinal perspectives on marriage. In D. H. Eichorn, J. A. Clausen, N. Haan, M. P. Honzik, & P. H. Mussen (Eds.). *Present and Past in Middle Life.* New York: Academic Press, 1981, Ch. 11.

Slack, N. V. & Porter, D. The Scholastic Aptitude Test: A critical appraisal. *Harvard Education Review,* 1980, *50,* 154–175.

Smith, M. B. On self-actualization: A transambivalent examination of a focal theme in Maslow's psychology. *Journal of Humanistic Psychology,* 1973, *13,* 17–33.

Spanier, G. B. Measuring dyadic adjustment: New scales for assessing the quality of marriage and similar dyads. *Journal of Marriage and the Family,* 1976, *38,* 15–28.

Spanier, G. B. & Lewis, R. A. Marital quality: A review of the seventies. *Journal of Marriage and the Family,* 1980, *42,* 825–839.

Spence, J. T., Helmreich, R., & Stapp, J. Ratings of self and peers on sex role attributes and their relation to self-esteem and conceptions of masculinity and femininity. *Journal of Personality and Social Psychology,* 1975, *32,* 29–39.

Spilka, B., Hood, R. W., Jr., & Gorsuch, R. L. *The Psychology of Religion: An Empirical Approach.* Englewood Cliffs, NJ: Prentice-Hall, 1985.

Stark, E. Mind openers. *Psychology Today,* 1988, February, 18.

Stroud, J. G. Women's careers: Work, family, and personality. In D. H. Eichorn, J. A. Clausen, N. Haan, M. P. Honzik, & P. H. Mussen (Eds.). *Present and Past in Middle Life.* New York: Academic Press, 1981, Ch. 14.

Super, D. E. Coming of age in middletown. Careers in the making. *American Psychologist,* 1985, April, 405–414.

Taylor, M. C. & Hall, J. A. Psychological androgyny: Theories, methods, and conclusions. *Psychological Bulletin,* 1982, *92,* 347–366.

Terman, L. M. The discovery and encouragement of exceptional talent. *American Psychologist,* 1954, *9,* 221–230.

Thomas, A. & Chess, S. *Temperament and Behavior Disorders in Children.* New York: New York University Press, 1969.

Thomas, C. B. Precursors of premature disease and death. *Annals of Internal Medicine,* 1976, *85,* 653–658.

Thomas, C. B. Stamina: The thread of human life. *Journal of Chronic Diseases,* 1981, *34, 41*–44.

Tocqueville, A. de. *Democracy in America.* New York: Knopf, 1945. (Originally published 1835.)

Vaillant, G. E. Antecedents of healthy adult adjustment. In D. F. Ricks, A. Thomas, & M. Roff (Eds.). *Life History Research in Psychopathology.* Minneapolis: University of Minnesota Press, 1974a, *3,* 230–242.

Vaillant, G. E. Natural history of male psychological health II: Some antecedents of healthy adult adjustment. *Archives of General Psychiatry,* 1974b, *31,* 15–22.

Vaillant, G. E. Natural history of male psychological health III: Empirical dimensions of mental health. *Archives of General Psychiatry,* 1975, *32,* 420–426.

Vaillant, G. E. *Adaptation to Life.* Boston: Little, Brown, 1977.

Vaillant, G. E. Natural history of male psychological health VI: Correlates of successful marriage and fatherhood. *American Journal of Psychiatry,* 1978, *135,* 653–659.

Vaillant, G. E. Natural history of male psychological health. Effects of mental health on physical health. *New England Journal of Medicine,* 1979, *301,* 1249–1254.

Vaillant, G. E. & McArthur, C. C. Natural history of male psychologic health, I: The adult life cycle from 18–50. *Seminars in Psychiatry,* 1972, *4,* No. 4.

Vaillant, G. E. & Vaillant, C. O. Natural history of male psychological health, X: Work as a predictor of positive mental health. *American Journal of Psychiatry,* 1981, *138,* 1433–1440.

Van Doren, M. *Liberal Education.* New York: Holt, 1943.

Verbrugge, L. M. Women's social roles and health. In P. W. Berman & E. Raimy (Eds.). *Women: A Developmental Perspec-*

tive. Washington, DC: U.S. Department of Health publication, NIH, 1982, #82-2298.

Veroff, J., Douvan, E., & Kulka, R. A *The Inner American: A Self-Portrait from 1957 to 1976.* New York: Basic Books, 1981.

Wallach, M. A. The psychology of talent and graduate education. Paper presented to Conference on Cognitive Styles and Creativity in Higher Education, Montreal, 1972, November.

Welsch, H. P. & Young, E. C. Research conducted at De Paul University, Chicago, IL, 1981.

Werner, E. E. & Smith, R. S. *Vulnerable but Invincible: A Longitudinal Study of Resilient Children and Youth.* New York: McGraw-Hill, 1982.

Westley, W. A. & Epstein, N. B. *The Silent Majority.* San Francisco: Jossey-Bass, 1969.

Whitaker, Kelly, E. L., & Uhr. A brief statement regarding the Michigan project on the prediction of professional competence in medicine. Unpublished article, 1956.

Williams, W. L. *The Spirit and the Flesh: Sexual Diversity in American Indian Culture.* Boston: Beacon Press, 1986.

Willingham, W. W. Predicting success in graduate education. *Science,* 1974, *183,* 273-278.

Willingham, W. W., Young, J. W., & Morris, M. M. *Success in College: The Role of Personal Qualities and Academic Ability.* New York: College Entrance Examination Board, 1985.

Winter, D. G., McClelland, D. C., & Stewart, A. J. *A New Case for the Liberal Arts: Assessing Institutional Goals and Student Development.* San Francisco: Jossey-Bass, 1981.

Yankelovich, D. New rules in American life: Searching for self-fulfillment in a world turned upside down. *Psychology Today,* 1981, April, 35-91.

Yeh, E.-K. & Chu, H.-M. The images of Chinese and American character: Cross-cultural adaptation by Chinese students. In W. P. Lebra (Ed.). *Youth, Socialization, and Mental Health.* Honolulu: University Press of Hawaii, 1974, Ch. 15.

Youniss, J. & Smollar, J. *Adolescent Relations with Mothers, Fathers, and Friends.* Chicago: Unviersity of Chicago Press, 1985.

Index

A

Academic grades, achievement, and aptitude tests. *See* Schools
Adaptation: definition of, 51, 66, 203; effects of successful, 36–37; and maturity, 38–59, 66, 120–121, 326–327. *See also* Adjustment; Self-fulfillment
Adelson, J., 305
Adjustment, 51, 120, 124, 257, 319, 326; definition of, 66
Adolescence: boy-girl comparisons of, 64, 300, 301–303, 360; and measures of maturity, 369
Adolescent predictors: of adult community involvement, 300–301; of adult maturity, 300, 344, 359, 360, 361; of adult success in personal relations, 300, 301; of adult virtue, 300, 301; of adult vocational success, 300, 301, 360–361; of adult well-being, 300–301, 344, 361, 384. *See also* Developmental History Questionnaire
Allen, Jane, 64–65, 177–186, 318; and community involvement, 227; and goals for children, 243–244; maturing of, 325; parents of, 179–180, 277–278, 280, 289; and success in personal relations, 181; and vocational success, 202, 206, 208, 210; and well-being, 246, 251
Androgyny: adolescent measure of, 306; and community involvement, 19, 227,
228; and creativity, 98–99; definition of, 19, 342; examples of, 29–33, 97–99, 109–110; and maturity, 116–117, 319; measure of, 29, 342, 374; personality correlates of, 18; and success in personal relations, 19, 127–128, 130, 159, 165–167, 171–173, 174; and virtue, 240, 262; and vocational success, 19, 184, 185, 192–193, 196, 205, 209, 211, 215; and well-being, 19, 247, 251, 261, 315
Autonomy, 36, 249; adolescent measures of, 301, 304, 307, 359; and adult maturing, 249, 257–258, 261, 312, 315, 318, 320, 325, 344; and community involvement, 229, 306; definition of, 54–58; immature, 57, 63, 72; male-female comparisons of, 211–214, 239–241, 255–259, 289; measures of, 169, 374, 375–376, 377, 379–380; and other-centeredness, 58, 63, 65, 318; personality traits of, 236, 240, 249, 250–251, 252, 258, 261, 262, 267, 306, 319; and stability, 54–58, 250–251, 301, 304, 315; and vocational success, 304. *See also* Cognitive skills; Interpersonal relations; Self-concept; Values

B

Baker, Karl and Jeannie, 122
Barnett, Eloise, 224, 225–226, 270, 271, 272

Barnett, Harry, 219, 223–230, 269–272;
and adolescent personality, 300–301;
and community involvement, 227;
and goals for children, 243; parents of,
272, 276, 280, 282, 284; and school
success, 293, 295; and success in personal relations, 269–271; and virtue,
238; and well-being, 246, 250–251,
260
Baruch, G., 189, 191–192, 346, 347, 350,
352, 354–355, 364
Bem, S. L., 172, 342, 374
Benjamin, 47, 48–49, 54–55, 69, 109, 143
Blake, Roger, 173, 331; and drive to grow
up, 5, 332; and insights into maturing, 113–114; maturity of, 39–42, 45,
47, 60, 61, 62, 63, 68, 129, 265, 312;
and views about generational changes,
131, 138, 158, 161, 184, 216, 284, 326
Brown, Martin, 164–165, 167

C

Calling. See Parental fulfillment; Parental role; Vocational fulfillment
Cannon, W., 60
Character. See Interpersonal relations;
Self-concept; Values
Children, maturity of, 238, 247, 253, 254,
268, 284; measure of, 368, 378; parental contribution to, 328–330, 337. See
also Developmental History Questionnaire
Citizenship. See Community involvement
Cognitive skills: autonomy of, 38, 54–56;
integration of, 38, 48–49, 312, 321,
343; maturity, 36; measures of, 369,
375–376, 378–379; and other-centeredness, 38, 43–45; stabilization of, 38,
54–56, 343; symbolization of, 38–39
Community involvement, 226–230; adolescent predictors of, 301, 306, 358;
definition of, 195, 226–227; determinants of, 274, 289, 297; male-female
comparisons of, 228–230; measures of,
226, 372; and other competencies,
227; personality correlates of, 19, 58,
191, 196, 227–229, 238, 253, 260;
rated importance of, 8, 224
Coping. See Ego strength
Corcoran, Dave, 50–51, 60, 66, 69, 177
Creativity, 98–99
Cunningham, M. E., 200–201

D

Developmental History Questionnaire,
23, 24, 96, 100, 104, 110, 140, 272,
273–290, 304–308; description of,
268, 368–369; reliability of, 299–300,
303, 356, 359–360; validity of, 300,
306–307, 369. See also Adolescent predictors; Maternal determinants; Paternal determinants
Dewey, J., 33, 38, 249
Douvan, E., 305
Drive to grow, 321, 332

E

Ego Developmental Scale, 23, 59, 78, 81,
276, 377, 383
Ego strength: personality correlates of,
30–31, 55, 249, 250–251, 256; and relation to model of maturing, 116
Einstein, A., 58, 294
Equilibrating principle: examples of, 58,
60–61, 185, 199, 217, 318, 321, 354;
male-female comparisons of, 64–65;
and relation to maturing, 60–64, 66,
106, 115–116, 316, 318, 321, 332
Erections, 153, 156, 255, 257
Erikson, E. H., 3, 57, 67, 227, 304–305
Ethical. See Values; Virtue
Exemplars of success, 20–32, 75–112,
177–181, 223–230, 269–272
Extracurricular activities. See Schools

F

Familial success. See Personal relationships, success in
Fels study, 364
Female maturing: barriers to, 316–320;
interpretations of, 109, 315–327; methodological issues about, 318. See also
Maturing of adults; Male-female comparisons
Femaleness. See Femininity; Menstruation
Feminine interpersonal skills: adolescent
measure of, 304–305; and community
involvement, 227; excessive development of, 318–320; and maturity, 45,
116–117, 319; measure of, 374–375;
and religiosity, 234; and success in
personal relations, 127, 128–132, 141,

156, 158–159, 161, 166, 168, 171–173, 268, 277; and virtue, 236, 239–241; and vocational success, 192–193, 205, 209, 211–213, 215; and well-being, 247, 251, 261, 319, 349

Femininity, 97–99, 111; definition of, 19, 29–30, 160; measure of, 374; and physical health, 76, 253–259. *See also* Male-female comparisons

Feminism. *See* Women's movement

Ferguson, J., 182, 186, 197

Freud, S., 12, 40, 41, 47, 66, 108, 116, 149, 306

Friendships with same sex, 161–168; and American males, 162–165; and androgyny, 19, 161, 165–167; ideal, 151–152; male-female comparisons in, 161, 162, 166–168, 283–284; and maturity, 161, 168; measure of, 166, 371–372; methodological problems in studying, 166–168; and other competences, 167–168, 191, 197; personality traits of, 165–167, 168, 238, 261; rated importance of, 8; transcultural differences in, 162–163

Fromm, E., 66, 276, 331–332, 336

Frost, R., 124–125

Fulfillment. *See* Judge ratings; Self-fulfillment

G

Gender role. *See* Sexual role

Gilligan, C., 318, 344–345

Good lover. *See* Sexual mutuality

Good marital partner. *See* Marital competence

Growing healthily. *See* Maturity

H

Handy, R. Y., 257, 258, 335

Happiness: adolescent predictors of, 308; in future marriages, 132–136; male-female comparisons in, 251–252; and maturity, 18, 245, 262; meaning of, 244–246; measures of, 94, 245, 375, 382, 383; and mental health, 246–247; parental determinants of, 274, 280–281; personality correlates of, 18, 58, 247, 251–252; and physical health, 246–247; rated importance of, 8, 243; and self-fulfillment, 352–353; success

in personal relations, 128, 140, 155, 168, 169–170, 173, 247; and virtue, 238; and vocational success, 183–184, 191, 201. *See also* Stage productivity; Well-being

Harvard Grant study, 363. *See also* Vaillant

Haverford College: alumni of, 10, 46, 365; effects of, 292, 305, 338; maturing of students, 305

Health. *See* Mental health; Physical health; Well-being

Health growth. *See* Maturing of adults; Maturity

Heath, H. E., 138, 143, 191, 374

Helson, R., 364

Henry, Barb and Bob, 16

Holt, R. R. *See also* Rorschach

Homosexual, 69, 119

Hope, 331–340; as predictor of success, 302; religious source of, 232–234; and schools, 337–339; and virtue, 235–236. *See also* Meaning for living; Schools

I

Identity: changing sources of, 3–7, 46, 223, 256–257, 319–320, 333–337; conflict within, 3–6, 145–146, 177–178, 206–208, 213–214, 229–230, 248–249, 289, 316–320, 322–325; male-female comparisons of, 7, 67, 143–149, 196–197, 206–208, 256–257; and Number 1 Self, 6–7, 9, 32, 68, 143, 145–146, 177, 193, 194, 199, 207, 212, 217, 304–305, 306, 312, 333, 336

IGS. *See* Intergenerational studies

Income, 187–194, 215; and familial success, 189; male-female comparisons of, 190–193; measure of, 371; and other competences, 190–191, 196; personality correlates of, 188–194, 248; rated importance of, 8, 187–188; and relation to vocational fulfillment, 178, 191, 200, 349; school determinants of, 293–294; survey results about, 188–189, 194. *See also* Vocational success

Incomplete sentences. *See* Ego Development Scale

Integration, 36; adolescent measure of, 359; definitions of, 47–54; and development in adulthood, 212, 310, 325,

343–344; and immaturity, 62–63, 79, 170, 193, 197, 214, 318, 323; measures of, 169, 324, 375, 376, 377, 379–380; and personality traits, 155, 156, 249, 252, 258; and success in personal relations, 50, 149, 155, 156, 159–160, 217; and vocational success, 178, 203–204, 216, 304. *See also* Cognitive skills; Interpersonal relations; Self-concept; Values

Intellectual strengths: examples of, 34, 38–39, 43–45, 48–49, 54–56, 182; importance of, 17. *See also* Cognitive skills

Intergenerational studies (IGS), 12, 13, 169, 189, 191, 254, 303, 304, 343, 344, 345, 346, 347, 349, 350, 354, 355, 358, 360–361, 362, 363, 364

Interpersonal relations: during adolescence as predictor of success, 360–361; autonomy of, 56–57, 211–214; being "alive," 331–333; importance of, 17; integration of, 49–50; measures of, 369, 372, 374–376, 378–379, 380; and other-centeredness, 45, 50, 127, 172, 211–214, 312, 321, 343, 354; and physical health, 355; and relation to maturity, 36, 45, 56, 116–117, 359; stability of, 56–57; symbolization of, 39–40

Interviews: about background, 22, 26, 52, 81, 91, 101–102, 150, 167, 178, 232, 269–272, 275, 278; description of, 379–380; on maturing, 42, 45, 46, 47, 49, 57, 106, 146, 310–312, 322–327; about sex role, 85, 380

Intimacy: and conflict with vocational success, 217–219, 346–347; determinants of, 273–274; male-female comparisons of, 67, 134–135, 156–157; measure of, 374; and other competences, 18, 129, 153, 155, 158, 168, 170–171, 173; personality correlates of, 18, 238, 249, 296; and relation to maturity, 18, 50

J

Jackson, Bruce, 127–128, 129, 131, 159, 160, 166, 185, 204, 205, 211, 277, 282, 285, 287

James, W., 6–7, 193, 207

Johnson, V. E., 154

Judge ratings: of adolescent mental health,

306–307; of community involvement, 227–229; of fulfillment, 18, 58, 128, 168, 169–170, 191, 229, 238, 375; of happiness, 18, 191, 197, 238, 251–252, 353; of leadership, 197, 227–229; of marital success, 121–123, 126, 128, 129–130; of maturity, 359, 361, 369; measures of, 370–371, 373, 380; of mental health, 250–251, 353, 361; of physical health, 255; of role competence, 19, 42, 126, 140, 153, 155, 168, 185, 197, 204–205, 227–228, 238, 247, 248, 253, 268, 355; use of, 13; of virtue, 237–238, 239–240, 351; of vocational success, 210–214. *See also* Personality Scale; Self-Image Questionnaire, Judge-rated

Judge selection, 10, 368

Jung, C. G., 19, 98, 107

L

Leadership success, 195–198, 216; definition of, 195; determinants of, 277, 287, 297; male-female comparisons of, 196; and managerial personality, 195–196; measures of, 195, 375; and other competences, 191, 197; personality correlates of, 197, 248, 253, 350–351; rated importance of, 8. *See also* Vocational success

Leighton, Billie, 19, 20–32, 106, 141, 208; adolescent personality of, 299, 300–301; and androgyny, 29–30, 116, 186; and community involvement, 227; and goals for children, 243; maturity of, 21, 30–31, 36, 38–39, 40, 43, 45, 46, 48, 49, 53, 56, 57, 62, 64, 66, 69; parent effects on, 31, 280; and success in personal relations, 21, 131, 171; and virtue, 21, 235; and vocational success, 21, 206; and well-being, 21, 246

Levinson, D., 67, 345, 364

Loevinger, J., 377

Longitudinal studies: examples of, 12, 363–364; methodological problems of, 13–16

Lover. *See* Sexual mutuality

M

Macho males, 117, 127, 129, 131, 156, 158, 159, 161, 162, 166, 172, 205,

211, 241, 256, 319, 346. *See also* Masculinity

Male-female comparisons: and adolescent predictors of success, 301–303, 360; and adults' parental relations, 316–318; and community involvement, 228–230; and goals, 8–9; and maturing, 64–65, 117, 309–314, 315–327, 344; and religiosity, 232; and success in personal relationships, 45, 124–125, 129–132, 134–135, 145–146, 152–153, 155–158, 162, 166–167, 168, 273–274; and values, 8–9, 239–241; and virtue, 236, 239–241; and vocational success, 184, 188–194, 196–197, 203–209, 211–214, 216, 350, 367; and well-being, 250–252, 253–259, 319, 326, 353–354, 362

Maleness. *See* Handy, R. Y.; Masculinity

Marital Adjustment Scale: description of, 92, 121, 373; and friendship, 168; male-female comparisons in, 129–132; and marital competence, 129; and maturity, 18, 127; as measure of marital fulfillment, 373; and parental success, 126, 140; personality correlates of, 18, 19, 126–128; and sexual success, 126, 153–155; and virtue, 232, 238; and vocational success, 191, 197, 204; and well-being, 128, 247, 253, 254. *See also* Marital fulfillment

Marital competence: and character of ideal partner, 123–124; and friendships, 168; and happiness, 126; male-female comparisons of, 124–125; and maturity, 127; meanings of, 118–121; measures of, 92, 121–123, 370–371, 381–382; and parental success, 126; personality correlates of, 126–128; and sexual success, 126, 153; and virtue, 238; and vocational success, 191, 204; and well-being, 247, 253. *See also* Judge ratings

Marital fulfillment: character attributes of, 126–131, 153; in the future, 131–136, 172; male-female comparisons of, 124–125, 129, 346; measures of, 373, 379; rated importance of, 8, 118. *See also* Marital Adjustment Scale

Marital success. *See* Judge ratings; Marital Adjustment Scale; Marital competence; Marital fulfillment; Personal relationships, success in

Masculinity, 85, 97–99, 217; changing meanings of, 144, 326–327; correlates of, 153, 185–186, 189, 192–193, 196, 211, 227, 253–254, 297, 319; definition of, 19, 29–30, 151, 160, 172; and macho index, 241; measure of, 374. *See also* Macho males; Male-female comparisons

Maslow, A. H., 12, 20–21, 33, 37, 63, 65, 123, 243, 337, 353

Masters, W. H., 154

Maternal determinants: of happiness and fulfillment, 280–281; of maturity, 268, 328–330; measure of, 368–369; of mental health, 279–280, 357; of success in personal relations, 274–277, 356; of virtue, 279–280; of vocational success, 277–279, 288. *See also* Developmental History Questionnaire

Matthews, Alice, 207–208, 248

Maturing of adults: barriers to, 316–320; determinants of, 26, 42, 43, 44, 45, 46, 47, 49, 57, 105–106, 115, 146, 227, 265–266, 280–281, 305, 310–311, 313–314, 321–327; impetus to, 331–333, 338; male-female comparisons of, 64–65, 248–249, 309–314, 315–327; procedure to determine, 26, 313, 379–380; rate of, 309–310; types of, 49, 68, 100–101, 223, 310, 312, 321, 343–344. *See also* Stage productivity; Maturity

Maturity: and adaptation, 18, 33–59, 67, 124, 170, 205, 207, 208, 217–218, 229; adolescent measure of, 307, 369; and androgyny, 99, 116–117; assumptions of model of, 31, 39, 60–61, 64–65, 68, 69–71, 99, 115, 243, 344–345; continuity over time in, 59, 266, 307, 309–310, 353, 359, 361; definition of, 33–59; disorganization and, 47–48, 51, 55, 63, 67–69, 323, 325–326; and educational goals, 51, 71–72, 98, 249, 301, 338–339; and ego strength, 55; and feminine interpersonal skills, 45, 116–117, 318–320; life-span stages and, 67–68, 310, 343; male-female comparisons of, 4, 45, 64–65, 319; and meaning for living, 336–337; measures of, 14, 99, 359, 377, 380; and mental health, 342–343, 353; methodological issues about, 59, 71, 344; myths about, 64–72; parental contributions to, 328–330; personality correlates of, 18, 42, 43, 45, 47, 50, 56, 58, 63, 127, 154, 155, 168, 239, 261; rated importance of, 8, 18, 33, 342; and relation to success, 31, 33, 47, 50, 59, 127, 168, 170, 173, 197, 204, 211, 215; religious views of, 33; transcultural studies of, 43, 53, 55, 57, 65, 162, 335, 342, 377; visible signs of, 36–37, 67, 323; and well-being, 18, 244, 352, 353. *See also* Developmental History Questionnaire; Equilibrating principle; Interviews; Judge ratings; Perceived Self Questionnaire; Self-Image Questionnaire; Valuator Test

Mead, M., 133, 265

Meaning for living, 48, 333–337; and maturity, 336–337. *See also* Hope; Religiosity; Values

Menstruation, 111, 255–256, 261, 316

Mental health: adolescent predictors of, 301, 306–308, 359–360; and androgyny, 251; feminine interpersonal correlates of, 251, 319–320; male-female comparisons of, 251–252, 253, 319; maternal determinants of, 274, 279–280, 355; and maturity, 250–251, 261, 342–343, 353; meanings of, 244, 343, 361; measures of, 14, 354, 359, 373, 381, 383; paternal determinants of, 274, 289–290, 355, 357; personality correlates of, 238, 246, 249–251, 261; and physical health, 246, 253, 261; rated importance of, 8, 243; relation to adult competences, 127, 247, 261; surveys of, 11, 120, 137–138; 188–189; and well-being, 246. *See also* Judge ratings; Maturity

Middle age: crisis, 4, 345; as determinant of maturing, 313–314

Miller, Andy, 72, 75–102, 103, 106, 345; androgyny of, 95, 97–99, 116; community involvement of, 227; and goals for children, 243; maturity of, 100; parent effect on, 95, 96–97, 276–277, 280, 285; school success of, 293, 295; and success in personal relationships, 92, 106, 120, 125, 128–129, 135, 138, 145–146, 149–150, 155, 166, 170; and virtue, 171, 235; and vocational success, 80, 186, 204; and well-being, 94, 246, 251

Miller, Marty, 72, 75–94, 95, 99, 101,

103–112, 135, 345; androgyny of, 104, 109–110, 116; and community involvement, 227; and goals for children, 243; maturity of, 116, 324–325; parent effect on, 104–106, 277, 280, 289; and success in personal relationships, 91–94, 120, 121, 128–129, 131, 138, 145, 149–150, 155, 160, 170, 171; and virtue, 235, 238; and vocational success, 82, 143, 145, 170, 186, 206, 208; and well-being, 94, 246, 251, 257

Miller, S., 164

Mind. *See* Cognitive skills; Intellectual strengths; Maturity

Minnesota Multiphasic Personality Inventory (MMPI), 59, 127, 173, 204, 247, 253, 255, 359, 369–370; and maturity, 369

MMPI. *See* Minnesota Multiphasic Personality Inventory

Moane, G., 364

Morale, student, 349

N

Neugarten, B., 364

O

O'Neil, John and Mary, 16

Other-centeredness, 36, 229, 249; adolescent measures of, 304, 307; and adult maturing, 218–219, 257, 260–262, 305, 310, 343; and autonomy, 58, 63, 318; definition of, 43–47; determinants of, 305; development in adulthood of, 227, 307, 312; immaturity, 62, 197, 320; male-female comparisons of, 62, 117, 211–214, 239–241, 255–259, 304–308, 344; measures of, 169, 374, 375–376, 377, 379–380; and personality traits of, 236, 239, 249; and relation to self-fulfillment, 352–353; and stability, 318; and success in personal relationships, 47, 127, 130–131; and vocational success, 212–213, 304. *See also* Cognitive skills; Interpersonal relations; Self-concept; Values

P

Parent Adaptation Scale: and community involvement, 227; description of, 374;

and friendship, 168; male-female comparisons in, 143–146; and marital success, 126; and maturity, 140; and parental calling, 143–147; and parental competence, 140; personality correlates of, 140–142; and virtue, 238; and vocational success, 191, 204, 227; and well-being, 147, 247, 253. *See also* Parental fulfillment

Parent, single, 277, 285

Parental competence: and child's maturity, 139–140, 268; definitions of, 138–140, 268; and feminine interpersonal skills, 268; and happiness, 268; and ideal parent, 139, 267, 268; judge ratings of, 268, 355; and marital success, 126; and maturity, 18, 268, 274; measures of, 93, 139–140, 268, 370–371, 378, 381–382; and mental health, 247; and personality correlates of, 268. *See also* Judge ratings; Personal History Questionnaire

Parental enmeshment, 316–318, 372

Parental fulfillment: as a calling, 143–146; measure of, 93, 143–145, 374; mother-father comparisons of, 140–147, 366; of working mothers, 346–347. *See also* Parental Adaptation Scale

Parental relation with participants, measure of, 372–373, 379

Parental role: and calling vs. job, 143–146; and effects on maturing, 45, 46, 47, 105; rated importance of, 8, 137, 146

Parental success, meanings of. *See* Parental competence; Parental fulfillment

Parents, effects of on women, 23, 317–318

Participants of study: description of, 10, 366–367; selection of, 10, 20–21, 366. *See also* Study

Paternal determinants: of community involvement, 287; of happiness, 282; of maturity, 268, 328–330; measure of, 368–369; of mental health, 289–290, 357; of success in adult personal relationships, 282–286, 356; of virtue, 282; of vocational success, 286–289, 356. *See also* Developmental History Questionnaire

Perceived Self Questionnaire: and child's maturity, 18; and extracurricular activity, 297; and fulfillment and happiness, 18; item examples from, 39,

45, 53, 101; male-female comparisons of, 116–117; as measure of model of maturity, 36, 110, 375–376; personality correlates of, 43, 116–117; and success in personal relationships, 18, 127, 140, 153, 154, 155, 168, 173, 268; transcultural validation of, 43; and virtue, 18, 238; and vocational success, 18, 184, 191, 197, 201, 204, 208; and well-being, 18, 244, 247, 253, 353. *See also* Maturity

Personal History Questionnaire, 23, 370–373

Personal relationships, success in, 164–174, 247; adolescent predictors of, 305–306; maternal determinants of, 273, 274–277; meaning of, 119–121; paternal determinants of, 274, 282–285; summary measure of, 382. *See also* Friendships with same sex; Marital success; Parental success; Sexual success

Personality Scale, judge ratings of: and academic grades, 293; and community involvement, 227–229; description of, 374–375, 381; of femininity, 29, 45, 374–375; of masculinity, 29, 374–375; of maturity, 45, 116–117; and religiosity, 234; and school achievers, 295–296; and success in personal relationships, 127, 129–131, 141–143, 153, 154–155, 165–167, 168, 171–173, 268, 346; and virtue, 18, 239–241; and vocational success, 185–186, 190, 192–193, 196–197, 205–206, 208–209, 211, 350; and well-being, 247, 249–254, 354. *See also* Self-Image Questionnaire, judge-rated

Physical health: adolescent predictors of, 301, 306, 361; male-female comparisons of, 255–259, 261, 362; measures of, 255, 373, 381, 382; and mental health, 246, 250; and personality correlates of, 238, 246, 250, 261, 355; rated importance of, 8, 243; and relation of to maturing, 255–259. *See also* Erections; Femininity; Masculinity; Menstruation

Piaget, J., 49, 55

Pryor, Jim, 52–53, 69–71, 233–234, 237, 240

PSQ. *See* Perceived Self Questionnaire

Psychological health. *See* Mental Health

R

Reflective awareness. *See* Symbolization

Religiosity: definition of, 231–232, 235; familial background of, 235; and maturity, 234, 336–337; measures of, 232, 351, 372, 377, 384; personality traits of, 234, 260, 351; rated importance of, 8, 218; and success, 232, 234, 260; and virtue, 234. *See also* Values

Rogers, C., 332, 353

Role competence, summary measure of, 370–371, 379, 381; personality traits of judge-rated, 42, 45, 47, 170, 173, 185, 295, 300. *See also* Judge ratings

Rorschach, 15, 22, 26, 42, 45, 58, 59, 110, 170, 173, 185, 204; and Holt scores, 378, 383; interpretive examples of, 28–29, 52, 53, 79, 96, 107, 110; as measure of psychological health, 359, 369, 378

S

SAT. *See* Schools

Schools: and academic grades, 18, 291, 292–294, 358; and achievement tests, 18, 295; effects of, 332, 338; extracurricular activities in, 292, 297–298, 304, 306, goals of, 249, 301; and hope, 302, 337–339; and scholastic aptitude scores, 18, 291, 295–297, 358–359; and student morale, 349; and teacher ratings, 293, 296

Schwartz, Sue, 275, 286

Sears, R. R., 118, 247, 356, 363

Self-actualization. *See* Maturity; Self-fulfillment

Self-concept: autonomy of, 57–58; 249, 252, 257, 312, 319–320, 321, 325, 344; determinants of, 42, 313–314; 321–326; integration of, 53–54, 199, 312, 321, 324–325; judged maturity of, 377, 381; and maturity, 36, 322; measures of, 369, 374–377, 378, 379–380, 381; and other competences, 141, 192, 198, 199; and other-centeredness, 46–47, 229, 321, 324; personality correlates of, 58, 59; self-esteem of, 141, 173, 192; stability of, 57–58, 250–251, 258, 312, 320–321, 324, 325, 344; symbolization of, 42–43, 198, 229, 303, 312, 321, 323–324. *See also* Interviews; Perceived Self Questionnaire; Personality Scale; Self-Image Questionnaire, judge-rated; Self-Image Questionnaire, self-rated

Self-esteem. *See* Self-Image Questionnaire, self-rated

Self-fulfillment: and adaptation, 18, 66, 120, 169–170, 184, 201; and androgyny, 19; and happiness, 352; meaning of, 20, 51, 245, 352–353; measure of, 245, 352, 375, 382; rated importance of, 8. *See also* Marital fulfillment; Parental fulfillment; Sexual fulfillment; Vocational fulfillment

Self-Image Questionnaire, judge-rated: and judged vocational fulfillment, 211; male-female comparisons on, 117, 251–252; and marital success, 129; and maturity, 42, 43, 45, 49–50, 117, 168, 204, 229, 234, 238; measures of, 376, 378, 381; and parental success, 141–142, 268; personality traits of, 117; and role competence, 42; and virtue, 239; and well-being, 248, 251–252

Self-Image Questionnaire, self-rated: integration of, 50, 127, 204, 249; measure of, 376, 378, 379; and other-centered empathy, 45, 204, 229, 247; and self-esteem, 42, 50, 141, 173, 191, 204, 211, 238, 247, 268; and self-insight (symbolization), 42, 43, 204, 229, 238, 247; and stability, 249

Self-insight. *See* Self-Image Questionnaire, self-rated

Sex vs. sexuality, 150–151, 154

Sex-Role Inventory. *See* Androgyny; Bem; Feminine interpersonal skills; Femininity; Masculinity

Sexual competence, 93; and being an ideal lover, 149. *See also* Sexual mutuality

Sexual fulfillment: amount of pleasure in, 152–153, 347; definition of, 151–152; frequency of, 152–153, 192, 347; male-female comparisons of, 148, 152, 153–154, 155–158; and maturity, 153; measures of, 93, 371; and other competences, 152, 153; personality correlates of, 153–154, 157; rated importance of, 8, 148

Sexual mutuality: definitions of, 152, 154; and friendship, 168; and good lovers, 158–159, 238; male-female comparisons of, 152, 155–158; and marital success, 126, 155; and maturity, 18, 50, 56, 154, 155, 156; measure of, 152, 371; personality traits of, 155, 157, 158, 295; and role competence, 154, 155; and virtue, 238; and well-being, 154, 155, 247, 253. *See also* Sexual fulfillment

Sexual role, 31, 217–218, 248–249; adolescent differences in, 303–306; bodily determinants of, 257–259, 316, 335–336; cultural determinants of, 85, 130–132, 196–197, 212, 217–218, 228–230, 303–306, 319–320, 322–327, 335–336; interview about, 26, 380; measure of, 380; women's conflict about, 316–320, 322–327. *See also* Erections; Menstruation

Sexual success: and cultural values, 148, 151, 157–158; male-female comparisons of, 132, 134; and maturity, 18. *See also* Sexual fulfillment; Sexual mutuality

Sheehy, G., 115, 364

SIQ. *See* Self-Image Questionnaire

Spaulding, Bill, 126, 127, 129, 131, 159, 160, 166, 185, 197, 217.

Stability, 36, 249; adolescent measures of, 304, 307; in adult development, 312, 318; and adult maturing, 250–251, 261, 318, 320, 343–344; and autonomy, 54–58, 250–251, 301, 304, 315; and community involvement, 229; definition of, 54–58; and immaturity, 63; measures of, 169, 374, 375–376, 377, 378, 379–380; and personality correlates of, 236, 240, 250–251, 258, 261, 319, 353; and success in personal relations, 154–155; and vocational success, 205. *See also* Cognitive skills; Interpersonal relations; Self-concept; Values

Stage productivity: correlates of success with, 128, 140, 155, 168, 184, 197, 204, 229; measure of, 370; and personality, 58, 238, 247

Strong-Campbell Interest Inventory, 29, 370

Study: background of, 363–365; and methodological issues, 12–14, 75, 367–368; participants in, 20, 366–367; preview of results of, 16–19; procedure and methods of, 368–384; purpose and organization of, 10–16, 365–366; summaries of results of, 31–32, 113–117, 160, 173–174, 215–219, 260–262, 328–330

Study of Values, 372, 377

Success, generalized: 17; adolescent predictors of, 300; and androgyny, 18; and maturity, 18; measure of, 370–371; meanings of, 3, 6–9; personality correlates of, 17–19

Symbolization, 36, 229, 299; definition of, 38–43; determinants of, 313; and development in adulthood, 310, 312; and immaturity, 40–42, 61–62, 198; male-female comparisons in, 312, 321; measures of, 169, 374, 375–376, 377, 379–380; transcultural study of, 43. *See also* Cognitive skills; Interpersonal relations; Self-concept; Values

T

Taylor, Marc, 15

Terman, L. M., 13, 297, 363

Thematic Apperception Test, 84, 109, 269, 379

Tocqueville, A. de, 163, 241

V

Vaillant, G. E., 12, 13, 46, 114–115, 169, 185, 205, 268, 283, 290, 308, 343, 348, 351, 356, 357, 361, 362, 363–364

Valuator Test, 238, 377

Values: autonomy of, 57, 344; and changing society, 334–337, 341–342; and ethics, 34–35, 338, 351; integration of, 36, 50–53, 321, 344; measures of maturity of, 238, 251–252, 369, 374–376, 377, 379–380; 384; other-centeredness, 45–46, 241; ranked importance of, 8; religion, 234, 336–337; stability of, 57, 312; symbolization of, 40–42, 312; types of, 232, 338, 373. *See also* Religiosity; Valuator Test; Virtue

Van Doren, M., 249

Vehrman, F., 333

Veroff, J., 137, 188

Virtue, 235–242, 261; adolescent predictors of, 300; autonomy of, 239; and community involvement, 227; determinants of, 274, 279–280; and feminine interpersonal skills, 236, 239–241; and judged vocational fulfillment, 211; male-female comparisons of, 236, 239–241; and maturity, 18, 35, 236, 238; measures of, 237–238, 377, 384; methodological problems studying, 236, 237–238, 351; and other competences, 171, 173, 236; personality correlates of, 18, 197, 234, 238; rated importance of, 8, 218, 236–237; and success in personal relations, 171. *See also* Judge ratings; Perceived Self Questionnaire; Personality Scale; Valuator Test

Vocational Adaptation Scale, judge-rated, 82, 210–214, 216; determinants of, 288; and feminine interpersonal skills, 211–212, 350; and friendship, 168; and income, 191; and leadership, 197; male-female comparisons in, 16, 204, 211–214, 216; and maturity, 18, 211; measure of, 373, 381; and mental health, 247–248; personality correlates of, 18, 19, 211–212; school determinant of, 293–294; and virtue, 211, 238; and vocational fulfillment, 204, 211. *See also* Judge ratings; Vocational fulfillment; Vocational success

Vocational Adaptation Scale, self-rated, 80, 82, 199–210; and androgyny, 204, 209; and income, 178, 191; and judge-rated vocational success, 204, 211; and leadership, 197; male-female comparisons in, 203–207, 211–214, 216, 248; and masculinity, 204; and maturity, 18, 184, 201, 205, 207, 208; measure of, 373; personality correlates of, 205, 208–209; and success in personal relationships, 204; and virtue, 238; and well-being, 201, 204, 247–248, 253. *See also* Vocational fulfillment; Vocational success

Vocational fulfillment, 199–210, 216, 248–249, 350; and calling vs. job, 57, 143, 145–146, 178, 199–202, 349; conflict between intimacy and, 206, 208, 217–219, 278, 349–350; and in-

come, 178, 200; measure of, 373; of teachers, 209, 350; of working vs. nonworking mothers, 278, 361. *See also* Vocational Adaptation Scale, self-rated

Vocational role: calling vs. job, 199–202; effects on maturing, 313; and male-female identities, 206–209

Vocational success, summary measure of, 181–186, 215; adolescent predictors of, 184, 301, 303, 304; ideal strengths for, 182–183; male-female comparisons of, 184; maternal determinants of, 274, 277–279; meanings of, 177–178; measure of, 178, 183, 371, 382; and other competence, 348; paternal determinants of, 274; personality correlates of, 183–186, 348, 350; and personality of physicians, 183, 294; rated importance of, 8; school determinants of, 297. *See also* Income; Leadership; Vocational Adaptation Scale, judge-rated; Vocational Adaptation Scale, self-rated

W

Well-being, 243–252; adolescent predictors of, 300; and androgyny, 249, 319; and autonomy, 249–250; male-female comparisons of, 248–249; maternal determinants of, 279–280; and maturity, 18, 244; meaning of, 244, 352; measure of, 246, 352, 354, 382; and other competences, 229, 247, 268; paternal determinants of, 289–290; personality correlates of, 19, 238, 246–252, 349, 355; rated importance of, 8, 242, 243; and vocational success, 247–249

Williams, C., 228

Wolfe, T., 148, 187

Women's movement, 4, 81, 108, 110–112, 132, 180, 320, 321, 322–327, 336

Working women, 213–214, 248–249, 278, 290, 303, 310, 346–347, 316